History of the Town of Durham

New Hampshire

(Oyster River Plantation)

With genealogical notes

(Volume I)

Everett S. Stackpole,

Lucien Thompson

Alpha Editions

This edition published in 2020

ISBN : 9789354008351

Design and Setting By
Alpha Editions
email - alphaedis@gmail.com

HISTORY

of the

TOWN OF DURHAM

NEW HAMPSHIRE

(Oyster River Plantation)

WITH

GENEALOGICAL NOTES

By EVERETT S. STACKPOLE
and LUCIEN THOMPSON

IN TWO VOLUMES

Volume One

NARRATIVE

PUBLISHED BY VOTE OF THE TOWN

CONTENTS

ILLUSTRATIONS

FOREWORD

The movement to publish a History of Durham was begun in 1885 by a vote in town meeting, authorizing the appointment of a committee by the selectmen for that purpose. The committee so appointed consisted of Joshua B. Smith, Winthrop S. Meserve and Lucien Thompson. In 1886, in response to a petition signed by this committee and by James W. Burnham, Benjamin Thompson, Hamilton A. Mathes, William P. Frost, Samuel H. Barnum, Henry B. Mellen, Albert DeMeritt, Joseph C. Bartlett, Ephraim Jenkins and John W. E. Thompson, the town voted an appropriation of $900 to assist in the publication of a History not to cost over $5 per copy, and added Ephraim Jenkins and Joseph W. Coe to the above mentioned committee. The committee had power to fill vacancies and was authorized to collect material and secure the publication of the history with such aid as they thought best. Printed circulars were issued, stating the scope of the proposed history, and also there were distributed five hundred circulars full of questions, especially soliciting genealogical information. To this circular there were but few replies. In 1887 Albert Young was chosen a member of the committee to take the place of Joshua B. Smith resigned. In 1889 Hamilton A. Mathes was chosen to fill a vacancy caused by resignation of Joseph W. Coe. Conferences were held with the Rev. Alonzo H. Quint, D. D., and Miss Mary P. Thompson relative to the preparation of the history. Dr. Ham of Dover offered all possible assistance. Thus the records close,—to be reopened over twenty years later.

In 1911 the matter was taken up again. Messrs. Albert De- Meritt, Arioch W. Griffiths and Charles Wentworth were added to the committee, in place of some who had resigned or passed away. These conferred with the Rev. Everett S. Stackpole, D. D., who agreed to write the proposed history. In 1912 the town voted anew to raise $150 for preliminary expenses, and the Hon. Lucien Thompson, who had been gathering material for a score of years, became interested as associate author of the proposed history. The money requisite for the printing of the History was voted by the town at its annual meeting, March 1913. At the request of Mr. Stackpole the name of Dea. Winthrop S. Meserve was added to the title page of the second volume, as associate author of the genealogical part.

BIRTH AND GROWTH OF THE TOWN

All truths, all facts and all men are related. To know completely a part of a system one must know the whole. The history
of a town is woven into the history of the world. To separate it
is like tearing off a piece of a garment. Since to know the whole
is forever impossible, we must content ourselves with partial
knowledge and with probabilities. To understand well the
history of Durham one needs to know the first discoveries of the
region of the Pascataqua, the causes that led to its settlement,
the antecedents and ancestry of the first settlers, the ends they
sought, the religious and political state of Great Britain especially at that time, as well as the deeds the colonists performed.
All this cannot be unfolded in a town history. Such matters
properly belong to a general history of New Hampshire, or of
Maine.

We are obliged to plunge into the stream of history somewhere,
not too far back, and to float down with the current. We care
mainly for men; their deeds interest us only as they show forth
the character of the actors or influence the lives of their successors.
When we know well and interpret rightly our antecedents, we
may with some degree of safety forecast the future and make
wise plans therefor.

The first settlers left but few records. They had little idea of
the historic importance of their undertaking. They foresaw
not the many thousands of descendants that would rejoice to
find scraps of information about their origin in the old countries
beyond the great sea. Perhaps many came as a temporary ven-
ture, thinking to return home soon. They stayed either from
stern necessity or because they learned to love the new country
and foresaw something of its future prospects. They sought not
so much religious and political liberty as to better their material
conditions. The gift of fifty or one hundred acres was a mighty
inducement to many, who could never hope to acquire a small
piece of land in any of the old countries. The desire of some
leaders to found great manorial estates in the new world was
rudely disregarded by men who had tasted of civil and industrial
freedom. We laugh now at the folly of trying to wrest away by

process of law the farms of the first settlers and restore them to
the English heirs of Capt. John Mason.   Any effort to enforce
such a claim would have brought on the Revolution earlier than
it came.   The King of England claimed all the land discovered,
just as William the First claimed and distributed all the lands of
England at the time of the Conquest.   His grantees could not
hold them.   A handful of men got together and formed a town
without any charter and then they made grants of land to themselves and to others whom they wished to join them.   Some
trifles were given to the Indians to quiet their claims, and so the
lands were seized, to have and to hold.

The fisheries, that had for rendezvous the Isles of Shoals for
many years, first attracted settlers to the mainland.   They
combined fishing with agriculture.   The Pascataqua and its
tributaries were full of salmon and sturgeon, that gave their
names to waterfalls and creeks.   There was abundance of lumber
for ship-building and commerce.   The settlers searched in vain
for mines of gold and silver, and iron ore was obtained with difficulty in small quantities.   Wild game filled the forests, and the
fur trade brought revenues to some.   But agriculture, the greatest and most necessary industry for man, soon came to be the
principal occupation, and swarming children pushed in further
from the shores, to which the first settlers clung cautiously and
for the only means of communication.   Every settler was almost
of necessity a boatman, fisherman, hunter, carpenter, mechanic
and farmer.   The women could spin, weave, make garments of
every sort, cook marvelously, and manage a dairy.   Necessity
made the weak strong.

How much we would like to know the number and names of
the men and women who came with David Thompson, in 1623,
from Plymouth, England, to Odiorne's Point and helped him build
his fish-weir near a point of land a little south of the mouth of the
Cochecho River, which has ever since borne his name.   Who
besides Thomas Roberts came with Edward and William Hilton
from London to Hilton's Point in the same year?   What were
the names of the eight Danes and twenty-two women who came
with Capt. John Mason's colonists from the south of England
to Strawberry Bank and Newichawannock between 1631 and
1634?   Who were all those that came from Bristol with Capt.
Thomas Wiggin to Dover Neck in 1633 and gave the name Bristol

to the little city they there attempted to found? These companies were the real pioneers of the Pascataqua region. We know the names of a few of them; we are well convinced that certain others must have been among them. Of Capt. John Mason's company Ambrose Gibbons, Francis Matthews, John Ault, and John Goddard settled in Oyster River Plantation, while James Nute lived on the west side of Back River, within the present limits of Dover. Among the companions of Capt. Thomas Wiggin were probably Elder Hatevil Nutter, Richard Pinkham, Thomas Leighton, Richard York, William Williams, William Beard, Thomas Beard, Thomas Stevenson, Samuel Haines, John Heard, John Dam, George Webb, Philip Chesley, William Pomfret, William Storer, Thomas Canney, Henry Tibbetts, George Walton, William Furber, and the Rev. William Leveridge. At least all these lived on Dover Neck within a few years of Capt. Wiggin's arrival, and they were joined not long after by Anthony Emery from Newbury, Joseph Austin from Hampton, John Tuttle who came in the Angel Gabriel, Job Clement from Haverhill, Ralph Hall, John Hall, Philip Cromwell, "Mr. David Ludecas Edling," Capt. John Underhill and the Rev. John Reyner.

It seems to have been the design of Capt. Wiggin to found a city or compact town on the hill-top of Dover Neck, giving to each settler three and a half or four acres for a home lot, while out lots or farms and pieces of marsh were assigned on the shores of Little and Great Bays and their tributaries, which they could easily reach by boat. Probably this was thought necessary at first for mutual defence, as well as to avoid insufferable loneliness. After land had been cleared and log houses built and flocks and herds began to multiply, it became quite necessary to quit Dover Neck and remain permanently on the farms. Thus by the year 1640 much of the best land along the shores and up to the head of salt water in the Shankhassick, as the Indians called Oyster River, was in the recognized possession of settlers, and clearing had well begun. The first comers got the best land. To him that had was given. Big grants went to the big men, and some families soon became prominent because their emigrant ancestor was fortunate enough to get possession of fertile land easily cultivated, while those who settled on poor and rocky soil and stayed there remained poor and of little account.

There were from the very beginning some order and recognized authority. There is no reason to suppose that Capt. Wiggin allotted lands, or that he was in any sense a Governor. He was the agent of a land company, and Ambrose Gibbons was as much a Governor of Maine as Capt. Thomas Wiggin was of New Hampshire. The company under the leadership of Capt. Wiggin were in effect from the start a democratic republic and regulated their own internal affairs much as the Pilgrims did at Plymouth. They assumed to be a town and did the chief business of a town at that time by granting lots and purchasing lands

SHANKHASSICK, OR OYSTER RIVER

of the Indians. William Hilton, in 1641, sold land that had been granted to him by the inhabitants of Dover. This was at the head of Oyster River. "The inhabitants of Dover alias Northam" granted land to the Rev. Thomas Larkham between the years 1639 and 1642. Darby Field was in quiet possession of Oyster River Point earlier than 1639. Ambrose Gibbons, Thomas Stevenson, William Williams and William Beard, all of Oyster River, had lands assigned to them by common consent before 1640. On the 18th of the 8th month, 1652, John Ault made a deposition as follows:

The deponent sayth that in the yere 1635, that the land about Lamprile River was bought of the Indians & made use of by the men of Dover & myselfe both for planting & fishing & feling of Timber.

John Ault and Richard York made oath to this statement
before George Smyth, and to similar effect testified Hatevil
Nutter and William Furber.   See depositions in N. H. Province Papers, Vol. 1, p. 204.   The original depositions may be
seen in the archives of Massachusetts, 112-14.

In the above statements "the men of Dover" and "the inhabitants of Dover" are mentioned collectively as having power to
purchase lands of the Indians and to grant lands to individuals
as early as 1635.   This was the beginning of town business, though
it was not till 1648 that they assumed to assess rates and became
a full-fledged town.

The Exeter Combination of 1639 was signed by two men of
Oyster River, namely, Darby Field and Francis Matthews, and
it is noticeable that these did not sign the Dover Combination of
the following year.   Indeed, none of the settlers at Oyster River
signed that compact.   It has been called Dover's Magna Charta
rather inappropriately, since it was no concession wrung from a
reluctant king, but a voluntary agreement of forty-two inhabitants of Dover Neck, Cochecho and what was afterward Newington.   It is a formal statement of what had been informally agreed
to from the beginning of the settlement of Capt. Wiggin and
company on Dover Neck, in 1633.   If "two or more persons
banded together to do good make a church," as I once heard a
Canon of the Church of England publicly declare, then two or
more settlers in a new country banded together for mutual protection and self-government make a town, and such a church and
such a town need no higher authorization.   The Combination
was as follows:

Whereas sundry mischeifes and inconveniences have befaln us, and more
and greater may in regard of want of civill Government, his Gratious Ma'tie
haveing hitherto setled no order for us to our knowledge:
   Wee whose names are underwritten being Inhabitants upon the river Pas-
cataquack have voluntarily agreed to combine ourselves into a body politique
that we may the more comfortably enjoy the benefit of his Ma'ties Lawes
together with all such Orders as shal bee concluded by a major part of the
Freemen of our Society in case they bee not repugnant to the Lawes of England
and administered in the behalf of his Majesty.
   And this wee have mutually promised and concluded to do and so to continue
till his Excellent Ma'tie shall give other Order concerning us.   In Witness
whereof wee have hereto set our hands the two and twentieth day of October
in the sixteenth yeare of our Sovereign Lord Charles by the grace of God King

of Great Britain France and Ireland Defender of the Faith &c. Annoq Dom. 1640.

John Follet	Thom. Larkham
Robert Nanney	Richard Waldern
William Jones	William Waldern
Phillip Swaddon	William Storer
Richard Pinckhame	William Furber
Bartholomew Hunt	Thos. Layton
William Bowden	Tho. Roberts
John Wastill	Bartholomew Smith
John Heard	Samuel Haines
John Hall	John Underhill
Abel Camond	Peter Garland
Henry Beck	John Dam
Robert Huggins	Steven Teddar
Fran: Champernoon	John Ugroufe
Hansed Knowles	Thomas Canning
Edward Colcord	John Phillips
Henry Lahorn	Tho: Dunstar
Edward Starr	James Nute
Anthony Emery	Richard Laham
William Pomfret	John Cross
George Webb	James Rawlins

The original of the above is in the Record Office at London. The clerk in copying may have made some mistakes. Edward Starr is doubtless Elder Edward Starbuck. Tho: Dunstar is probably Thomas Dustin, afterward of Kittery, whose son Thomas lived in Haverhill. Thomas Canning is Thomas Canney. Henry Lahorn may be Henry Langstaff. Hansed Knowles is the Rev. Hansard Knollys.

Why did no man in Oyster River Plantation sign that Combination? Already that section of ancient Dover began to feel itself separate from and independent of the rest of the town. It was geographically distinct and soon began to clamor for parish and township rights. Local convenience made this almost a necessity.

In the above Combination no name is given to the town. It was yet undecided whether it should be called Bristol, Northam or Dover. The last name became fixed about the year 1642.

There is another reason why nobody from Oyster River signed the so-called Dover Combination. At this time the inhabitants of Exeter were claiming that the northern limit of their town was the Oyster River or a mile beyond, by virtue of a deed obtained by Parson Wheelwright from an Indian chief. In the first allotment of land in Exeter, December 1639, it was declared that the meadows "from Lamprey river to the head of Little Bay should be equally apportioned into four parts." This is all the region of Durham afterward known as Lubberland. Under date of 12 November, 1640, it is recorded in Exeter thus:

It is agreed upon yᵗ Mr. William Hilton is to enjoy those two marshes in Oyster River wᶜʰ formerly he hath possession of & still are in his possession and the other marsh wᶜʰ Mr. Gibbies [Ambrose Gibbons] doth wrongfully detayne from him with the rest of those marshes wᶜʰ formerly he hath made use of soe far forth as they may be for the publique good of this plantation, and so much of the upland (adjoining) to them as shall be thought convenient by the neighbores of Oyster River, wᶜʰ are belonging to this body.

This must refer to William Hilton's eighty-eight acres at the head of salt water in Oyster River, where the public school building in Durham now stands, and to the two hundred acres belonging to Ambrose Gibbons, that formed later the Burnham farm, on the south side of the river. The inhabitants of Oyster River were wavering between allegiance to the Exeter Combination, that two of their number had signed, and to the so-called Dover Combination. Commissioners decided that the southern limit of Dover extended down to Lamprey River. The boundary was long disputed. [See Bell's History of Exeter.]

In 1652 the Commissioners appointed to determine the bounds of Dover reported that

They have thus agreed that the uttmost bound on the west is a creek on the east side of Lamprell river, the next creek to the river, and from the end of that creek to lamprell river first fall and so from the first fall on a west and by north line six miles,

from nequittchewannock first fall on a north and by west line fower miles,

from a creeke next below Thomas Cannes his house to a certaine Cove near the mouth of the Great Bay called hogsty cove and all the marsh and meadow lying and butting on the great bay with convenient byland to sett there hay. Mass. Archives, 112. 53

John Alt, "aged about seventy-three years," deposed, 2 March 1677/8, that Robert Smart, senior, of Exeter did own and possess all the meadow on the southwest side of John Goddard's Creek "and yᵉ said Smart did possess it twelve years before Dover was a township and he did possess it sixteen years together." How shall this be interpreted? When did Dover become a township? According to this deposition it was not in 1640, the time of the Combination, for twelve years before that date would carry us back to 1628, some years before John Ault arrived in Dover, or Robert Smart in Exeter. The latter was a resident of Hingham, Mass., in September, 1635, and probably came the following year to that part of Exeter which is now Newmarket. He needed marsh grass for his cattle and so took it where he could find it most conveniently. Twelve years after his arrival, that is, in 1648, the first taxes were levied, according to an order of Court at Boston. Was the authority of the Town of Dover then first recognized by the inhabitants of Oyster River Plantation, among whom was John Ault? There are certainly records which speak of the town of Dover as early as 1642, but then Oyster River Plantation was debatable land. Selectmen were chosen in 1647 and Ambrose Gibbons of Oyster River was one of them.

In 1639 a committee of three persons from Dover appeared at the General Court in Boston, proposing that Dover come under the jurisdiction of Massachusetts. Their offer was eagerly accepted and the terms were all that Dover desired. They were to have their own court at Dover like the courts at Salem and Ipswich; they were "exempted from all public charges other than those that shall arise among themselves or from any occasion or Course that may be taken to promote their own proper good and benefit"; they were to have all the privileges of towns, and church membership was not required to make inhabitants freemen, though this was the rule in Massachusetts. In fact the General Court granted everything for mere supremacy. May 10, 1643, the County of Norfolk was formed, with Salisbury as the shire town. Sessions of the court were held annually at Dover, and the records of the same are now at Concord, N. H. Norfolk County ceased to exist 8 September, 1679, when the territory lying between Massachusetts and Maine was made a separate royal province, in order to try the claims of Capt. John Mason's heirs to the improved lands of New Hampshire farmers. The claims seem to us ridiculous but were founded upon laws made for the benefit of the privileged class. The courts allowed the claims, but the attempt to collect rents was unsuccessful. Some Oyster River settlers were by legal process dispossessed of their estates, but practically they continued to possess them and to transmit them to their heirs.

Whatever records once existed of town proceedings in Dover until 1648 have been lost, except a few unimportant leaves. In

1647 William Pomfret was chosen recorder, or as we now say town clerk, and thereafter the records are of great historical importance. "Dicesimo Septimo die 10mo, 1647, it was ordered concluded and agreed upon that the inhabitants of Dover should condescend unto a form of levying rates and assessments for raising of public charges according to an order of court made and held at Boston." Funds for the ministry and other public expenses must have been raised before that time by voluntary contributions. We have the first rate list, which has been repeatedly published. We here copy only the names of those who lived in Oyster River Plantation.

The Towne Rate Made the 19th 10th mo [16] 48.

	£ s. d.	£ s. d.
George Webb, Rated	0046:00:00	
and to pay 4d p£ is		0000:12:08
John Goddard, Rated	0129:10:00	
and to pay 4d p£ is		0002:02:02
Richard Yorke, Rated	0072:08:00	
and to pay 4d p£ is		0001:04:00
Ambrose Gibbons, Rated	0086:00:00	
and to pay 4d p£ is		0001:08:00
Willm Beard, Rated	0076:10:00	
and to pay 4d p£ is		0001:05:06
Tho: Stephenson, Rated	0050:00:00	
and to pay 4d p£ is		0000:16:04
William Drue, Rated	0070:00:00	
and to pay 4d p£ is		0001:03:04
Matthew Gyles, Rated	0194:10:00	
and to pay 4d p£ is		0003:03:02
Mrs Matthews Rated	0139:10:00	
and to pay 4d p£ is		0002:03:02
Jonas Binns, Rated	0042:00:00	
and to pay 4d p£ is		0000:14:04
Charles Adams, Rated	0031:00:00	
and to pay 4d p£ is		0000:10:04
John Bickford, Rated	0115:10:00	
and to pay 4d p£ is		0001:18:06
Philip Chasely, Rated	0078:10:00	
and to pay 4d p£ is		0001:06:06
Tho: Willey, Rated	0071:10:00	
and to pay 4d p£ is		0001:03:06
John Allt, Rated	0069:00:00	
and to pay 4d p£ is		0001:03:00
Darby ffeild, Rated	0081:00:00	
and to pay 4d p£ is		0001:07:00

	£ s. d.	£ s. d.
Oliuer Kent, Rated	0070:10:00	
and to pay 4d p£ is		0000:011:4
Tho: Johnson, Rated	0040:00:00	
and to pay 4d p£ is		0000:13:04
Geo:Branson, Rated	0030:00:00	
and to pay 4d p£ is		0000:10:00
Willm Roberts, Rated	0046:10:00	
and to pay 4d p£ is		0000:15:02
Tho: ffootman, Rated	0060:00:00	
and to pay 4d p£ is		0001:00:00
John Martin, Rated	0041:10:00	
and to pay 4d p£ is		0000:13:10

This Rate within specified Is to bee paid in such commodities, time and place, as followeth, vizt. One fourth part in Corne, to bee pd and brought in at the rates as followes vizt. Indian Corne at 4s p bushell, wheat and pease at 5s p bushell, and to bee paid by the 10th day of the next m^o at the house of Wm Pomfrett and the rest of the rate to bee pd in by the 10th day of March next ensueing at the saw pitt below Tho. Cannys, for one place of receipt, for part of the said rate, and the other to bee paid in at the back Cove, to the Constable or his Assignes. All pipe staues are to bee delivded in at the rate of 3:10:0, and hh staues at 02:05:0. And for default of paym^t in either or eny of the said paym^{ts} in p^t or in all contrary to the forme aforesaid Wee doe hereby authorize and giue vnto the Constable full pow^r to arrest and attach the goods of such pson or psons as shall make denyall. Witnes o^r hands, this 19th day of 10th m^o 1648.

> Ambrose Gibbons
> Hatevill Nutter
> William Pomfrett
> Anth^o Emerey
> Tho: Layton.

This list shows that twenty-three out of fifty-three inhabitants of Dover lived at Oyster River. The next year two new names appear at Oyster River, John Hill and William Follett, and in 1650 we first find the names of Rise Howell and Mr. Valentine Hill.

The following first appear in the rate list of 1657, Ed Patterson, John Meader, Patrick the Scot [Patrick Jameson], Robert Burnham, William Williams, James Bunker, Robert Junkins, Mathew Williams, Richard Bray, John Davis, John Woodman, Joseph Field, William Pitman, and John Hance.

In the rate list of 1659 appear the following new names, Thomas Humphrey, William Graves, James Jackson, Walter Jackson, Henry Browne, Thomas Doughty, James Oer, James Middleton,

Edwin Arwin, John Barber, Benjamin Matthews, Benjamin
Hull, John Diuill, William Jones, and Steven ye Westingman
(?) which may mean either Stephen Jones or Stephen Robinson,
both of whom appeared about that time.

In 1661 we first find Hugh Dunn, Alexander McDaniel, Henry
Hollwell or Halloway, Teague Riall or Royall, Joseph Smith, and
Davey Daniel.

In 1662 the list shows the new names of Philip Cromwell or
Crommett, William Perkinson or Perkins, James Smith and
John Smith.

In 1663 appear Thomas Morris and Patrick Denmark. William Durgin was first taxed in 1664.

In 1666 we find Nicholas Harris, Robert Watson, Joseph
Stimson or Stevenson, Salathiel Denbo, Arthur Bennet, Thomas
Edgerly, Abraham Collens, Zachariah Field, Michael Simmons,
James Huckins, Edward Leathers and Thomas Chesley.

In 1681 appear as new names, Samuel Burnham, Dennis
Bryant, Jerimie Crommet, Abraham Clarke, John Davis, junior,
Nicholas Doe, James Derry, John Derry, Nicholas Follett,
George Goe, Joseph Hill, Samuel Hill, Charles Landeau, Joseph
Kent, Nathaniel Lumocks [Lamos], John Meader, junior, John
Mickmord [Muchmore?] John Pinder, John Rand, John Simons,
Robert Smart, junior, Edward Small, Bartholomew Stevenson,
William Tasket or Tasker, James Thomas, John Tompson,
William Williams, junior, John Willie, Stephen Willie, and John
Yorke.

In 1682 we notice David Davis, Nicholas Dunn, Nathaniel
Hill, William Hill, William Hucklie, William Jonson, Ezekiel
Pitman, Francis Pitman, Roger Rose, Joseph Stevenson.

This is not the place to enter into details concerning the troubles
of New Hampshire with Massachusetts, with the heirs of Capt.
John Mason, and with the Cranfield administration. The
following brief citation from an article in the *Granite Monthly*
of February 1902, written by the Hon. Frank B. Sanborn of
Concord, Mass., sufficiently sets forth the part Oyster River had
in those affairs. Robert Burnham, who was born at Norwich,
England, in 1624 and married in Boston in 1646 or earlier "was
in 1664 a petitioner to King Charles for a separation from Massachusetts and appears to have been then a Church of England
man; but in 1684 he refused to pay Mason his quit-rents and was

nominally ejected by Mason from his farm in Durham. Moreover, at the time of Monmouth's rebellion and after the death of
Charles II it was testified by Philip Chesley of Dover, April 26,
1685, 'that he heard Robert Burnham of Oyster River say there
was no speaking treason at present against the king, for there was
no king, and that the Duke of Monmouth was proclaimed and
crowned in Scotland and gone for Ireland, and that the Duke of
York was not yet crowned, and it was a question whether he ever
would be.' In 1665 Burnham had joined with Champernoon
and John Pickering of Portsmouth, and Edward Hilton and John
Folsom of Exeter in petitioning that King Charles 'would take
them under his immediate protection and that they might be
governed by the known laws of England,' and one reason for
this request was 'that they might enjoy both the sacraments,
which they have been so long deprived of.' In 1684 he joined
with the Waldrons, Wiggins, Sanborns, etc., in petitioning against
the exactions of Cranfield and Mason, and among his fellow-
petitioners was Joseph Stevenson of Oyster River, who said, not
long after, 'I owe the governor nothing, and nothing will I pay
him; I never knew him, nor had any dealings with him.'"

Exasperated by the arbitrary methods of Cranfield the people
of Exeter, Hampton, Portsmouth and Dover decided to make
complaint to the king, and Nathaniel Weare of Hampton was
appointed their agent and sent to England in 1685. In the
petition that he carried from Dover are found the following
Oyster River names, John Meader, Philip Chesley, Joseph Steven-
son, Thomas Chesley, Stephen Jones, Edward Small, Nathaniel
Lamos, James Huckins, Zacharias Field, Robert Burnham,
Samuel Burnham, Jeremiah Burnham, Samuel Hill, Peter Mason,
John Woodman, senior, John Woodman, junior, Jonathan Wood-
man, John Davis, senior, John Davis, junior, Joseph Field, John
Bickford, Thomas Edgerly, John Hill, Charles Adams, Charles
Adams junior, William Parkinson [Perkins], Joseph Hill and
Nathaniel Hill. [See N. H. Province Papers, Vol. I, p. 561.]

It is worthy of note that during Cranfield's administration
the Rev. Joshua Moody was tried at the Quarter Sessions before
Capt. Walter Barefoot, Nathaniel Fryer, Henry Green, Peter
Coffin, Henry Robie and Thomas Edgerly, the last being a well
known name of Oyster River. The justices debated a little;
four of them entered their dissent, viz., Messrs Fryer, Green,

Robie and Edgerly; but Barefoot and Coffin were for Mr. Moody's condemnation. In the morning, after outside influences had been used, Green and Robie consented to his condemnation. Justice Edgerly was cashiered and bound over to the Quarterly Sessions. By the governor's order he was discharged from being Justice of the Peace and from being in any other public employment. In the records of the Quarter Sessions the Clerk of the Court gave the substance of the debate as follows: "Justice Edgerly—that since his Majesty has been pleased to grant liberty of conscience to all Protestants here, the said Moody is not liable to the penalty of the statutes for refusing to administer the sacraments according to the form thereof."

A petition dated 20 February, 1689/90, was addressed to the Massachusetts authorities by the inhabitants and train soldiers of New Hampshire, requesting that they might be taken under the government and protection of Massachusetts Among the petitioners are the following names of men then residing at Oyster River. Those followed by a cross thus ✕ made their mark Philip Duday ✕, James Thomas ✕ William Perkins ✕, Steven Robeson, Francis Pitman, Robert Burnam, Jeremiah Burnum, John Buss, Joseph Meder ✕, John Meder junior, Stephen Willey ✕ Joseph Davis Moses Davis, Thomas Bickford, Charles Adams, C. A. his mark, Benjamin Mathews ✕, John Bunker ✕, Joseph Kent, Salathiel Denbow ✕, William Durgin by order, John Bickford, John Davis, James Smith, Nathaniel Hill, John Woodman, Thomas Edgerly, Zacharias Field, Thomas Chesley, Philip Chesle, Robert Watson, Stephen Jones, Thomas Arsh ✕ [Ash], Edward Lethers ✕, Philip Chesley ✕, John Pitman, James Derry ✕, John Davis junior, Samuel Burnum, Thomas Davis ✕, and William Pitman.—[N. H. Province Papers, Vol. II, pp. 34-39.]

The fruitless petition of Oyster River in 1669 to the General Court of Massachusetts may be seen in the chapter on Church History. Another petition was made to the General Court of New Hampshire in 1695, asking that Oyster River be made a township.

To the Honble John Usher Esqr., Leut. Governor, Comandr in Chief of his Majesᵗˢ Province of New Hampshire and to the Honble Councill,

Wee the Subscribers, Inhabitants of Oyster River, Humbly Petition and Pray

That whereas his most Sacred Majesty King William has been pleased through his grace and favor to grant unto yoʳ Honʳˢ by his Royall Comission with yᵉ Councill full powers and authorities to Erect and Establish Townes within this his Majesties Province, and whereas wee yoʳ petitioners have by divine providence Settled and inhabited that Part of his Majesᵗˢ Province Commonly called Oyster Riuer, and have found that by the Scituation of the place as to distance from Douer or Exeter, but more especially Douer, wee being forced to wander through the Woods to yᵗ place to meet to and for yᵉ Management of our affaires are much Disadvantaged for yᵉ Present in our Business and Estates, and hindered of adding a Town & People for the Honʳ of his Majesty in the Inlargement and Increase of his Province, Wee humbly supplicate that yoʳ Honʳˢ would take it to yoʳ Consideration and Grant that wee may have a Township Confirmed by yoʳ honours, wᶜʰ wee humbly offer the bounds thereof may extend as followeth, to begin at the head of Rialls his Cove and so to run upon a North west line Seven Miles, and from thence with Douer line Paralell until wee meet with Exeter line that yoʳ Honʳˢ would be pleased to grant this Petition, which will not only be a great benefit Both to the settlement of our minestrey, the population of the place, the ease of the Subject, and the Strengthening and Advantaging this his Majisᵗˢ Province, but for an engagement for yoʳ Petitioners ever to pray for the Safety and Increase of yoʳ Honʳˢ and prosperity.

John Woodman	William Jackson
Stephen Jones	Joseph Bunker
———— Davis X	John Smith
Samson Doe	Joseph Jones
James Bunker Sen X	John Doe
Jeremiah Cromet	John Williams
James durgin X	Thomas Williams
William willyoums	William durgin X
Elias Critchett	Henry Vines (?)
Nathaniell Meder	Philup Cromel X
John Cromell	John Meder Jr.
Jeremiah Burnum	William tascet X [Tasker]
John Smith	James dere [Derry]
Thomas Bickford	philip duly X
John Pinder	Ele meret [Eli Demeritt]
francis mathes	Joseph Jengens
Henry Nock	Jems Bonker X
John Willey	James Thomas
Thomas Edgerly	———— Pitman
Edward Leathers X	John Edgerly
Henry marsh	William durgin X
Joseph Meder	Joseph Smith
Edward Wakeham	Thomas Wille
Philip Chastlie Sin	Thomas Chastlie
Thomas Chastlie Jun	francis Pitman
George Chastlie	

This petition as printed in the Memoranda of Ancient Dover has been compared with the same as found in N. H. Town Papers, Vol. IX, p. 234, and appears to be more correct, especially as to names of inhabitants.

Nothing resulted from this petition, and the thought of making Oyster River a separate township passed out of mind for more than a generation. The rights of an independent parish, secured in 1716[1], satisfied the inhabitants for a time, and the dispute between the people at the Point and those at the Falls and the western part of the parish concerning the location of the meeting house engaged attention for a long time. In 1729 a dispute arose about the division line between Oyster River Parish and the rest of Dover, and a committee was appointed by the General Assembly to run the line. Parties living near the border desired to be included in the Oyster River precinct, where they had considered themselves as belonging and where it was more convenient for them to attend church. The following petition of "sundry aggrieved inhabitants of Oyster River" best explains the situation

To the Honorable John Wintworth Esq[r] Lieu[t] Governor and Commander in Chief in and over his Maj[tes] Province of New Hampshire in New England and to the Honorable his Majs[tes] Council and Representatives for said province.

The Humble Petition of Sundry aggrieved Inhabitants of the parish of Oyster River most humbly Sheweth Whereas we the Subscribers in Habitance of said parish Have allways been Constant hearers and Paid our Rats to the Minister of said Parish as by the Rait List of assessment Will make appear and Likewise Sundry of us have Been at a Consederabel Charge in Bulding a Meating House in said parish it being Nier and more Convenent for us to attend upon the Publick Worship of God at Oyster River Meeting House then at Cochecho Meeting House which is a great way further for us to go tho Never the Less as we understand we are in Danger of Being Excluded from our said Priviledges by such an Unequal Line of Boundary between the parish of Oyster River and Cochecho which if being so stated will be greatly to the Damage of yo[r] Petitioners.

We do therefore Humbly Crave Liberty of the more Mature and Superior Judgment of your honours in the General Assembly praying yo[r] honours to take it in Consideration that there may be a more Equal Line of Bound'ry Set so that yo[r] aggrieved petitioners may not be under such Grat hardships, and yo[r] petitioners shall ever pray,

JOSEPH JONES in behalf of the rest whose
names are to be given in.

[1] See chapter entitled Sketch of Church History.

Joseph Daniel	Zachrah Edgerly
William Brown	William Glines
James Jackson	Samuel Davis
Thomas Lethers	Joseph Hiks
John Tasker	James Busell
Samuel Chasley	Morres Fouller
Joshua Chasley	John Busell
Joseph Parkins	Eli Demerett
Thomas Bickford	William Demerett
Ralph Horll [Hall]	John Demerett
Samuel Parkins	John Huckins
Joseph Jones Junr	Job Demerett
Benj Jones	Derry Pitman
John Jones	Thomas Willey Jun
John Rand	Joseph Daniel the third
John Remiss [Remick?]	Noel Crose
Timothy Moses	John Daniel
Thomas ———	Benjamin Evens
Samuel Chesle	Harvey Buswell
John Allan	William Buswell
Dec. 10, 1729.	

As a result of this petition a hearing was granted, and the matter was put off until the spring session. Mr. Jones petitioned a second and a third time, and still no action was taken. September 18, 1731, the Rev. Hugh Adams asked for a hearing with reference to the division line of the parishes, and a hearing was ordered for 23 September, but no record of the result is to be found. September 24, 1731, Stephen Jones, Hubbard Stevens and John Woodman petitioned for a hearing on the same matter, representing that they were a committee authorized by the Oyster River Parish and that the previous hearing had not been held as ordered. In response to this petition a hearing was ordered for 6 May, 1732, which by adjournment was held 9 May, 1732. As a result a bill was drawn up and in a few days passed, incorporating Durham as a Township. The Journal of the House calls it the Parish of Durham. The records of the Council call it a Township. The Charter calls it a Township. The name Durham was suggested by the Rev. Hugh Adams, as claimed by him in an address to the General Assembly in 1738. See N. H. Province Papers, Vol. V, p. 35. See also Miss Mary P. Thompson's Landmarks in Ancient Dover, p. 67.

The Charter as given below is copied from the Town Record Book, the first thing recorded in the book that contains the records from the year 1820 to the year 1841. It has been compared with a copy made from the original in 1828. The original act was found among the papers of Secretary Richard Waldron in the hands of Richard Russell Waldron of Portsmouth, February, 1827. It does not bear the Province Seal:

Anno Regni Regis Georgii Secundi Quinto.

An act for making that part of Dover formerly called Oyster River into a township by the name of Durham.

Be it enacted by his Excellc⁷ the Governor, Councill and Representatives conven'd in General Assembly and by the authority of the same, That all those lands lying on the southerly side of a west north west halfe a point north line from Johnsons Creek at the bridge (in the county rhoad) to the head line of Dover township, and from the said bridge southeast and by east down to a pine tree on a point or neck of land called Cedar Point on the west side of the mouth of the Back River in Dover be erected and made into a distinct and separate town by the name of Durham by the bounds aforesaid: all the lands lying within the township of Dover on the southerly side of the lines aforesaid from Johnsons Bridge: And that the inhabitants of Durham have, use, exercise and enjoy all such powers and privileges which other towns have, and do by law use, exercise and enjoy so that theykeep & maintaine a learned orthodox minister of good conversation among them: and make provision for an honᵇˡᵉ support and maintenance for him and that in order thereto they be discharged from payment to any other minister: and that all the common land within said town of Durham to be the present inhabitants as the majᵗ part thereof shall grant and that (if there be occasion to call a town meeting for making choice of any town officers for the present yeare) that Capt. Francis Mathes is hereby impowered and directed to notifie and summon the inhabitants duely quallified for voters to assemble & meet together for the choosing such officers or making such rates as are needfull for the present yeare untill theire annuall meeting.

And be it further enacted, That the said town of Durham have power to send a Representative to the Genˡˡ Assembly from time to time.

In the House of Represenˢ May 13th 1732.
Read three timᵉ in the House of Representatives and passed to be enacted.

ANDREW WIGGIN, *Speaker*

In Counᵉ *eod die* Read and Concurr'd.

R. WALDRON, *Sec'ry*

May 15, 1732. I assent to the enacting this bill.

J. BELCHER.

The first town meeting was called by Capt. Francis Mathes and held 26 June 1732. It was voted to divide the common and undivided lands among the present inhabitants, and a committee for that purpose was appointed 28 January 1733/4. The warrant of 6 March, 1733/4. under the hands of the select-

2

men, called a meeting of the freeholders and inhabitants, who were so in 1732, to assemble at the meeting house, where the Sullivan monument now is, on Monday, 18 March 1733/4, to pass votes relating to the division of the common lands. It appears that the previous committee did not act. The meeting chose Jonathan Thompson as Moderator and the following committee to make the division, viz., Job Runals, Joseph Jones, Jr., Stephen Jones, Ichabod Chesle, Thomas Stevenson, Samuel Smith, Elezar Bickford, Daniel Davis, Francis Mathes, Joseph Thomas, John Smith, Jr., John Williams, Jon^a Tomson, John Burnum and John Woodman.

DURHAM VILLAGE AS SEEN FROM BROTH HILL
"Distance lends enchantment to the view."

Samuel Smith was chosen Proprietors' Clerk, and 19 December 1734, it was voted "that not any person that was not an inhabitant in town when the charter was given and granted should have any part or share of the common or undivided lands in said town."

On 20 December, 1734, the committee "voted that no person under the age of twenty one years of age when the charter was given & granted should have any part or share of the common & undivided lands in said town."

At a subsequent meeting it was decided that twenty-five acres should constitute a whole share, and that whoever had farmed or improved any of the common lands since 1701 and before the charter was given should have the privilege of laying it out "when it comes their turns by the numbers that they draw," and íf they refused then the others could lay out the same. The Rev. Hugh Adams, in a petition to the Governor, Council and Assembly, in 1738, states that "the inhabitants of said town proceeded by their chosen committee at their most general meeting to divide their commons, voting the minister aforesaid should, as he did, draw lots for them all." The division was made in the meeting house, the land divided being largely located near Little River, in that part of Durham which is now Lee. Later it was voted by the town that "each whole Share man pay ye Comite eight shillings & each lesser Share man according to their proportion & to pay when their lots are drawn." The division was made 18 March, 1733/4, and the following is a list of those who received lands:

Acres		Acres	
12½	Joseph Atkinson	25	Wm Clay
16⅔	Saml Adams	25	Elias Critchet
25	Hugh Adams	8⅓	James Conner
3½	Joseph Baker	25	Joseph Davis
25	Joseph Bickford	25	Ephraim Davis
25	Benjn Bickford	25	Joshua Davis
25	John Bickford	25	John Davis
25	Elizer Bickford	25	Benjamin Davis
16⅔	Walter Briant	12½	Jeremiah Davis
25	John Burnum	12½	Samuel Davis
25	James Burnum	25	James Davis Jr.
25	Robert Burnum	25	Daniel Davis
3⅛	Charles Bamford	16⅔	Solomon Davis
25	Joseph Bunker	25	James Davis
25	James Bunker	16⅔	Jabez Davis
25	Abraham Bennick	16⅔	Ebenezer Davis
12½	John Buss	25	John Drew
16⅔	John Buss Jr.	25	Joseph Drew
25	Jonathan Chesle	25	Wm Drew
25	Ruben Chesley	25	Thomas Drew
25	Joseph Chesle	16⅔	Joseph Durgin
25	Ichabod Chesle	25	Francis Durgin
25	Philip Chesle	25	John Durgin
25	Joshua Chesle	16⅔	James Durgin Jr.
25	Lemuel Chesle	25	James Durgin
25	Eli Clark	25	William Durgin
25	Joshua Cromet	16⅔	Wm Durgin Jr.
25	John Cromat	16⅔	Jonathan Durgin

Acres	
12½	Benjamin Durgin
16⅔	John Doo Jr. [Doe]
25	John Doo
16⅔	Joseph Doo
25	John Daniels
25	Joseph Duda
25	Joseph Daniels Jr.
12	Peter Dennio [Denbo, now Dinsmore]
25	Richd Dinbo
12½	Benjamin Daniel
6¼	Joseph Daniels
25	Samuel Emerson
25	Timothy Emerson
25	John Edgerly
25	John Edgerly Jr.
25	Joseph Edgerly
25	Joseph Edgerly Jr.
25	John Footman, deceased
25	John Footman
25	Joseph Footman
25	Thomas Footman
3⅛	Samuel Folloy
25	Ichabod Follet
16⅔	John Foolet
25	John Gray
6¼	Joseph Gilman
1	Nathaniel Gookin
25	Henry Hill
25	Valentine Hill
25	Nathaniel Hill
25	William Hill
12½	John Hall's Estate
12½	James Hall
6¼	James Heald
25	Robert Huckins
25	Joseph Jones
25	Stephen Jones
25	Stephen Jones Jr.
25	Eben'r Jones
25	John Jenkins
25	Wm Jenkins
25	Stephen Jenkins
12½	Samuel Jackson
25	Wm Jackson
6¼	Moses Kenning
6¼	John Kelly

Acres	
25	Robert Kent
12	Joseph Kent
25	John Kent
12½	Naptheli Kinket [Kincaid]
1	Christopher Korest (?)
12½	Ezekiel Leathers
16⅔	Edward Leathers
12½	Abednego Leathers
25	William Leathers
3⅛	James Leary
16⅔	Thomas Langley
16⅔	James Langley
8⅓	John Mason
16⅔	Isaac Mason
25	Peter Mason
6¼	Wm Mills
25	Peter Mondro
16⅔	John Muncy
3⅛	Robert Mack Daniel
1	Randel Mack Donel
25	Samuel Meder
25	Joseph Meder
25	John Meder
25	Nathaniel Meder
25	Daniel Meder
25	Nicholas Meder
25	Francis Mathes
25	Francis Mathes
6¼	John Moore
25	Hezekiah Mash
25	John Pinder
25	Benjn Pinder
25	Samuel Perkins
25	John Pitman
6¼	Abel Peve
8⅓	Mathew Percy
25	Solomon Pinkham
25	Wm Rains
25	John Rawlings
25	John Ranals
25	Job Ranals
16⅔	Jon Randel
16⅔	Wm Randell
6¼	Richard Rooks
8⅓	John Seias Jr.
16⅔	Samuel Sias
16⅔	Solomon Sias

Acres	
1	Benjamin Stevens
16⅔	James Stevens
25	Hubord Stevens
8⅓	Ebenezer Spencer
8⅓	Wm Shepperd
12½	Clement Sias
25	John Sias
25	John Smith
25	John Smith Jr.
25	John Smith ye 3d
25	Samuel Smith
25	Samuel Smith Jr.
25	Samuel Smith ye 3d
25	James Smith
25	Archabel Smith
25	Benjamin Smith
6¼	Joseph Smart
12½	Joseph Simons
25	Joseph Stevenson
25	Thomas Stevenson
25	Abraham Stevenson
25	John Tomson's Estate
25	John Tompson
25	Jonathan Thompson

Acres	
25	Joseph Thomas
16⅔	Joseph Wormwood
16⅔	Jacob Wormwood
25	Wm Wormwood
25	Jonathan Woodman
25	Jonathan Woodman Jr.
25	Joshua Woodman
16⅔	Edward Woodman
16⅔	Arclas Woodman
25	John Woodman
8⅓	John Welsh
5	Joseph Wheler
25	John Wille
25	John Wille Jr.
12½	John Wille ye 3d
16⅔	Wm Wille
16⅔	Stephen Wille
15	Ye Estate Wm Wakham decd
25	Samuel Williams
25	John Williams
25	John Williams Jr.
25	John York
6¼	Richard ——— [York?]

Additional Grants, March 23, 1737.

Acres	
25	Thomas Leathers
8⅓	Joseph Glidden
6¼	Salathiel Denbo

Acres	
25	Lemuel Chesley
12½	John Laskey
	George Chesley

The business of the Proprietors was not closed up for many years. In 1765 Jonathan Woodman and Hubbard Stevens, Proprietors' Committee, called a meeting, as some grants conflicted with each other. John Thompson, Jeremiah Burnham, Jr., and Moses Emerson were impowered to sell the balance of land and examine the doings of the former committee. A committee consisting of John Woodman, Capt. Joseph Sias, and Capt. Benjamin Smith were chosen to examine the papers brought from the former clerk's office and determine what of said papers is proper to be recorded. Ebenezer Thompson was elected clerk 31 March 1766, which position he filled until 28 March 1774.

When the parish of Lee was established in 1765, the town of

Durham thus voted to protect the interests of the proprietors, "That the said parish shall not in any Respect Interfere with any Lands belonging to the proprietors in said town." See N. H. Town Papers, Vol. XI, pp. 584-85.

In 1772 John Woodman, "survivor of the Proprietors' Committee," called a meeting, and Major Stephen Jones was chosen moderator and Nathaniel Norton Clerk *pro tem.* Action was taken to eject William Caldwell from land. The records show lawsuits. The end is not recorded.

The aim of this chapter is to state merely the most important steps in the municipal history of Durham. We pass on, therefore, to the division of the town and the incorporation of Lee. It is thus stated on high authority, "January 16, 1766, the town was divided and the westerly part incorporated as a Parish by the name of Lee, with full town privileges." It is questionable whether Lee had at first full town privileges, for the Journals of the House of Representatives do not show that Lee was impowered to send a representative to the General Assembly while New Hampshire was a royal province. Lee sent as delegates to the first Provincial Congress at Exeter Joseph Sias and Ebenezer Jones; to the second Congress, Joseph Sias and John Layn; to the third, Joseph Sias and Smith Emerson, and also to the fourth; to the fifth, Capt. Hercules Mooney. This Congress met 21 December 1775 and was organized as a House of Representatives in January 1776.

Moreover, the town records of Durham show that in the spring meeting after the incorporation of Lee the town elected three selectmen for Durham and also Nicholas Duda and Robert Thompson for Lee, and in 1767 the town meeting of Durham elected Miles Randall and Nicholas Duda as selectmen of Lee. Also on the 28th of March 1774, when trouble was brewing with Great Britian, the town of Durham elected Joseph Sias, Esq., and Capt. Hercules Mooney on an important town committee, "to prepare instructions to be given their Representatives and report to the adjournment of the meeting."

A town meeting was held at the Falls meeting house in Durham, 3 September 1764. A committee consisting of Lieut. Joseph Sias, Miles Randall and Nicholas Duda on the part of those desiring incorporation, and Capt. Stephen Jones, Thomas Chesley and Capt. Benjamin Smith on the part of Durham, was appointed to run a line from Paul Chesley's house near the Madbury line to the house of John Smart on the Newmarket line, according to the request of sundry persons of the town. The meeting was adjourned to the 24th instant, when the committee made their report and unanimously recommended,

That a Strait Line, Beginning one hundred and Twenty four Rods above the Dwelling house of paul Chelsey, on Madbury Line, and So to Run a Strait point across to Newmarket Line. to one mile and a half above the Dwelling house of John Smart, may be a Suitable Line.

N. B.   It is the intent of the above Resolve, that the Line Fixed upon run from the house of paul Chesley, North 6 degrees East to Madbury Line & then to Measure up 124 rods, by said Madbury Line.

The town meeting was adjourned to 8 October next, when Capt. Benjamin Smith and Lieut. Joseph Sias were appointed a committee to "draw a Vote in writing for the western part of the town to Be Sat of as a parish and Bring it to the Town, at Some publick town meeting." This committee brought in their report to a town meeting held 18 November 1765, in writing, as follows:

That the west End of Said Town of Durham be voted to be Sat of as a parish, Agreeably to the Result or a Report of a Committee, (Chosen and appointed for that purpose) and Brought into publick Town meeting the 24th day of Sept. 1764—with this addition, thereto, that the Said parish, when an act may be Obtained for that purpose, Shall take their proportionable Part of the poor now Supported by the whole town, and Likewise That the Said parish Shall not in any Respect Interfere with any Lands belonging to the proprietors in Said Town.—Voted that the above vote, Brought by Capt. Smith and Sias, is agreeable to the Sense of the Town and that it be Recorded accordingly." See N. H. Town Papers XI. 584-5, or Town Records of Durham.

The following petition is of value especially for the genealogist, since it shows who were living in Lee in 1765:

To his Excellency Benning Wentworth Esqr Governor and Commander in Chief in and over his Majesty's Province of New Hampshire, to the Honourable his Majesty's Counsel and the House of Representatives in General Assembly Convened, *The Petition* of Sundry of the Inhabitants of Durham most humbly *Sheweth* that in said Town of Durham there are Inhabitants Sufficient for two Parishes and to maintain and support the Charge thereof That many of the Inhabitants live more than Eight miles from the Place of Publick Worship and where all Town meetings and the Publick of Affairs are holden and Transacted which Renders it very Difficult for them to Attend there at any time but more Expecially in the winter Season that the consequence thereof it is Probable will be that many of the Youth in said Town will be brought up in great Ignorance unless the Difficulties be removed and the Petitioners are in a great measure prevented the use of their Privilidges in their present Situation—

Wherefore your Petitioners most humbly pray your Excellency and Honours,

that there may be two Parishes in said Town and that the Dividing Line between the two Parishes Beginning at Paul Chesles house at Beech Hill so
(Called) then North Six Degrees East to the line Between said Durham and
Madbury then running westerly on said line one hundred and twenty four
Rods then Beginning and Running from thence to New Market line to one
mile and half above the Dwelling House of John Smart, which line was agreed
upon by a Committee Chosen by the said Town of Durham in the year one
thousand Seven hundred and Sixty four and Voted in Publick Town meeting,
and so to Include the whole of said Durham above this line. *We therefore
humbly* pray your Excellency and your Honours to take our Case into your
wise Considerations and Set said Parish off by said line with the powers and
privileges of other Towns or Parishes in this Province and your Petitioners as
in Duty bound shall ever pray.

Dated at Durham November 18th 1765.

Hercules Mooney	Joshua Woodman Junr	Israel Randel
Gideon Mathes	John Giles	Francis Durgin
Winthrop Durgin	Joseph medar	Joshua Burnam
Elijah Denbo	Thomas Huckins	Samuel Carter
Samuel Jackson	Nicholas Duda	Thomas huckins Jr
Joseph Thomson	Ebenr Lethers	Solomon Sias
James Hall	William Renely	ffrancis Allen
Jonathan runnels	ffrancis Eliot	William Cashey
Samuel pitman		Edweard Scales
John follett	Benjamin Bickford	Samuel bickford
Benjamin Bradly	mason Rendel	William Rendel
Joseph Jackson	Joseph Clay	Job Runels
Josiah Johnson	Nathaniel Stevens	John Clark
Timothy Davis	Jun	David Davis
thomas Yourk	Bartholomew Smart	George tutle
stoten tutle	Nichole Tuttel	Jonathan Stevens
Miles Randal	Samuel Burley	Zaccheus Clough
Samuel Langley	Nathaniel Randal	John Davis
Moses Davis Junr	Reubin Hill	James Giles Bunker
Willm Waymoth	Clement Davis	Robert York
James Davis	James Watson	Jonathan Stevens
Hanary tufts	Nathaniel frost	Ebenezer Dow jun.
nathaniel Watson	Samuel Watson	Nathaniel Watson jur
Andew watson	Josiah Durgin	Joseph Huckins
Isaac Small	John Durgin	John Shaw Junr
Joseph Hicks	John Shaw	Ichabod Denbow
John Sanborn	Benjamin Woodman	Thomas Wille
Edward Hill	Samuel Sias	John Snell
Thomas Snell	David munsey	Eli Clark
Eli Clark Juner	Benja Clark	hunkin Dam
Eben Randel	Moses Dam	Thomas Noble
Micah Emerson	Joseph doe	Nathel Sias
Joseph Clark	Benja Durgin	Nathaniel Stevens
Joseph Sias	Ebr Jones Juner	
John Elliot		

John Cartland, a Friend, is said to have come from Lee, Scotland, early in the eighteenth century and to have had the privilege of naming Lee after his native town.

No further change was made in the boundaries of Durham till 2 July 1870, when the western portion of Lubberland stretching along the north shore of Great Bay was set off and annexed to Newmarket. Thus that part of ancient Exeter received a portion of its original claim, and Durham lost some historic places. This portion, however, is included in the descriptive history of this book.

No complete tax list has been found between the years 1682 and 1783. There is a "Ministers Counterpein for the year 1760" in the possession of S. H. Shackford, Esq., of Boston, which gives the names of those then living on the "North Side" of Oyster River. The names alphabetically arranged are as follows:

Doc⸢ Joseph Atkinson	Jonathan Davis Jr.
Abner Bickford	Jeremiah Davis
Benjamin Bickford	Moses Davis
Samuel Bickford	Nehemiah Davis
Benjamin Bodge	Robert Davis
Joshua Burnum	Zephaniah Davis
Solomon Burnum	Aaron Davis
Thomas Bunker	Samuel Demeritt
Isaac Bussel	Clement Denbo
Andrew Carter	Ichabod Denbo
George Chesle	Joseph Doe
Jonathan Chesle	Samuel Dyer
Joshua Chesle	Benj Durgin
Lt. Ichabod Chesle	Josiah Durgin
Paul Chesle	Moses Emerson
Lt. Philip Chesle	Solomon Emerson Esq.
Samuel Chesle	Abraham Fernald
Thomas Chesle	Jonathan Fish
Thomas Chesle Jr.	John Follet
Joseph Clark	Widow Prudence Follet
Joseph Clay	John Giles
Jonathan Clough	Stephen Glashier
Zacheus Clough	John Glover
John Crocket	Richard Glover
Moses Dam	Samuel Gray
David Daniel	Edward Hill
Ephraim Davis	Eliphalet Hill
John Davis	Jonathan Hill
Jonathan Davis	Nathan⸢ Hill

Robert Hill
Samuel Hill
Samuel Hill Jr.
Valentine Hill
Widow Abigail Jones
Benjamin Jones
Ebenezer Jones
Ebenezer Jones Jr.
Richard Jones
Capt. Stephen Jones
Benjamin Jackson
Widow Patience Jackson
William Jackson
Mark Jewel
David Jonson
Thomas Jonson
John Huckins
Joseph Huckins
Joseph Huckins Jr.
Thomas Huckins
Thomas Huckins Jr.
Aaron Hunscomb
Elias Lad
John Langley Jr.
Samuel Langley
John Laskey
Samuel Langmaid
Abednego Leathers
Ebenezer Leathers
Edward Leathers
Edward Leathers Jr.
Ezekiel Leathers
Jonathan Leathers
Robert Leathers
Stephen Leathers
Thomas Leathers
Gideon Mathes
John McCoy
Nathan¹ Meder
Thomas Noble
Wm. Odiorne Esqʳ.
Abijah Pinkom
Walter Philbrick
Quick Priest
Ebenezer Randal
John Randel
Jonathan Randal
Mason Randal

Widow Mary Randal
Miles Randal
William Randal
Thomas Rines
Thomas Rollins
Abraham Runals
Job Runals
Job Runals Jr.
Jonathan Runals
William Runals
Edward Scales
Lt. Joseph Sias
Nathaniel Sias
Samuel Sias
Samuel Sias Jr.
Solomon Sias
John Shaw
Benjamin Small
Benjamin Small Jr.
Edward Small
Isaac Small
Joseph Small
Joseph Small Jr.
John Snell
Abednego Spencer
Hubbard Stevens
Hubbard Stevens Jr.
Joseph Stevens
Samuel I. Stevens
Jos. Stevenson
Docʳ Ebenezer Thompson
John Thomson
Ens. Jonathan Thomson
Widow Sarah Thomson
Nathaniel Thomson
Robert Thomson
Robert Thomson Jr.
Seth Thomson
Solomon Thomson
John Tasker Jr.
Samuel Tod
Archalaus Woodman
Edward Woodman
Jonathan Woodman
John Woodman
Jonathan Woodman, Jr.
Joshua Woodman
Shadrach Walton

Thomas Whitekom
Paul Wille
Samuel Wille
Thomas Wille

John Williams
John Williams Jr.
Joseph Williams

The following names are found on a counterpart for the Parish of Madbury for the year 1758 and may be of use to genealogists. Many on this list belonged to Durham families.

William Allen
Elijah Austin
Benjamin Bickford
Charles Bickford
John Bickford Jr.
Thomas Bickford
Benjamin Bodge
Nicholas Brock
James Brown
Azariah Boodey
Benjamin Bussell
Henry Bussell
Ebenezer Bussell
Isaac Bussell
John Bussell
Joseph Bussell
Samuel Bussell
William Bussell
Stephen Bunker
Richard Caswell
Ichabod Canney
James Chesleys Estate
Jonathan Chesley
Joshua Chesley
Samuel Chesley
Samuel Chesley Jr.
Paul Chesley
Reuben Chesley
Lemuel Chesley
Abraham Clark
James Clark
Rememᶜᵉ Clark
James Clements
Hezekiah Cook
John Canney Jr.
Wid Sarah Dam
Lt. James Davis
Maj. Thomas Davis
Samᵘ Davis & son Thomas

Ephraim Davis
Nathaniel Davis
Samᵘ Davis, Jr.
Joseph Daniels
Joseph Daniels Jr.
Jacob Daniels
Eli Demerit
Job Demerit
Ebenezer Demerit
John Demerit
& his son John
Solomon Demerit
William Demerit
Job Demerit Jr.
Clement Drew Jr.
Clement Drew
David Drew
James Drew
Joseph Drew Estate
Joseph Drew
Francis Drew
Meshech Drew
Obediah Drew
Paul Drew
Silas Drew
Samuel Drew
Thomas Drew
& son John
Thomas Drew Jr.
Thomas Drew 3rd
Lt. Zechʳ Edgerly
Solᵒ Emerson Esq.
Daniel Evens
John Evens
Joseph Evens
Micah Emerson
Stephen Evens
Thomas Evens
Ebenʳ Garland

Capt. Paul Gerrish
William Glidden
Wid. Mary Glover
John Ham
John Ham Jr.
James Hanson
Jonathan Hanson
Nathaniel Hanson
Stephen Hanson
Timothy Hanson
Samuel Hanson
Ichabod Hayes
Daniel Hayes
Capt. Joseph Hicks
Israel Hodgdon
John Huckins
Robert Huckine
Benjamin Hill
William Hill
Daniel Jacobs
Wid. Hannah Jackson
James Jackson
James Jackson Jr.
Daniel Jacobs Jr.
Joseph Jackson
William Jackson
William Jenkens
Anthony Jones
Benjamin Jones
Richard Jones
Abraham Jonson
Wid. Hannah Laighton
Isaac Laighton
John Laighton
John Laighton of Barrington
Gideon Laighton
Samuel Laighton
James Lammus
Nath'll Lammus
Benjamin Leathers
Thomas Leathers
Joseph Libby
John Malory
John Malory Jr.
James Malory
Daniel Meader
Joseph Meader

Daniel Misarve
Daniel Misarve Jr.
Joseph Misarve
John Misarve
Timothy Moses
David Muncey, Durham
Stephen Otis
Stephen Otis Jr.
Conor Pitman
Zechariah Pitman
Amos Pinkham
James Pinkham
Moses Pinkham
Paul Pinkham
Stephen Pinkham
Solomon Pinkham
Richard Pinkham Jr.
Samuel Pinkham Jr.
Simon Rendel
John Roberts
Ens. Joseph Roberts
Samuel Roberts
John Smith
Abednego Spencer
Ebenezer Tasker
John Tasker
John Tasker Jr.
William Tasker
Daniel Tibbets
Henry Tibbets
Jeremiah Tibbets
Nathaniel Tibbets
Isaac Twombly
Joseph Twombly
William Twombly 3d
John Winget Jr.
Dennet Waymoth
Moses Waymoth
John Whitehorn
Joseph Woodman
Abner Young
Eleazer Young
Daniel Young
Jonathan Young
Samuel Young
Samuel Young Jr.
James Young

Durham has sent out colonies from time to time to found and develop other towns. New Durham was incorporated, 6 December 1762, as the result of a petition signed in 1748 by ninety-six petitioners from Durham, many of whom settled in the new town. Many of the founders of Rochester went from Durham, and the earliest meetings of the proprietors were held in Durham. Canterbury had a goodly number of settlers from Durham, whose names are found in the list of proprietors. Holderness, Barrington, Barnstead and Nottingham were indebted to Durham for many of their early men of enterprise and leadership. In later years the broad West has been dotted here and there with settlers from the vicinity of Oyster River, and some of these have risen to places of distinction and power.

EARLY SETTLERS AND ESTATES

In locating the first settlers in Oyster River Plantation it may be convenient, for the sake of clearness, to begin at the western extremity of the shore line, at the mouth of Lamprey River, the earliest boundary between Dover and Exeter.

Richard York deposed in 1652 that he was living in Dover in 1635. He had a lot on Dover Neck as early as 1642. The following town grant is without date, but it was made probably about this time. "Richard York, a house Lott conteyning by Estimacon eleaven acres more or less, butting upon the high street East and on the Durty Lane west on John Dams Lott on the South and uppon the lane from Elder Nutters North, more all the m' she in a Creeke called by the name of Little Johns Creek, more one small marsh conteyning by estimation eleaven acres more or less in the great Bay butting upon two small Islands southwest, more one spott of marsh lying to the northwest ioyning to ye other only a small point of Land making some division." In 1656 there were granted to him one hundred acres next to John Martin's "bounded as followeth, that is to say, by lambrill River side North west 96 Rood and from the marked tree Betwixt John Martin and Richard York 200 Rood South west and be west and the head line 96 Rod nor west & be nor and from that marked tree to the River again 200 Rood south west and be west." This he willed to his son Benjamin in 1672. This land is now in Newmarket, forming the southerly part of the neck of land lying between the mouth of Lamprey River and Goddard's Creek.

Next north of Richard York lived John Martin, who married Hester, daughter of Thomas Roberts of Dover Neck. On the 26th of 7th month, 1664, there was granted to John Martin "the land which now he posseth where his dwelling house standeth to be maed up forty ackers Beginning at the water sied taking all the land Betwixt John Godder and Richard Yorke and so running up into the woods not intrenching upon ani former Grant."

The location of John Martin's lot is still further defined, 28 February 1664, when it was ordered that Capt. Ralph Hall and

Deacon John Hall lay out a highway from Lamprey River Fall
to the water's side in the Great Bay. They accordingly "layd
it out as followeth, that is to say, from the fall above sayd to
Goe as the old way goeth tell it Cometh to a great Roke with a
tree groeing on the top thear of on the left hand of the old waye
goeing from the said fall to John Godders, neir to wich Roke are
two trees marked with H thus betweine wich trees the way is to
goo straite Downe to a letell freshett and over it strait to another
and over it and soe betwixt two trees marked with H like the
former two trees and soe betwixt a letell swampe and the Rokey
hill side thet lieth behind John Martins house and soe strait to the
laen that is betwixt John Godders fence and John martins fence
of the Corn fields that now lieth befoer thear doers or houses tell
it cometh to the lower Corner of John Martins fence next the
foer menshened laen and thear to turne and goe as the old way
goeth at the present to the usuall landing plase tell John martin
mak a way from the sayd Corner of his fence lower downe toward
the water side then the way goeth at the Present. The way is to
be fower poll wied all the way saueing between the two foer
mentioned fences. John Martin is to make the way soe as shall
be to the Towns Content belowe his feilld befoer it be
Altered."

John Martin and wife Hester conveyed, 20 September 1667,
to Thomas Mounsell his dwelling house "now standing in Luberland in ye Great Bay," together with forty acres of upland lying
between Richard York's and John Goddard's lands, and the
following year Mounsell sold this to Nicholas Doe, whose son,
Sampson Doe, inherited it and added adjacent lands thereto.
John Martin and family removed to Piscataway, New Jersey.

On the 10th of the first month, 1673/4, the bounds between
Nicholas Doe and John Goddard were fixed as follows, "from
high water mark at the usuall landing place A high waye of fower
poele wid up to John Godder his land at the marsh on the one
side and soe to the Corner of John Godders orchard on the west
and that fence of the orchard to stand and soe to a heape of
Rockes on the west of the heigh waye and Nicholass Does garden
on the Est of the high waye and all the Newe fence att Does
garden to be wholley taken a way and from the Corner of Does
garden in to the woods upon the west sid of the hill this high way
to goe into the woods of fower pole wide upon a North and be

west line and is the bounds of the land betwixt John Godderd and
Nichlos Doe."

It is impossible to locate precisely the ten acres granted to Hugh
Dunn, 17th of first month, 1663/4. "Whereas hew doenn hath
Buellt a house neir lampril River and having now writ [no right]
to anie land thear we doe Grant him ten ackers thear, Exchange
of ten Ackers from his thirty Ackers at Sandey Banck, which tenn
Ackers at Sandey Banck is to Remaine the Townes." The land
at Sandy Bank had been granted to him in 1656. It is located up
Lamprey River, on the north side of Lee Hook. Dunn sold this
to Philip Crommett about 1666 and went to New Jersey with
John Martin and others. See New Jersey's Indebtedness to
New Hampshire, by O. B. Leonard of Plainfield, N. J., in N. H.
Gen. Record, Vol. 1, pp. 145-50.

The next lot northeasterly of John Martin's was originally
granted by the town to the Rev. Thomas Larkham, between 1639
and 1642, who conveyed the same to Joseph Miller. On the 21st
of September 1647, Joseph Miller conveyed to John Goddard
the "house where Miller now liveth and five acres of land," also
twenty acres given by the inhabitants of Dover, alias Northam
to Thomas Larkham, "lyinge on the west side of Backe River,"
also thirty acres of meadow ground lying "on the westerlie side
of the greate baye neere unto a cove called the greate Cove,"
excepting ten acres given unto John Ault by the said Thomas
Larkham, also one hundred acres on the easterly side of the said
marsh ground given by Dover to said Larkham. Goddard paid
for all this land 16,500 of merchantable pipe staves. Goddard's
Creek, an often mentioned landmark, ran through the thirty
acres of land above mentioned.

John Goddard was one of Capt. John Mason's colonists, who
came over in the *Pied Cow* in 1634. He aided in erecting the
first saw mill and grist mill run by water in New England, at
what is now Great Works, South Berwick, Me. It would seem
from what is said above that his house, which was a garrison,
stood south of the creek.

Mention has been made of land butting upon two small islands
granted to Richard York. His son John inherited this land and
islands and, 1 June 1676, he and wife Ruth sold to Michael
French of Oyster River "all that tract or point of land lying and
being in Lubberland, bounded by the Great Bay on the South

3

east side, by the lands of Nicholas Doe on the North west side, by the lands of the said John York on the North east side, and by the creek called Goddards Creek on the South west Side," "with a parcel of marsh on the South side and two little Islands containing by estimation six acres be it more or less." One of the witnesses was Thomas Ladbrook. October 14, 1680, John York conveyed to Roger Rose eighty acres granted to York's father, with all meadows, flats, creek, thatch-bed, islands, and islets belonging to said grant. Roger Rose sold this land to John Rawlins of Newbury, and Rawlins sold it to John Smith, 20 July 1705, "a tract of land and salt marsh, houses, ffeilds and

DAVIS-SMITH GARRISON, LUBBERLAND

orchards scituate, lying and being in Lubberland." Roger Rose died 6 August 1705, leaving no issue, so far as learned. He was born about 1638 and married in 1661 Abigail, daughter of Christopher Grant of Watertown, Mass. In early life he was a servant of William Hudson. He is called "tailor."

Joseph, son of John Smith, sold above mentioned land and islands to Nicholas Doe, and Sampson Doe, his son, sold the same to Joseph Chesley, 27 March 1707. The latter is said to have had a garrison house here and the islands were called Chesley's Islands. Some have supposed that the first Philip Chesley lived here, but the evidences are all against that supposition.

John Alt, "aged about seventy-three years," deposed, 2

March 1677/8, that Robert Smart senior of Exeter did own and possess all the meadow on the southwest side of John Goddard's Creek "and yᵉ said Smart did possess it twelve years before Dover was a township & he did possess it sixteen years together." This takes us back to 1636. Others testified to the same effect in a controversy that arose. A part of this marsh came into the possession of Sampson Doe, and the rest was sold by Robert Smart to Joseph Smith and his son John, 8 April 1706.

It has been said above that the Rev. Thomas Larkham gave ten acres to John Ault before 1642, lying next to Goddard's land. The town also granted to John Ault, 10 August 1653, eighty acres at "yᵉ Great Cove above needums poynt, 40 rods in length upon yᵉ Cove." This was laid out to him in 1669, beginning at Richard York's marked tree and running thence by the water side forty rods toward Needoms point. The place is called Broad Cove and also Needham's Cove. It seems that John Ault did not live here. He sold this land, in 1670, to John Cutt of Portsmouth. Ault's home lot will be shown further on.

It was in this vicinity that David Davis, who was taxed in 1680, built his garrison house in 1695, which until recently stood about a quarter of a mile west of where Warren Smith now lives. The road has been changed so as to run over the site of the old garrison. Davis was killed by Indians, 27 August 1696. John Smith got possession of this land also and kept adding to his landed estate till he owned a stretch of about four miles along the northerly shore of the Great Bay, and here his descendants have lived unto the present day.

Needham's Point, called later Jewell's Point, derived its name probably from Nicholas Needham of Exeter, though no record has been found of land owned by him here. Needham's Cove is northeast of the Point, and the point of land at the easterly extremity of the Cove was anciently called Pinder's Point. The next point of land was called Morris's Point, and between the two points was Clift Cove. John and Ruth York 14 October 1680, sold to John Pinder, brickmaker and bricklayer, "land beginning at the little point in Clift Cove adjoining to Thomas Morris and so over the neck to a pine tree by the path going to Lubberland." John York had bought this land of Thomas Roberts, senior, 1 July 1669. Here lived the Pinder family for several generations.

Lubberland seems to have been a name given first to the region
between Lamprey River and Goddard's Creek and to have gradually been applied to all the adjoining region along the north
shore of Great Bay.

Thomas Morris was taxed in 1663 and died 30 July 1707, as
Pike's Journal says. His will gives his land to his friends James
and William Durgin. James Durgin's son, John, sold to John
Smith, 2 January 1735, twenty acres of land "with one dwelling
house thereon situate lying & being in Durham ajoining on y^e
north west side of ye Great bay & bounded by John Pinders land
on ye Southwest & on ye North by John Smiths land & on y^e
northeast by ye Creek call Thomas Morrys [Morris's] Creek."

Next east of Thomas Morris came land of Thomas Footman,
granted to him in 1653. He first lived on the shore of Little
Bay, as we shall soon see. An island, still called Footman's
Island, was granted to him on the 19th of 8th month, 1653, con-
taining one acre of land more or less, in the mouth of the Great
Bay. The island, "laying against the house," is mentioned in
Thomas Footman's will, 1667. The site of the Footman house
is easily found in about the middle of the field.

Next to Thomas Footman lived William Durgin. This appears from the following citation. December 20, 1723, Francis
Durgin of Exeter sold to John Smith his right, title and interest
in "one certain neck of land situate lying & being on ye norwest
side of great bay & aioyning to Matheses Creek so called which
being y^t half of s^d neck of land which my father William Durgin
lived on in his life time & died in ye Persetion." December 11,
1694, William Furber was licensed to keep a ferry from his house
at Welchman's Cove, to transport travelers over to Oyster
River, at the rate of three pence for each person and eight pence
for man and horse, if landed "at Mathews his neck," and six
pence for each person and twelve pence for man and horse, if
landed "at Durgins the west side of Mathews his neck." See
N. H. Province Papers, Vol. II, 146-47.

Eli Edgerly has long lived on the old Durgin farm. In front
of his house and about two rods distant there was a cellar where
now is a large cherry tree. Here was probably the Durgin garrison mentioned in 1695. The ferry landing seems to have been
in a little cove at the southeast corner of the field. The site of

Thomas Footman's house is plainly seen from Mr. Edgerly's doorway.

South of Crommett's Creek and west of the road a winding road near the creek led to the home of the Daniel family in the old days. Certainly John Daniel lived here and probably his father, "Davey" Daniel. The cellar can be found easily.

On the 23d of the 10th month, 1654, a grant was made to Francis Matthews of "all the marsh in the Great Creek on the norwest side of the Great Bay, being the first creek, and one

ADAMS POINT, FIRST CALLED "MATTHEWS NECK"
In the distance, beyond Crommett's Creek, is the old Durgin farm

hundred acres of upland adjoining to it." This creek was for many years called Mathes Creek, till Joshua Crommett and his son, Jacob, settled on the north side of it and west of the road, where a Mr. Quimby has recently lived. They managed the grist mill, the ruins of which may be seen on the west side of the creek, south of the road. Crommett was living here before 1772. It is still known as Crommett's Creek.

All that neck of land, which is almost an island, has been known since 1654 as Matthews, or Mathes, Neck. Benjamin Matthews

had a grant, 10th of 2d month, 1654, of "a Little Plott of marsh
at the head of the Little Bay, with the neck of land there."
Matthews Neck is now called Adams Point, from the name of the
present owner. This is now a beautiful summer resort. The
view of the extensive meadow, of Great and Little Bays, and of
Furber's Point opposite in Newington is one of the best in all
this region of fine scenery. The present house is the fourth that
has stood on the same site. Here lived Capt. Benjamin Mathes
for a time.

Next north of Matthews Neck and stretching from Crommett's
Creek to the head of Little Bay is the old Kent farm, where eight
generations of the Kent family have lived. There were laid out
to Oliver Kent, 3d of 2d month, 1658, seventy acres of land,
"bounded betwixt William Drewes and Mrs. Mathes and Charles
Adamses by the cricke side commonly called Mr Mathews
Cricke." Oliver Kent was taxed in Dover in 1648 and perhaps
had lived here from even earlier than that date, since grants of
land were often made years after occupation and improvement.
His house stood on the hilltop westerly of the present barn of
Mr. Eben Kent, and the old Kent burial-ground is southeasterly
of said barn. It contains marble headstones of some of the later
generations and rough unlettered granite stones to mark the
resting places of the early families. The outlook from the Kent
lawn is alone enough to make life happy. Oliver Kent's son,
Joseph, added to the original grant the above mentioned lot of
Charles Adams by purchase from his heirs, 15 February 1714/5.
It had been granted to Charles Adams as an out lot in 1656,
"one necke of land lying on the south side of Bronsons Crick
bounded from the western branch upon a south line to the Great
Bay." Oliver Kent bought of George Smythe, administrator
of the estate of George Webb, in 1651," an acre and a half of
land in Oyster River Plantation heretofore in the possession of
said George Webb," who in 1642 was presented at court "for
living idle like a swine." This is all we need to know of him.
He probably lived as a fisherman, in single wretchedness, on the
south shore of Branson's Creek.

Jonas Bines had a grant of "an out lot being on the south west
side of a Creeke caled by the name of Bransons Creeke being
ten acres, the west side ioyning to George Webb, from a great
white Oke marked and the east side coming to a little gutt,

right over against a place called the hay stack and lyeth next to Charles Adams Lott." This lot was sold to John Hill, 26 February 1668, by John Bickford, senior, who may have acted as executor of the estate of Jonas Bines, since there is no record of Bines after that date. It was laid out to John Hill thus "The head line begins at a pine tree by Bransons Crick and runs south west 29 or 30 rod along Georg web his lot to the corner tree and from the pine tree down the Crick 40 rod Est South Est to a letell gut by the Crick and from that gut it Runs south west 37 rods to a little Pine tree marked and from that tree it Runs west south west 60 rod to a marked tree and from that marked tree it Runs to the upper Corner of George Webes lot." This lot seems to be now a portion of the Kent farm.

Branson's or Bronson's Creek next engages our attention, a small inlet, about the size of Willey's Creek, which is better known. It is on the south side of the old Thomas Drew farm and was named from George Bronson, or Branson, who was taxed in 1648 and was killed by a bull, 2 July 1657. John Ault testified that "Bronson went well out of his house and he went after him and found Bronson lying on the ground crying that the bull had killed him." He left nothing to perpetuate his name but this creek. There is no grant or sale of land in his name. Even the creek is called Brands Krick in 1691 and half a century later it is called in a deed Blanchard's Creek. Let the old name be retained. It is better than a tombstone for George Branson.

The next lot was granted to William Drew, 10th of 8th month, 1653, "sixty acres of upland being on the north side of Bransons Creeke joining to his marsh." This was assigned to his son, Francis Drew, and laid out in 1669, "on the north side of Bransons Crieck from the marsh thirty rods north est to a marked tree at the cricke next to Thomas Willes land and from thence 160 rods northwest to a marked tree and from thence 90 rods southwest to a marked tree." Francis Drew deeded this to his son Thomas, 9 October 1691. Some time after the return of Thomas from captivity in Canada he settled here with his wife, Tamsen, but the other heirs of Francis Drew long afterward claimed some right in this farm. This explains a deed of Elijah Drew, son of Thomas and Tamsen, dated 15 May 1744, when he conveyed to Joseph Wheeler and Zachariah Edgerly "all right in lands and tenements which did belong unto Mary Green of

Stratham, being a fifth part of sixty acres of land lying by ye Little Bay & by Bransis Creek."

John Drew, brother of Thomas and son of Francis, escaped from a window in the old Drew garrison at Drew's Point, on the south side of Oyster River, at the time of the massacre in 1694, and was slain by Indians in 1706. He left two daughters, as a deed shows, Mary, who married Joseph Wheeler, and Joanna, who married Zachariah Edgerly. A deed of partition, dated 13 July 1747, between Joseph Drew and John Drew, sons of Thomas, and Joseph Wheeler and Mary his wife and Zachariah Edgerly and Joanna his wife, gives to Joseph and John Drew their part of sixty acres, "Beginning at a stake and stones standing half a rod south west from the south corner of the old house cellar & from said stake and stones it runs south fifty Degrees and a half Degree east to the Salt River, with lands, buildings and appurtenances thereto belonging," and to said Wheeler and Mary his wife & Zachariah Edgerly and Joanna his wife all on the other side of a line, "with all that Land which Thomas Drew late of Dover afores⁴ son of Francis Drew late of the same place purchased of Margaret Squire." This land also reached down to the salt river. Margaret Squier, widow of Bernard Squier probably, conveyed to Thomas Drew, 24 July 1701, eighteen acres on the northwest side of little bay, joining to lands of aforesaid Thomas Drew. This land had been granted to her first husband, Thomas Willey.

This old Drew farm many years ago came into the possession of Richard Kent. The buildings now standing unoccupied were erected by him, but the old Drew residence could not have been far from the same site. Old residents in this vicinity say that it stood a little lower down, eight or ten rods from the present barn. It was demolished about one hundred years ago and Mr. Joseph Adams has now one of its doors. The Drew burial-ground is in the field below the house, on the west side of a gulley through which flows a small brook into Branson's Creek. The cemetery is unfenced. The inscriptions on two headstones can be read with some difficulty. Many rough granite stones appear. Here sleep the ashes of Thomas and Tamsen Drew and many of their fourteen children and more numerous grandchildren.

In 1653 there were granted to Rice Howell twenty acres "next to William Drews grant." This he exchanged with Thomas

Footman for land further north, and Footman sold these twenty acres to Thomas Willey, who, 4 August 1666, sold land adjoining to Henry Hollwells to William Perkins, who seems to have added thereunto, for, 10 June 1694, William Perkins and wife, Elizabeth, who had removed to Exeter, conveyed to their daughter, Elizabeth Wheeler, sixty acres of land with house, "over against Little Bay," reserving a moiety of mowing land and of growth of apples during lifetime. Here lived John Wheeler and wife, Elizabeth, till they were killed by Indians, in 1706. His son, Deacon Joseph Wheeler, inherited the farm, added more to it and passed it along to his son, Benjamin Wheeler. The old cellar near the stone house, belonging to Mr. Edward Rollins of Boston and formerly belonging to Charles H. Mathes, and built by James Fernald, perhaps seventy-five or one hundred years ago, on the farm next north of the old Drew estate, is probably that of the Wheeler family. October 30, 1765, Benjamin and Elizabeth Wheeler of Gardners Town, Lincoln County, Mass. (now Gardiner, Me.), Daniel Edgerly and Hannah, his wife, of Madbury and Abigail Wheeler, spinster, of Durham (who married William Buss), children of Joseph Wheeler, tailor, sold to Daniel Warner all right in half of a certain farm joining on Little Bay, "between the land of John Edgerly and Joseph and John Drew." The farm then contained one hundred and twenty acres.

In 1658 the selectmen laid out for the use of the town a grove of pine trees, "lieinge and beinge on the north west sied of the letell Bay half a mile or thereabout from a creeke called the Long Creek, bounded upon the South by Tho Willey his grant." On the 10th of the 2d month, 1654, Thomas Willey had a grant on the northwest side of Little Bay, "threescore rods by the Water side to begin at the mouth of the Long Creeke and so upwards eight score rods into the woods." Willey sold this to William Perkins, and, 28 January 1669, William Perkins and Elizabeth, his wife, conveyed to Thomas Edgerly a parcel of land "lying & being on the northwest side of the Little Bay and on the southwest side of the long creek in the town of Dover afores[d] containing twenty pole by ye water side, being marked and bounded by the long creek afores[d] on the north east side of said parcell of land and by a hemlock tree on the other side which standeth by the water side. . . . containing twenty acres more or less, the which parcell of land is a part of the sixty acres

purchased of Thomas Willey." These twenty acres passed to
Thomas Edgerly's son John, and, 4 February 1711, John Edgerly
and wife, Elizabeth, conveyed to Samuel Edgerly (his brother)
twenty acres on the northwest side of Little Bay, bounded on the
north "by the Creeke called and known by the name of the Mill
Creek, bounded on the east with the aforesaid Little Bay, bounded
on the South with the land of John Wheelers lately deceased."
Thus it seems that John Wheeler had acquired before 1711 the
land laid out in 1658 for a pine grove for the use of the town. This
land of Edgerly's is now in the possession of James Meader,
and Long Creek is called today Meader's Creek.   A two-branched

MOUTH OF LONG CREEK

brook flows through the field in front of Meader's house and
empties into the head of Long Creek, called also Mill Creek in
some deeds, because a mill was erected at an early date near the
mouth of it.

Long Creek winds up into the woods that conceal it perhaps
less than an eighth of a mile.   It is broad and deep, an admirable
refuge for fishing craft in the old days.   Just south of it, on the
elevated land, amid the woods that may have formed a part of
the pine grove reservation, have recently been built some summer
cottages.

North of Long Creek it is difficult to locate with precision the
first settlers, because there were so frequent transfers of small

grants of land. The following citation from Dover records will aid us. The record has been slightly mutilated. "The grant of land by the Town of Dover to Thomas Footman of twenty acres, as appears by ye date of . . . of the first month, 1651, and also a grant of ten acres granted to John Hill, granted to him by ye town of Dover at a meeting they had ye 10 of ye 8 . . . These two grants are laid out and bounded as follows, 65 rod along ye shore from Thomas Humphreys next John Alts long creek near ye mill and from thence west nor west 90 rods to a marked tree marked T. C. and from y^t tree it runs north northeast 50 rods to a red oack tree marked again with T. C. and from thence it runs east south east till it comes to ye same brook where it began, and whereas the Town intended a high way & landing place att long Creek it is ordered y^t there . . . all be three rod in bedth as it is now marked to the end of the lott and what wast land is between the high way and ye creek, eqall with ye creek, is Thomas Edgerlys in consideration of ye high way. This land we find to be Thomas Edgerlys by ye consent of his father in law John Alt and John Bickford of Oyster River senior, so then we finde that the brook that is between John Alts and Thomas Edgerlys is the bound given by John Alt to ye said Edgerly his land and is laid out and bounded this 18 of November 1678." Signed by John Davis and Robert Burnum.

Here mention is made of a mill on Long Creek and a highway therefrom. These are again mentioned in a deed from Thomas Edgerly, senior, and his wife, Rebecca, to their son, Samuel Edgerly, dated 21 May 1700. It conveyed fifteen acres "bounded from a marked pine tree at ye head of ye old dam, seated between the long Cricke brook and the high way that goeth out into ye Commons, lying to ye west of ye little bay in Oyster River."

January 28, 1711, Thomas Edgerly and wife, Rebecca, sold to their son, John Edgerly, seventy or eighty acres of land on the northwest side of the Little Bay, "bounded on the north by land of John Rand. It fronteth on the aforesaid little bay and is bounded on the south by the creek called and known by the name of the mill creek, at the water side and from there into the woods."

Thus we see that Thomas Edgerly owned land on both sides of Long or Mill Creek. That on the north side came to him by marrying Rebecca, widow of Henry Hallwell, and daughter of John Ault. The marriage took place in 1665. His garrison house was evidently north of Long Creek, now Meader's Creek, and was burned by the Indians in 1694. Shortly afterward he petitioned that the neighboring house of John Rand should be made a garrison. Rand had married Remembrance, the other daughter of John Ault, and so had half of the original estate of John Ault, who was one of Capt. John Mason's colonists and must have settled at Oyster River about the year 1635. His farm lay between Long Creek and the next brook north called in ancient deeds Plum Swamp Brook. John Ault conveyed to his son-in-law, John Rand, 21 April 1674, "all yᵉ place or plantation whereon I now live."

SHORE OF LITTLE BAY
Durham Point on the left, Fox Point on the right

November 17, 1718, John Rand, son of the John Rand, who with wife, Remembrance, was probably killed by Indians in the massacre of 1694, conveyed to Francis Mathes thirty acres of "Rands Plantation," "on the northwest side of yᵉ Little Bay," between John Edgerly's land on the south and John Ambler's land on the north.

November 26, 1720, Job Runnels sold to John Ambler land which John Ault gave to his son-in-law, John Rand and wife, Remembrance, in 1764, which land Runnels bought of Nathaniel Rand and Francis Rand.

In August, 1912, Hon. Lucien Thompson and myself carefully explored this region. We found what seems to have been the landing place at the mouth of Long Creek, on the north side, where in later times bricks were made. The mill dam may have been that of a tide mill, at the very mouth of the creek, where upright ledges form natural abutments and where a dam could have been built at little expense. The supply of water from tide and brooks would have been abundant for those times. An excavation on the hilltop, perhaps ten rods from the mouth of the creek and on the north side, probably marks the site of the Edgerly garrison, burned in 1694. The pasture land around it is now overgrown with small pines and bushes, yet traces of the old road from the landing to the main road are easily discovered. Walking in a northerly direction over this wooded and hilly pasture one comes to a large field of the John Emerson farm, where Mr. Bela Kingman has a camp. In the southeast corner of that field, a few rods from the shore, not far from a fine spring of water, is a depression that marks the cellar of the house built by John Ault, given to his son-in-law, John Rand, and used as the garrison of this region after 1694. A portion of a brick was found near the surface.

On the 17th of the 4th month, 1667, Thomas Seabrook and wife, Mary, conveyed to John Ault, for twelve pounds paid by Thomas Edgerly, all right, title, and interest in "all such lands that John Hill did purchase of Thomas Footman, did purchase and pass over to Richard Bray, situate & lying in ye Little Bay on ye south west side of ye Brooke wch runneth between ye lot of s^d Richard and ye Lott of Thos Humphreys near John Aults land wth ten acres of land more ajoyning to the land afores^d." N. H. Deeds, III, 149a.

It would seem, then, that Thomas Humphreys' land began at the mouth of Plum Swamp Brook, near the "Falling-off Place," where, on the north side, there is a very old stone wall, that may have been a division fence. How Thomas Humphreys acquired this does not appear in the records. His name does not appear in grants or sales of land. He was taxed at Oyster River in 1659 and is called "Thomas umfirie the stiller," or distiller. He evidently furnished the liquid then deemed almost indispensable. He took the oath of fidelity in 1661. He married, 1 December 1665, Hannah, daughter of John Lane of Hingham Mass., where his sons had families recorded. He was constable, sergeant and clerk of the writs at Sagadahock, Me., in 1674. He and James Middleton, once of Oyster River, sold land on the Kennebec in 1676. Mention is made of his house at Oyster River, near which Thomas Canyda was killed by the falling of a tree in 1660, as said a coroner's jury.

It may be conjectured that Thomas Humphreys got possession of a small lot on the shore in this way: Thomas Footman owned land a little north of Plum Swamp Brook. He conveyed to Rice Howell, 29th of the 10th month, 1654, one messuage or tenement of land on the northwest side of Little Bay next to John Ault's lot, seven or eight acres, bounded by a freshet that runs on the southwest side of said land. This land probably passed from Howell to Humphrey. The "freshet" spoken of is Plum Swamp Brook, on the farm formerly of the late John Emerson.

Mention has been made of Richard Bray, who had a small lot just south of Plum Swamp Brook, probably acquired from John Ault. He had a grant, in 1658, "of twenty acres of upland at the head of his lot." He was taxed in Exeter in 1664, and there is no record of how he disposed of his land at Oyster River. He died in 1665, and his estate was administered by his widow, Mary, appointed administratrix 10 April 1665, then of Exeter and having children, John and Mary. This John Bray was of Middletown, N. J., 31 May 1689, when he sold to John Sleeper of Exeter eighty acres in Exeter. The deed is also signed by his mother, then Mary Whitlock.

April 3, 1674, John Ault sold to his son-in-law, Thomas Edgerly, "one fourth of an acre of land at west end of a field called Hilliards" and joining Edgerly's land, near Plum Swamp. Did Emmanuel Hilliard once live here, he who was later of Hampton and perished in the Wreck of Rivermouth, as sung by the poet Whittier? He seems to have been the only known Hilliard in New England at that time.

We have learned that Thomas Footman exchanged a small piece of land with Rice Howell. The latter was taxed in 1648 and in 1657. The following deposition throws some light on his pathway: "The Deposition of Philip Chesley this deponent witnesseth that hee Being at a Bargain making between Thomas Johnson of Oister River and Rise Howell of the said river which was to this effectt that if the said Howell would leave the places

hee was then in where he had good wages and come and live with
the said Johnson hee should have fouer Ackers of Land joyning
to his feild the said Howell Breaking of it up and house Roome
to dwell in all wch the said howell was to in Joye as Long as he
lived and further saith not." Deposed 27 July 1661. N. H.
Court Records, I, 87.

It has been shown that Thomas Footman owned a small piece
of land north of Plum Swamp Brook. He had land from Henry
Symson in York previous to 15 April 1640, and lived there as
late as 1648. He had a grant on the northern shore of Great
Bay in 1653 and there he made his home. It is questionable
whether he lived for a short time on the shore of Little Bay, although he owned several pieces of land there.

There were granted to John Hill, in 1655, "six acres between
the land of John Ault on the southwest and land of Jonas Bines
on the northwest, joining to a point of land bought of Charles
Adams." Here we meet with Jonas Bines again. Apparently
about 1648 he had not only a grant near Branson's Creek, as we
have seen, but also "One house and In lott conteyning sixe acres
or there aboutes which hee bought of Thomas Stephenson being
next to the point at the entrance into Oyster River, Compassed
wth the river evrie way only the South side and that joines uppon
the land of Mr. ffrancis Matthewes, . . . alsoe a Little
Island conteyning two acres or there aboutes being at the entrance into the little Bay over against a point called by the name
of Charles point." On the 10th of the 8th month, 1653, Jonas
Bynes had a grant of ten acres of "upland in the head of the
Creeke, joining to his Marsh, on the east side of the Creeke,"
and he had ten acres more granted the 11th of the 2d month,
1654. These grants were on Johnson's Creek. Thus he had
at least five small pieces of land widely scattered over the plantation of Oyster River. He seems to have lived on a small lot of
land nearly opposite Ambler's Islands. I have found no record
of the administration of his estate, nor of transfers of his lands,
nor of any family.

Charles Adams bought of John Ault, 10 April 1645, "a messuage or tenement in the plantation of Oyster River," for £20,
and also "so much marsh ground as will keep three cows in the
winter time." This seems to be the land sold by Adams to John
Hill, and here probably Charles Adams first lived and gave his

name to "Charles Point," later called "Ambler's Point." Tradition locates one or more old habitations here, opposite Ambler's
Islands, which three islands are spoken of in old deeds as one
island of two acres, the division into three having been made by
erosion of connecting lands by the waves.

In 1685 Joseph Hill sold to John Smart the farm which he
bought of his father, John Hill, "by ye Little Bay between the
plantations of Joseph Kent and John Ault." Joseph Smith,
attorney for John and Elizabeth Smart of New York, conveyed,
26 March 1703, to John Ambler land and buildings which said
Smart bought of Joseph Hill, on the westerly side of Little Bay.
Here lived the Ambler family for a long time. The cellar of the
house probably built by John Hill and lived in by John Ambler
is easily found, in the edge of a grove in Hon. Jeremiah Langley's field. The site is sufficiently elevated to afford a fine view
of the bay and the opposite shore.

January 10, 1739, John Ambler conveyed to his son-in-law,
Ephraim Libby, of Kittery, all his lands including the "home
place" and Island, and, 27 March 1776, Ephraim Libby sold
the same to his son-in-law, Thomas Langley, Jr.

Next north of the Hill-Ambler farm was the homestead of
Thomas Willey, that descended to his son, Stephen, to grandson,
Thomas, to great grandson, Stephen, and to great, great grandson Stephen. Thomas Willey, who married Margaret Crawford,
deposed in 1680 that he had lived at Oyster River forty years.
This takes us back to 1640, and he must have been one of the
first settlers. He was twenty-three years old in 1640 and may
have lived in the family of Darby Field. Traces of his dwelling
place are pointed out in the field now belonging to Mr. Edward I.
Langley, perhaps thirty rods from the shore of the bay. The road
to Oyster River Falls is sometimes called the highway from Willey's Creek, sometimes the highway from Bickford's Ferry. In
1658 Thomas Willey was appointed to keep the "ordinary" in
place of John Bickford. Three of the Willey family were carried into captivity in 1694, and the house where Thomas Willey
lived may then have been burned.

Much research has been made to thus make plain the loca-
tions of Branson's Creek, Long or Mill Creek and Plum Swamp
Brook, because Miss Mary P. Thompson, in her indispensable
Landmarks in Ancient Dover, has made these Creeks the same as

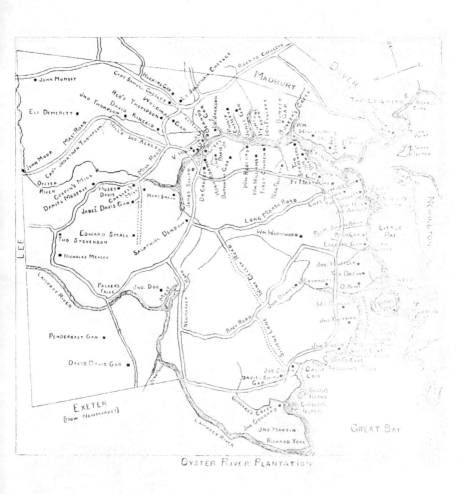

OYSTER RIVER PLANTATION

the Great Creek, Matthews Creek, or later Crommett's Creek, which is near the outlet of Great Bay This occasions confusion in locating the earliest inhabitants. When Miss Thompson wrote, the Provincial Records of New Hampshire had not been indexed, which fact sufficiently explains the errors of that painstaking and entertaining writer.

Once at least Matthews Creek is called the Long Creek, when, in 1653, ten acres were granted to John Hill "between Thomas Footmans grant & the long creeke on the Nor west Side of the *great* Bay."

South of Willey's Creek and some distance from the shore there are traces of graves, and here was probably the burial ground of the Willey and Bickford families.

Next north of Thomas Willey and at the extremity of Durham Point lived as early as 1639 Darby Field, who signed the so-called Exeter Combination and was the first to explore the White Mountains. He was licensed to sell wine in 1644. Doubtless he kept the ordinary at the Point, since we know that John Bickford did a little later, to whom Field conveyed, 16 July 1645, his house and lot, except the breadth of a lot in possession of Thomas Willey. Here lived several generations of the Bickford family. The garrison, that Thomas Bickford successfully defended in 1694, stood near the water, as traces of a cellar indicate, in a place beautiful for situation. Here terminated Bickford's Ferry. Before his door passed the extensive commerce and travel of a wide region. Some locate the Bickford garrison "a third of the distance from the shore to the brick house, looking from said house toward the west side of the nearest of the Ambler islands."

Next northwest of John Bickford and just within the mouth of Oyster River were the six acres granted to Jonas Bines, which he bought of Thomas Stevenson. The place is still known as Jonas' Point, sometimes corrupted to Jones' Point. Thus the name of a comparative nobody is perpetuated, while many great and worthy persons are soon forgotten. What is fame? There is no discoverable trace of a habitation on this point, and the soil is comparatively barren. It was acquired by the Bickford family, and, 8 June 1774, John Bickford conveyed to his son, Winthrop Bickford, his homestead and six acres "commonly called Jonas's Point."

4

Next let us try to locate the garrison house of Charles Adams, who very early lived at Charles Point, or Ambler's Point, opposite Ambler's Islands. January 30, 1711/12, Rebecca Edgerly, daughter of John Ault, aged 71, deposed "that Charles Adams did possess land within the mouth of Oyster River joining to Francis Mathes above sixty years ago [about 1650] and ever since till Oyster River was destroyed and then the said Adams was killed and his house burned by the enemie." John Meader, senior, aged 82, testified at the same time to the same effect. In 1656 the town of Dover granted to Charles Adams twelve acres of land. "It beginneth at a marked tree behind his house lot about a hundred Rode by the hieway side that goeth to Oyster River Falls and runneth from that marked tree forty eaght Rod to A marked tree west and from that tree it Runneth south sixty Rode to another marked tree and from that marked tree where it begune it runneth south Twenty eaght Rode and from that tree it Runeth uppon a straight line west and be south or thear aboutes to the other Corner." This was laid out in 1671. On the 10th of 2d month, 1654, there were granted to John Bickford ten acres "behinde the Lott of Charles Adams" and the same day ten acres were granted to Thomas Willey "behinde the Lott of Charles Adams."

In 1711 Joseph Dudy, or Durrell, who had married Rebecca Adams, granddaughter of the first Charles Adams, together with his wife and her sister Esther Adams, conveyed to Francis Mathes the home plantation of Charles Adams, estimated to contain eighteen acres, "bounded on the north with the highway that leads from Willeys Creek to Oyster River Falls," together with the twelve-acre grant of 1656 above described. These conveyances make it perfectly plain that Charles Adams' garrison stood south of the present road, which is the same as the ancient one, and the logical place, indeed the only suitable place for a house, is the site of the brick house built by Washington Mathes and now in ruins. Fourteen of the Adams family perished in the massacre of 1694, and one at least, Ursula, was taken to Canada, never to return. The bodies of the fourteen were buried under a little mound close to the tomb on the east side of the Mathes burial ground, a pathetic reminder of the hardships and sufferings of those who prepared this beautiful land for us.

The next lot of land west of Darby Field, or John Bickford, and abutting on Oyster River, originally belonged to William Beard, who conveyed it to Francis Matthews, in June 1640. Francis Matthews was one of Capt. John Mason's colonists in 1634, the same who married, 22 November 1622, Thomasine Channon, at Ottery St. Mary, Devonshire. Since 1640 the land has been in the unbroken possession of the Matthews, now Mathes, family. The first house is said to have stood a little north of the site of the present one. It withstood the attack of the Indians in 1694.

COMFORT MATHES CAMP

Owned by Miss Fannie Pendexter Mathes. Once the residence of the late Benjamin and Comfort (Smart) Mathes

Matthew Giles first owned the next lot up the river, and the middle of the channel of the little creek was the dividing line between the two lots. "Giles old field lying between two creeks" is repeatedly mentioned in old deeds. He died in 1666 and his estate was divided between Matthew Williams and Richard Knight. The latter sold it to William Pitman, who willed it to his son, Francis, and Francis Pitman sold it to Edward Wakeham, weaver, 2 May 1695. Wakeham had married Sarah Meader from the other side of the river and at its mouth, and

here his son, Caleb, lived till he perished in a storm, in 1770,
"supposed to be much in liquor," as Schoolmaster Tate says.
The creek on the west side of Wakeham's lot was long known
as Wakeham's Creek, earlier as Giles Creek.

Francis Pitman sold a portion of the old Giles farm to Nicholas
Dunn, who was taxed at Oyster River in 1680. On the 18th
of October 1699, Elizabeth Dunn, "who was y⁰ wife of Nicholas
Dunn," of Oyster River, conveyed to Edward Wakeham land
joining to said Wakeham's land, that was bought of Francis
Pitman. N. H. Prov. Deeds, X, 369.

The next lot west of Wakeham's Creek was first owned by
Darby Field, conveyed by him to William Roberts, and by him
to William Drew before 1648. Doubtless Drew was the first
one to live here, and the place was long known as Drew's Point.
The cellar of his garrison house may be plainly seen and traces
of the orchard around it. The house was burned in 1694.
Stephen Jenkins acquired this place, 10 May 1712, and sold
it to James Langley, 5 November 1714, and here lived several
generations of the Langley family. This with the Wakeham
farm eventually came into the possession of the Mathes family,
who seem to have gradually bought everything that joined them.

Between this lot and the next a road was laid out in 1715
on petition of James Langley. His next neighbor up the river
was Bartholomew Stevenson, son of Thomas. On the 11th of
the fifth month, 1644, three acres at the Oyster Point were
granted to Thomas Stevenson, and the neck of land opposite.
September 3, 1680, Thomas Willey, aged 63, and Margaret
Willey his wife, aged 65, deposed that they had lived in Oyster
River forty years or thereabouts, that Thomas Stevenson
cultivated his neck of land forty years ago near the Oyster
Bank, commonly called Stevenson's Neck. This carries Thomas
Stevenson back to 1640, evidently one of the earliest settlers,
who had cultivated land here some years before he received a
formal town grant. The western boundary of Stevenson's land
was called Stevenson's Creek, into which flowed Stoney Brook
from the southwest. Two acres of marsh near the mouth of
Stevenson's Creek very early belonged to Joseph Field and is
repeatedly mentioned in deeds.

On the neck of land between Oyster River and Stevenson's
Creek, at the extreme point is the cellar of Thomas Stevenson,

a deep excavation, with split stone around it and an old wall
and apple tree behind it. The gently sloping ledge in front of
it served as a convenient landing. The place is now surrounded
by woods. On the highest point of this neck of land are found
in the edge of the grove bricks and indications that here may
have once been a house. The view up the river is one of the
very best. In about the center of the spacious field is a low
mound, and here are found several rough oblong granite stones
similar to those used to mark graves in early times.

Above Stevenson's Creek a lot was granted, 10 August 1653,
to John Pillin, called also Pillion, Pillon, and Pelline in deeds,
"forty acres of land beinge upon the noe west side of Stoney
Brooke." Little is known of John Pillin. John Goddard may
have administered his estate, for he sold this lot, 6 April 1659,
to William Williams, senior, forty acres on the south side of
Oyster River, "butting upon a creek commonly called Stimpsons
Creek, which was John Pillions with ye necke of land wch lyes
betweene Stoney Brooke & the Meeting house Lott." William
Williams and wife Agnes conveyed this lot, bounded in like
manner, 18 June 1674, to Joseph Field. Zachary Field, brother
to Joseph, sold it to John Davis, 11 December 1710. On the
22d of July 1680 there was an agreement made between Nicholas
Follet and Joseph Stevenson about bounds of land "neare to
ffollets now dwelling house & adjoining to Joseph Fields marsh
and s^d Stevensons land." This appears to be the land lying
between Stevenson's Creek and Stoney Brook, not extending
down to the river. See N. H. Prov. Deeds, III, 158a.

March 26, 1701, Nicholas Follett and wife, Mary, sold to
Nathaniel Meader all lands of his father in Oyster River, including that fenced land he died possessed of, bounded with
the land of Joseph Stevenson "on ye east and land of Joseph
Field on ye north and ye lands of Thomas Drew on y^o south."
Meader sold this to Thomas Footman, and it descended to his
son, Francis Footman, and from him to his son, Thomas Footman, by division of estate in 1774, forty acres bounded on the
west by Daniel Davis. This lot now contains the eastern
field of Mr. Clarence I. Smart's farm, and on a little hill in this
field may be seen the deep cellar of what tradition says was a
garrison house. It is somewhat concealed by a clump of trees.
Here, doubtless, lived Nicholas Follett. Not far distant in a

northerly direction and just where Stoney Brook broadens
into Stevenson's Creek are plain evidences of an old wharf or
landing place, where the boats of Nicholas Follett, mariner,
must have been moored.

On the lot originally that of John Pillin and later belonging
to Daniel Davis a house once stood on a hilltop in Mr. Smart's
field. The cellar has been filled till not a trace remains. At
this point of view one looks down upon the slate tombstone in
the field, where rests the body of Ivory H. Willey, who died
30 September 1832, aged 22 years and 5 months. As much
further beyond one sees a clump of trees and close beside it,
at the extreme point of land, is a very old landing place, repaired
by Dea. James Munroe Smart in his day. From this place
have been shipped to Portsmouth many loads of quarried stone
and of brick dug out of this farm.

Not far from the main road and east of Mr. Smart's house
is the cellar of the house where lived Abijah Pinkham, whose
burial place with broken down marble tombstones is hidden
from view by overgrowing shrubbery. It was walled in, a
short distance northerly of where the old barn stood. Here
also lies the body of his wife, Rachel (Huckins) Pinkham, and
there are indications of several other graves. The inscriptions
that can be read appear in the genealogical notes on the Pinkham family, in this history.

We come now to the meeting house lot. A meeting house
was built here by Valentine Hill, in 1655, and a parsonage was
built the following year, but the formal grant for the use of the
ministry was not made till 20 September 1668. Then sixty
acres were granted by the selectmen "for the meeting house and
burying place." "It runes from ye water side next to William
Williams sener his Lot and it Runs thear along the highway
from the water side south west 324 rods to a whit oak tree marked
on both Sids and from the tree it Runes south east 35 Rods to
a pitch Pine with 4 Rod alowed ye Length for a high way and
from that tree it Runs northeast to John Palles Lot and soe
by it to the water side by the same point and we have alowed
fower Rod in the Length of it for A high way to go across the
lot. This is the Towne Lott only exsempting Joseph Fields
marsh which is in some part of the front of it." In 1762 there
is an article in the warrant for town meeting, "to see whether

the town will choose a committee to settle the boundary of the parsonage Lott near the Oyster Bed where the old meeting house formerly stood." Agreeably to this a committee, consisting of Joseph Smith, Jeremiah Burnham, and Ebenezer Thompson, renewed the boundaries of the lot, 7 May 1774. "We began at the River side by a small alder And run South west 324 Rods (going across a Rock near the house formerly Stephen Jenkans Deceased) to a Saplin pine and spotted it on four sides and then South East 35 Rods to a Picked Rock and marked it T. L. and then North East 324 Rods to the River and then to the first bounds and we find that in runing these points we include about one acre of Fields Marsh (so called)." . . . "We have also run out Two acres of Land for the use of the Town aforesaid that is now in possession of the heirs of Daniel Davis Deceased by their liberty. We began by the water side adjoining said Town lot at the place where was the old Burying place & Run South west 29 Rods, and then began again at said water side and run south 67° East 12 rods then S. W. 25 rods and then to the place where the 29 rods ended." Here, then, were the first church and parsonage and the oldest burial ground in Durham, on a little plot of ground in the part of the parsonage lot that lies close to the river. Here is a slightly elevated ridge of land now covered with a clump of trees and bushes. Search failed to disclose any signs of graves. The first church must have stood near by on the river bank. The parsonage was probably on higher ground, but no trace of a cellar has been discovered. Here lived the Rev. John Buss.

The road which formed the western part of the meeting house lot was only a bridle path. The next lot was that of William Williams. Just when he settled here is unknown, but he came with Thomas Wiggin to Dover Neck in 1633. There were granted to William Williams, senior, 24 August 1651, twenty acres bounded then by lands of John Bickford and Mr. Ambrose Gibbons, "from William Williams his house to the next creek westward and from his house to the eastward eight rods." In 1665 he had a grant of twenty acres more, "to be joined to his house loot bounded twelve pooll by the water side next to the meeting house and the rest adjoining to his former loot backwards." William Williams and wife, Mary, and Samuel Hill and wife, Elizabeth, 23 March 1686, conveyed

to Stephen Jenkins of Kittery land "on which the aforesaid
William Williams now liveth, containing fforty acres as it is
bounded between the lands called Roberts his Land on the
North west and the High way or the Ministers Lot on the South
east, and butting upon Oyster River." Here the Jenkins family
lived a long time. Stephen Jenkins' house stood on or very
near the site of the old house now standing on the hilltop, and
William Williams lived, as the above citation shows, near the
river bank, twenty rods west of the parsonage lot. The Mathes
brickyard accounts for the disappearance of the cellar.

March 6, 1743 4, John Jenkins and Rebecca, his wife, sold
to Valentine Mathes thirty acres which he purchased of his
father, Stephen Jenkins, bounded on "ye west or norwest side
by land now in possession of Jeremiah Burnham and Robert
Burnham, on ye north or northeast side by ye town Lot, on east
or south side by a high way y^t leads from ye town Lot to a Place
called Long Marsh."

William Roberts lived on the next lot west, the same who was
killed by Indians in 1675. He sold a piece next to the road,
on the back side of his lot to Thomas Doughty, who sold it to
John Cutts of Portsmouth in 1667. The place still goes by the
name of Cutts' Hill. In 1664 Roberts gave a deed of his remaining land to William Pitman, who had been living there since
earlier than 1657 and had, perhaps, married Roberts' daughter,
Ann. In the sale to "William Pitman & to his Eldest son
Ezekiel Pitman" the land is described as adjacent to "Robt
Burnhams lands on the north west side of it And Thomas Dow-
ties on the South east side to a marked tree at ye lower end
of the fresh marsh & from thence along the brow of ye Hill till
it meet with Robert Burnhams line and from thence along
his line to Oyster River & ye River bounds ye other end." The
price was sixteen pounds. Here lived the Pitman family many
years. The southerly end of the farm on the south side of the
main road is still known as the Pitman field.

The next lot west of Roberts' land was originally owned by
Ambrose Gibbons, the leader of Capt. John Mason's colony
in the settlement at Great Works, now in South Berwick, Me.
He settled here before 1640, and on the 5th of the 10th month,
1652, he had a grant of land adjoining his marsh from the "creek
between his land and William Roberts" to the "western creek."

This grant of two hundred acres he willed to Henry Sherburne of Portsmouth, who had married his only child, Rebecca Gibbons. On the 12th of May 1657, Henry Sherburne, for £100, conveyed to Robert Burnham of Oyster River "one dwelling house with the out howses appertayning thereto with all the lands which the said Ambrose Gibbins Dyed possessed off," "betweene the Creeke upon the lands of William Pitman, formerly William Roberts, toward the South East and a certayne Creeke towards the west abutting upon said River called Oyster River towards the east and so runneth up into the woods towards the South to the quantity of about two hundred acres," "and also all the meadow lying in Oyster River aforesaid which the said Ambros Gibbins Dyed possessed off." See Suffolk Deeds, III, 17. The original deed is in the possession of S. H. Shackford, Esq., Boston. The land was laid out to Robert Burnham in 1661, one hundred rods on the river and running southwest 388 rods, "from the head of the creeke near William Pitmans house upon a south west line 388 rods long and it lieth from Benjamin Mathewes his lote sid south so west the breadth of this lote," as the Dover records say. The Burnham garrison house,—and probably this was the house of Ambrose Gibbons, stood on the hilltop, where the old cellar may be plainly seen, as well as the cellar of a smaller house or out-building near by. Ezekiel Pitman lived within gunshot at the time of the massacre in 1694 and hearing cries of alarm escaped with his family to the Burnham garrison, while his own house was burned. See Landmarks in Ancient Dover, p. 180.

The land between the grant to Ambrose Gibbons and the Sullivan place was originally granted to Benjamin Matthews. June 26, 1682, John Mighell of Newbury sold to John Davis, junior, forty acres which he bought of Benjamin Matthews, 2 January 1673, which deed is not recorded. John Davis, junior, was here killed by Indians, with wife and two children, in the massacre of 1694. Jeremiah Burnham was made administrator of his estate in 1702. He left a daughter, Sarah, who returned from captivity in Canada and married Peter Mason. She conveyed to John Sullivan, 26 September 1771, thirty acres of the homestead on the south side of the highway from the parsonage house to Durham Point. See Landmarks in Ancient Dover, by Miss Mary P. Thompson, p. 260.

The fact that Benjamin Matthews owned this land is further
evidenced by a town record, dated 9th of 9th month, 1661,
when the lot of land granted to Ambrose Gibbons was laid out
to Robert Burnham, "from the head of the creek near William
Pitman's house," 380 rods long, "and it lieth from Benjamin
Mathews his lote sid south so west," the breadth being one hundred rods.

The early history of the next lot north of John Davis' is best
told in the following citation from a deed, dated 29 March 1682.
John Mighell (pronounced M-i-l-e) of Newbury sold to Samuel
Burnham "a certain house Lott with a Dwelling house on it
ye Lott is Layd out & bounded for ten acres as will appear by
the return of it of ye Lott Layers, according to ye grant of y^e
s^d Towne, this dwelling house wth ye Lott & all other priviledges
& app^tnances there unto belonging with a grant of four acres
more adjoining to ye s^d ten acres at ye south end of it, if it be
to be found in ye records of ye Town of Dover afores^d. This
Lott was granted to Joseph Field by ye Town of Dover & by
him sold to James Smith of ye same town & ye s^d James Smith
sold this portion of land to Thomas Mighell as doth appear by
a bill of sale under his hand the 28th day of 8th mo 1668 &
this bill of sale was assigned to Jno Mighell his brother to be
as good to him, his heirs & success^rs as it was to Thomas Mighell."
Witnesses, James Huckins and William Johnson. N. H. Prov.
Deeds, III, 173b.

This John Mighell took oath as constable of Dover 30 June
1674. He witnessed a deed in 1669 and was a juror in 1672.
The Mighell family still has representatives in Rowley, Mass.

April 24, 1718, James Burnham, son of the Samuel Burnham
just named, sold to Samuel Smith eighteen acres which were
sold by John Miles to Samuel Burnham, except one and a half
acres sold to Hugh Adams. October 22, 1718, James and Mary
Burnham sold to Jonathan Crosby land and buildings south
of Oyster River, which had been sold by John Miles to Samuel
Burnham. August 7, 1717, James Burnham and wife Mary
sold to Hugh Adams, minister of the Gospel, one acre and a
half "near to ye new meeting house near the falls," bounded
"northward on the s^d Oyster River, northwest on ye Landing
place adjoining to and behind the s^d meeting house by a straight
line running from ye Corner of ye same at the s^d River south

westerly to an heap of stones by a pine bush distant from the south east corner of the said meeting house just two rods five feet and one inch, southwestward by other lands belonging to me" nine rods, then northeastward twenty-eight rods, thence seven or eight rods northwest by north to a flat rock at the edge or brinke of the River. Witnesses, Nathaniel Hill, John Smith, and Joseph Buss. N. H. Prov. Deeds, X, 325.

April 12, 1720, Dr. Jonathan Crosby and wife, Hannah, sold to "Hugh Adams Cler. minister of the Gospel, one and three quarters acres 'near ye uper Meeting house at ye first falls,' three rods to the eastward of his said land and two rods to ye southward thereof, from the southeast corner of his homestead land one and a half rods east southeast unto a Larg Pitch Pine, thence twenty-three rods to a Larg Black Oak, thence north and by west thirteen rods to the river, thence three and a half rods to a flat rock." Witnesses, Humphrey Sullivan, Thomas Wille, William Pitman. N. H. Prov. Deeds, XI, 402.

February 4, 1741, Hugh Adams and wife, Susanna, sold to John Adams of Boston, merchant, a parcel of land at "ye Landing place near the meeting house, bounded southerly on land belonging to Daniel Rogers and Samuel Smith, beginning two rods and five feet from the southeast corner of the meeting house, on a straight line and southeast course twenty-two rods easterly to a pine tree, thence northerly by a stone wall sixteen rods, thence westerly by a straight line to the landing place twelve feet distant from ye south end of ye house belonging to Samuel Adams, thence on ye landing place southwesterly to ye first bounds by ye meeting house, with ye Dwelling house, Barn, orchard, etc." N. H. Prov. Deeds, XXV, 467.

This was sold, 3 October 1764, by John and Annee Adams of Boston to Joseph Drew, who had married Elizabeth, daughter of the Rev. Hugh Adams, and Joseph Drew sold it, 4 October 1764, to Daniel Warner.

June 2, 1743, Hugh and Susanna Adams, for fifty pounds, sold to Samuel Adams, physician, "all ye remainder part of my homestead Lot or Tract of Land lying & being in Durham nigh ye falls Meeting house." bounded "by land I sold to my son Jn° on ye South, by land of Samuel Smith Esq on ye East, ye River on ye North, & westly by ye High way or Landing place so called, on which my s⁴ son Sam¹ has built an house

& barn." Witnesses, Joseph Drew and Elizabeth Drew. N. H. Prov. Deeds, XXVIII, 143.

Dr. Samuel Adams lived here, in a house which he himself built, till his death in 1762. His widow, Rebecca Adams, 19 December 1764, sold to John Sullivan, for 2300 pounds, old tenor, three acres bounded "Northwesterly on the high Way or landing place, South Westerly on lands in Possession of Joseph Drew, South easterly on lands of Joseph Smith Esqr Easterly by Oyster River (so called), with the Buildings & appur^s thereunto belonging." Witnesses, Joseph Smith and Winborn Adams.

Thus we have the history of the lot of land on which stands the old Sullivan house so-called, built by Dr. Samuel Adams some time before 1741.

James Smith and his descendants lived on the west side of the road that ran in front of the meeting house after it was built about 1716, and here his son, John, kept an "ordinary." Later Winborn Adams bought a small lot here and he, too, had an ordinary. The Smith land extended toward Broth Hill, where Valentine Hill's "seven Scots" had a small grant, extending down to the "freshet" or mill-pond. Here lived John Hudson, Edward Patterson, Henry Brown, James Oar and other Scotchmen. Later James Smith acquired all this land. Still further west, on the road to Lamprey River, now Newmarket, we come to Denbow's Brook, near which lived Salathiel Denbow, or Dinsmore, as later generations write their surname.

The land at the mouth of Oyster River, on the north side, was granted to Valentine Hill, 5 May 1643, "land from a Creeke over against Thomas Stephenson at Oyster River that hath an Island in the mouth of it to the head of that Creeke in Royalls Cove, to y^t part of the North East of Mr. Roberts his marsh, reserving to Mr. Roberts Marsh and twenty acres of Upland, all the rest of that Neck we give to Mr. Hill & one hundred acres more up in the country." The first grant included what is now known as Tickle Point, where the boundary lines of Durham, Madbury and Dover converge to a point. The place is called in old records "Hills Neck." The second grant to Hill was at Wheelwright's Pond, in what is now Lee.

The neck of land between the mouth of Oyster River and Royall's Cove was acquired in part by John Meader by purchase

GOAT ISLAND, SEEN FROM FOX POINT, NEWINGTON

Beyond is "Bill's Neck," or Tickle Point, and Atkinson hill is on the horizon

from Valentine Hill, 20 September 1660, and a part was a grant to him and William Sheffield in 1656. On the northeast were lands of Thomas Leighton. Here John Meader had a garrison house and here lived several generations of the Meader family, many of whom were Quakers. The adjoining Leighton farm stretched toward what is now called Atkinson's Hill, from the top of which is gained one of the most beautiful views in New England.

BUNKER GARRISON

Valentine Hill conveyed the rest of his land on the north side of Oyster River and next west of Meader's land, sixty acres, to John Davis of Haverhill, Mass., 14 August 1654, "beginning at the mouth of a creek and extending west southwest to Stoney Brook Cove." The cellar of his garrison house that his son, Col. James Davis, successfully defended in 1694 is easily found close to the west side of a little creek and on elevated ground. The family burial ground is in the field near by.

Next west of John Davis was a grant of forty acres, made to Matthew Williams, who sold it to Joseph Smith, 14 September

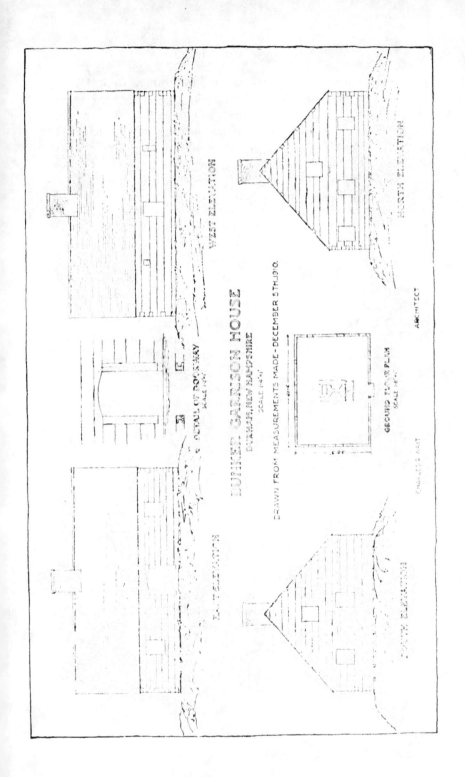

WEST ELEVATION

NORTH ELEVATION

DETAIL OF DOORWAY
SCALE 1¼"

LUTHER GARRISON HOUSE
DURHAM, NEW HAMPSHIRE
SCALE ¼"=1'

DRAWN FROM MEASUREMENTS MADE - DECEMBER 5TH, 1910.

GROUND FLOOR PLAN
SCALE ⅛"=1'

EAST ELEVATION

SOUTH ELEVATION

CHARLES E. HART   ARCHITECT

1660. On the 31st of the 7th month, 1660, there were "given and granted unto Joseph Smith his heirs and assigns one small parcel of wast land on the north side of Oyster River for a house lot, provided it intrench not upon anie former grant, which sayd land lyeth Between the lott of Matthew Willyames and the lot of Wm Willyames Juner." In 1693 he had a grant of ten acres more adjoining his land on the northwest.

William Williams, junior, had his grant of twenty acres 10 August 1653, beginning at the mouth of a creek below Oyster Point. It is now known as Bunker's Creek. Oyster Point lies between the west side of this creek and the river. Here and on the opposite side of the river were the oyster beds that gave name to the river and plantation. Oysters may be found here at the present time.

The land between Bunker's Creek and Johnson's Creek was granted 10 August 1653, to James Bunker and William Follett and later it all came into the possession of the Bunker family, containing 236 acres. The remains of the old Bunker garrison on the hill west of Bunker's Creek are sadly visible. It is a shame to let such a historic landmark go to ruin.

Johnson's Creek was so named from Thomas Johnson, who sold a lot on Dover Neck to William Pomfret in 1639. He had a grant of one hundred acres of upland next to Philip Chesley's land. Ambrose Gibbons had permission to erect a saw mill at the head of this creek in 1652. Johnson died intestate and left no children, and his land was regranted to Stephen Jones in 1672, and thereafter the lower portion of the creek was called Jones' Creek. William Storey, or Storer, had one hundred and forty acres on the east side of the creek, not fronting on the river, one hundred acres of which were owned later by Joseph Jenkins, neighbor to Nathaniel Lomax, Lamos or Lummis, and the rest was bought by Abraham Clark.

Jones' garrison stood on the upper, or west side of the creek, not far from the river. It was burned before 1732. The site of the garrison is made known by a depression containing broken bricks, pieces of pottery and of flint. It is about five or six rods north of the road leading to "Piscataqua Bridge" and about ten or twelve rods from the Chesley division line, on the plain below the walled burial place of the Jones family. The present house on the Jones farm was built about one hundred years ago. The farm is now owned by Dr. Alice Chesley of Exeter, whose mother was Harriet Dustin Jones, wife of Lafayette Chesley. Next west of Jones and between him and William Beard's land was the home land of Philip Chesley. He had a grant of twenty acres near Cochecho in 1644 and still earlier he had a house lot of three and a half acres on Dover neck, which he sold to Thomas Leighton. No evidence has been found that he ever lived at Lubberland, as some have asserted. He had a conditional grant in Exeter at an early date but never fulfilled the conditions. In 1664 he deeded to his son, Philip, the "neck of land" whereon he lived, excepting the half already given to son, Thomas. April 23, 1675, there were "laid out to Thomas Chesley ten acres of land bought of the Towne at the head of his fathers land upon yᵉ neck on yᵉ north side of yᵉ highway on yᵉ west side of his brothers land joining to his brothers land on the west side and runs in length forty eight rods and yᵉ lines run thirty five rods east and west." The following mutilated record is found in the Dover Town-book: "Laid out unto Philip Chesley Jr. . . . at the head of his fathers land upon . . . joins unto Walt Jaxons land . . . in breadth ye line runs east and . . . laid out and bounded by us this . . . ." All of which goes to show that Philip Chesley had a "neck of land" between land of Stephen Jones and land of Walter Jackson, reaching down to Oyster River. Here was the old Chesley garrison about half way between the Dover road and that to Pascataqua Bridge, twenty rods west from the Jones division wall, on a little elevation in the field of Mr. Daniel Chesley. A door-stone with the name of Alpheus Chesley upon it was taken from this place. The old Chesley burial place is north of this spot, on more elevated land and joining to the westerly side of a stone wall.

Beard's Creek is so called from William Beard, who, as we have seen, sold land near the mouth of Oyster River to Francis Matthews in 1640. His garrison house was east of the creek on the road to Dover. Here he was killed by Indians in 1675. He sold a lot to three Scotchmen, which is thus described in the town records:

Be it knowne unto all men By thes Presence that I William Beard to geather with my wife Elizabeth Beard dwling in the towne of Dover in the County of Norfolke for and in consideration of three and Twinty pounds starling have

5

Given granted Barganed and Soold A Sertayne Parsell of Upland and
Meadowe lying in Oyster Rever in the presinkes of Dover in the County of
Norfolkell unto Robert Junkinge Edward narving and Henrey Browne to
them thear heires and asines Exequtores and Admincstratores to have and
to hold for Ever. The land y⁴ Bounded by Consent of Evrey of thes parties A
Bove minshened the River lyinge on the won end of it about Este and West
the won sied of it Bounded by Thomas Johnsons land y⁴ lyinge near North
Est and south west the other seid of it is Bounded By the sayd William Beards
land and the aforesayd Robert Edward and henrey to have free Egres and
Regres therrowe my land toward the Common Witnes my hand and Seall the
9th 12th 1657.

the marke of WILLIAM BEARD.

Sealled and Delivered in the presence of ROBERT BURNUM, the marke of
JOHN DUELL, JOSEPH SMIETH.

This lot was soon in the possession of Walter Jackson, another
Scotchman, who had a grant of twenty acres, in 1666, "at the
head of his one [own] lot betwixt the Cow path and the swamp."

Walter Jackson sold land to Robert Watson, 14 December
1668, and after Watson was killed by Indians and his widow,
Hannah, had married John Ambler they sold this land, 26 March
1703, to Philip Chesley. It measured twenty-seven and a half
rods on Oyster River and twenty-five rods on the other end,
which bordered on "the Cochecho path," bounded on one side
by Philip Chesley and on the other by Walter Jackson's land.

April 10 1675, William Beard and wife, Elizabeth, gave to
James Huckins "gratisly and freely" a tract of land near Beard's
Creek, adjoining land of John Woodman. There is a mutilated
record of a grant to James Huckins, without date, as follows:

James Huckins ten acre lott .   .   . is layd out and bounded as followeth two   .   .   .   joining to y⁰ north end of his whom lott ye south
.   .   .   brook which runs into y⁰ freshet att y⁰ head of y⁰ creek and thence
n   .   .   .   and by west fifteen rods to a ash tree by y⁰ bridg marked with
I. H. and   .   .   .   y⁰ tree north north east by y⁰ high way y⁴ comes from
Thomas Chesley   .   .   .   it come to y⁰ high way y⁴ goes to y⁰ head of
Thomas Johnsons Creek   .   .   .   eastern corner of his whom lott y⁰
other eight acres begins att a tree in y⁰ angle of y⁰ high way and runs nor
nor east forty two rods by y⁰ high way that goes to Thomas Chesleys to a
tree marked with I. H. and from y⁴ tree it runs east northeast forty rods to
a tree by y⁰ brook marked with I. H. it runs down y⁰ brook being y⁰ east
north east side bound till it come to y⁰ high way y⁴ goes toward y⁰ head of
Thomas Johnsons Creek.

The estate of William Beard was divided between his widow,
Elizabeth Beard, and Edward Leathers, whose family long lived
here.   Edward Leathers sold, in 1697, land on the north side of

Oyster River to Joseph Smith, and Smith sold the same to Jonathan Chesley. In both deeds it was described as twenty-seven and a half rods on the river and two hundred rods deep, next northerly of Beard's Creek, extending to the brook on which was Huckins' mill, with marsh on the west of Jackson's land. Jonathan Chesley's old garrison house is probably the one now standing on the northerly side of the road to Madbury, a short distance east and on the opposite side of the road from Dea. W. S. Meserve's house. The date, 1716, has recently been found on one of its interior timbers, but the house was probably built before that date. The garrison of his brother, Capt. Samuel Chesley, stood three or four rods east of Dea. Meserve's house.

The following may be of interest, copied from an old paper in the possession of S. H. Shackford, Esq., of Boston:

Know all men by this presence that I Elizabeth Beard of Oystariver in yͤ towne of Dover in yͤ County of Dover & Pouchmoth doe make over my hole Estat which I now poses in Oyster River yͭ is to say my housing & lands two oxsen too cous three hefers too calves too mears seven sheep six swine unto Robert Burnum of oystar River in yͤ towne of Dover in yͤ County of Dover & Porchmoth to improve or let out with my Consent for my nose & benefit in wittness whear of I have set to my hand & Seale in yͤ year of our Lord: 1676 & on yͤ 13th day of ye 8: month   ELIZABETH BEARD
                                                     Her E marke

Sined seld & Delivered
in yͤ presenc of us witness
JAMES HUCKINE
EDWARD LETHERS
His E marke.

Beard's Creek is fed by a brook that ran through James Huckins' land and hence is called Huckins' Brook. From the west it is fed by Stoney Brook (the third brook of that name that we have seen in our rambles about old Oyster River), and between Stoney Brook and Beard's, or Woodman's Creek lay the old estate of Capt. John Woodman, who bought land here of Benjamin Matthews in 1663, having had in 1660 a grant of twenty acres, "at the head of William Beard's creek." Here was a public landing place, and south of it, on a commanding hill, may be seen the ruins of Woodman's garrison house.

The tract of land lying between Beard's Creek and Valentine Hill's grant of five hundred acres was originally owned by William Hilton, who had a grant here of eighty-eight acres from the town of Dover and sold it, 7 July 1641, to Francis Matthews.

The widow of Francis Matthews, with the consent of her son, Benjamin, sold it to Valentine Hill, who conveyed it to Patrick Jameson, 11 May 1659. Jameson conveyed it to Thomas Mighill, 29 July 1669, who with wife, Bethula, sold it to John Webster of Newbury, Mass., 29 December 1670. John Webster and wife, Anne, conveyed it to George Chesley, 16 October 1699. At the request of his widow, Deliverance Chesley, and of James Davis the land was rebounded, 21 May 1711, eighty-eight acres on the north side of Oyster River, according to deed from William Hilton to Francis Matthews:

Beginning at a point of land at the Creeks mouth next belo the falls on the north side of Oyster River Running northward towards Jonathan Woodmans and from the aforesd Poynt on the west side of the sd Creeks mouth it Runes near west and be south by the River seventy two Rods to a fence now standing between Land now in the possession of deliverance Chesle and an orchard in the Possession of bartholomew stephenson from thence it Runs nor west 2' westerle six Rods and from that extent it Runes west and be south Twenty nine Rods to the top of the hill on the south side of bartholomew stephensons house from thence Leaving the sd stephensons house on the north side and the Landing Place and highway at the falls with the land joining to the saw mill on the south side of this line and from that Extent it Runs west and be south 4'westerle sixty one Rods to a stake set in the ground and from that Extent it Runes nor nor west ninety six Rods to a stump markt W H and from that stump East and be north to stonie brook on the south side of Jonathan Woodmans orchard and so downe the affore mentioned Creek and from thence the sd creek bounds this Land on the East till it comes to the Poynt where we begun.

Mention is made above of the fact that Bartholomew Stephenson lived near the landing at the falls. He seems to have settled here by right of squatter sovereignty, and in 1710 Nathaniel Hill claimed the land that Stephenson was living on. The case in court brought out several depositions that are worth more to the historian than the land. Peter Coffin, aged about 79, testified that Valentine Hill lived on the north side of Oyster River near the Mill and employed a great many men on his 500 acres and that Coffin himself was one of the employees and afterward was agent of Hill's estate.

William Leathers of full age testified, 19 October 1710, that Bartholomew Stevenson built a house upon "ye upland 23 years ago, on land now in controversy between Nathaniel Hill and sd Stevenson, and was never interrupted in sd time."

The Deposition of Joseph Meader sen[r] & Stephen Jones both of full age Testifieth & saith that Capt Nath[ll] Hill built a house & erected Fences upon a Tract of Land att y[e] head of Oysterriver the salt River on the north side of y[e] River & lived there Peacably without any molestation by any Persons for twenty eight years ago or thereabouts & when Oysterriver was Part of it cut of by the enemy John Dean was killed by y[e] enemy who lived in said Hills house & y[e] s[d] House was Burned by y[e] enemy which land s[d] Hill sueth Bartholomew Stevenson for & now is in controversy and further saith not. [See Court Files at Concord, N. H. No. 15657.]

February 23, 1709/10:

The Deposition of Capt. Benjamin Matthews of Dover, aged 80 years or thear about, that sixty years ago or thear about my mother asked my consent to sell Valentine Hill that tract of land my father purchased of Mr. William Hilton as appears by a dede of sale under his hand and my mother told me that she sold that land to the said Hill by my consent and by surety of that sale the sayd Hill built upon that land for sixty years ago or theare about and the said Hill lived and died in peacebell possession of that land without any molestation by any persons to the best of my knowledge, which land lieth at the hed of Oyster river the sallt river on the north side of that river joining to the saw mill that was bought by Capt. Woodman and Ste. Jones and Nathaniel Hill and furder saith by information Bartholomy Stevenson has bewelt upone and improved part of the same land and furder saith that he never heard that the sayd Hill was molestet in his possession of the fresh meddowe att Whelrits pond and thear about by person or persons. [Court Files No. 17101.]

February 13, 1709/10:

The testimonie of John Medder sen[r] of Dover beeing eighty years of agge testifieth and saith that the five hundred ackers of Land granted to Mr Valentine Hill by the town of Dover at the head of Oyster river adjacent to his sawmill the North Line of y[t] land running near aboutt the foott path going from the falls to Stoney Brook near Capt. Woodmans orchard soe running up the hill northerly between Capt. Woodmans house and A Littell barn westerly of the house, I being lately upon the Spote and acquainted to the above premises, aboutte sixty foure years, and further saith the westerly bounds of that land Mr Valentine Hill sold to Patrick Jemison begins at the salt river between a fence and a Littell Hill wher plume trees grow and soe running upon a straight Line to Stony Brook to an elm standing near Capt. Woodman Dece[sd] orchard And the land wich Mr Valentine Hill sold to Patrick Jemison is noe part of that land wich Capt. Nath[ll] Hill and Bartholmew Stevenson is now in controversy with And I asked Mr Valentine Hill why hee would sell that land to Patrick Jemison, Hee answered mee because hee was A usefull man to mee aboutte my mills hee was my Serv[tt] and I would have him settled by mee and further saith not. [Court Files, No. 17101.]

It appears from the above that Valentine Hill built a house on the north side of the river and lived in it, that his son, Nathaniel Hill, built another house about the year 1682, that John Dean was living in said house in 1694, when Dean was killed and the house was burned. Nathaniel Hill probably was then living in the house his father built, and tradition says that the house built by Valentine Hill forms a part of the Ffrost house on the hill. This, then, must be the oldest house in Durham, and it is doubtful whether there is another so old within the limits of ancient Dover. This house must have been a garrison capable of resisting the Indian attack of 1694.

As a result of the aforementioned suit possession was delivered, 15 March 1710, to Nathaniel Hill of "six acres of land

HEAD OF TIDE WATER, OYSTER RIVER

bounded easterly with land now in the occupation of the widdow Chesly, on the southerly and westerly side with the publick high way and a lane northerly."

It appears as though Bartholomew Stevenson lived on the hill, within the limits of the town landing as afterward laid out, about where now stands an old white house, that a century ago was occupied by Widow Elizabeth Dutch. The house in which John Dean lived and which was burned in 1694 may have been under the hill, where an old cellar is even now plainly visible.

The bounds of the Landing Place as laid out by John Tuttle, Jeremiah Burnham, Tristram Heard and James Davis, in 1703, further describe this region:

Beginning att high water mark by George Chesley his fence, so from high water mark by yᵉ fence eight rods northwesterly or as the said fence now layes, which is near thereabouts, from thence west and be south twenty nine Rods to the Top of the hill by Bartholomew Stephenson his house, from thence nor nor west to a pitch pine markt H standing on yᵉ east side of yᵉ mast path which leads from Oyster River falls, from thence west to the fence on the west side of the aforesaid path, then southward as yᵉ sᵈ fence now goes tell it comes to the fresh River above the sawmill, all which Land thus Laid out to Lay open for a Public Landing Place.

Thus we come to the large estate of Valentine Hill. On the 29th of the 9th month, 1649, there was granted to Valentine Hill and Thomas Beard " the fall of Oyster River," "for the Erickting and setting up of a sawe mill," with accommodations of timber for the mill. The annual rent for the same was ten pounds, to be paid to the town, beginning the following September or earlier if the mill began to run before that time. A little later Thomas Kemble owned a large share in this mill. On the 14th of the 5th month, 1651, the town granted to Valentine Hill five hundred acres for a farm, "adjacent to his mills at Oyster River, provided it doth not annoy the inhabitants, and laid out and bounded in yᵉ year 1660, yᵉ 3rd day of yᵉ 11th mo. bounded upon a N and S line from Oyster River 200 rods, and from that bound N W half a point westerly 320 rods and from yᵗ to Oyster River upon a S. W and by S line 210 rods to yᵉ River and yᵉ River is yᵉ bounds."

This tract embraced the greater part of the site of the present village of Durham and was long in possession of the heirs of Valentine Hill. In the mill he employed his "seven Scots" and had a grant of four acres for their use, as has been before said. Though he had a house near the mill, and probably it was a part of the present Ffrost house, — yet in 1660 "the house of Mr. Valentine Hill, which is his now dwelling house at Rockey Point," is mentioned in fixing the division line of Oyster River parish. This was probably near the mouth of the river, on the north side, since we have already seen that Hill owned a large tract of land there at this time. He also had a grant of the mill privileges at Lamprey River, in 1652, with accommodations of timber on land a mile wide on both sides of the river, for which he was to pay the town twenty pounds annually.

John Thompson, who married Sarah, daughter of Capt. John Woodman, about 1679, lived not far from his father-in-law. He had a grant of land, 2 April 1694, on the north side of Mast Road in Follett's swamp. The first Thompson house was on the present farm of Lucien Thompson, and the road leading thereto from the Mast Road was just west of the new Boston and Maine Railroad station. His land extended to the King's highway leading from Oyster River to Dover through what is locally known as Bagdad. This was a strip directly north of the Kincaid and Hill lands. Here John Thompson, senior, and succeeding generations were buried. He had a grant of two acres against Woodman's land in 1702 and an additional grant of land adjoining in 1720. Another grant was made to him in 1733. Successive

UPPER END OF COLLEGE RESERVOIR, IN "FOLLETS MARSH"

generations had extensive grants and made purchases of a considerable part of the Woodman farm. Robert Thompson built his house on the corner of Thompson land nearest to the Woodman garrison for protection.

West of the Thompson land, in Follett's swamp, was land granted to Eli Demeritt, 30 May 1699, in exchange for land which had been granted to him near John Derry, 11 April 1694. This grant was laid out, 31 May 1699, "in follets swamp and is bounded by four rods of Land Left for a path for cattle into the

woods and Jonathan Woodmans Land Lying on the north side
of it the first bounds being four rods south from a marked Hemlock tree and runs south west and by south forty rods to A Bass
tree marked and from thence norwest or there about eight score
rods to A marked Hemlock tree marked E J and from thence it
runs east and be north forty rods to A Hemlock tree marked
E J and from thence where it began.'' Signed by John Woodman, Jeremiah Burnum and John Smith, Lott Laiers.

The above grant is now a part of the three hundred acre farm
owned by Albert DeMeritt. The farm of Capt. George P.
Demeritt adjoining has also been in the family many generations, perhaps back to the first settler, Eli Demeritt.

The location of other settlers will best be told in the chapter on
roads.

EXILES FROM SCOTLAND

The fact is well known that Oliver Cromwell took ten thousand prisoners at the battle of Dunbar, 3 September 1650, and as many more at the battle of Worcester, just one year later. Those taken at Dunbar were marched down to Durham and Newcastle by way of Berwick and entrusted to the care of Sir Arthur Heselrig. Many perished on this march, and some were shot because they could not or would not march. They had little to eat for eight days. Disease swept off 1,500 in the course of a few weeks. One hundred and fifty were sent over to Boston, Mass., in the ship *Unity*, and since a score or so of them settled at what is now South Berwick, Me., that place was first called the Parish of Unity. Many more of these Scotch prisoners were sent to Virginia, and more still were sent to West India islands.

The prisoners taken at Worcester were marched up to London and there confined for a few months in the artillery grounds at Tuthill Fields, perhaps half a mile west of Westminster Palace. Here they were allowed for daily rations a pound of bread and half a pound of cheese. Shelter seems to have been provided for the sick only. Two hundred and seventy-two of these prisoners were sent to Boston in the ship called the *John and Sara* and were consigned to Thomas Kemble, a merchant of Charlestown, Mass.

This Thomas Kemble was part owner with Valentine Hill in the mills at Durham Falls and Lamprey River. He also owned lands in Maine and did an extensive business in lumber. He saw that the young Scotch prisoners would be useful men in sawmills and so he disposed of many of them in this way. Richard Leader had charge of some Scotchmen at the Lynn Iron Works and later, in 1652, took some of them with him to work in the mills at South Berwick, then called Great Works.

All the Scotchmen brought in the two ships above mentioned were sold to planters and others who needed workmen throughout New England. The usual price paid was twenty pounds per man, and after working from five to eight years, nominally to pay their passage money, and to learn some trade as appren-

75

tices, they were given their liberty. Many of them received grants of land in the towns where they had worked.

The records of Dover, under date of 5 October 1652, have the following: "Given & granted unto Mr. Valentine Hill, his heires Executors administrators or assigns foure acres of land adjoining to Goodman Hudsons Lott for his Scots." Later, about 1663, we find another record as follows, "Layd out and Bounded to henrey Brown and James Ore fower ackers which were given and granted unto Mr. Valentine Hills seven Scotes in the yeir 1652. Said land lyeth on the northern side of the land that was granted to Hudson and now in the hands of Edward Patterson." It bordered on the "freshet," that is, the mill-pond above the dam at Durham Falls, and was on the south side of the river, and on the Newmarket road. It is probable that they worked by shifts in the mills, having three days in the week to work in their gardens. They were not allowed to marry till they got their liberty. Some of them never married. Some married daughters of their employers. Some married Irish maids who had been kidnaped and brought over as house servants and to swell the population of the colonies.

A study of these Scotchmen clears up a lot of mystery heretofore connected with certain names that appear in early taxlists of Dover and in court records. Let us see who they were.

Nyven Agnew, called also Nivin Agneau, is called "Nivin the Scot" in the Dover tax-list of 1659, shortly after he got his freedom. He administered the estate of James Barry, another Scotchman of South Berwick, Me., about 1676, and lived on the land that Kittery had granted to Barry. Agnew's will, 16 September 1687, mentions debts due to him from James Barry, his predecessor. He divides his property between Peter Grant and John Taylor, two other Scotchmen. In the inventory of his estate is this item, "To a sword that Peter Grant did say he would give ten shillings for." Neither Barry nor Agnew married.

John Barber was taxed in Dover in 1659 and was received as an inhabitant of Exeter in 1678. He had wife, "Sisly," and a seat was assigned to him in the church at Amesbury, Mass., in 1667. He had at least two sons, John and Robert. John Barber, Jr., married Anne, daughter of Robert Smart and lived on Hilton's Mill Grant in 1696. He had a grant of fifty acres in 1725. His wife, Anne, made a deposition, 23 June 1759, aged

83. They had sons, Joseph who was a soldier at Crown Point in 1756, and John, who was living in 1768. Perhaps this was the John Barber who married Jane Davis in Durham, 19 January 1736/7.

Robert Barber, son of John, senior, was born in Amesbury, Mass., 4 March 1669 70. He had a grant of fifty acres in Exeter in 1698 and was killed by Indians 1 July 1706. He had children, Abigail, Mary, Daniel and Robert.

Henry Brown and James Orr, Oar, or Ore, lived together all their lives, unmarried. They were admitted as inhabitants at Oyster River, 10 November 1658, and were taxed in 1659. They and Edward Errin bought in 1662 "a farm at Bradboate Harbour in Pischataq River at the Wadeing place, with 50 acres of upland." This was near the line between Kittery and York, called long afterward "Scotchman's Neck." In 1686 Brown and Orr brought suit against John Bray for carrying away their grass at Brave Boat Harbor. June 3, 1675, "Henry Brown and James Oare, Scotchmen & now residents in the township of Wells", bought 200 acres of Henry Sayward, at "Mowsome." In 1662 Brown and Ore had a grant of eight score acres near "Moharmits marsh." October 9, 1669, James Ore of Saco Falls belonging to Winter Harbor, for himself and Henry Brown, sold to James Smith of Oyster River, tailor, land granted to them by Dover, a "mile and a halfe or there abouts" from Oyster River, on the south side of said river, eight acres. Brown and Orr lived many years in Wells, Me., and ran a sawmill, having learned the trade of Valentine Hill. They associated with them one Robert Stewart, another Scotchman, and left all their property to him.

Thomas Canyda has been already mentioned as killed by the falling of a tree upon him near the house of Thomas Humphreys, in 1660.

John Curmuckhell came in the *John and Sara* from the battlefield of Worcester. John Cernicle, called also Carnicle, was taxed at Oyster River in 1657. John Chirmihill bought land of John Pearce of York, 26 December 1660, and married Pearce's daughter, Ann. He had a grant of upland at York Bridge in 1671. Ann, wife of John Cyrmihill, was presented at court, 6 July 1675, "for not frequenting the publique worship of God on the Lord's days." He died soon after this, and his widow married Micum McIntyre of York.

"Davey Daniel" is suspected of being a Scot. He is first mentioned in the settlement of a Scotchman's estate. It is known that James Daniels was one of the thirty-five Scots employed at the Lynn Iron Works in 1653. He is also called Danielson and his son founded the town of Danielson, Conn. The Daniels family of Durham was first called Daniel. The name originally might have been McDaniel. The Mc was dropped, as in many other names, when the Scotchmen came to New England. Later its equivalent was added to the name, making Danielson, or shortened to Daniels. See Daniel family in Genealogical Notes.

Patrick Denmark was taxed in Dover in 1662. He had wife, Hannah, and children found in records of Dover, viz., Patrick born 8 April 1664 and James born 13 March 1665. He is once called Patrick Denmor. He removed to Saco, Me., soon after 1665, where children are recorded. In 1685 he petitioned for a grant of 100 acres in Saco, "having now a great Charge of Children." His son, James, married Elizabeth Littlefield of Wells.

Thomas Doughty was received as an inhabitant of Dover in 1658. He was born in 1630, as a deposition shows. In this deposition he delares that he worked for Valentine Hill and cut a road for Hill to his meadow at Wheelwright's Pond, where said Hill built a house and kept cattle. Hill paid Doughty ten pounds for cutting the road. Doughty removed to Great Works, South Berwick, and managed the sawmill there a short time. He married, 24 June 1669, Elizabeth Bulie of Saco. The Indians drove him from Wells to Salem, Mass., where he died about the year 1705. He left children, viz., James who married, 10 April 1707, Mary Robinson in Hampton, N. H., and settled in Cape Elizabeth, Me.; Joseph of Salem; Elizabeth who married Thomas Thomes and went to Falmouth, Me.; Benjamin; Margaret, who married Samuel Wilson of Malden, Mass.; Abigail who married in Lynn, Mass., 28 October 1717, Robert Edmonds; and Patience who married Benjamin Follett of Salem, Mass. The descendants of Thomas Doughty are many in Maine and Massachusetts.

Edward Erwin was received as an inhabitant of Dover in 1658. He was taxed as Edward Arrin in 1659. He with Henry Brown and James Oar bought land in Kittery in 1662. "Edward Irwin and Company" were taxed in Dover in 1662. Edward Eurin died in Exeter, 9 November 1667. He is called Duren and Dowreing in the administration of his estate. James Kidd and George Veasey were administrators, and John Roy, a Scotchman of Charlestown, seems to have been his heir. I think he was the Edward Dulen, so erroneously reported in the passenger list of the *John and Sara*, and that he was captured at the battle of Worcester, 3 September 1651.

William Furbish was taxed in Dover in 1659 as William Ferbush. The statement that he was taxed in Dover in 1648, made in Old Kittery and Her Families, is an error, the result of the misreading of the name William Furber. William Furbish was in Scotland probably William ffarrabas, and a family of the same surname in Massachusetts is now called Forbes, once pronounced in two syllables. William Furbish owned land in Kittery, now Eliot, before 1664, and had a grant from the town in 1668. He died in 1701, having had seven children. He was punished in 1681 for calling His Majesty's authorities "Divills and hell bound," thus showing his lasting antipathy to the rule of Englishmen. The fight at Dunbar was not yet ended in his breast. His descendants are very numerous. See Old Kittery and Her Families, pp. 121, 437.

William Gowen, alias Smith, was taxed as William Smith at Oyster River in 1659. William Smith, alias Gowin, was fined "for fighting and bloodshed on ye Lords day after ye afternoone meeting," 30 June 1668. He was on a coroner's jury at Oyster River in 1660. The Scotch word *gowen* means a smith, hence the change of his name. "Elexander Gowing," perhaps the same man, was taxed at Oyster River in 1661. William Gowen, or Smith, was a carpenter. He first appears in Kittery, now Eliot, in 1666. There he married, 14 May 1667, Elizabeth, sister of Major Charles Frost, and had a grant of a house lot in 1670. He died 2 April 1686, leaving eight children. See Old Kittery and Her Families, p. 468.

Peter Grant was taxed at Oyster River in 1659. He had previously been employed in the Lynn Iron Works. He bought land at what is now South Berwick, 21 October 1659. A deposition, made 13 September 1701, calls him "upwards of 70 years old." He married, about 1664, Joan, widow of James Grant of York, though court records show that both of them had wives in Scotland, to whom they could not return. Peter Grant left eight children and his descendants are numerous. See Old Kittery and Her Families, p. 472. He was a member of the Scotch Charitable Society in Boston in 1657.

John Hudson came in the *John and Sara*. He is mentioned at Oyster River, 5 October 1652. He settled at Bloody Point, Newington. There were granted to John Hudson, 19 March 1693/4, ten acres joining to land he bought of William Furber. He married, 25 July 1689, Mary Beard. This was probably a second marriage. He died about 1717, leaving most of his property to his grandson, Hudson Peavey.

Walter Jackson came in the *John and Sara* and was received as an habitant at Oyster River in 1658. He had wife, Jane, in 1663, and, Ann, in 1667. For family see Genealogical Notes.

James Jackson also came in the *John and Sara*. He was taxed at Oyster River in 1663. June 27, 1661, James Jackson was freed from training "by reason he hath lost one of his fingers." Did he lose it at the battle of Worcester or in Valentine Hill's sawmill? He married a daughter of John Smith of Cape Nedick, York, where he had a grant of twenty-eight acres in 1667, next to land of his father-in-law. He was probably killed by Indians, with his wife and two children, in 1675. He left a daughter, Elizabeth, who in 1685 acquits her uncle, John Smith, Jr., of York, from any incumbrance, dues or demands concerning her father's estate or concerning herself. See York Deeds, VII, 262.

Patrick Jameson came in the *John and Sara*. He seems to have been the one who is called "Patrick the Scott" in the Dover tax-list of 1657. Valentine Hill sold to "Patrick Gimison of the same town," 11 May 1659, land on the north side of Oyster River, that later was the estate of George and Deliverance Chesley. The village school house is on this lot. Hill declared that Jameson had been a servant of his and was useful in his mills and, therefore, he sold the land to Jameson. In 1664 Patrick Jameson was chosen with Philip Chesley to lay out a road from Oyster River to Cochecho. Patrick Jennison, his mark, probably the same man, witnessed a deed at Kennebunk, in 1674. He was accused of crime at Oyster River, in 1669, and ordered to be sent to Boston for further trial, but the case seems not to have been pushed. In 1677 the administration of the estate of Patrick Gynnison, deceased, was granted to Samuel Austin of York, as court records at Alfred, Me., say. There is no record of any family.

Robert Junkins was taxed at Oyster River in 1657, and as
"Robard Junkes" in 1663. He removed to York before 1674
and took the oath of allegiance there 22 March 1681. He had
a garrison house in the upper part of York, that was standing in
recent years. The region is called "Scotland" unto this day.
November 31, 1715, "Sarah Junckins, aged seventy years, living
at her father's house at Cape Nedick on the north east side of
Cape Nedick river, near the ferry place, testifieth that her father
John Smith senior lived there 48 years agoe, as she can well remember, that he lived near where Samuel Webber now lives."
This was found among the Court Files at Alfred, Me. His wife,
then, was Sarah, daughter of John Smith of York. He died
about 1699, leaving widow, Sarah, and three sons, Alexander,
Daniel and Robert. Alexander married Catherine, daughter of
James and Margaret (Warren) Stacpole. Daniel married Eleanor, daughter of Deacon Arthur Came, another Scotchman, as
was also James Warren, father of Margaret. The Junkins name
still exists and must be distinguished from the surname Jenkins
of Kittery and Durham.

John Kye, Key, Keiay, or Keays, was taxed in Dover in 1657
and was living at Salmon Falls, in what is now South Berwick in
1667. He and his son John and daughter Abigail were captured
by Indians and carried to Canada about 1689. His son, James,
was then killed. The name of his first wife is not known. He
married (2) Sarah, widow of Jonathan Nason and daughter of
Reynold Jenkins. He and son, John, were prisoners at Quebec
in 1695. Very likely this was the John Mackey, who came in
the *John and Sara*. The name might be pronounced in different
dialects like Ke and Ki, with long sound of the vowel. July 1,
1703, John Key senior, aged about 70 years, deposed that James
Barry, Niven Agnue and John Taylor owned in succession a
farm in upper Kittery, now South Berwick. In his will, 1710/18,
he is called both Key and Kye. For family see Old Kittery and
Her Families, p. 568.

James Kidd was fined and taxed in Dover in 1657. He had
a grant of 100 acres, near the great pond, in 1656, laid out in
1714. He had a grant of four acres for a house lot, on Back
River, next to Lieut. Ralph Hall, 1 February 1658. He removed
to Exeter and was one of the executors of the estate of Edward
Erring, or Erwin, 1673. He took oath of fidelity, 30 November

1677. In 1665 he had a grant of twenty acres in Exeter, next to
Henry Magoons, another Scotchman. He is repeatedly called
James Skid in Exeter records and as a witness to one of the York
Deeds. His name and his associations with Scotchmen create
the impression that he also was one of Cromwell's Scots. He
died before 1712.

Allexander Mackdouel or McDaniel, was taxed at Oyster
River in 1661, and his estate was taxed in 1663. He was drowned
between York and Dover, 16 January, 1663, and his property
was awarded to a kinsman, John Roy of Charlestown, Mass.
His estate was appraised by John Tod, John Alt, Walter Jackson
and Henry Brown. There were bills from Edward During
and William ffurbush. The debts were to Walter Jackson, Philip
Chesley, Thomas Dowty, Patrick Denmark, and David Danniell.
The following deposition is found in Boston among the papers
pertaining to the settlement of his estate: "The testimony of
phillip Cheasly aged about forty six years saith that about ten
dais before Ellexander magdunell was drowned being att the sd
deponents house heard the sd magdunell say that if he died
that he would give all that he had to his cosen John Roye livinge
att Charlestown and further saith not." Dated 2 February, 1663.

Micum McIntire appears in the Dover tax-list of 1664 as "Mi-
come the Scotchman." Micum appears to be Highland Scotch
for Malcolm. I think that he worked in the mills at Cochecho.
He had a grant in Kittery, above Salmon Falls, 11 December,
1662. He settled in the upper part of York, or Scotland Parish,
and his garrison house is still standing. Micum appears in the
Dover tax-list of 1659. He was twice or thrice married and there
are a host of descendants. The tradition has floated down that
after he was taken prisoner in Scotland he was drawn up in line
with others, that every tenth man might be shot. He saw that
death was coming to him, broke rank and ran for life. A mounted
officer pursued and wounded him, but his life was spared.

James Middleton was received as an inhabitant at Oyster
River in 1658. He was appointed administrator of the estate of
Mrs. Ludeces of Dover Neck in 1664. He may have worked in
the home of David Ludecas Edling, as he is called, whose widow,
Elizabeth. died 16 November 1663. James Middleton was convicted, 3 June 1659, of frequenting the taverns and quarreling
and fighting. He was fined twenty pounds, and Valentine Hill

was surety on his bond for good behavior. Philip Chesley, Thomas Footman and William Smith (Gowen) were convicted of quarreling with James Middleton at the same time and were fined. Also George Vezie was convicted of being more than half an hour in the tavern, at the same time, and was fined two shillings. James Middleton was east of the Kennebec in 1665, and 16 September 1676, he, being then a resident of Great Island in Pascataqua River, sold to William Gowine, alias Smith, all right to lands on the Kennebec, especially "at Small Point, which I lately bought of Patricke Denmarke." See York Deeds, III, 67. James Middleton of Newichawanock, laborer, brought suit for debt against George Jeffrey of Great Island in 1683.

James Morrey, or Murray, was received as an inhabitant in 1658. He died at Oyster River, 11 November 1659. A jury of inquest, impaneled by John Bickford, found that James Morrey was killed by the limb of a tree falling on his head. Among the jurors were William Smith (Gowen), Niven Agnew, Jonas Bines James Bunker, Thomas Stevenson, Matthew Williams and others, all of Oyster River. See Court Files at Concord.

Edward Patterson was taxed at Oyster River in 1667/9. He is mentioned in 1660 as a voter. The following is found in Dover Town records: "31:10:1660, Granted to Edward Patterson a trackt of land lying between his land and the Brooke which Runneth out of the long marsh on the est side of the highway from Oyster River fall to lamperell River and on the west side by the South branch of Oyster River, not intrenching on anie former grant, always provided that thear be a Convenient way alowed to the Scochmen to thear lott." He sold this lot to William Roberts. Edward Patterson was a grand juryman in 1660. There died at New Haven, Conn., 31 October 1669, Edward Patterson, "one of the south end men." Had he wandered so far to join some of his own countrymen there?

William Thompson was another Scotchman, without doubt, as were George Thompson of Reading and Alexander Thompson of Ipswich, Mass., by convincing evidence. For his family see Genealogical Notes.

Later Scotchmen in Durham were David Kincaid, probably from Campsie, in the parish of Stirling; Eleazer Wyer, son of Edward Wyer, tailor, from Scotland, who lived in Charlestown, Mass. Eleazer Wyer married Sarah, widow of James Nock and daughter of Charles Adams.   Another son of a Scotchman was Dr. Samuel Merrow, born at Reading, Mass., 9 October 1670, son of Henry Merrow, who married Jane Wallis, 19 December 1661.   Dr. Merrow practiced medicine at Durham from 1720 to 1733.

DEPREDATIONS BY INDIANS

The story of the Indian wars in New England has been told so many times and embellished by fancy so plentifully that it is very difficult to add thereto statement of fact or pleasing form. Yet the history of Durham would be incomplete without the full story, and so effort has been made to bring together the scattered narrations of the past.

The causes of the wars with the Indians have been sought in the injustices of white settlers, overreachings in trade, treachery of supposed friends, maltreatment of Indians, their sale into slavery, and like offences. There were exceptional misdeeds on the part of white men, and it must be remembered that not all the Indians were examples of childlike innocence and good-will. Yet there were some good Indians that were not dead Indians, and the majority of the white settlers treated them with justice and kindness. For fifty years there was little trouble with them, and no war would have been waged with them, in all probability, had it not been for conflict between the people of France and Great Britain. These nations carried their quarrels and ambitions into their foreign possessions. One prize at stake was a continent, or a large part thereof, though neither party then knew the value of the prize. The French stirred up some Indian tribes against the English, and the English retaliated, whenever they could, in like manner.

The first clash of arms was in what is known in history as King Philip's War. In 1675 began the depredations in Maine and New Hampshire. Hubbard records that in that year the Indians burned five or six houses at Oyster River and killed two men, namely William Roberts and his son-in-law. This William Roberts lived on the south side of the river, about two miles below the Falls. There is no record that any of his neighbors were disturbed, and he may have been away from home. Who the son-in-law was has not been ascertained. Five sons-in-law are mentioned after this date as living, and only five daughters have been found. He had a son, William Roberts, Jr., who is mentioned in Court Records before this as a simple-minded youth, and is not mentioned anywhere after 1675. He may have been the one who was killed with his father.

Soon after this, in the same year, the Indians "assaulted another house at Oyster River, the which, although it was garrisoned, yet meeting with a good old man, whose name was Beard, without the garrison, they killed him upon the place and in a barbarous manner cut off his head and set it upon a pole in derision. Not far off, about the same time, they burned another house and barn."[1] The man slain was William Beard, whose garrison stood "east of Beard's creek, between the turnpike road and the highway to Dover, a short distance from the corner." Probate records declare that he died about the first of November, 1675. Hubbard goes on to say that the same year the Indians "burned two Cheslies houses about Oyster River and killed two men that were passing along the river in a canoe and carried away an old Irishman with a young man taken from about Exeter." The two escaped later. History does not tell us who the men slain were. The Chesley families were nearest neighbors to Beard and probably were in his garrison, when their houses were burned, for they survived this raid.

The following letter was written shortly after the well known massacre at Cochecho, when Major Waldron and twenty-two others were killed and twenty-nine were carried into captivity. It seems that the Indians then made an attack upon some part of Oyster River Plantation, though the historians have made no note of it. The letter is found in the Massachusetts Archives:

HAMPTON, July 30, 1689.

MAJOR PIKE SIR: thes are to informe you that this last night There came news to me ffrom Exeter that one of Phillip Cromwells Sons came yesterday from oyster River where were 20 Indiens Seen and seueral Houses Burning. About 20 English ishued out to beat them off a many guns were herd go off but he coming away while it was a doing we have not as yett any account of what harme is ther done and we thank you for your care about our . . . . Although no help could be procured there is but a few could be procured with us the notice was so suddaine but thos that are gon went yesterday when it was almost night they were willing to stay no longer. When I have account farther from Oyster River I will send it to you not Els at present.

ffrom your ffriend

SAMUELL SHERBURNE[2].

[1]Hubbard's Indian Wars, Vol. II, pp. 110, 116, 118. Cf. Landmarks in Ancient Dover, by Miss Mary P. Thompson, p. 178.
[2]Memoranda of Ancient Dover, p. 269.

The messenger above mentioned may have been a son of Philip Crommett, who is sometimes called Cromwell in the old records. He lived at this time near the northern border of Exeter, now Newmarket.

The next attack of the Indians upon Oyster River was in 1689. Then the Rev. John Pike records in his Journal that in August "James Huggins [Huckins] of Oyster River was slain, his garrison taken and 18 persons killed and carried away." James Huckins was a lieutenant and had been one of the selectmen of Dover. He had a garrison-house, which stood a few rods south of the house now owned by heirs of the late Andrew E. Meserve, east of the railroad and on the north side of the second road crossed by the railroad as it runs from Durham to Dover. The men slain were at work in the field which lies southeast of the garrison, beyond Huckins' brook. They were all buried under a mound which still exists in the southeast corner of the field which now belongs to the Coe family. The Indians then attacked the garrison-house defended by only two boys and some women and children. They managed to set fire to the roof of the garrison but the boys held out till the Indians promised to spare the lives of all. Yet they killed three or four of the children and carried away the rest of the inmates of the garrison, except one of the boys, probably Robert Huckins, who escaped the next day. The garrison-house was destroyed. Lieut. Huckins' widow was recovered after a year of captivity at Fort Androscoggin, which was located on Laurel Hill, Auburn, Me.

Some details of this attack have been preserved in a letter of Jeremiah Swayen to Governor Simon Bradstreet, dated at Salmon Falls "7ber 15 1689." He says, "a house poorly fortified at Oyster River was taken by ye Enimie being about Sixty in ye company; though part of capn Gardners Compa lodged the night before at said house and were moved away about half an hour before ye assault and were got to Cocheacha where a post overtooke them and they faced about & persued ye Enimy but could not find them. . . . One of ye captives made his escape two days after he was taken, whom ye Indians tould that they had beleagerd ye place three days and when they knew how many men belonged to ye house & seeing ym all gathering corn came and killed them first, and then sett upon ye house where were onely Woomen children & two Boyes, they killed and Cap-

tivated Eighteene persons none escapeing." Coll. of Maine
Historical Society, IX, 57.

On the fourth of July, 1690, seven persons were slain and a lad
taken at "Lamperell River," that is, in the vicinity of the present
village of Newmarket. Two days later, 6 July, occurred the
battle, when "Capt. Floyd fought the enemy at Wheelwright's
Pond but was forced to retire with loss of 16 men," as Pike says.[1]
It was a very hot day and the men of Oyster River made all
haste to arrive at the scene of action. Among them was James
Smith, who lived near the Falls. Of him it is recorded that he
"died of a surfeit which he got by running to assist Capt. Floyd
at Wheelwright's pond."

History gives but few details of the battle at Wheelwright's
Pond, which was a running fight through woods, after Indian
fashion, beginning, as local tradition says, at Turtle Pond in
Lee and extending to the southeast side of Wheelwright's Pond
in the same town. One hundred men, under command of Capt.
Noah Wiswall and Capt. John Floyd, set out from Dover. The
fight was on Sunday. Captain Wiswall, Lieut. Flag, Serg.
Walker, and twelve privates were killed, when both parties withdrew from the conflict. Capt. Converse found seven wounded
men yet alive and brought them to the hospital by sun-rise the
next morning, says Mather. Probably all of the men at Oyster
River who were enrolled in the militia had a part in this battle,
as we may infer from the following petition, found in the Massachusetts Archives.

PETITION OF THOMAS FOOTMAN
March the 29th 1692.

To the honorable court now sitting in Portsm° the humble peticon of thomas
ffootman humbly shueth that your petitioner being Imprest almost two years
past to serve their magstys and on the first expedition was Listed under the
honorable Capt. John floyd whereupon y° first ffight our commander had (which
was at osteriver New town) your petitioner was wounded, of which wounds
your petitioner is not healed, nor cannot Expect to be ever Able to work to
get a Competent Living, your peticoner being Reduced to so weake and Low
Estate nothing to help himself for present nor for futuer no wages Reserved,
nor non to pitte a poore wounded soulder, Charritye also grone cold the doctors
they demand money, your peticioner having for himself nether meat nor drink
nor Cloths, makes your peticoner humble address his poore and miserable Lowe
Condition to this Honorable Court humbly praying Releff not doubting but

[1]Mather's Magnalia, App. Art., VI.   N. E. Reg. VII, 156. Id., XVIII, 161. Pike's Journal.   Thompson's Landmarks in Ancient Dover, p. 180.

this honorable Court will bee pleased to Consider Your peticconers Case and find a way that your petitioner may be Releved & your petitioner shall pray

THOMAS FFOOTMAN.[1]

John Davis certified that he impressed Thomas Footman on the 20th day of June 1690, by order of Major Vaughan, for the expedition to Winipisiocke. Accompanying this petition is an account of "Lowis and Cristan Willames," [Lewis and Christian Williams of Portsmouth] "of ther Charg to Thomas fottman for his tendance and seven months diate during the Cure in which time the said fottman was not able to put on his Cloathes which is 7 shillings and 16 pence a week." John Davis certified that the bill of the "Cerorgon" [chirurgeon, surgeon] was six pounds.

It appears from the above that the fight began at "Newtown," an undefined locality, north of Turtle Pond and extending to the upper part of Oyster River and towards Wheelwright's Pond.

The French and Indians seem to have had little regard for solemn treaties of peace. That made at Pemaquid was suddenly broken by the attack upon Oyster River, 18 July 1694, said by captives to have been talked of in the streets of Quebec two months before. Pike's Journal records the terrible event in the following laconic sentences: "The Indians fell suddenly & unexpectedly upon Oyster River about break of day. Took 3 garrisons (being deserted or not defended) killed & carried away 94 persons, & burnt 13 houses. This was the first act of hostility committed by them after ye peace concluded at Pemiquid."

There were warnings that led some persons to be apprehensive of danger, warnings which were long remembered and interpreted with suspicion. Col. Richard Waldron wrote to Governor Dudley, under date of 22 September 1712, thus: "Capt Davis tells me yt last night at oyster river in the dead of ye Night there were doors knock'd at & Stones flung at Some Garrisons, to find out who liv'd in their houses & whether any watch was kept in their Garrisons, as the enemy did ye Night before Oyster river was Destroy'd & Wee are well assured Some Scouts of the Enemy are now near us."[2]

The account of this attack as given by Dr. Belknap in his History of New Hampshire is said to have been drawn from manuscripts in the possession of the Smith family of Durham.

---

[1] Collections of the Maine Historical Society, 2d Series, Vol. 4, pp. 382-3.
[2] Collections of the Maine Historical Society, IX, 330.

But little can be added thereto from public records and published histories. On Tuesday evening, 17 July, the enemy to the number of about 250 concealed themselves in the woods and divided into two bands, one for the north side of the river and the other for the south. The latter began the attack somewhat prematurely. John Dean, who lived near the Falls, on the north side of the river, arose before day to catch his horse, intending to leave home in the morning. He was fired upon and killed. The report of the gun was heard and warning was thus given to some households. The undefended fled to the nearest garrisons, and some were killed in their flight. Mrs. Dean and her daughter were captured and her house was burned. They were taken to a spruce swamp and left in the care of an old Indian who had a violent headache. He asked her for a remedy and she replied, "occapee," the Indian term for rum. He drank freely and she and her daughter made their escape. They hid in a thicket during the day and then went down the river in a canoe to Burnham's garrison, where they found protection.

The next house attacked seems to have been that of Ensign John Davis, who lived perhaps half a mile below the Falls. He surrendered on the promise of safety, yet he, his wife and several children were killed, and his house was burned. Two daughters were made captive, one of whom became a nun in Canada and never returned. The other returned and became the wife of Peter Mason. A sister of Ensign Davis, who was the widow of James Smith before mentioned, was living at the house of her brother and was killed at the same time with her sons, James and Samuel, after having been carried into the woods. The statement has been made that the oldest son of Mrs. Smith escaped to the river but was there shot. This may be doubted, since John Smith, her son, lived to marry Elizabeth Buss and have a numerous family. Two daughters also were spared, as subsequent deeds clearly show.

The next house below Davis' was the Burnham garrison, on a hilltop, easily defended by its situation. Hither fled Moses Davis, who had heard the first shot that killed John Dean. Ezekiel Pitman and family, who lived only a gun-shot's distance from Burnham's, were alarmed by shouts. They escaped through one end of the house while the Indians were entering the other, and, protected by the shade of trees, made their way to the Burnham

garrison, on which no serious attack seems to have been made.
Tradition in the Burnham family says that the yard-gate had been
left open that night, and ten Indians were sent to surprise the
garrison. They were fatigued and fell asleep on the bank of the
river near the house. John Willey with his family spent that
night at the Burnham garrison. He had been kept awake by
toothache and heard the first gun fired. He immediately closed
the gate and shouted to the Pitman family. The shout awaked
the Indians, who at once made the attack upon the Pitman
dwelling.

The next house below Ezekiel Pitman's was that of Stephen
Jenkins, who had bought the place of William Williams. He
lived on the hill, about where the present old house of Benjamin
Mathes stands. On the 26th of July 1694, only eight days after
the massacre, it was recorded in the Probate Court, that "administration on the estate of Stephen Jenkins of Oyster River,
who was killed by the Indians and left several small children, was
granted to his brother, Jabez Jenkins of Kittery, Maine." Ann,
wife of Stephen Jenkins, was carried into captivity and returned
in time to give testimony in the trial of the noted Indian chief,
Bomazeen, at Boston, who escaped with his life at this trial and
was slain in the attack on the village of the Norridgewocks, in
1724. The deposition of "Ann Jenkins, her within written
testimony," dated 11 June 1695, gives many details of this
massacre.

Ann Jenkins, of full age, Testifieth & saith, that at Oyster River, on the
eighteenth of July last past, in the morning about the dawning of the day my
husband being up went out of the dore, & presently returning cried to me & our
children to run for our lives, for the Indians had beset the town: whereupon
my husband & myself fled with our children into our corne field, & at our
entrance into the field, Bomazeen, whoume I have seen since I came out of
captivity in the prison, came towards us & about ten Indians more: & the sd
Bomazeen then shot at my husband and shote him down, ran to him & struck
him three blows on the head with a hatchet, scalped him & run him three
times with a bayonet. I also saw the said Bomazeen knock one of my children
on the head & tooke of her scalp & then put the child into her father's armes;
and then stabbed the breast. And Bomazeen also then killed my husband's
grandmother & scalped her, and then led me up to a house and plundered it
& then set it on fire & carried me & my three children into captivity, together
with the rest of our neighbors, whose lives were spared, being at first forty nine:
but in one miles goeing, or thereabouts, they killed three children, so there
remained forty six captives. & that night the company parted & the captives
were distributed, but before they parted I, this deponent, numbered one

hundred and fourty of Indians & fourteen frenchmen & then, when I tooke account, there were more fireing at Woodmans garrison & at Burnhams garrison,
but the number unknown to me. Myself with nine captives more were
carried up to penecook & were Left with three Indians, & that party went
to Greaten, Bomazeen being their Commander. In nine days they returned
& brought twelve captives: & from thence with their canoes, sometimes
a float, & sometimes carried, untill that we came to Norridgeawocke, which
took us fifteen dayes, & staid about two months there, then dispersed into
the woods, twoe or three families in a place, & kept moving toe & froe, staeing
about a week in a place, until they brought us down to pemaquid & delivered
us to Capt. March. Bomazeen was my Master; his wife my Mistriss, untill
Bomazeen was taken at pemaquid; after that I belonged to his wife, untill
about two months before I was brought down to pemaquid; for then the
Indian Minister, called prince Waxaway, bought me, when I was brought to
great weakness and extremity by their bad usage, and showed me great kindness; by whose means, under God, my life was preserved. My mistriss was
very cruel to me & I was cruelly whipt seaven times & they intended so to
proceed, once a week, untill they had killed me; but that the Indian Minister
had compassion on me & rescued me. That Indian Minister also bought
three captives more, and freed them from their hard usage. Their names
are Nicholas Frost, Sarah Braggonton and Thomsand Drue.

The mark of W An JENKINS.

Notice that the manual sign of Ann Jenkins was W. Was
her maiden name Williams? The Nicholas Frost mentioned in
her deposition was the beaver-trader of Kittery, now Eliot, Me.
Sarah Braggonton was doubtless of the family of Arthur Bragdon
of York and Thomsand Drue was Thomasine, or Tamsen Drew
of whom we shall learn more a little later.

Mention is made in the above deposition of a house near to
Jenkins' that was plundered and set on fire. This must have
been the house of the Rev. John Buss, who was at the time away
from home. His house, which was the parsonage, together with
the church, stood near the bank of the river, or perhaps a few
rods therefrom, on higher ground. His family hid among the trees
till the enemy withdrew. The church, which stood near the
parsonage, was not burned at this time and religious services
were held there after 1718.

The fact that Bartholomew Stevenson was appointed, 4 August
1694, administrator of the estates of his brothers, Thomas and
Joseph Stevenson, leads to the inference that these two brothers
perished in this massacre. They lived near the garrison of Thomas
Drew, who, according to Probate Records, "was killed by Indians
and left no will." Administration was granted to his widow

Mary, 30 July 1694. Thomas Drew has been confused with
Francis Drew, who married Lydia Bickford. The latter surrendered the garrison at Drew's Point, on promise of quarter.
He is supposed to have killed an Indian, whose bones were found
in the house after it was burned. Francis Drew attempted to
escape and ran towards the Adams garrison but was overtaken
by the Indians, bound and tomahawked. His wife was carried
away and was rendered so feeble by hunger that she was left to
die in the woods. "Administration on the estate of Francis
Drew of Oyster River, who was killed by the Indians and left
no will, granted to his brother, John, Nov. 16, 1694." Two
years later administration on the estate of Francis Drew was
granted to his oldest son, Thomas, he being "now returned out of
the hands of the Indian Enemy." This Thomas Drew had
been married about six months to wife, Tamsen, and lived with
his father. He was taken to Canada and his wife to Norridge-
wock, whence she returned after about four years, to become the
mother of fourteen children. The following deposition by her
sheds further light on the massacre of 1694:

The Deposition of Damsen Drew lately dwelling att Oyster River in Piscataqua.

This Deponent maketh Oath that on or about the last day of August [evi-
dently an error of memory] in the year 1694 she this Deponent being in Bed
with her Husband they heard a great Tumult and Noise of firing of Guns which
awakened her out of her sleep, and she understanding that the Indians were in
arms & had encompassed the House, willing to make her escape, she endeavored & att last got out of the window and fled, but the Indians firing fast after
her she returned to the House and her father in law took her by the hand and
haled her into the House again, where upon she endeavored to get out at
another window, but the Indians had besett that, so she returned to the other
Room where her friends were, and the window of that Room being open an
Indian named Bombazine (as she was then informed & has since seen and
known him in the Prison at Boston) caught hold of her Arm and pulled her
out att the Window & threw her violently upon the ground, she being then
with child & when he had so done he went into the House to plunder, when
another Indian named Assurowlaway (who could speak good English) came
to her & told her she would receive no hurt & took her and carryed her into
the woods, And further this Deponent saith not.

The mark of DAMSON x DREW.
Boston, May 23ᵈ 1698.

Tamsen Drew "was delivered of a child in the winter, in the
open air and in a violent snow storm. Being unable to suckle
her child or provide it with food, the Indians killed it. She lived

fourteen days on a decoction of the bark of trees. Once they
set her to draw a sled up a river against a piercing northwest
wind and left her. She was so overcome with the cold that she
grew sleepy, laid down and was nearly dead when they returned;
they carried her senseless to a wigwam and poured warm water
down her throat, which recovered her." Belknap's History of
New Hampshire, p. 141. Footnote by John Farmer, giving
traditionary information obtained from John Smith.

There were fifteen in the Drew family at the time of the massacre. John Drew was put out of the window and escaped, probably to be killed by Indians a few years later. Benjamin Drew
was about nine years old. He was carried over Winnipiseogee
and made to run the gauntlet till he was cut down with toma-
hawks. Thomas Drew and his wife, Tamsen, lived to very old
age and, dying about the same time, were buried in the same
grave.

The Matthews, or Mathes, garrison seems to have resisted
attack and probably sheltered some of the neighbors. All houses
between this and the Burnham garrison were, doubtless, burned.

The Adams garrison stood south of the road to Durham Point
and not far from the ruins of the brick house built by Washington
Mathes. This garrison was burned, and Charles Adams and
wife, his son, Samuel, and wife, and eleven others were killed.
The wife of Samuel Adams, being then pregnant, was ripped up.
They were all buried in one grave, near the Mathes Cemetery.
A son, Charles Adams, survived his father but a few months, and
so this branch of the Adams family ceased to transmit the surname, though descendants of the first Charles Adams are many
in the Tasker, Nock, Durrell and Bickford lines.

After setting fire to the Adams garrison the Indians attacked
the garrison of Thomas Bickford at the extremity of the Point.
Bickford's defence of his house seems to have been about the only
item of special interest in this massacre that the Rev. Cotton
Mather thought worthy of being recorded in his *Magnalia Christi
Americana*. He says:

Several persons remarkably escaped this bloody deluge, but none with more
bravery than one Thomas Bickford, who had an house, a little pallisadoed, by
the river side, but no man in it besides himself. He dexterously put his wife
and mother and children aboard a canoe, and, sending them down the river,
he alone betook himself to the defence of his house, against many Indians that
made an assault upon him. They first would have persuaded him with many

fair promises, and then terrified him with as many fierce threatenings, to yield himself; but he flouted and fired at them, daring 'em to come if they durst. His main strategem was to change his livery as frequently as he could; appearing sometimes in one coat, sometimes in another, sometimes in an hat and sometimes in a cap; which caused his besiegers to mistake this one for many defendants. In fine, the pitiful wretches, despairing to beat him out of his house, e'en left him in it; whereas many that opened unto them upon their solemn engagements of giving them life and good quarter, were barbarously butchered by them.

Abigail, Judy and Elizabeth Willey were captured and were still in captivity in 1699.

John Edgerly, grandson of the first Thomas Edgerly, is the authority for the statement that his uncle, Thomas Edgerly, lived at Ambler's. That must mean that he lived where John Ambler afterward lived, who bought, in 1703, the place where now lives the Hon. Jeremiah Langley. This Thomas Edgerly, Jr., married Jane Whedon in 1691. The above named authority relates that "upon hearing the Indians he, his wife, and her sister jumped out of bed and got down cellar, leaving their children in bed; the Indians came in, killed the children, and one or two persons living in the other end of the house were taken; they looked into the cellar, but did not go down. They rifled the house and fired it; as soon as they were gone he put the fire out." This Thomas Edgerly removed to Exeter in the year 1700.

Thomas Edgerly, senior, sent a petition to the Governor and Council at Strawberry Bank. It has no date but it was considered in Council 20 July, so that it must have been written the next day after the massacre. It is as follows:

Whereas it has pleased God to cast affliction upon him and his Neighbours by the sudden incursion of the Indian Enemyes, having his Son wounded, now Remaining at Strawbery Bank under Capt. Packers hand, and his dwelling house burned, and his goods Destroyed.

Humbly Desires your Consideration of his Low Condition and that you would Graunt him and his Neigh⁾ Liberty to make the house of John Rand Deceased a Garrison ffor the Security and defence of some of the Remaining ffamilies adjacent, and to Graunt us supply of six men, and we shall always pray ffor your happiness and Prosperity. [N. H. State Papers, Vol. XVIII, p. 640.]

John Rand, mentioned in this petition, married Remembrance, daughter of John Ault, and sister to Rebecca, wife of Thomas Edgerly. The old farm of John Ault, bordering on Plum Swamp brook, had been divided between Edgerly and Rand. It stretched

from Little Bay back into the woods, and on this farm was the
Rand-Edgerly garrison, wherein soldiers were quartered after the
time of the massacre, soldiers impressed from Hampton. The
Probate Records declare that administration on the estate of
John Rand and Remembrance Rand was granted to John Rand,
probably their son, and that his bond, dated March 1694/5, had
for sureties Thomas Edgerly and Edward Leathers. It is probable that John Rand and his wife, Remembrance, perished in the
massacre. A boy, named Samuel Rand, was redeemed from
captivity in 1695 and Remembrance Rand was still a captive in
1710. Thomas Edgerly, senior, his son Joseph and a daughter
were taken captive. The rest of the family got into a canoe and
as they were setting off the Indians fired upon them and mortally
wounded his son, Zechariah. Among the captives returned,
17 January 1698/9, were Elizabeth Edgerly and Susanna Edgerly,
while Joseph Edgerly was then remaining in captivity. He
returned in 1706. See Coll. of the Maine Historical Society,
2d Series, Vol. V, 516.

Early tradition records that one Kent (it must have been
Joseph Kent, if the tradition be true), upon hearing firing, got
up and looked out, when he saw Indians waiting for him. He
was so surprised that he did not stop to awake his family, but
secured himself in a drain that led from the house, where he lay
all day. His family were soon after aroused by the firing, about
which time the Indians that were around the house retired to
assist their companions, who were besieging the Drew garrison.
This gave Kent's wife an opportunity to escape with her children.

It seems that the Indians also molested at this time the inhabitants along the shore of Great Bay and those living on the road
from Oyster River Falls to Lamprey River. Peter Denbow was
carried into captivity, where he yet remained in the beginning of
1698/9. The Indians seem to have hastened back by the same
way they came, the main road leading from Bickford's Ferry to
the Falls. They assembled with their captives in the meadow
west of the Burnham garrison and, making some insulting signs,
one of them was shot at long range.

The following petition implies that the Indians attacked
another part of the town:

January 8th 1694/5
To ye honored President & Council now sitting at New Castle, in ye Great
Island.

The humble Petition of William Graves humbly sueeth y⁺ your honours
would please to take into your consideration yᵉ distressed estate and condition
of your poor Petitioner, who at yᵉ last desolation at Oyster River was wounded
by yᵉ enemie & his eᵗtate demolisht, who since hath been a long time with the
Chirurgeon for cure & by yᵉ blessing of God hath arrived to a good measure
of health; but hath not wherewithall to answear yᵉ Doctor, nor to help himself, humbly craveth some succour & reliefe therein; whereby you will do a very
charitable Deed and oblige him to pray for your honours prosperity,

Your humble Petitioner

WILLIAM GRAVES.

[N. H. Province Papers, II, 147.]

There was another petition, without date but considered in
Council 20 July, 1694, together with that of Thomas Edgerly,
so that both must have been written 19 July 1694, the next day
after the massacre. It shows that all the families at Lubberland
were driven away, perhaps through fear of an attack. It shows,
too, that in 1694 the whole shore line from Mathes', or Crummett's
Creek, to Lamprey River was known as Lubberland.

The condition of Luberland is such: we had a good Garrison last summer
but was cut down and Burnt, and for want of a Garrison the Inhabitants are
forced to leave the place and flie for Refugg. If itt were possible to save
the place wee who know the vallue vallues itt at about four hundred pounds
of provisions and movables: provided the cattle Breaks in yᵉ Corn, itt will be
much damage. It is yᵉ generall vote yᵗ Capt. Matthews should comᵈ the
Garrison. Our request is for 15 or 20 souldiers to assist this place.

Belonging to the place, Betwixt Capt Matthews and Lamp . . . River,
the contents as follows:

Capt. Mathews	Wm Durgin and three sons.
Fran: Mathews	Tho. Morris
Joⁿ Benicke [Bennett]	Joⁿ Piner [Pinder]
Joⁿ Doe	Hen. Marsh
Samson Doe	David Davis
Elias Critchett	Abra Benicke [Bennett]
	Joⁿ Cromwell [Crommett]
[N. H. Prov. Papers, II, 147.]	Jerⁱ Cromwell [Crommett]

Now we may follow the other party of Indians in their work of
slaughter and burning on the north side of the river. Remember
that all this savagery was justified under the name of war between
Christian nations and their allies and was about as civilized and
"glorious" as any wars have been till within recent years. We

7

do not tomahawk and burn enemies now; we blow them to pieces with shells and bombs.

In the Jones family the tradition has been preserved that Ensign Stephen Jones "in the night heard the barking of dogs and thought the wolves were about. He got up and went some distance from the house to take care of swine. Returning he went into a flanker, got on the top of it and sat there with his legs hanging down on the outside. An Indian fired at him; he fell back, and the bullet entered the flanker betwixt where his legs hung. A band of Indians from behind a rock a few rods from the garrison kept firing on the house." The inhabitants of ungarrisoned houses in that vicinity fled to Jones' garrison. Some were killed in the attempt, among them a woman named Chesley. Tradition says that Hester Chesley, who married John Hall, escaped by jumping from an upper window, with a babe in her arms. One account says that five by the name of Chesley were shot, but these may have been killed in subsequent raids, tradition not being careful as to chronology. Robert Watson, who lived about a quarter of a mile away on land he bought of Walter Jackson, was killed with others of his family. His wife, whose maiden name was Hannah Kent, returned from captivity and married Dea. John Ambler. Accompanying the inventory of her first husband's estate are items of expense, among which are twenty pounds "for my ransom "and two pounds" to a frenchman who promised to redeem my son therwith," "besides Cloathing my self when I came naked out of Captivity."

In connection with this the following information, found in the records of Canada, is of interest. On the 8th of April 1697, there was baptized, "sous condition," an Englishman named Joseph Houatson, aged 17. On 3 June 1715, the curate of Boncherville baptized Marie Josef Robert Ouetsen, daughter of Joseph Robert Ouetsen and Marie de Mers. On the 11th of April 1717, J. R. Ouatsenne, son of Robert Ouatsenne and of Anne hesemenre (?) an Englishman of the village of Piscataqua was married to Angelique Benard Carignan. Here we may have a clue as to who was the first wife of Robert Watson of Oyster River, and we learn that Robert's son, Joseph, married and remained in Canada.

The wife of Edward Leathers was killed and some of her

children.   A woman named Jackson was slain, perhaps Ann, wife
of Walter Jackson.

Edward Small found refuge in Jones' garrison.   He married
Mary, daughter of Capt. John Woodman, and soon after this
massacre removed to Monomoit, now Chatham, Mass.   The
following letter is of historic interest:

>Son Edward and daughter mery Smalle: A store of Love to you: by thes
you may knowe that I received yours and that we ar not without feres of
further trobeles by the Indons: by Reson there of: I cannot yet aduyss you: to
macke Anny preparation: Hom ward: until wee heve further proued: thayr
keeping of the peace: Lest your Returen should be so unsesonebl that it might
be As much dameg to you: as your Remouing thether: thay haue not as yet:
yousd anny Hostilety: tourds ye Englesh I have sent you A thousend of good
bords by William Eldrege your brother Jonathan cannot yet sell your Hors:
any thing Lick to the worth of Him: senc His order to sell Him wee ar all in
Resonebel good Halth threw gods marsy: your brothers and sisters Remember
thayer Loues to you:

from your Louing father
JOHN WOODMAN

Oyster River
  July 26: 1700

This for Edward
Smalle at monamey

Mrs. Judith (Davis) Emerson was taken and held in captivity
several years.   Tradition says that her aged mother, whose
maiden name was Jane Peasley of Haverhill, Mass., was captured
and dismissed by one band of Indians.   She hid in a field of corn
and another band discovered and slew her.   Among the captives
remaining in the hands of the Indians, 17 January 1698/9, was
Judah [Judith] Emerson.   See Coll. of Maine Historical Society,
2d Series, Vol. V, p. 516.

The tradition is still told in Durham that Judith Emerson was
redeemed from captivity by a Mr. Morrill for two shirts, one of
which he took from his back.   Samuel Emerson, thinking his wife
was dead, went to Portsmouth to complete arrangements for a
second marriage.   There he met an old acquaintance and told him
his designs.   The acquaintance, knowing that some captives had
just arrived from Canada and that Mr. Emerson's wife was
among them, said, "I bet a double drink of grog your wife is in

---

¹ In 1889 Mr. Lucien Thompson learned of the existence of the original letter in the possession of Mrs. M. A. Sanborn of Barnstead.   Her grandfather was Samuel Pitman of Durham,
who married Sarah, daughter of Edward Small, and removed to Barnstead.   Mr. Thompson
had the letter photographed and has presented a copy of it to the N. H. Historical Society.

town." The bet was taken, whereupon Mr. Emerson was conducted into the presence of his wife. It is needless to say that
the second marriage was indefinitely postponed, and it faded
into a traditionary possibility. The Emerson family were living
at this time at Back River, Dover.

Old Mr. Robert Huckins, many of whose family had been slain
in the massacre of 1689, was killed at this time. The Jones
garrison was burned before 1732.

Below Jones' garrison were those of Bunker, Smith and Davis,
all of which were successfully defended. Lieut. James Davis
sent his family away by water and with the help of his brother,
Serg. Joseph Davis, defended his garrison, extinguishing the fire
applied to it. Sergt. Davis was fired upon by three Indians.
He stooped and a bullet split a sappling just above his head.
He shot an Indian, whose bones were found in a swamp soon after.

The Meader garrison was abandoned and was burned. The
family escaped by boat. Near by a man named Clark was shot
and another man named Gellison, while he was going from one
house to another for powder. A brother of the latter jumped
into a well for safety and was unable to get out. He died next
day soon after having been rescued from his hiding place.

Three Indians were sent to attack the house of William Tasker,
at the foot of Moharimet's Hill in what is now Madbury. An
Indian looked into a small window and inquired if it was not time
for them to get up. Mr. Tasker replied with a shot from his
gun which mortally wounded the Indian, who with bitter screeches
was carried off by the other two. The family immediately fled
through the woods to the Woodman garrison.

Probate Records inform us of another family broken up at this
time, not mentioned in any of the traditional accounts. It was
that of John Derry, who lived near William Tasker, in Madbury.
Administration on his estate was granted, 18 May 1698, to his
widow, Deliverance, who married Nathaniel Pitman before 7
January 1698. Her petition of the latter date "humbly showeth,
that in the years 1694 yor petition^{rs} House was burnt by the
Indians and our cattle killed, as also most of our children; my
husband, o:.e child, and yor Petition^r taken Captives, in which
Captivitye my husband dyed; none but your Petition^r returned."
The child was Joseph Derry, and what became of him is not
known. John Derry's name is among the list of captives returned

17 January 1698 9, but this may be an error, since there is no subsequent mention of him.

Both parties of Indians met at the Falls after their raids on the south and north sides of the river and made an attack on the garrison of Capt. John Woodman, which resisted the attack and remained, with bullets in its timbers, till 1896, situated at the head of Beard's Creek.

The following letter, dated 21 July 1694, adds some historical touches to the picture. It tells us who the Indian was that got drunk on "occapee," at the suggestion of Mrs. Dean. Mass was said by each of the two priests, who accompanied this expedition, just as Chaplains went with British and American regiments, and for a similar purpose. We may suppose they did what they could to prevent cruelty and to soften the ferocity of savages. We know on good evidence that some Roman Catholic priests and missionaries among the Indians in Maine were kind to captives, bought them out of slavery, and secured their release. The place where mass was said is thought, by Miss Mary P. Thompson, and with good reason, to have been on a ledgy hilltop, not far from the Woodman garrison. The tradition that the priests made chalk-marks on the pulpit of Parson Buss' church is interpreted by her as the writing of some verse from Holy Writ or from the Credo. The fact that the meeting house was not burned during this raid is evidence that they had some respect for the place.

To Gov. Phipps,
May it ples yo' Excell.

Since the Lft Govern** of 18th inst anoth'is come to our hand. The Indians verie numerous. Not less than three hundred. Douie who signed the Peace was there, a woman who was Douies servant made her escape, by reason of his being drunck. Saith Douie did tell her that they did expect 600 Indians more, that the Mangwaits were joined with them, and judge some Southern Indians were there. There is two Fryars among the Indians who after victory said Mass twice, the Indians did spred 6 or 7 miles and engaged all at once. Oyster River in a manner Ruined, only about 20 houses left, the rest layd waste. Unless we have a supply of men from yourself Oyster River must be deserted. If Oyster River be deserted, the Enimie will have an inlett to the whole Country, for the Majest* Service and Security of the Country desire you would forthwith Supply us with one hundred men, with ammunition & Provision to be posted for preservation of these Out places. We are dispatching some souldiers into our Outward garrisons, according to the ability of this Province upon the alarms with all expedition. We dispatched from the Severall Towns one third of the Militia in this Province for Releafe of

Oyster River, but before they came here the Enimie was drawn of and could not be met with; its judged Eighty persons killed & taken, abundance of cattle killed. Last night three Indians seen, severall Guns fired. Judge the Enimie is still bordering upon us, but we want assistance to pursue them, the Enimie being so numerous. Desire that orders may be given to Justices and all Constables for the Dispatch of Expresses. Not doubting of yor Rediness to assist us, we being ready to afforde our assistance, according to our ability, to your parts in case the Enimie should invade yours,

    We crave your answer by this—ers.

By order of the Lt. Govern^r & Councill

WM. REDFORD: *Dept. Secry.*

[N. H. Province Papers, II, p. 129]

To sum up the results of this Indian raid, it may be positively stated that the houses of the following persons were burned, three of them being garrisons, viz., house owned by Nathaniel Hill and occupied by John Dean (The houses of Nathaniel Hill and Bartholomew Stevenson near by were not destroyed), houses of Ensign John Davis, Ezekiel Pitman, Stephen Jenkins, Rev. John Buss, Charles Adams, Thomas Edgerly, Joseph Meader, Robert Watson, John Derry, William Leathers, John Drew, William Jackson, and probably houses of the Chesley, Stevenson, and Willey families. Thus we have the sixteen houses and garrisons mentioned by the Rev. John Pike in his Journal.

Among the slain were John Dean, Robert Huckins, Robert Watson and two or more children, the mother of Mrs. Judith Emerson (who was Jane Peasley Davis), sister of Mrs. Emerson, Ensign John Davis, wife and two children, Widow James Smith and two sons, a Mr. (Abraham?) Clark, two men named Gellison, Stephen Jenkins and child, Francis Drew and wife, Lydia, Benjamin Drew, fifteen in the family of Charles Adams, two children of Thomas Edgerly, Jr., grandmother of Stephen Jenkins, Mrs. Edward Leathers, Mrs. Jackson, Zacheriah Edgerly, several children of John Derry, and probably Thomas and Joseph Stevenson and John Rand and wife, Remembrance. Thus forty-nine or more are known.

Among those carried into captivity were certainly John Derry and his wife and son, Joseph, Hannah Watson and her son, Joseph, Sarah Davis and her sister, Mary, Ursula Adams, Mrs. Ann Jenkins, Thomas Drew and wife, Tamsen, Abigail and Judy and Elizabeth Willey, Elizabeth and Susanna and Joseph Edgerly, Mrs. Judith Emerson, Peter Denbow and Remembrance Rand, making twenty known captives. Thus sixty-nine or more out of the ninety-four reported by the Rev. John Pike are accounted for. There were probably some captives, unknown by name, who never returned.

Twenty soldiers were sent to defend garrisons at Oyster River, and Capt. John Woodman reported, 6 January 1695/6, that they were posted as follows: at his own garrison, 2; at Meader's, 3; at Davis', 2; at Smith's, 3; at Burnham's, 2; at Bickford's, 4; at Edgerly's [where John Rand had formerly lived], 3; at Durgin's, 2; at Jones', 2; at David Davis', 2.

In his fourth return, 5 February 1695/6, he reports soldiers posted as follows: at Meader's, 2; at Smith's, 1; at Bunker's, 3; at Jones', 2; at Burnham's, 2; at Edgerly's, 2; at David Davis', 2.

The account of Oyster River people for their maintenance of soldiers from 24 May 1697, unto 4 October 1697, was rendered by Capt. John Woodman as follows:

Joseph Smith for 2 soldiers, 18 weeks,07:04:00; James Buncker for 1 soldier, 18 weeks, 03:12:00; Ensign Jones for 1 soldier, 18 weeks, 03:12:00; Mr. Thomas Edgerly, 1 soldier, 18 weeks, 03:12:00; John Woodman, 2 soldiers, 18 weeks, 07:04:00. [See N. H. Province Papers, II, 253.]

The Indians seem to have had a special spite against the inhabitants of Oyster River, or their attacks there were so little opposed that they returned often for easy spoils. We are indebted to Pike's Journal for the following brief items of subsequent molestations:

August 27, 1696, "David Davis killed by the Ind[ns] at Lubberland."

November 15, 1697, "Tho: Chesley Sen: slain by y[e] Indians not far from Johnsons Creek. Will Jackson taken at the same time & at same time made his escape."

April 25, 1704, "Nath. Meader was slain by y[e] Indians at Oyster River, not far from the place where Nicholas Follet formerly lived."

June 1, 1704, "Samuel Tasker was slain by 8 or 9 Indians at Oyster River."

August 10, 1704. "Joseph Pitman slain by the Indians, as he was guarding some mowers, not far from Oyster River Meetinghouse."

November 4, 1705, "Sab. Nath Tibbetts of Oyster River was carried away by the Indians about sun-set."

April 27, 1706, "The Indians came in upon the south part of Oyster River, by the Little Bay, & killed ten persons, the chief whereof were bro: John Wheeler & his wife, John Drew, etc. Tis thought this was done by Bommazeen." Belknap says that two children of John Wheeler were slain and four sons escaped by taking refuge in a cave by the bank of the Little Bay.

May 22, 1707, "Two young girls were carried away by the Indians from Bunkers Garrison at Oyster River, viz. the daughter of Thomas Drew (near 13 years old) & Daughter of Nath[1] Laimos (Much younger). This was the first mischief done by them in y[e] year 1707." Marie Anne was baptized in Canada, 12 September 1709, as daughter of Thomas and Mary (Bunker) Drew, and she was naturalized there 25 June 1713. Elizabeth Lomax was baptized in Canada, 11 September 1707, as daughter of Nathaniel and Deliverance (Clark) Lomax. Thus the two little lost girls are found, and we learn incidentally who their mothers were.

July 8, 1707, "John Bunker & Ichabod Rawlins (both of Dover) going with a cart from Zech: Fields Gar: to James Bunkers for a Loom were assailed by many Indians & both slain. The enemy (supposed 20 or 30 in num.) slaughtered many cattel for the Jones's (at same time) to the number of 15 or more."

September 17, 1707, "Capt. Samuel Chesley, his bro: James Chesley & 6 more stout young men were slain by the Indians as they were cutting and halling timber, not far from Capt. Chesleys house. The Indian y[t] killed James Chesley was slain on y[e] spot by Rob: Thompson. Philip Chesley and 3 more escaped." The Council voted, 22 October 1707, that five pounds be given to Robert Thompson, and the Governor signed an act in these words, "ordered that Robert Thompson[1] be paid five pounds out of the present tax for an Indian scalp lately taken by him at Oyster River," 10 May 1708.

September 18, 1708, "David Kinked of Oyster River was assaulted by 3 Indians at his house, some considerable distance from Woodmans Gar: Three Guns were fired at him and his Lad, but (through mercy) both escaped well."

June 30, 1709, "Bartholomew Stimpson Jun: of Oyster R. was Slain by an Ambuscade of Indians near Capt. Woodmans Gar." The Rev. Hugh Adams records that "on Friday the first day

[1] Great, great, great-grandfather of Col. Lucien Thompson.

of May 1724, our worthy & Desireable Elder James Nock was most surprisingly Shott (off from his horse) Dead and Scalped by three Indian Enemies. O that Christ Emmanuel may speedily avenge his blood upon them." This sounds like an imprecatory Psalm and shows that in all ages good men feel the demands of retributive justice. He adds, "June 17, 1722, On Wednesday, it being our Preparation Lecture,—Turned into a Fast on account of the Indian War, so severe on our Church by the sudden Death of another of our Members, that was slain the last Wednesday, Namely Moses Davis, Senr & his son Moses. And in the evening by the Indians was killed by a Shott in his head Poor George Chesley & Elizabeth Burnam was wounded." She died four days later, as the following record, dated 27 May 1724, shows, "Elizabeth Burnam who was wounded by the Indians the 24th, the day George Chesley was killed, the evening before she died I baptized at her penitent request." Miss Mary P. Thompson, in her Landmarks in Ancient Dover, rather discredits the tradition that this George Chesley was engaged to be married to Elizabeth Burnham and conjectures that he must have been forty-five years of age, but the church records state that "George Chesley, batchelor," was baptized 24 December 1721, about two years and a half before this event, so that the tradition of their engagement might be well founded. He must not be confused with an earlier George Chesley, who was killed by Indians on his way to mill, 8 June 1710, leaving widow, Deliverance.

The Rev. Hugh Adams says in a petition that "five persons in Oyster River were cut down in the Indian war that begun in 1722."

Miss Thompson tells of another "young Chesley" who was returning from meeting with a Miss Randall of Lee, when they were slain upon the Mast Road. The rock on which the maiden fell is said to be stained with blood "unto this day," and some poet has lamented her fate. This seems to be a variant of the tradition recorded in Historical Memoranda of Ancient Dover, page 85. The Thomas Chesley there mentioned may well have been the Thomas Chesley, junior, born 1688. See Genealogical Notes under Chesley and Randall, where it appears that there was no Miss Randall of Lee at the time mentioned and that all subsequent Miss Randalls of Lee are accounted for. The tradition is that Miss Randall was returning from the Falls with a party of friends, when they were attacked by Indians. She tried to escape into a barn and was shot just as she was entering it. She fell across the stone at the door and there bled to death. Mr. Chesley was greatly grieved at her death and declared that he would spend his life in fighting the savages. He soon had an opportunity to kill eleven out of a bunch of twelve, and the tradition properly closes with the statement that he himself was afterward killed by Indians. So many members of the Chesley family met their fate in this way, that it is not surprising that some conflicting reports have come down.

To this list of the slain may be added the name of Jeremiah Crommett, who was killed and scalped by Indians, in 1712, at the upper branch of Oyster River. See Genealogical Notes.

MILITARY HISTORY.

This chapter can contain but little more than the names of the citizens of Oyster River, or Durham, that served in various wars that afflicted the colonies, after the Indian depredations already described. Every able-bodied man was enrolled in the militia, and doubtless many served in active campaigns whose names are unrecorded. The New Hampshire Province and State Papers are the sources from which the following names have been gleaned.

May 10, 1710, the report, to the General Assembly, of the committee on claims allowed five pounds to Robert Thompson for killing an Indian and endorsed the accounts of George Chesley, and Captains Abraham Bennick, James Davis, and Nathaniel Hill.

There is an interesting claim for "several persons under named for their snow shoes and mogasans which were imprest for her Maj^{tys} service by Capt. James Davis, by order of Col. Hilton." These marched to the eastward, to "Picwacket and Mariwock," and none of the snowshoes were returned:

Serg. Jonathan Woodman	Abraham Bennet
John Ambler	James Durgin
Joseph Smith	Mr. Thomas Edgerly
Left. John Smith	Thomas Drew
Jeremiah Burnam	Philip Chesle
En. Francis Mathes	Capt. James Davis
En. Stephen Jones	Samuel Waymouth
William Jacson	John Cromet
Lt. Samuel Edgerly	John Williams

Ensign Mathews' muster roll was allowed 19 November 1712. The amount was £2 s14 d4.

The following appear on the roll of a scouting party, under command of Capt. James Davis, in 1712. Capt. Davis served twenty-one weeks; the men here named, selected from the rolls and arranged alphabetically, served ten days and their wages were eight shillings and six pence apiece. The men from Oyster River were "John Ambler, Jeremiah Burnham, Robert Burnham, Eliezer Clark, Timothy Conner, John Chesley, Jonathan Chesley, James Davis, Moses Davis, John Davis, Timothy

Davis, Sampson Doe, Thomas Drew, Jr., William Drew, Joseph Dudey, Cornelius Drisco, Eli Demerrit, Ichabod ffollit, John Footman, John Kent, Benjamin Mathews, Benjamin Pinner, William Pitman, John Rand, Thomas Rynes, Thomas Stephenson, John Tasker, Jonathan Thompson, Robert Thompson, Samuel Wille, and Samuel Williams."

Salathiel Denbow, called also Denmore, served in the French and Indian War and had his thigh broken and skull fractured at Spanish River, Cape Breton. In response to his petition he was granted ten pounds, 18 January 1716/7, and a pension of ten pounds was granted him, 1 December 1730.

The account of Sergt. James Nock's muster roll was allowed in 1723. He was deacon in the church at Oyster River and soon after was killed by Indians.

June 24, 1724, Robert Burnham was admitted into the Council Chamber and presented an Indian scalp to the board and made oath that it was *bona fide* the scalp of an Indian slain two days before at Oyster River by a party of men under the command of Mr. Abraham Bennick, and that he believed the said Indian was an Indian enemy, etc. Whereupon, it was ordered that pursuant to act of General Assembly the slayer be paid one hundred pounds out of the treasury and that the clerk further prepare a warrant accordingly, the said sum being made payable to Capt. Francis Mathews at the request and on the account of the said slayers. N. H. Province Papers, IV, 140.

The manuscript of Rev. Hugh Adams says that 10 June 1724, occurred "the smiting of four Indians and getting the Scalp of a Chief Captain among them, who was by all circumstances of his learning in his writings of Devotion and lists of names of nine score Indians found in his minuta which I saw, and his Scarlet-Died, Four-Laureate Coronet, with a Tassel of four small bells, by the small tinkling whereof in the thickets of bushes his Indian souldiers might follow him," etc. Adams conjectures he must have been a son of Sebastian Rasle, an unwarranted conclusion.

Abraham Clark's Scouting party, July 1724, contains the names of John Bunker, James Davis, John Brown, Clement Drew, William Clay, Nathaniel Denbo, Joseph Perkins, William Raines and Samuel Williams.

This copy of Capt. Samuel Emerson's commission will serve as a sample of those issued at that time:

SAMUEL SHUTE ESQ.: Captaine General and Governour in chief, in and over His Majesty's Province of New Hampshire in New England, and Vice Admiral of the same.

To Captain Samuel Emerson—Greeting:

By Virtue of the Power and Authority in and by His Majesty's Royal Commission to Me Granted, to be Captain General &c., over this His Majesty's Province of New Hampshire aforesaid. I do (by these Presents,) Reposeing especial trust and confidence, in your Loyalty, Courage and good Conduct, Constitute and Appoint you the said Saml Emerson to be a Capt. of a foot Company of the north side of Oyster river in Dover in ye regiment whereof Richd Waldron Esq is Colonel. You are therefore carefully and diligently, to discharge the Duty of a Captain in Leading and Ordering and Exercising, said Company in Arms, both Inferior Officers and Soldiers, and to keep them in good Order and Discipline, hereby commanding them to Obey you, as their Captain and yourself to observe and follow such Orders and Instructions, as you shall from time to time receive from Me, or the Commander in Chief for the time being, or other your Superior Officers, for His Majesty's Service, according to Military Rules and Discipline; Pursuant to the Trust reposed in you.

Given under my Hand and Seal at Portsmouth the Twelfth day of May in the fourth Year of His Majesty King George His Reign.

Annoque Domini 1718
By His Excellency's Command

SAML SHUTE.

RICHD WALDRON, Clercon.

The following list of trained soldiers on the south side of Oyster River, dated 5 May 1732, only ten days before Durham was incorporated as a town, was furnished by the late Ballard Smith about sixty years ago, for publication in the *Dover Inquirer*. The original paper was then in his possession. It was the third company in Col. Gilman's regiment and was under the command of Capt. John Smith, Jr. The names are here arranged alphabetically for convenience.

Abraham Bennet	Solomon Daveis
Eleazer Bennet	Joseph Daveis Jr.
Eli Clark	Benjamin Daveis
Joshua Crumit	Samuel Daveis
Joseph Chesly	Joshua Daveis
Thomas Chesly	Salathiel Denmore Jr.
Jabues Daveis	Richard Denmore
Jeremiah Daveis	Francis Drew
John Daveis, Jr.	John Drew
Ebenezer Daveis	Thomas Drew, ye third

Thomas Drew Jr.
Eliphalet Daniel
Benjamin Doo
John Doo
Joseph Doo
Daniel Doo
Benjamin Durgin
John Durgin
James Durgin
Joseph Durgin
Jonathan Durgin
Francis Footman
John Genkins,
John Jenkens Jr.
Stephen Genkins Jr.
George Gray
John Gra
Robert Kent
John Langley
John Laski
Thomas Langley

Hezekias Marsh
Peter Mason
Nathaniel Meader
John Moor
Jeremiah Pender
John Pitman
William Randal
John Randal
John Runls
Benjamin Smith
James Smith
John Smith ye third
Samuel Smith
William Sheperd
Joseph Thomas
Stephen Wille
Theoder Willey
Joseph Woodman
Jacob Wormwood
Joseph Wormwood.

The above list may be compared with the following made a few years later. "A list of all the Soldiery that be under my Command from sixteen years old and upward as the law directs." This, too, includes only those living on the south side of Oyster River.

"JOHN SMITH Junʳ, *Capt.*"

Sargt Thomas Stevenson
Sarg Samuel Willey
Sarg John Crummet
Sarg John Edgerly
Cor. Joseph Wormwood
Cor. Joseph Davis
Cor. Joseph Edgerly
Cor. John Durgain
John Footman
Joseph Footman
Samuel Smith
Benja Smith
Joseph Chesly
Ebenezer Smith
Benjᵃ Pender
Francis Durgain
Eliphalet Daniel
Reuben Daniel
John Kent

John Kent Jun.
Abrahan Mathews
John Drew
Elijah Drew
Tho Bickford
Robert Kent
Tho Langley
William Lord
Stephen Willey
Benjᵃ Mathews
Volintin Mathews
Abraham Mathews Jun.
Joseph Stevenson
Abraham Stevenson
Caleb Wakham
Francis Footman
Daniel Davis
Tho Footman Jun.
John Genikins

Benja Genikins
Joseph Smith
Tho Yorke
Samue Watson
Joseph Gleden
Robert Burnham Jun.
John Burnham Jun.
Richard Dunmore
Benja Davis
Jabez Davis
Jeremiah Davis
John Davis
Solomon Davis
Ebenezer Davis
Samuel Meeder
James Burnham
Ichabod Denmore
Joseph Bickford
John Langley
Jobe Langley
Hezekiah Marsh
Will= Willey
John Mason
Daniel Doo
John Doo

Joseph Doo
Benj= Doo
Will= Wormwood Jun.
Will= Jncks
Joshua Crumet
Abraham Bennet Jun.
James Durgain Jun.
Will= Durgain
Phillip Crommet
Benj= Bennet
Isac Mason
David Davis,
Samuel Joy
Joshua Davis
Joseph Dudy
Joseph Dudy Jun.
Benmore Dudy
Tho Willey
Theodor Willey
James Smith
Joshua Woodman
John Cretchet
John Willey
James Burnham Jun

A true copy of the List Roll taken ye Last Training Day and coppyed out July ye 29th 1740.   Total 86.

JOSEPH DREW, *Clerk*

[N. H. Town Papers, IX, 240, 241.]

A scouting party under Samuel Miller, from 29 June to 13 July 1744, contains the following men from Durham, Abraham Runals, Joseph Durgin, James Lomas, and Thomas Tash. A muster roll of troopers, under command of Capt. Joseph Hanson, dated 5 August 1745, contains the names of men from Durham, who scouted in the woods and found themselves horses, provisions and ammunition, viz., Samuel Tasker. Valentine Mathes, Samuel Demeritt, Thomas Willey, Thomas Leathers, Henry Hill, and James Chesley.

The principal event in King George's War was the capture of Louisburg, on Cape Breton Island. 17 June 1745. This was, next to Quebec, the strongest and most important French fortress in America. The land forces in this expedition were commanded by Col. William Pepperrell of Kittery, who was knighted for the exploit. Many of his troops were collected from Maine and New Hampshire. Col. Samuel Smith of Durham was a member of the provincial council of New Hampshire at that time and of the joint committee "on the subject of Govr Shirleys letter and some other papers laid before the Assembly by his Excellency." This committee reported in favor of the Louisburg expedition and recommended the raising of money to defray charges and liberal pay to volunteers, as well as the furnishing of provisions and transports. Col. Smith was at the same time chairman of the board of selectmen of Durham, town clerk, part of the time moderator and also the chief military officer in the vicinity. As councillor he had a prominent part in the emission of money to pay the expenses of the expedition, being on the committee to print the money and have custody of the plates and keys. The provincial records show that he was clerk and commissary of the various scouting parties in his vicinity and had charge of the snowshoes and moccasins, of which the House voted that one hundred pairs of each should be kept in Durham, ready for any emergency.

The rolls of the New Hampshire regiments in this expedition have not been found. Hon. George A. Gilmore, as special commissioner under legislative authority, has published a "Roll of New Hampshire Men at Louisburg, Cape Breton, 1745," and he gave the residences of the men as nearly as he could ascertain the same. Durham is given as the residence of the following men, Benjamin Bunker, Eleazer Bickford, Eliphalet Daniel, and Moses Meader.

Benjamin Bunker was clerk of Capt. Samuel Hale's company, enlisting as a private 13 February 1745, and was promoted to be Ensign, 10 August.

Eleazer Bickford petitioned the General Assembly for some allowance on account of sickness, losses, etc., and was allowed two pounds. Daniel Doe at the same time was allowed two pounds, ten shillings, because of medical treatment by Dr. Samuel Adams after his return. The first was a private and the second a mariner, both enlisting 13 February 1745. Daniel Doe was son of John Doe and lived near the Moat.

Moses Meader petitioned for relief because of sickness at Louisburg, which caused his return to New Castle in August, where he was confined by sickness for three weeks, and in consequence he states that he has been able to do but little for the support of himself and family. He was allowed five pounds, though his expenses at New Castle alone had been over ten pounds.

Col. Gilmore does not give the residences of many of the soldiers, but one familiar with the records of Durham can easily pick out the following names of Durham men, Abraham Bennet, Moses Davis, Benjamin Daniel, John Edgerly, John Ealet [Eliot], Thomas Jones, Thomas Johnson, William Lapish, David Kinkett [Kincaid], John Perry, William Randall, James Smith, John Smith, Corp. Samuel Thompson, James Thompson, and John Welch.

The town voted to exempt from taxes for that year those who went on the Louisburg expedition.

Scouting parties were sent out during the winters of 1744 and 1745. Capt. Benjamin Mathes had command of one, 11 January 1745. The men were Joseph Wormwood, Gershom Mathes, William Emerson, Abraham Mathes, James Thompson, Joseph Coleman, John Leighton, Reuben Heard and Samuel Bickford. They served twenty-one days for eighteen shillings and nine pence each.

On "the muster roll of eight men under the command of John Huggins of Durham who begun July ye 11th 1745 to scout in ye woods from Rochester to Winnipissoke" are the names of John Huggins, Edward Leathers, Abel Leathers, James Brown, Moses Varney, Joseph Langley, Daniel Hays, Charles Baker and Ephraim Alley. Some of these men lived in Dover. They served fourteen days for twelve shillings, six pence.

Capt. Jonathan Chesley had command of another party of scouts that ranged "the frontiers about Merrimack" in 1745. He was elected Representative and served in the House during most of King George's War.

"Seargeant John Thompson" commanded another scouting party of eleven men around Barrington and Rochester twenty-eight days in 1746 and earlier. Four times money was voted to him and his men for such services.

December 2, 1747, the House "voted that ye Muster Roll of Joseph Thomas & twenty men under his Command scouting from Durham to Chester, Epsom & Nottingham, amounting to twenty two Pounds fifteen Shillings & 9d in full be allowed."

Scouting parties were commanded also by Samuel Randall and Joseph Sias. More will be said of these men elsewhere.

8

Capt. Jonathan Chesley was paid for guarding the frontiers, in 1748, with seventy-three men. Other men who served in such scouting parties were Ephraim Davis and Nathaniel Huggins [Huckins].

Capt. Joseph Bickford's muster roll, 1756, for defense of Epsom, contains names of Durham men, Joseph Randall, Ed. Pendergast, Benjamin Hall, Gideon Leighton, Joseph Doe, and Samuel Bickford.

For further information about the military rolls of this period see Adjutant General's Report, Vol. II, 1866, and N. H. Province Papers.

The following documents are copied from the historical collections of Col. Lucien Thompson and may be of interest to the reader. The first document has no date, but, from the names in it, appears to have been written before 9 September 1757:

Provinc of   } To Quarter
New hampshire } Samuel Demeritt

In his Majstys name you are Required to See that the men that are apinted to go on Duty are fited as the Law Directs Emeadately to march att a quartr of an ouer notis heare of faill not and you will oblige your Humble Servant
                                        Daniel Rogers Capt.

the men apinted are
    Stephen Wille   9 men   under your
    Joseph wormwood Junr   command from
    Edward Hill   Durham are
    Stephen Sweet [Swett]
    Stephen Leathers   Stephen Wille Junr
    Thomas Leathers   Benjam Buzell
    Jonathan Langly   Stephen Leathers
    Benjamin Buzell   Edward Hill
    Jonathan Rendal   Joseph Wormwood Jun
                                    to march according to order

The two following documents contain, in the original, the autograph signatures of the subscribers. They show the military spirit that prevailed and the undesigned preparation for the approaching conflict with Great Britain. For drill in time of peace they seem to have preferred cavalry to infantry. They were "Gentleman Troopers," getting ready to be future officers, as many hoped.

We the Subscribers Do hereby Signify our Consent & Desire to Join in a Company of horse that may be Raised in the Town of Durham & Parish of

Madbury under Such officers as may be Appointed by the Honourable Benning
wentworth Esqr Governor & Commander in and Over the province of newhampshire & Do hereby manifest our Desire that Such a Company may be
Raised & that we will be properly Equipt in a Reasonable Time to Join in
Such a Company in witness whereof we hereunto Subscribe our names this
27th Day of Sep^t 1764.

Daniel Meserve Jun	Job Demerit Junr
Robert Hill.	Samuel Emerson
Beniamjn Gerrish.	Joseph Demerit
Jonathan meserve	Solomon Demerit
Samuel Jones	Zachariah Boodey
John Emerson	Robert Hill
John Roberts Junr	John Demerit
Timothy Moses Junr	Clemet Meserve Jun
John Hill	Ebenezer Miserue.
Beniam Chesla Junr	Abednego Leathers.

DURHAM, April 17, 1765.
We the under Named Subscribers do hereby Inlist our Selves under the Com-
mand of Captain Samuel Demerit Esqr. in a Troop of horse in the Province of
New Hampshire to Ride as Troopers under his Command of which Troop the
Honourable Clement March Esqr. is Colonel.

Solomon Demeret	Timothy Moses Junr
Samuel Clark	John Emerson
Joseph Jackson.	Trumpeter of this Trope
Stephen Wille Junr	Richard Hull
Giordon Mathes	James Bonely
hezekiah randel.	Alpheas Chesley
Robert Hill	Joseph Wormwood
David Davis ^{54}	Volintine Mathes Junr
Edward hill	Nathe Daniels
Thomas Lathers	Clement Meserve.
James Davis Junr	Ichabod Bussell
Mason Rendel	John Edgerley
Joseph Lebbey	Joshua Wiggin
Jonathan Meserve	thomas gorge
william Rendel Junr	John Williams
Job Demeret Junr	David Daniels
John Ring	Jonathan Williams
Philip yeaton	Samuel Snell
Benning Brackett.	Josiah Burley
Samuel Emerson.	George tutle.
	Gentleman Troopers.

THE REVOLUTION

On the eighteenth day of July 1774, Ebenezer Thompson, Esq., and John Sullivan, Esq., were elected to attend a convention at Exeter for the purpose of choosing delegates to attend the General Congress to be held at Philadelphia the first day of September next. This was the first step taken by Durham as a town toward the liberation of the American Colonies from the oppressive yoke of Great Britain.

Soon after contributions were sent by various towns for the relief of those who suffered from the Boston Port Bill. The following letter, dated 21 November 1774, shows Durham's sympathy with "suffering brethren in Boston."

GENTLEMEN: We take pleasure in transmitting to you by Mr. Scammell a few cattle, with a small sum of money, which a number of persons in this place, tenderly sympathizing with our suffering brethren in Boston, have contributed towards their support. With this, or soon after, you will receive the donations of a number in Lee, a parish lately set off from this Town, and in a few days those of Dover, Newmarket, & other adjacent Towns. What you herewith receive comes not from the opulent, but mostly from the industrious yeomanry in this parish. We have but a few persons of affluent fortunes among us, but those have most cheerfully contributed to the relief of the distressed in your metropolis.

This is considered by us, not as a gift, or an act of charity, but of justice, as a small part of what we are in duty bound to communicate to those truly noble & patriotic advocates of American freedom, who are bravely standing in the gap between us & slavery, defending the common interests of a whole continent and gloriously struggling in the cause of liberty. Upon you the eyes of all America are fixed. Upon your invincible patience, fortitude & resolution (under God) depends all that is dear to them and their posterity. May that superintendent gracious Being, whose ears are ever open to the cry of the oppressed, in answer to the incessant prayers of his people, defend our just cause, turn the counsels of our enemies into foolishness, deliver us from the hands of our oppressors and make those very measures, by which they are endeavoring to compass our destruction, the means of fixing our invaluable rights & privileges upon a more firm & lasting basis.

While with the most painful sensations we reflect that prior to the commencement of the evils which now surround us, supineness & inattention to our common interests had so far prevailed, as almost wholly to sink in luxury & dissipation the inhabitants of these Colonies; we are bound to acknowledge the divine wisdom & goodness, which by these calamities roused us from our lethargy, and taught us to defend those inestimable liberties, which otherwise must have been forever lost to us & our posterity; and to evince his determina-

tion to save America, directed the attacks of our enemies to that quarter
where the virtue & firmness of the inhabitants could brave the shafts of military tyrants, and set at defiance the threats of an exasperated & despotic
minister.

We are pleased to find, that the methods by which the ministry sought to
divide, have happily united us, and by every new act of oppression, more &
more strengthened union. And we can, with truth, assure you, gentlemen,
that in this quarter we are engaged, to a man, in your defence, and in defence
of the common cause. We are ready to communicate of our substance largely,
as your necessities require; and, with our estates, to give our lives & mingle
our blood with yours, in the common sacrifice to liberty. And since we have
no asylum on earth, to which we may fly: before we will submit to wear the
chains of slavery a profligate & arbitrary ministry are preparing for us, we are
determined upon an emigration through the gate of death, in hope of inheriting
the fair land of promise and participating with our forefathers in the glorious
liberty of the Sons of God.

That Heaven may support you, under your distressing circumstances, and
send you a speedy and happy deliverance from your present troubles, is the
earnest prayer of, Gentlemen, your cordial friends and very humble servants,

JOHN ADAMS,
JOHN SULLIVAN, *Committee.*

[Mass. Hist. Col'., Fourth Series, Vol. I., p. 144.]

It is probable that this letter was composed and written by the
Rev. John Adams, in consultation with John Sullivan and many
others in Durham. Note the unanimity of sentiment expressed.
It is a noble document, and the church and town should be proud
and grateful that a man of such spirit and abilities was a leader
among them at a critical time. John Sullivan wielded the sword
and earned all the honors he has received. John Adams remained
in the work of the Christian ministry, serving his country as
faithfully as the other, and four years later was forced out of
Durham by a false and slanderous tongue. Is the pen mightier
than the sword? This eloquent epistle is worthy to be ranked
with the utterances of the most famous orators and patriots of
revolutionary times.

On the twenty-third of the following November a town meeting was called "to make choice of committee to observe the conduct of All persons touching the association of the late American
Congress held at Philadelphia and to proceed with those who
Violate the same in the way pointed out by the said Congress."
This meeting convened at two o'clock of the afternoon of 28 November 1774 and adjourned to the house of Lieut. Winborn

Adams, who lived just across the road from the meeting house, possibly because it was late in the year and those assembled could keep warm more easily in Adams' house, for meeting houses then had neither stoves nor chimneys. The record of the meeting is as follows, lacking somewhat in clearness. No Association Test, signed by inhabitants of Durham, is found in the office of Secretary of State of New Hampshire, though eighty-six towns are so represented:

There James Gilmor Esqr. Valentine Mathes Esqr. George Frost Esqr. Jno Sullivan Esqr. Ebenezer Thompson Esqr. Capt. Thomas Chesley, Jno Smith 3d. Majr Stephen Jones. Voted that Majr Jones be Excused from serving Thos Hardy chose. Mr Jonathan Chesley Lt. Winborn Adams Mr Moses Emerson Mr Alexander Scammell Mr Stephen Cogan Mr Joseph Stevens— chosen a Committee for the purpose within mentioned. Maj⁴ Stephen Jones put to Vote again and rechosen and Mr. John Griffin Jeremiah Burnum Lt. Samuel Chesley Doctor Samuel Wigglesworth Jonathan Woodman 3d Nathl Hill Timothy Medar Nathl Demerit & Francis Mathes—Voted Revd John Adams Ebenezer Thompson Esqr Major Sullivan Jno Smith 3d and Mr Moses Emerson be a Committee of Correspondence to Correspond with the Committees of the severall Towns in this and the other Governments in British America, the Determination of three of the sd Committee to be suffi-cient. Resolved that the select Men of Durham ought forthwith to add to the Town stock of Powder so as to make it up 200 lbs and to lay in 400 lb bullets & 500 flints.

Last Monday of each month to meet. Mr Emerson chosen Chairman of the Committee of Inspection. [Town Records, Vol. II, p. 94.]

The opportunity to add to the town's stock of powder soon presented itself. Down at New Castle, at the mouth of the Pascataqua River, stood Fort William and Mary, known to con-tain valuable military stores. On the thirteenth of December, 1774, Paul Revere brought to Portsmouth a message from the Committee in Boston, that troops were to be sent to reinforce the fort, and that orders in the King's Council prohibited the ex-portation of gunpowder and military stores to America. Gov. Wentworth sent word to Captain John Cochran, who commanded only five men at the fort, to be on his guard. He put three four-pounders where he thought they would do the most good and awaited the expected assault.

On the fourteenth of December about four hundred men assembled in Portsmouth under the leadership of Hon. John Langdon. Tradition says that Thomas Pickering also had a

leading part, for which the evidence is not so full. They went
to the fort in gondolas and naturally did not face the cannon's
mouth, when there was an easier way of approach. The cannon
and small arms were discharged at command of Capt. Cochran,
but nobody was hurt. Indeed, he probably aimed so as to hurt
nobody, thus saving himself and his men from harm. Capt.
Cochran reported in writing, "Before we could be ready to fire
again, we were stormed on all quarters, and they immediately
secured both me and my men, and kept us prisoners about one
hour and a half, during which time they broke open the powder-
house and took all the powder away, except one barrel; and having put it into boats and sent it off, they released me from
confinement." This was written the very day of the assault and
is, doubtless, literally true.

About one hundred barrels of gunpowder—the number varies
a little in different statements—were sent to Maj. John Sullivan
at Durham, which he deposited in places of security, as he afterward wrote. He further says, "I went down with a large number
of men and in the night following went in person with gondolas,
took possession of the fort, brought away the remainder of the
powder, the small arms, bayonets, and cartouch-boxes, together
with the cannon and ordnance stores; was out all night, and
returned to Portsmouth next day. I might here add that I
bore the expense of all the party. The gondolas, with the stores,
were brought to Durham, after several days spent in cutting the
ice, Durham river being then frozen over; the cannon, etc., was
then deposited in places of security. These are facts known to
almost every person in the State." This was published in the
New Hampshire Mercury, 3 May 1785.

It appears, then, that the Durham people had no part in the
first assault on Fort William and Mary, and that the second assault, by the company from Durham under the leadership of
Maj. John Sullivan, during the night of 15 December 1774, met
with no resistance. Effort has been made by writers of prose and
of poetry to magnify this deed and to secure honor therefor to
various towns. That four hundred men should overcome six
men, who made only a feint of resistance, is not in itself a deed

THE MAJOR JOHN DEMERIT RESIDENCE, MADBURY

Here was secreted powder taken from Fort William and Mary, 1774.

to boast of. There was no fighting, no danger, no display of bravery. The courage required was not physical, but moral. It was an aggressive act of rebellion against the strongest nation on earth. If the revolt failed, the leaders at least knew that they would lose their lives, but they knew well that the thirteen colonies were with them in this enterprise. It was one of the first public acts in the great struggle for national independence. If there had been a little blood shed on both sides, this would have been celebrated even more than the fight at Concord and Lexington. Somebody must be killed before war becomes glorious. Such at least is the verdict of history.

The powder was stored first in the meeting house at Durham Falls, as uniform tradition says; some have said under the pulpit; others, in the cellar; but the meeting houses of that time had no cellars. One hundred barrels of gunpowder would probably not remain in or under the meeting house over the Sabbath. The thought of it would disturb the peaceful devotions of the worshipers. It was speedily removed and distributed in several towns. Some of it was stored at the house of Hon. Ebenezer Thompson, and more was carried to the home of Maj. John Demerit, who lived in Madbury. The exact site of the building, where the powder entrusted to him was kept, is now pointed out. The tradition that he hauled with an ox-team some of this powder to be used at the battle of Bunker Hill seems to be trustworthy. That some of it was sent later to Winter Hill at the request of Gen. Sullivan is clear by historical evidence. The arms brought from the fort to Durham were repaired and put in order, as appears from a town record under date of 31 March 1783. "Voted that the select men Be directed to allow Thomas Wille 20 9 in full for repairing the guns brought from Fort Wm and Mary."

The men who went down to the fort from Durham are mentioned in part by Gen. Sullivan in an article published in the *New Hampshire Spy* of 17 March 1789. He says that Ebenezer Thompson went with the party to Portsmouth, but did not go down to the fort. Among those who did go to the fort were "the Rev. Mr. Adams, Dea. Norton, Lieut. Durgin, Capt. Jonathan Woodman, Mr. Aaron Davis, and, I think, Mr. Footman of Dover, and many others." Capt. Eleazer Bennett, the

last survivor of those who took part in the capture of the military
stores, who lived to be over one hundred years old, gave an account
of the affair to the Rev. Mr. Tobey of Durham, which was published in the *Congregational Journal* of 18 February 1852. Besides being there himself he mentioned John Sullivan, Winborn
Adams, Ebenezer Thompson, John Demerit of Madbury, Alpheus
Chesley, Jonathan Chesley, Peter French, John Spencer, Micah
Davis, Edward [Ebenezer] Sullivan, Isaac Small and Benjamin
Small. Gen. Sullivan wrote in 1785 that he was assisted by his
three clerks in bringing the stores up the river, and these clerks,
or law-students, were Alexander Scammell, Peter French and
James Underwood.[1]

January 2, 1775, the town again chose Ebenezer Thompson,
Esq., and John Sullivan, Esq., as deputies to attend a convention
at Exeter, to chose delegates to the General Congress to meet at
Philadelphia, and 26 April 1775, a special meeting of the inhabitants of Durham chose Moses Emerson as Moderator and
voted as follows:

That Ebenezer Thompson Esq' Mr. Moses Emerson and John Smith 3ᵈ
be Deputies to attend the Provincial Congress at Exeter forthwith. Lt.
Samuel Chesley added to the Committee.

Voted that the Town would Pay any men that Should Set off Equipt as
Soldiers for Boston according as the Provincial Congress shall determine, if
they vote anything otherwise the Town to Allow them a reasonable sum.

Voted that those persons who are about to march and not able to furnish
themselves be furnished by the Select Men.

This was seven days after the battle of Lexington. It is evi-
dent that some men from Durham went to Boston soon. How
many were present at the battle of Bunker Hill cannot be told.
There is official record that Alexander Scammell was there as
brigade major. Moses Emerson was appointed commissary
for the army 25 May 1775. Under date of 28 June 1775 he writes
from Medford, Mass., "Ever since the engagement they have
been all hurry and confusion; busie intrenching & preparing to

[1]Much that is based only in the imagination has been written about this event. The
account here given is taken in substance from Prof. Charles L. Parsons' *The Capture of Fort
William and Mary*, reprinted from Proceedings of the N. H. Historical Society. His statements are so supported by historical evidences that they can scarcely be questioned.

receive the enemy. The troops that were in the late engagement lost their blanketts & Clothes." The reference is to the engagement at Bunker Hill, 17 June.

On 20 May 1775, the convention at Exeter voted to raise three regiments one of which was commanded by Col. Enoch Poor. The term of service was to expire in December of the same year. This regiment was afterward designated as the Eleventh Continental Foot. Durham contributed nearly a full company, under command of Capt. Winborn Adams. Col. Poor's regiment was stationed on the seacoast, from Odiorne's Point to the Merrimack River. The very day of the battle of Bunker Hill the Committee of Safety at Exeter directed Gen. Folsom to order two of the companies in Col. Poor's regiment, including that of Capt. Adams, to march to Exeter for further orders, and the next day, "upon receiving the news of the engagement at Charlestown directed Col. Poor to order all the companies in his regiment, except Capt. Elkins', to march immediately to Cambridge."

The following is a list of Capt. Winborn Adams' company, 2 June 1775:

MEN'S NAMES.	AGE.	OCCUPATION.	TOWNS IN WHICH THEY LIVE.
Capt. Winborn Adams			
John Griffin			
Zebulon Drew			
Stephen Jones Thomas	24	Gent.	Durham
Micah Davis	34	Husbandman	Durham
Trueworthy Davis Durgin	21	Husbandman	Durham
William Adams	19	Taylor	Durham
John Neal	33	Carpenter	Barnstead
John Starboard	21	Husbandman	Durham
Samuel Demerit	19	Husbandman	Durham
Charles Bamford Jr.	36	Husbandman	Barrington
John Drisco	21	Husbandman	Durham
Tobias Leighton	37	Joiner	Durham
Robert Leathers	40	Husbandman	Durham
Eph'm Tibbits	21	Joiner	Madbury
David Rand	28	Blacksmith	Durham
Daniel Nute	22	Husbandman	Madbury
David Cops	25	Turner	Durham
Robert Wille	22	Husbandman	Durham
James Leighton	25	Taylor	Durham
Thomas Ellison	21	Husbandman	Barrington
James Thomas	34	Husbandman	Durham
John Collins	25	Taylor	Durham

Jeremy Young	18	Husbandman	Durham
Joseph Rendall	19	Taylor	Durham
Samuel Sayer	21	Taylor	Durham
Eliphalet Durgin	22	Joiner	Durham
Solomon Runnals	23	Tanner	Durham
Abijah Blaisdell	21	Cordwainer	Durham
Ezekiel Wille	51	Carpenter	Lee
John Pemerit	26	Blacksmith	Madbury
Ebenezer Chesley	18	Cordwainer	Durham
Samuel Hill Clark	22	Husbandman	Durham
Sam' Clough	23	Husbandman	Durham
Joseph Bickford	21	Husbandman	Durham
Josiah Burnham	23	Taylor	Lee
Dudley Davis	27	Husbandman	Barrington
John Williams	28	Husbandman	Lee
Thomas Davis	27	Husbandman	Durham
Nath' Jenkans	26	Husbandman	Barrington
Sam' Smith	23	Husbandman	Madbury
John Johnson	20	Husbandman	Durham
Joseph Smith	21	Husbandman	Durham
Daniel Pinkham	21	Husbandman	Madbury
Eli Bickford	21	Husbandman	Lee
John Clough	26	Husbandman	Durham
John Colbath	22	Husbandman	Durham
John Buss	33	Husbandman	Durham
Winthrop Wiggan	30	Carpenter	Newmarket
John Glover	24	Husbandman	Durham
Lemuel Nutter	35	Joiner	Newington
Joseph Leighton	22	Husbandman	Newington
Thomas Thompson	23	Husbandman	Durham
Moses Meader	23	Husbandman	Durham
Enoch Green	19	Hatter	Durham
John Sias	21	Husbandman	Lee
Thomas Polluck	25	Husbandman	Durham
Daniel Shaw	22	Husbandman	Lee
John Leathers	22	Husbandman	Lee
William Sm art	20	Cordwainer	Durham
Nicholas Tuttle	22	Husbandman	Middletown
Enoch Rcnrals	21	Husbandman	Lee
Isaac Tuttle	22	Husbandman	Dover
Lewis Kyraston	24	Taylor	Newmarket
Joseph Buzzel	46	Husbandman	Madbury
Simon Batchelder	18	Husbandman	Northwood
Benj* Johnson	23	Husbandman	Northwood
Amos Fernal	24	Cordwainer	Lee
James Thompson	26	Joiner	Durham

Total 68 men including the Captain, which said men are good effective able bodied men mustered & received by me June 2ᵈ 1775,

per SAMˡ HOBART.

N. B. The aforesaid men took the oath proposed by the Honˡ Congress, at the same time, before me

SAMˡ HOBART *Jus Pacis.*

Moses Meader was received by the committee instead of John Johnson. Another Roll shows that John Griffin and Zebulon Drew were lieutenants, Tobias Leighton, Micah Davis, John Neal, and Daniel Shaw were sergeants; David Cops, John Stirbourd, John Drisco and Enoch Green were corporals; John Collins was drummer and William Adams was fifer.

A pay roll of this company omits these names, viz., Thomas Ellison, Josiah Burnham, Dudley Davis, John Clough, and Joseph Leighton. It adds, however, the names of John Couch, Timothy Davis, Hatevil Leighton of Newington, Stephen Noble, Samuel Runolds, Peter Stillings of Newmarket, Benjamin Small of Lee, John Shepherd of Barrington, Samuel Thompson, Vincent Torr, James Underwood, Jonathan Williams, Samuel Yeaton, and Thomas Footman. All were of Durham except the four otherwise designated.

Tradition says that many people in Durham escorted Winborn Adams' company as far as the Newmarket line, where prayer was offered by the Rev. John Adams, cousin to Winborn. At the close of the prayer half the military company were in tears. We can well believe this tradition after reading John Adams' letter to the patriots of Boston.

Association Test of Lee, 1776

It is said above that the soldiers of Winborn Adams' company took the oath proposed by the Honorable Congress. No other Association Test of Durham has been found. The Rev. John Adams in his letter to the patriots of Boston says of the people of Durham, "We are with you to a man." Perhaps this is the reason why there was no test. That of Lee is here presented because it contains the names of so many persons belonging to Durham families. All these promised to oppose the British forces, to the utmost of their power, at the risk of their lives and fortunes. The names are here arranged alphabetically for convenience of the reader.

Thomas Arlen
Philbrook Barker
Josiah Bartlet
Micajah Bickford
Samuel Bickford
William Bly
James Brackett
Joseph Brackett
Benjamin Braily?
Benjamin Bodge
Mr. Samuel Bodge
Josiah Burley
Samuel Burley
Ebenezer Burnum
Joshua Burnam
Joshua Burnham Jr.
Benj. Clark
Isaac Clark
James Clemens
George Chale
Daniel Chele
Lemuel Chesley
Zaccheus Clough
James Davis
Clement Davis
John Davis
David Davis
John Davis
Moses Dame
Hunking Dame
Cornilus Dinsmore
Elijah Dinsmore
Jonathan Dow
Benjamin Durgin
Josiah Dergien
Samuel Durgin
Joseph Doe
George Duch
John Emerson
Samuel Emerson
Smith Emerson
Anthony Fling
John Follett
Joseph Follett
Peter Folsom
Elijah Fox
Nathaniel Frost
William French

Dimond Furnald
Amos Furnald
Eli Furber
Jonathan Fisk
Ruel Giles
William Gliden
John Glover
William Goen
Edward Hill
Reuben Hill
Samuel Hill
Richard Hull
Thomas Hunt
Sam. Hutchin
Thomas Huckins Jr.
Jeremiah Hutchins
Bennan Jackson
Samuel Jackson
Ebenezer Jones
E. Jones Jr.
Benjamin Jones
George Jones
John Jones
Joseph Jones
Benjamin Jones
Matthias Jones
John Kinnison
Josiah Kinnison
Samuel Langmaid
Samuel Langley
Thomas Langley
Edward Leathers
John Leathers
John Layn
Gideon Mathes
Samuel Mathes
Nicholas Meder
John Mendum
Timothy Moses
Timothy Muncy
Thomas Noble
Robert Parker
Joseph Pitman
John Putnam
Ebenezer Randel
Miles Randel
Simon Rindel
Enoch Runels

Job Runels
Moses Runales
Jonathan Runals
Job Runels Jr.
John Sanborn
Edward Scales
Ephm Sherburne
Daniel Shaw
John Sias
Joseph Sias
Samuel Smith
Samuel Snell Jr.
Isaac Small
Jonathan Stevens
Nathaniel Stevens
Stephen Stevens
Samuel Stevens
William Stevens
Jonathan Thompson
Tolman Thompson
Henry Tufts
Thomas Tuffts

George Tuttle
Thomas Tuttle
Henry Tufts Jr.
Nicholas Tuttle
Andrew Watson
Eleson Watson
Joseph Watson
James Watson
William Waymouth
Ezekiel Wille
Stephen Wille
Thomas Wille
Zebulon Wiley
Zekiel Wille
Samuel Wille
John Williams
Edward Woodman
Samuel Woodman
Joshua Woodmarch
John Wiggin
Robert York
Thomas York

The following men in Lee refused to sign the Test, some for conscientious reasons, because they were Friends. Among the latter were the Cartland, Jenkins, Meader and Bunker families. The Association Test papers were signed by Ichabod Whidden and William Laskey, as Selectmen:

William Calwell
Joseph Emerson
James Bunker
Joseph Cartlin
Richard Glover
Aaron Hanson
William Jenkins

William Jenkins Jr.
Joseph Meder
Samuel Lamas
David Muncey
Charles Rundet
Robert Thompson
John Srell

The following is a copy of a paper that was in the possession of the late Stephen Millett Thompson and needs no explanation:

We the Subscribers, thinking it a Duty incumbent upon us at all Times (but more especially at this alarming Juncture) to lend our Aid & Assistance as far as in us lays for the Defence of our Country and of those Priviledges & Liberties which God & our Ancestors of happy memory have handed down to us; and as our restless and implacable Enemies are forceably endeavoring to deprive us of them: Therefore it behooves us to exert ourselves to the utmost of our Power in their Defence, which cannot be done unless we are properly officer'd and fixed with Arms and Ammunition. In Consideration of the above we have come unto the following agreement —

Viz. That we will assemble and meet at Durham Falls, on Monday the tenth
day of July next ensuing, at two of the Clock in the Afternoon, then and there
to choose a Chief Officer and two Subalterns, and such other under Officers as
the Company then met shall think proper, which said Officers shall be chosen
out of the Subscribers to this Agreement, and shall have it in their Power to
order Meetings for the future, as often as they shall think necessary and convenient. And we engage that we will do our utmost Endeavor to provide ourselves with well fixed Firelocks, Powder and Balls sufficient for them, as can
be procured, and that without any Delay. And further we engage that we will
when ordered to assemble, and while assembled, pay proper Regard, & be under
due Subordination & Subjection to our said Officers, in as full and ample manner, as we should were they commissioned by the highest Power.

In Confirmation of all and every Part of the above Agreement, we have set
our Hands this twenty ninth Day of June A. D. 1775.

Jere Folsom Jur, Edward Winslow[1] (?), Josp Stevens, Alpheus Chesley,
Ephraim Folsom, Solomon Davis, Jonathan Woodman Jun., Robert Hill,
Lemuel Jackson, Jonathan Bickford, Steven Jones, Wilam Cotten, E. Thomp-
son, John Folsom, Theophilus Hardy, Albert Dennier, Nath¹ Hill, Timothy
Medar, Enoch Jackson, Jona Chesley, John Welsh, Jona Woodman 3d, Patrick
Cogan, Sam¹ Wigglesworth, Thos Pinkham, John Hill, Thomas Edgerly, Samuel
Chesle, John Thompson, John Crockit, Jonathan Woodman, Arch Woodman,
Timothy Emerson, Eliakim Bickford, Abednego Spencer, Daniel Rogers,
Benja Chesle Jur.

The remainder of the paper, containing additional names,
has been lost. The whole list is thought to have had about one
hundred names. Many of the above afterward served in the
Revolutionary Army.

At a town meeting held 11 December 1775 "Ebenezer Thompson Esqʳ was chosen to Represent the Town of Durham in General
Congress to be held at Exeter on the 21st Day of December current at 6 o'clock in the afternoon and impowered to act in sᵈ
Capacity for the Term of one Year. Either as a member of the
Congress or if such a Government should be assumed by a
Recommendation from the Continental Congress as would require
a House of Representatives, the sᵈ Thompson to become a member of the House agreeable to the within Notification." Here,
then, is Durham's first representative in the State's revolutionary
government.

Durham kept sending men to the front and supplying their
families while they were in the army. At first the volunteers
were many and for short periods of service. Later it was more
difficult to get men to inlist for three years or during the war.
Bounties were offered to volunteers. March 31, 1777, Col.

[1]Probably Edward Winslow Emerson.

(ham "for any sum they in their prudence may think sufficient

Samuel Chesley, Capt. Timothy Emerson and Capt. John Burnam were appointed a committee to draw upon the selectmen of Durham "for any sum they in their prudence may think sufficient to use and apply for hiring men to compleat our quota." The men so hired helped to fill up three Continental Battalions then raised in New Hampshire.

The inflation of prices caused by the war made it necessary to fix the prices of necessary provisions for the families of soldiers, and the price of Indian corn was fixed at four shillings per bushel, of salted pork at seven pence and a half per pound, and of beef at three pence and a half per pound, the town paying the balance, if such articles could not be obtained at such prices. The town records declare that Widow Sarah Colbath was aided like the wives of soldiers and that "John Hull have the Cow that was purchased by the town committee for his family in his absence, he paying the s⁴ Committee Eighteen Dollars for the Use of the Town." The committee were instructed at the same time to buy sixty bushels of corn and two thousand pounds of beef for the use of the families of soldiers. A bounty of $300 was paid to David Kynaston in 1779, and in 1781 Jonathan Chesley was voted "4600 Dollars" for advancing the money to the said Kynaston, or Kenniston, showing the rapid inflation of currency. March 29, 1779, the town voted to "pay the Wid⁰ Susanna Crown twenty Dollars toward her support she having lost her Husband in the service of the United States." This is the first time the United States are mentioned in the town records. In 1779 five men volunteered to join the expedition to Rhode Island, and the town paid them $100 above the State bounty. Two of the men were James Thomas and Trueworthy Davis Durgin.

The Committee of Safety, Inspection and Correspondence for 1777 and 1778 consisted of Ebenezer Thompson, Esq., John Smith, 3d, Esq., Moses Emerson, Esq., Valentine Mathes, Esq., Benjamin Smith, Esq., Joseph Stevens, Esq., Col. Alpheus Chesley, Capt. Thomas Chesley, Mr. John Thompson, James Gilmor, Esq., Mr. Jonathan Woodman, Jr., Mr. Nathaniel Hill and Capt. Timothy Emerson. The committee for 1779 was the same except that Lieut. Benjamin Chesley was substituted for his father, Capt. Thomas Chesley, deceased. The committee for 1780 consisted of Ebenezer Thompson, Esq., Mr. John Thompson, Valentine Mathes, Esq., Capt. Timothy Emerson, Col. Alpheus

9

Chelsey, Joseph Stevens, Esq., James Gilmor, Esq., Lieut.
Benjamin Chesley, Mr. Nathaniel Hill, John Smith, 3d, Mr.
Jonathan Woodman, Hon. Gen. Sullivan, and Col. Samuel Ches-
ley. The committee for 1781 included Mr. Jonathan Chesley
and Capt. John Grifin, and omitted John Thompson and Alpheus
Chesley.

In 1779 a committee appointed to consider the inflated prices
and depreciation of paper currency reported a series of resolves
to be signed by voluntary subscribers, to the effect that they
would not ask more for certain commodities than the prices
established by the committee and that such prices should be
changed only in agreement with Portsmouth and neighboring
towns. The following persons signed the agreement, Alpheus
Chesley, Jacob Joy, Ebenezer Chesley, William Jackson, Enoch
Jackson, Samuel Chesley, Philip Chesley, Thomas Dame, Jonathan Williams, James Gilmor, James Leighton, Lem Jackson,
Benjamin Bunker, Ebenezer Meserve, Jeremiah Burnham,
Samuel Hicks, Eliphalet Wiggin, Benmor Duda, Samuel Joy,
Joseph Chesley, Jr., Ephraim Clough, Benjamin Doe, Jr., James
Drisco, Joseph Rendal, Pike Burnam, Samuel Nutter and Robert
Lapish.

On the 18th of October, 1779, the report of a committee was
accepted, fixing the price of merchandize and country produce
in pounds and shillings of greatly depreciated currency. Silver
and gold coins were not in circulation, having been bought up
by speculators. The following list is instructive as showing the
necessities of life and their comparative values:

West India Rum per gallon, £6.12; New England Rum, 5.2; Molasses per
gal, 4.13, Coffee per pound, £0.18; Sugar from 12s to 14s per pound; Tea per
pound, 6.6, Chocolate, 1.7; Cotton Wool per pound, £2; salt of the best quality
per bushel, £9; New England made salt, £6; Indian Corn, per bushel, 4.10;
Rye, 6; Wheat, 9; Oats, 2.5; Peas, best quality, 9; Beans, 9; Beef, Mutton,
Lamb and veal by the quarter, 4 shillings per pound; Hides per pound, 3.6;
Pork by the Hog, per pound, 6 shillings; Butter, per pound, 12 s; Cheese, 6s;
English Hay per ton, £30; German Steel per pound £1.16; Bloomery Iron per c,
£30; Cider at the press per barrel, £5.8; Flax well dressed per pound, 12s;
Sheep wool, £1.10; Sole Leather per pound, £1.1; Upper Leather, well cured,
per side, £12; Green Calf Skin, £2.14; Calf Skin dressed at a medium, £6;
Side of Leather Suitable for Saddles, £13.4; Laborer per day found as usual,
£2.2; Tradesmen that work abroad and are found as usual, £3.3; Blacksmiths
for shoeing a horse all round, steel corcks, £6; Shifting a set of shoes, £1.16;
Axes, £7.10; Mens Shoes of the best quality from £7 to £8 per pair; Best Womens

shoes, £6; Cabinet makers to have no more than 20 for 1 from the price of 1774; Felt Hats, £6; Tailors to have £18 for a suit of plain Cloaths and other work in like proportion; Innholders, for Dinners, £1;for Breakfasts and suppers, 15s; Horse keeping to Hay, £1.4; Toddy per bowl, 15s; Cyder per mug, 5s; Oats per mess, 7s; Tallow candles per pound, 15s; Letters of horses to have 4s per mile out and nothin in; Potatoes and Turnips of the best quality, 24s per bushel; Wood per cord, £13.10; Good Saddle, £52.16; Bridle,—; Poultry —; Hogs fat, per pound, 13s; Winter apples per bushel, 18s; All articles of country produce, manufacture, or labour not herein enumerated to be at 20 for 1 from the price in the year 1774.

In this list the relative price of labor is the most interesting item. A laborer would have to work three days to get a gallon of rum, then considered more a necessity than molasses, or three days for a pound of tea, or two days for a bushel of corn, or nearly four days for a pair of shoes. Who will say that labor is not better paid today? But is the shoemaker of the factories today better off than the independent cordwainer that went from house to house in those times? Is the sweat-shop of modern tailors to be preferred to the changing work-shops of those who then made clothes? Have times improved? It is the comparative inequalities that distress and oppress wage-workers.

From various sources, chiefly from the Revolutionary Rolls, as published in the State Papers of New Hampshire, have been gathered the names of the men from Durham and Lee who served as soldiers in the War for the Independence of the Colonies.

Adams, Lt-Col. Winborn	Burnham Josiah (Lee)
Adams, William, fifer	Burnham Edward
Adams, Ensign Samuel	Burnham, Ensign James
Applebee, Joseph	Burnham Pike
Applebee Thomas	Buss John
Branscomb Arthur	Burnham Paul
Adams Peter (negro on ship Raleigh)	Burnham Samuel
Bennett Ebenezer	Carson Robert
Bickford, Eliakim	Chesley, Aaron,
Bickford Eli (Lee)	Chesley, Col. Alpheus
Bickford Ephraim (Lee)	Chesley Ebenezer
Bickford Josiah (Lee)	Chesley Jonathan
Bickford Joseph	Chesley Samuel
Bickford Samuel	Clark Samuel Hill
Blaisdell Abijah	Clough John
Boffe Jesse	Clough Samuel
Bunker Zacheus	Clough Lt. Zacheus
Bunker Enoch, Corp.	Cogan Patrick
Burnham Benjamin (Lee)	Colbath Benjamin

Colbath Dependance
Colbath Downing
Colbath John
Colkins John, Drummer
Copps David, Corp.
Couch John
Critchet Elias (Lee)
Crommit Moses
Crommett James
Crommett Philip
Crommett Ebenezer
Crommett Thomas, Ens.
Cromwell Samuel
Creecy William
Crown William
Dame, John
Daniels Eliphalet, Capt.
Daniels Nathaniel (Lee)
Davis David
Davis Micah, Sergt.
Davis Clement
Davis Philip
Davis Thomas
Davis Timothy
Davis John (Lee)
Doe Jonathan
Doe Joshua
Duda Lemuel
Drew Andrew
Drew Zebulon Lt.
Drew Francis
Drisco John
Demeritt Samuel
Durgin Benjamin
Durgin David
Durgin Joseph
Durgin Josiah (Lee)
Durgin Henry
Durgin Levi
Durgin Philip
Durgin Trueworthy D.
Durgin Eliphalet Lt.
Dunsmore Elijah Capt. (Lee)
Dutch Jeremiah
Dutch John
Edgerly Sergt. Thomas
Edgerly James
Emerson Moses, Commissary

Emerson Capt. Smith
Emerson Timothy
Fernald Amos (Lee)
Fowler Philip
Frost Nicholas (Lee)
Frost Nathaniel (Lee)
Frost Winthrop (Lee)
Footman Thomas
Footman John
Green, Corp. Enoch
Gerrish Timothy
Glidden Gideon
Glover John
Griffin, Lt. John
Hall Benjamin (Lee)
Hall Sergt. James (Lee)
Hall John
Hicks Benjamin (Lee)
Hill Wille (Lee)
Hill Thomas (Lee)
Hull John
Jenkins Nathaniel (Lee)
Johnson John
Johnson Andrew
Kinnistin Josiah (Lee)
Kynaston David
Kent Robert
Kent, Ebenezer
Langley David
Layn Capt. John (Lee)
Leathers, Enoch
Leathers John
Leathers Jonathan
Leathers Edward (Lee)
Leathers Thomas
Leathers Robert
Leighton James
Leighton, Lt. Tobias
Leighton, John?
Leighton Valentine
Mann David
Martin Dan (Negro)
Martin Sidon (Lee)
Mathews Gideon
Mallin Mathew
McDaniel James (Lee)
Meader Moses
Meader Nicholas

Mitchell John
Mooney Benjamin
Mooney, Col. Hercules
Mooney John
Munsey Timothy (Lee)
Neal John
Noble Stephen
Noble John
Norton John
Norton Thomas
Pendergast Edmund
Perry Abraham
Pinder Sergt. Jeremiah
Pinkham Abijah
Pinkham Isaac (Lee)
Pinkham Paul (Lee)
Pinkham Thomas
Polluck John
Pinder Benjamin
Rand David
Rand John
Randall Joseph
Rogers Daniel
Reynolds Abraham
Richards Bartholomew
Runnels Enoch (Lee)
Runnels Capt. Samuel
Runnels Israel (Lee)
Runnels Moses (Lee)
Runnels Stephen
Runnels Solomon
Ryan James
Ryan Michael
Scales Samuel (Lee)
Scammell, Gen. Alexander
Sawyer Samuel
Shaw Daniel (Lee)
Sias John (Lee)
Sias, Capt. Benjamin
Smart William
Smith Benjamin
Smith Edward
Smith John
Smith Joseph
Small Benjamin (Lee)

Small Isaac (Lee)
Spencer John
Starboard, Ens. John
Starboard Stephen
Spencer Abednego
Spencer Moses
Spencer Robert
Stevens John (Lee)
Stevens Nathaniel (Lee)
Sullivan, Gen. John
Tash, Col. Thomas
Torr Vincent
Thomas, Lt. Joseph
Thomas Stephen Jones
Thomas, Sergt. James
Thompson James
Thompson Samuel
Thompson Thomas
Tobnie Patrick
Tucker Stephen B.
Tuttle Capt. George
Tuttle Nicholas
Tuttle Isaac
Tufts Henry
Underwood, James
Ward Samuel
Wille Robert
Wille Ezekiel
Wille Thomas
Williams Joseph
Williams Jonathan
Williams Samuel
Weeks Jedediah
Welch Benjamin (Lee)
Whitten Mark (Lee)
White James
Williams John (Lee)
Wigglesworth Surgeon Samuel
Woodman Lt. Archelaus
Woodman Edward Jr.
Woodman Sergt. Joshua
Yeaton Samuel
Young Jeremy
York Samuel

It is impossible to trace the military record and life history of all the men of Durham who took part in the struggle for national

GEN. JOHN SULLIVAN

freedom. It would not be fitting, however, to publish a history of Durham without saying the few words that space permits about some of the soldiers of the Revolution.

Gen. John Sullivan was born in Berwick,[1] Me., 17 February 1740, son of the Irish schoolmaster, John Sullivan, and his wife, Margery Browne. He was educated mainly by his father and studied law with Judge Samuel Livermore of Portsmouth, settling in Durham as its first lawyer soon after 1760. He purchased of the heirs of Dr. Samuel Adams, 19 December 1764, the house since known as the Sullivan house, near the monument that the State erected to his memory. He is mentioned in the town record in 1771, when he was chosen overseer of the poor. He soon became well known as a lawyer of learning, eloquence and forensic ability. Prosperity enabled him to purchase the water privilege at Packer's Falls and to erect, soon after 1770, six mills, including corn-mill, saw-mill, fulling-mill, and scythe-mill. We have seen the part he took in the capture of military stores at Fort William and Mary. He was commissioned major in 1772. He was delegate to the Continental Congress in 1774 and 1775, where he took an active part and urged the declaration of independence. He was appointed brigadier general in 1775 and served at the siege of Boston, after which he served in the expedition to Canada and conducted the retreat. He was promoted to be major general 29 July 1776. He took part in engagements about New York, where he was captured but soon exchanged, and in the battles of Trenton, Princeton, Brandywine and Germanton. He spent the winter at Valley Forge and commanded the expedition to Rhode Island. He scourged out of the Susquehanna Valley the Indian murderers of Wyoming, for which service monuments have been erected in his honor. Through impaired health and the pressing needs of his family he resigned his office, 9 November 1779. He was again delegate to Congress in 1780 and 1781. The office of attorney general was conferred upon him in 1782 and was held till 1786. It is remarkable that a son and a grandson held the same office. He had a prominent part in the formation of the

[1] The Rev. Alonzo Quint D.D., in his oration at the dedication of the Sullivan monument in Durham, claims that Gen. John Sullivan was born in Somersworth. The evidence seems insufficient to the present writer. Berwick points out the exact spot where he was born. In 1737 the parish of Somersworth voted "that Mr. John Sullivan be the schoolmaster for the ensuing year, voted John Sullivan to sweep and take care of the meeting house & to have thirty shillings,"—See Knapp's Historical Sketch of Somersworth, p. 28. This was three years before Gen. John Sullivan was born.

Sullivan Monument

Constitution of New Hampshire and was thrice elected president, or governor, of the state, 1786-87, 1789. He was also speaker of the House. He was made by President Washington first Judge of the United States District Court of New Hampshire, in which office he died. He was also the first Grand Master of the Grand Lodge of Free Masons of New Hampshire.

It is of equal interest to the inhabitants of Durham to know how he served his town. He was chosen agent for the proprietors of Durham, 22 May 1769. He was moderator of town meetings eight times, 1781-1788, on the Committee of Correspondence, Inspection and Safety, 1774-1781, overseer of the poor, 1771, 1784, assessor and commissioner, 1788, on the school committee for the Falls District, 1780.

He was the first president of the New Hampshire branch of the Society of the Cincinnati, and meetings of that society were held in Durham in the years 1788-1792.

The Sullivan Lodge of Knights of Pythias is so named in honor of an illustrious townsman.

His patriotism and ability in war and peace have been recognized in the erection of the monument in front of his old residence, 27 September 1894, with the following inscription:

In Memory of
JOHN SULLIVAN
Born February 17, 1740
Died January 23, 1795
Erected by the state of New Hampshire
upon the site of the Meeting House
under which was stored the gunpowder
taken from Fort William and Mary.

The reader, doubtless, will be interested to see a picture of another monument that commemorates the victorious campaign of Gen. Sullivan in the Susquehanna Valley. The illustration is here presented through the courtesy of the American Irish Historical Society, which published a full report of the proceedings at the dedication of the monument. On that occasion, Lynde Sullivan, Esq., of Boston, whose summer residence is in the old Sullivan house in Durham, gave the principal historical address, in which many interesting details are given of

the life of Gen. John Sullivan. A noble poem was read by Joseph
I. C. Clarke, and here is a little sample of it:

I see through a tangled, wooded glen
The glint of weapons shine,
And a long array of stalwart men
Marching in warlike line.
They stretch 'twixt the hills from crest to crest,
Their sweat is thick upon brow and breast,
Their muskets trailing low.
They peer through the forests round about
For pitfalls of the foe.
Their horses tug at the traces stout
Of cannon rumbling slow.
And swarms of boats and rustic floats
Up the babbling river come,
And I catch the thrilling of bugle notes
And the rolling of the drum.
On through the thickets a way they trace;
They pause at the river's bars.
They follow a man of the Fighting Race,
And he follows a flag of stars.

The inscription upon the monument is as follows:

NEAR THIS SITE
SUNDAY AUGUST 29 1779 WAS FOUGHT
THE BATTLE OF NEWTOWN
BETWEEN
CONTINENTAL TROOPS COMMANDED BY
MAJOR GENERAL JOHN SULLIVAN
AND A COMBINED FORCE OF
TORIES AND INDIANS UNDER
COLONEL JOHN BUTLER
AND
JOSEPH BRANT
AVENGING THE MASSACRE OF
WYOMING AND CHERRY VALLEY
DESTROYING THE IROQUOIS CONFEDERACY
ENDING ATTACKS ON OUR SETTLEMENTS
AND THEREBY OPENING
WESTWARD THE PATHWAY OF CIVILIZATION.

Gen. Alexander Scammell, son of Dr. Samuel Scammell, who
came from Plymouth, England, in 1738, and settled at Milford,
Mass., was born in 1744. He graduated at Harvard, in 1769.
He taught school at Kingston, Mass., in 1770, at Plymouth,
Mass., in 1771 and at Berwick, Me., in 1772. For a year he was
employed as a surveyor in exploring the territory of Maine and

NEWTOWN BATTLEFIELD MONUMENT
Elmira, New York.   Dedicated August 29th, 1912

New Hampshire, and was one of the proprietors of Shapleigh, Me.
He then became a student in the law office of Maj. John Sullivan
at Durham. The will of Samuel Meader of Durham was witnessed
in the law office of Gen. John Sullivan, 18 May, 1773, by John
Smith, Alexander Scammell and Jn° Sullivan. He is first mentioned in the records of Durham as one of the committee to apply

GEN. ALEXANDER SCAMMELL

the Association Test, 28 November 1774. Tradition says that he
pulled down the flag at the capture of Fort William and Mary,
December 1774. He was at the battle of Bunker Hill as brigade
major and served under Gen. Sullivan in the siege of Boston. He
was promoted to deputy adjutant-general in 1776. He crossed
the Delaware in the same boat with Washington as his special aid,
and took part in the battles of Trenton, Princeton and Saratoga.

In the campaign against Gen. Burgoyne he was colonel of the First and then of the Third New Hampshire troops and was by the side of Lieut-Col. Winborn Adams when he fell at Bemis Heights. He himself had been wounded yet kept the field and witnessed the surrender of Burgoyne. In 1778 he was commissioned adjutant-general of the army. At the battle of Monmouth he was aid to Washington, rallied the troops and led the charge. Washington said of him, "The man who inspired us all to do our full duty was Alexander Scammell." He commanded the Light Infantry in the march into Virginia, was wounded and captured at the battle of Yorktown and died of his wound six days after, 6 October 1781, aged 35. He was buried at Williamsburg, Va.

He was six feet and two inches in stature, of fine proportions, graceful and attractive, full of ardor, courage and perseverance, a favorite with Washington, popular with the officers, honorably remembered by Lafayette. His was a brief, brilliant and noble career, and it reflects honor on the town where he lived and loved. Some permanent memorial erected in Durham is due him. The Scammell Grange is named in honor of him and thus honors itself also.

The following letter, written to Maj. John Sullivan, then in the Continental Congress, well shows the quality of Scammell's heart and mind, as well as the commotion caused at Durham by news of the battle of Lexington:

PORTSMOUTH, N. H., May 3, 1775.

HONOURED SIR: Your leaving New Hampshire at a time when your presence was so extremely necessary to cherish the glorious ardour which you have been so instrumental in inspiring us with, spread a general gloom in Durham, and in some measure damped the spirit of liberty through the Province; and nothing but the important business in which you are imbarked would induce us to dispense with your presence with any degree of patience or resignation.

But when the horrid din of civil carnage surprised us on the 20th of April the universal cry was—Oh if Major Sullivan was here! I wish to God Major Sullivan was here! ran through the distressed multitude.

April court which was then sitting adjourned immediately. To arms! to arms! was breathed forth in sympathetick groans.

I went express to Boston, by desire of the Congressional committee, then sitting at Durham, proceeded as far as Bradford, where I obtained credible information that evening. Next morning I arrived at Exeter, where the Provincial Congress was assembling with all possible haste. There I reported what intelligence I had gained; that the American army at Cambridge, Woburn and Charlestown was more in need of provisions than men; that fifty thousand had assembled in thirty-six hours; and that the Regulars, who had retreated from Concord, had encamped on Bunker's Hill in Charlestown.

The Congress, upon this report, resolved that the Durham company, then
at Exeter (armed completely for an engagement, with a week's provisions)
should return home and keep themselves in constant readiness. All the men
being gone from the westward and southward of Newmarket and men-of-war
expected hourly into Portsmouth, it was with the greatest difficulty your Durham soldiers were prevailed upon to return. Six or seven expresses arrived at
Durham the night after our return; some desiring us to march to Kittery; some
to Hampton; some to Ipswich, etc., which places, they said sundry men-of-war
were ravaging. The whole country was in a continual alarm, but suspecting

that the marines at Portsmouth might take advantage of the confusion we
were in and pay Durham a visit, we thought proper to stand ready to give them
a warm reception and supposing that your house and family would be the
first mark of their vengeance, although I had been express the whole night before, I kept guard to defend your family and substance to the last drop of my
blood. Master Smith being under the same apprehensions, did actually lay
in ambush behind a warehouse and came very near sinking a fishing boat
anchored off the river, which he supposed heaped full of marines. Men,
women and children were engaged day and night in preparing for the worst.

Many towns in this Province have enlisted minute-men and keep them
under pay; and the Congress before this would actually have raised an army

had they not waited for the General Court which sits tomorrow, in order to raise as much money as they can to pay off their army when raised.

I am extremely mortified that I am unable to join the army at Cambridge. The particulars of the skirmish between the Regulars and the Americans will, long before this, have reached you.

In longing expectation your safe, happy and speedy return is hoped for by all your friends but by none more sincerely than

Your dutiful humble servant,

ALEX. SCAMMELL.

To John Sullivan at Philadelphia or New York.

Col. Hercules Mooney is said to have been a tutor in the family of a nobleman in Ireland. A person of his name was in Trinity College, Dublin, in 1732. He is described as a "tall, stately man." He came to America in 1733 and began teaching in Somersworth. He signed the petition to make Madbury a parish in 1743. He removed to Durham, where he taught from 1751 to 1766. He received a captain's commission in 1757 and took part in the Crown Point Expedition, being captured and robbed when Fort William Henry was taken. Was selectman in Durham in 1765. After the separation of Lee he taught in that town and was selectman there, 1769-75, and represented Lee several times in the General Assembly. March 14, 1766 he was appointed major in Col. David Gilman's regiment, and on the 29th of September was promoted to be lieutenant-colonel and marched to Ticonderoga with his regiment. June 23, 1778 he was appointed colonel in the expedition to Rhode Island. He served on the Committee of Safety in Lee, was a justice of the peace and a grantee of Holderness, whither he removed in 1785. Here also he was selectman and representative four times. He died in April 1800, and was buried on his farm about a third of a mile from Ashland village, under a willow tree. The farm is now owned by Samuel H. Baker. A rough slab marks his grave. His sons, Benjamin and John, served in the Revolutionary Army, the former as lieutenant. Col. Hercules Mooney was one of Ireland's many precious gifts to young America, a leader in thought and activity, a moulder of character in the training of youth, a wise builder of the Granite State, a valiant commander in battle, a peaceful and highly useful citizen in the towns he served.

Col. Thomas Tash, born 5 July 1722, was of a family that came from near Belfast, Ireland, according to tradition. The original name was McIntash. His father was Jacob Tash, who married (2) Patience, daughter of James and Mary (Smith) Thomas, in

1727. Col. Tash married (1) Mrs. Anne Parsons, the wealthy widow of Capt. Parsons of Portsmouth, (2) Martha, daughter of Joshua and Elizabeth (Kenniston) Crommett. He appears in a scouting party, under Samuel Miller in 1744. He was a captain in 1758, in the French and Indian War. September 17, 1776, he was appointed colonel of a regiment that served near New York. He removed to New Durham in 1783 being one of the original proprietors and their clerk in 1765. His children were Thomas, James, Jacob, William, Martha, Betsey, Mary who married Josiah Edgerly 12 July 1793, and Patience. Col. Tash died in October 1809, aged 87 years.

He lived for a time in Newmarket being engaged in trading and shipping and represented that town in the legislature in 1776. He erected the first saw- and grist-mill in New Durham. He was taxed for real estate in Durham as late as 1783. He represented New Durham, Wolfeboro, etc., in the legislature in 1778. He was a justice of the peace and actively engaged in manufactures and agriculture, a busy leader in stirring times.

Lieut.-Col. Winborn Adams was born in Durham, son of Dr. Samuel Adams, grandson of the Rev. Hugh Adams. He was, doubtless, named for his uncle, Winborn Adams, a schoolmaster, who died in 1736, thus perpetuating the maiden name of his grandmother, Susanna Winborn. He is often mentioned in the records of Durham as surveyor of lumber and innholder. The house he built and used for an inn stands on the south side of the road, opposite the Sullivan monument. He was at the capture of the military stores at Fort William and Mary, December 1774, and was commissioned captain of the first company raised in Durham for the Revolutionary Army. He was promoted to be major in 1776 and lieutenant-colonel 2 April 1777. He commanded the Second New Hampshire Regiment at the battle of Stillwater, called also the battle of Bemis Heights, and fell mortally wounded, 19 September 1777. His name was long preserved in several branches of allied families. He seems to have been a brave and popular man. He was a member of the lodge of St. John (Portsmouth) of Free and Accepted Masons, and so also were Gen. Sullivan and Gen. Scammell. In a deed dated 1756 he is called "Chirurgeon."

He married Sarah Bartlett and she continued to keep the inn for some time after her husband's death, and town meetings were held at her house. The following petition may be of interest:

To the Honble the Council and House of Representatives of the State of New Hampshire. Gentlemen, Your Petitioner humbly sheweth that her Husband late Lt. Col° Adams of the 2nd New Hampshire Regt fell in battle on the memorable 19th of Sept 1777, and left her a helpless widow destitute of the means of procuring a Livelihood as her sole dependence was on her Husbands pay, her only son having been ever since in the service of this state. —That it has been with extreme difficulty she has since procured a scanty subsistence with her own industry & the Charities of her friends.—That she has delay'd petitioning hitherto in hopes that the Honble Legislature of the State would have made a general provision for the mourning widows & helpless orphans of those who fell in defence of the Liberty & Property of their Friends & Country.—

LIEUT.-COL. WINBORN ADAMS' INN

But that she is compelled to the disagreeable Necessity of imploring the assistance of that Country in defence of which her late husband fell, and humbly requesting that the Honble Legislature would grant her the half pay of her late husband or such other allowance as they in their superior Wisdom shall think proper, so as to raise her above the pinching hand of poverty and enable her to support a Life rendered melancholly and unhappy. And your Petitioner as in Duty Bound will ever pray &c.

[N. H. Town Papers, XI, 596.] SARAH ADAMS.

Samuel Adams, only son of Lieut.-Col. Winborn Adams, served as lieutenant under Gen. John Sullivan in the campaign against the Indians and was after the war lieutenant-colonel in the militia.

Capt. Smith Emerson served in Col. Wingate's regiment at Seavey's Island. This company was enlisted in October 1775. It served also at the siege of Boston and was discharged in March 1776. He was appointed captain of Company Six in Col. Thomas Tash's regiment which was raised in September 1776 and sent to New York to aid the Continental Army. His commission was signed by Gen. Washington, under whom his regiment served, taking an active part in the battles of Trenton and Princeton. Capt. Emerson settled in Lee, where he was one of the selectmen.

Capt. John Layn was living in Durham as early as 8 March 1760, when he enlisted in Capt. Samuel Gerrish's company, Col. John Goff's regiment, for the Canada expedition. John Layn, gunsmith, of Durham, in a petition of 26 May 1761, states that he was employed as armorer for that regiment and furnished his own tools, but had received no extra pay for this service. He was allowed four pounds sterling. [See N. H. Town Papers, XI, 581.]

He was appointed captain in Col. John Waldron's regiment, 6 March 1776, for six weeks of service at Winter Hill.

He lived in Durham village where now resides Hon. Joshua B. Smith. He acquired land at Newtown, in what is now Lee, in 1763 and 1766, and established the first inn in that town. The old signboard, bearing the name of Washington and the date 1779, is still to be seen, but the painting of Washington on horseback has been effaced therefrom by the elements. He owned mills at Newtown, where he was living in 1790. He died before 12 May 1811, when his son, John, was appointed administrator of his estate. Descendants of the name still live in that vicinity.

Col. Alpheus Chelsey, born in Durham, was one of the party that went to Fort William and Mary in December 1774. He was recommended to the authorities as captain, in 1775, by Gen. John Sullivan. He had orders to enlist a company of 61 able bodied men, 2 December 1775, to serve under Washington. He appears as lieutenant-colonel in Col. John Waldron's regiment 6 March 1776. He is repeatedly called colonel in the records of Durham. He married Deborah Meserve and died in Barnstead in 1792.

Andrew Drew was born in Dover 25 March 1758, and died at Durham Point, 19 December 1854. At age of 18 he enlisted in Capt. Caleb Hodgdon's company, in Col. Joshua Wingate's regiment, stationed on Seavey's Island in December 1775. He took part in the expedition to Rhode Island and was in the battle of Newport. He served nine months in Capt. Peter Drown's company, Col. Stephen Peabody's regiment. He received a bounty from the town of Durham and was a pensioner from 1836 till the time of his death. He was buried in the Smith cemetery, near the south shore of the mill-pond.

Samuel Demeritt was born 17 June 1756. He enlisted in Capt. Winborn Adams' company, 2 June 1775 and served near Boston. In 1776 he was on the roll of Capt. William McDuffee's company, Col. Tash's regiment, and probably joined the army in New York. He entered the naval service and was on the ship *Raleigh* as a marine, time of entry 31 July 1777, stature, five feet, eight inches and three fourths. He died 1 November 1801 at Wednesday Hill, Lee. [See Genealogical Notes.]

Henry Durgin was a private in the Eighth Company, Second regiment in 1780-1781, having enlisted for the war. Supplies were furnished him by the town in 1781. He certified, 30 January 1786, that he was a soldier from Durham in Capt. Fogg's company and was wounded in one foot "when at home on a furlough in the year 1782 & that Doct' Nathaniel Kidder of Newmarket had the care of the wound until it was healed." [N. H. Town Papers, XI, 591.]

James Leighton was born in Dover 12 October 1749 and died 22 February 1824. He was buried in the village cemetery at Durham. He was a tailor by trade, and enlisted in Capt. Winborn Adams' company in 1775 and remained in service during 1776. Afterward he entered the naval service and served three years under Commodore John Paul Jones, on the *Ranger* and on the *Bon Homme Richard*. He was one of the marines who took the plate from Lord Selkirke on the coast of Ireland, and when it was ordered to be returned he was one of the party sent to deliver it. He was quick tempered, fearless and always ready for adventure.

Lieut. Tobias Leighton, born in Dover 9 May 1736, enlisted as sergeant in same company as his brother, James. Was lieutenant 19 September 1776 and marched with Col. Long's

regiment to Ticonderoga.   He married Ann Tuttle and died in
Madbury, in 1812.   [See Genealogical Notes.]

Valentine Leighton of Durham was mustered into Col. Mooney's regiment 1 July 1779.   He was in the expedition to Rhode
Island serving five months and twenty days.   He afterwards enlisted for the war and 2 June 1781 was in Capt. Rowell's company,
in Col. Reid's regiment.   He married, 15 April 1784, Sally Wille,
who was buried 3 February 1785.   An only child was buried 14
November 1785.

Lieut. John Griffin was born at Gloucester, Mass., 25 July 1740.
He was lieutenant in Capt. Winborn Adams' company, in 1775.
He married, 18 May 1767, Hannah Gerrish of Berwick, Me.,
born 20 June 1746.   She died 11 March 1830.   The following
children were recorded in Durham: Adoniram, born 28 March
1768, married 18 August 1799, Ruth Currier, and died 20 June
1851; Nancy, born 5 November 1769, married Isaac Chesley,
Jr., 17 November 1796; Hannah, born 18 September 1771,
died young; William, born 13 October 1772, died young; William,
born 6 April 1774; Winborn, born 13 October 1776; Mary, born
23 September 1780; and John, born 17 June 1782, published to
Keziah Jenkins of Lee, 18 November 1806.   Lieut. Griffin died
in 1788 and was buried in Durham.   He is called captain in
1782 and was selectman 1782–87.   In the taxlist of 1787 he is
"Col. John Griffin."

Ens. John Starbird, born 7 February 1755, was the son of
Lieut. John Starbird, who died 17 October 1811, aged 87 years,
eight months, a soldier in the French and Indian Wars.   He
enlisted as corporal in Capt. Winborn Adams' company, 1775.
He appears as ensign in Capt. Caleb Hodgdon's company,
Col. Pierce Long's regiment 25 September 1776.   His company
was stationed at Portsmouth and marched to Ticonderoga in
1777.   After the war he was made lieutenant and was a pensioner.
He lived not far from the old railroad station and was a shoemaker.   He died 17 October 1841 and is buried in the village
cemetery, without a gravestone.   His wife, Rebecca, died 9
February 1825, aged 68.   Their children were Sally, who married
Stephen Hodgdon in 1810; Lois, who married (1) Calvin Pickering, (2) ———— Hazen, (3) Levi Cram; Stephen, who married
(1) Tamsen Nute who died 24 February 1848, (2) Caroline
(Teague) Davis, widow of Daniel Davis.   Stephen Starbird died

15 December 1869, aged 81 years, 8 months. Other sons of Ens. John Starbird were John, who married 23 December 1836, Olive, daughter of Edward Winslow Emerson, and Samuel, a sea captain in merchant service, who died 15 November 1825, aged 44 years. All the sons took part in the War of 1812, Stephen on the Canada frontier, and John and Samuel in the privateer service.

Samuel Scales was born in Durham, 1754. He was a private in Capt. Smith Emerson's company, 5 November 1775, enlisting from Lee. He died in March, 1778. His wife was Hannah Langley, who married (2) 1784 Samuel Hill of Loudon, N. H. Samuel Scales was buried in the old town cemetery in Lee. A common field stone, with the initials S. S., marks his grave. A posthumous son, Samuel, was born April, 1778.

Samuel Thompson was born in Durham about 1755. He served seven years in the Revolutionary Army, eighteen months in Col. Poor's regiment and five years in Maj. Whitcomb's rangers. In 1820 he was living in Sandwich, N. H., aged 64. He then had a wife, aged 50, and daughter, aged 13. He was a farmer and much troubled with rheumatism.

James Thompson, brother to the above, son of James and Mary (Clark) Thompson, was in Capt. Winborn Adams' company in 1775, then aged 26. He served three years in the army.

Vincent Torr enlisted at the age of 17 in Capt. Winborn Adams' company, 20 July 1775, and served at Winter Hill, Mass. He reënlisted for three years, 8 February 1777, in Capt. Frederick M. Bell's company, Col. Hale's regiment. He was at Ticonderoga and in the battle of Stillwater, or Bemis Heights, and wintered at Valley Forge. Died in Newmarket, 11 May 1829. [See Genealogical Notes.]

Samuel Williams was on the muster roll of Lieut. Piper's company, at Portsmouth in 1780. He enlisted 20 July of that year for six months. He or his family received supplies from Durham, March 1778 and onward till 1781. His wife's name was Sobriety (Bamford?). He was of Barnstead in 1781 as a recruit for Durham.

Lemuel B. Mason, son of Robert and Susanna (Bickford) Mason, was born in Durham, February 1759. He was an infant when his father died and was but sixteen years old when he enlisted, probably from Newington, soon after the battle of Bunker Hill. He remained in the army eight years, till the proclamation of peace. He participated in the battles of Trenton, Princeton, Monmouth, and Stillwater. He was present at the surrender of Burgoyne and was with Gen. Sullivan in his expedition against the Indians. His captain taught him to read and write and he became sergeant, clerk and lieutenant. In leading scouting parties against the Indians he had bullets put through his coat and hat but was never wounded. Once he saved himself by hiding in a hollow log all night. He returned to Newington penniless and despoiled of his inheritance. Here he married (1) Sarah Nutter, who died childless. He married (2) 16 November 1786 Mary Chamberlain in New Durham and had thirteen children. He removed from New Durham to Alton, where he served several years as selectman, and thence to Gilford. He served one year as captain in the War of 1812. He lived at Gilford many years, receiving in old age a pension of $320. He had a justice's commission in 1838. He died in Moultonborough, 30 March 1851, aged 92 years, 2 months. His wife died 4 February 1851, aged 82 years.

David Davis, born 25 August 1760, was a pensioner. He served in Capt. Archelaus Woodman's company, Col. John Waldron's regiment in January 1776. In August of that year he enlisted in Capt. Smith Emerson's company, Col. Thomas Tash's regiment, and in December of the same year he was in Capt. Samuel Wallingford's company, Col. David Gilman's regiment. In August 1777 he again entered service as private in Capt. George Tuttle's company, Col. Stephen Evans' regiment, which took part in the battle of Saratoga. In June 1778 he enlisted for eight months in Capt. Stephen Jenkins' company, Col. Thomas Poor's regiment. In July 1779 he enlisted for the sixth time in Capt. Samuel Runnels' company, Col. Hercules Mooney's regiment. He died at Packer's Falls, 19 November 1835.

THE WAR OF 1812.

The War of 1812 called but few soldiers from Durham and led to the building of two privateers. The following, who served in that war, are buried in the village cemetery: Joseph P. Burnham, Zachariah Bunker, George Hull, Capt. Joseph Richardson, Capt. Alfred Smith, Stephen Starbird and Rufus Willey. Burnham and Bunker married twin sisters, Esther and Mercy Varney,

and both served in the same company. Bunker was wounded
at Fort Erie in upper Canada by the bursting of a shell and had
to have his left leg amputated. He drew a pension of $8 per
month, which was later increased to $15. He lived between
the Ffrost house and the landing, at the Falls. George Hull
was confined for a time in Dartmoor prison, England. He was
captured on board a privateer.

The privateer *Harlequin* was built in Durham, near the Pascataqua bridge, by Andrew Simpson. It was built of good white
oak, one hundred and four feet in length of deck, and pierced for
twenty-two guns. The cost was $25 per ton, carpenter's measure-
ment, and most of the seventy-five shares were taken by people
in Portsmouth. The *Harlequin* was captured 21 October 1814,
after about two years of service. Also the privateer, *Andrew
Jackson*, was built by Mr. Simpson but delivered too late, 24
August 1815, to be of service in the war.

The military rolls of 1812–15 contain the names of Durham men
who served from the 11th to the 28th of September 1814, when
it was feared that the British forces would attempt the capture
of Portsmouth. In the roll of Capt. John Willey's company
appear the names of Ebenezer Cromit, first lieutenant, and private Stephen Bodge, who both served sixty days. In Capt.
Andrew Nute's company are found the names of Moses Emerson
3d, Joseph Burnham, Ely Demeritt, Eben Demeritt and Stephen
Demeritt, the last three probably from Madbury, who served
sixty days. In Capt. William Wiggin's company are found
Lieut. Stephen Paul, Ens. Larkin P. Edgerly; Sergts. Ebenezer
Doe, Mark Willey, Robert Furness, and James Willey, Jr.;
Corporals Stephen Willey, Daniel Cram, David Rand; Supply
Johnson, and Musicians Francis Drew and Joseph Ellison. The
privates in the same company were Thomas Chesley, Benjamin
Doe, William French, Samuel Stacey, Jonathan Dockhum,
Joshua Drew, Joseph Applebee, Jacob K. Watson, George Wood-
man, Hervey Presson, Samuel Drew, Joseph Thomas, Jr., Eliot
Burnham, Samuel Savage, Daniel Willey, Robert Willey, George
Libby, John Burnham, Nathaniel Ham, Phineas Willey, Asa
Durgin, Timothy Pendergast, Jacob Garland, Daniel Pinkham,
Joseph Langley, David Davis, Noah Willey, Samuel Edgerly,
William Smith, Stephen Cogan, Nathan Keniston, Joseph Doe
and John Downing.

In Capt. Alfred Smith's company are found the names of
1st Lieut. George Hull, 2d Lieut. Nathan Woodman, 3d Lieut.
Benjamin Dame, Sergts. George Dame, Stephen Twombly,
Daniel Young, Henry Wiggin, John Yeaton and Moses Wood-
man, Corporals, Jacob Odell, James Durgin, John Pinkham,
George Frost, Jr., and Musicians Francis Butler, Moses
Hanscom and Edward Mason. The privates in the same
company were Benjamin Tuttle, Bradbury Thomas, Daniel
Edgerly, Ebenezer Joy, Enoch Holt, Enoch Durgin, Jacob Ben-
nett, Jeremiah Elliot, James Smart, Levi Thompson, Willet
Wedgewood, Samuel Chesley, Timothy Emerson, Thomas James,
Samuel Mathews, William Footman, Edward Griffiths, John P.
Jones, Reuben French, James Pendergast, Daniel Lakin, Samuel
Lamos, Adoniran Griffin, John Smith, Daniel Taylor and John
Bean. This was, without doubt, a Durham company.

Nathaniel Sias of Newmarket, born in Durham, appears as
major of the Fourth Regiment in 1814. Ebenezer Cromit was
adjutant, inspector and brigade major of detached battalion.
Col. George Sullivan, son of Gen. John Sullivan, appears as
aide.

Some Durham names appear in Capt. Charles E. Tobey's
company, such as Stephen Starbird, Joseph Burnham, Joshua
Chesley and James Chesley.

THE CIVIL WAR.

Just now the Sons and Daughters of the American Revolution
are glorifying their ancestors. The time may come when the
descendants of those who fought for the preservation of the great
American republic will be equally proud of their ancestry. It is
fitting that a record of the soldiers of the Union Army should be
preserved, though little more than their names can be mentioned
here. There seems to be good evidence that the first two men
in New Hampshire to enlist were Col. John L. Kelley and Capt.
Hollis O. Dudley. Mr. Kelley was a native of Madbury and spent
his youth in Durham, whence his father had removed soon after
his birth. Mr. Dudley lived some years in Durham after the
war. They both enlisted 16 April 1861.

Capt. John B. Sanders of Durham commanded a company
of volunteers sent from this town to join the Sixth Regiment and

was presented with a sword by some of the citizens of the town, "desirous of showing our appreciation of his energy and patriotism," as the subscription paper says.

Of those who died in the army and were buried in Durham the following list has been made:

George W. Bunker, enlisted 8 November 1864; buried at Mast Road cemetery. He served in the Navy.

Charles S. Davis, Company M, First Cavalry; enlisted 23 December 1861; discharged for disability 27 June 1862; promoted to corporal. He was transferred to the Navy. Buried at the Albert Young graveyard.

John F. Langley, corporal, Company H, Sixth Regiment; enlisted 30 November 1861; died 8 March 1862; buried at Durham Point.

Alphonso Pinkham, corporal, Company H, Sixth Regiment; enlisted 28 November 1861; promoted to sergeant; died at Durham while on a furlough, 28 August 1863, buried in the village cemetery.

Samuel Stevens, wagoner, Company H, Sixth Regiment; enlisted 28 November 1861; discharged 27 November 1864; buried in graveyard on Martha A. Stevens' land. James M. Stevens, his brother, is buried in the same yard.

Samuel E. Smith, wagoner, Company H, Sixth Regiment; enlisted 28 November 1861; reenlisted 2 January 1864; died 15 April 1865; buried in village cemetery.

Amos M. Smart, Company K, Eleventh Regiment; enlisted 2 September 1862; died 6 April 1863 of typhoid fever; buried in the village cemetery.

Enrollment of all Able-bodied Male Citizens in the Town of Durham, Made by the Selectmen, August 20, 1862.

AGE.	NAMES	OCCUPATION.	AGE.	NAMES.	OCCUPATION.
28	Abbott, Horatio P.	Tanner		Bunker, Daniel C.	
24	Adams, Joseph M. R.		28	Bunker, John J.	Carpenter
		Farmer	25	Bunker, George W.	Shoemaker
23	Allen, William H.	Laborer	23	Bunker, Charles H.	Farmer
38	Atherton, Bradbury	Miller	21	Bunker, George F.	
			18	Bunker, Charles A.	
39	Butler, James	Farmer	19	Brock, Haley D.	Farmer
	Broderick, John	Laborer		Bickford, D. Page	Farmer
	Butler, George W.		44	Bickford, D. Prescott	
37	Bunker, William H.	Farmer			Farmer
32	Bunker, James M.	Farmer	24	Bickford, John F.	Shoemaker

Age.	Names.	Occupation.
40	Burnham, George W.	
		Farmer
26	Berry, Samuel	Laborer
36	Berry, Richard	Laborer
28	Brown, Jacob K.	Farmer
30	Chadwick, William	
	B.	Clerk in P. O.
23	Chesley, John S.	Farmer
	Chesley, George E.	Farmer
24	Colman, Oliver W.	Laborer
27	Colman, Daniel S.	
	Cummins, Charles D.	
36	Corson, John	Farmer
30	Corson, Aaron	Laborer
26	Corson, Charles H.	
	Channel, William J.	Farmer
	Coffin, William R.	Shoemaker
40	Church, Israel R.	
26	Dame, George E.	Farmer
26	Dame, Moses G.	Stone Cutter.
28	Dame, Levi	Shoemaker
26	Dame, Hunkin H.	Farmer
24	Dame, Sylvester	Farmer
18	Dame, Asa G.	Farmer
39	Drew, John	Farmer
44	Demeritt, John C.	Farmer
21	DeMeritt, George P.	Farmer
18	DeMeritt, Charles	Farmer
37	DeMeritt, Oliver P.	Overseer in
		Factory
23	Doe, Olinthus N.	Farmer
24	Doe, Horace B.	Farmer
34	Doe, Ebenezer F.	Farmer
31	Doe, Andrew J.	Farmer
	Dowe, George M.	
30	Davis, Ebenezer M.	Miller
34	Davis William H.	Tin Pedlar
39	Durgin, John W.	Farmer
27	Drew, John F.	Farmer
	Drew, Henry A.	Farmer
34	Emerson, Ebenezer T.	
		Farmer
19	Emerson, Charles W.	
30	Emerson, John P.	
21	Emerson, John	Farmer

Age.	Names.	Occupation.
24	Emerson, Samuel	Farmer
28	Edgerly, Eli	Farmer
26	Edgerly, George	Shoemaker
21	Edgerly, Richard	Farmer
	Edgerly, James B.	
18	Frost, George S.	Student
41	Foss, Leonard	
43	Fowler, Joseph	Farmer
28	Fowler, George	Mason
31	Francis, Robert W.	Farmer
33	George, Isaac B.	Depot Master
	Gleason, Albert	
40	Glidden, David S.	Farmer
	Greene, Samuel H.	Physician
	Gerrish, Ferdinando	Physician
20	Griffiths, Edward B.	Farmer
19	Griffiths, William H.	Farmer
19	Hanson, John A.	Laborer
30	Hayes, Ezra	
21	Hayes, John S.	Farmer
	Hall, Lafayette	Machinist
40	Haley, Michael	Laborer
41	Ham, John F.	Butcher
43	Hull, Cyrus G.	Mason
36	Hodgdon, Joseph H.	Laborer
39	Hobbs, William R.	Machinist
27	Jackman, Charles	Shoemaker
44	Jones, William F.	Farmer
23	Joy, Charles	Teacher
18	Jones, Charles O.	Laborer
22	Kent, Ebenezer, Jr.	
29	Kent, James M.	
32	Kent, George W.	
26	Keniston, George O.	
41	Kingman, John W.	Counsellor
	Lancaster, Edward M.	
		Teacher
33	Langley, Samuel	Farmer
21	Langley, Jeremiah	Shoemaker
	Langley, Moses B.	
35	Langley, William D.	Farmer
26	Langley, John E.	Carpenter
22	Langley, Charles F.	Farmer

Age.	Names.	Occupation.
	Langmaid, William B.	
	Langmaid, Charles A.	
	Langmaid, Jacob H.	
38	Long, James W.	
	Long, James H.	
	Long, George W.	
26	Long, John	Alien-Laborer
24	Lucus, James	Brickmaker
21	Marden, Bartholomew	Laborer
41	Mathes, John M.	Farmer
44	Mathes, Clark	Farmer
21	Mathes, John H.	Brickmaker
24	Mathes, Burnham	Brickmaker
21	Mathes, Mark H.	Farmer
19	Mathes, Hamilton A.	Farmer
20	Mathes, John A.	Farmer
24	Meserve, Winthrop S.	Farmer
42	Meader, Stephen	Farmer
27	McKone, Peter	Laborer
43	Moring, Andrew D.	Carpenter
22	Nute, Albert M.	Sailor
19	Nute, Augustus P.	Farmer
	Odell, Albert	Student
41	Odiorne, John H.	Farmer
41	Paul, Stephen	Carpenter
29	Paul, Charles H.	Machinist
27	Paul, Alfred F.	Shoemaker
32	Palmer, James B.	Shoemaker
23	Perkins, Marcellus	Shoemaker
35	Perkins, Thomas H.	Laborer
25	Rand, Stephen	Shoemaker
23	Ransom, Reuben M.	
23	Ransom, Alonzo	
	Roberts, Blake	
32	Savage, Sylvester	Carpenter
43	Savage, Henry F.	Carpenter
37	Shepard, Jacob	Shoemaker
35	Stevens, Nathaniel	Farmer
38	Stevens, Nathaniel, Jr.	Farmer

Age.	Names.	Occupation.
19	Stevens, David A.	Farmer
	Stevens, Darius	
	Stevens, Federal B.	Farmer
	Stevens, Parker, Jr.	
	Stevens, David	
38	Smart, John	Laborer
27	Smart, Amos M.	Laborer
	Smart, Charles H.	Farmer
40	Smart, James M.	Farmer
39	Smith, Joshua B.	Farmer
	Smith, Joseph	Farmer
25	Sullivan, David	Farmer
37	Sullivan, John	Alien-Laborer
	Smith, John S.	Ordained Minister
25	Thompson, Andrew B.	Shoemaker
39	Thompson, Samuel W.	Farmer
41	Thompson, Ebenezer	Farmer
22	Thompson, John W. E.	Farmer
	Thompson, Daniel G.	Student
	Thompson, True W.	Teacher
27	Thompson, Charles A. C.	Farmer
	Trickey, John F.	
	Twombly, John R.	Laborer
34	Twombly, Reuben H.	Farmer
19	Tuttle, William, Jr.	Farmer
	Tuttle, Charles H.	
27	Tufts, Willard C.	
36	Tufts, Samuel B.	
36	Watson, John	Farmer
23	Whitehorn, Charles H.	Farmer
21	Whitehorn, Alphonzo L.	Farmer
26	Wentworth, John N.	Farmer
27	Wiggin, George T.	Teacher

AGE.	NAMES.	OCCUPATION.	AGE.	NAMES.	OCCUPATION.
42	Wiggin, Nathaniel P.		26	Willey, Charles H.	Carpenter
		Carpenter	38	Wigglesworth, James L.	
19	Wiggin, Charles E.	Farmer			Shoemaker
33	Wiggin, William	Farmer	19	Walker, Charles W.	Farmer
22	Woodman, Daniel A.				
		Farmer	41	Yeaton, Nathaniel	Fisherman
42	Woodman, William	Farmer		Young, Josiah B.	
44	Willey, Ira	Carpenter	25	Young, Albert	Farmer
24	Willey, Mark E.	Carpenter	36	York, John B.	Mason.

Alphabetical List of Durham Soldiers in the Civil War.

Those names marked with a cross + were residents of Durham as shown by town records, the others were probably persons who enlisted to help make up Durham's quota of soldiers. List made out by Lucien Thompson from Adjutant General's List, Regimental Histories and Durham Records.

NAME.	CO.	REGT.	NAME.	CO.	REGT.
+Abbott, Horatio P.	E	13	Clark, James	I	4
Adams, Charles		14	Clayton, Wilton H.	(C	10
+ Adams, Enoch G., 1st				(C	2
U. S. V.	D	2	Cleves, John (alias John		
Ainsworth, Charles	B	10	Averill)	C	6
+ Allen, William H.	K	11			
Armstrong, James	E	4	Conley, James	F	14
Averill, John (alias John			+ Dame, Joseph W.	G	H
Cleves)	C	6	+ Davis, Alfred E.	H	6
			Davis, Charles	K	5
Baptiste, Oudin Jean	F	11	+ Davis, Charles S., Co. M.,		
	F	6	1 Cav.		
+ Barrett, John	C	6	+ Davis, David O.	D	2
+ Berry, Samuel	A	2		F	5
+ Bickford, Charles H.	B	5	+ Demeritt, George P.	K	11
+ Bickford, Dudley P., Jr.			Dexter, Charles R.	C	5
+ Bickford, John E.	K	5	+ Doeg, George P.	D	3
Boudy, Anthony, 1 Cav.			+ Doeg, John H.	A	9
+ Britton, James (also in	B	17	Dority, John C.	F	6
Navy)	K	2	+ Dowe, George M.	E	13
Burns, Harry	A	2	+ Edgerly, Charles E. B.	D	12
Carroll, John	C	3	+ Edgerly, George E.		
+ Chadwick, William B.	D	15	+ Edgerly, Joseph	D	3
+ Chapman, Joseph H.	E	13	Ellison, George W.	H	6
	B	2			
+ Chesley, Alfred E., U. S.			+ Francis, Robert W.	E	13
Army 17th.					
Chidsy, Fred S., V. R. C.			Gammon, Charles	K	3

NAME.	CO.	REGT.
+ Gerrish, Ferdinando E.	E	13
Gleason, John	F	13
Golliez, Edward	K	5
+ Goodrich, John	E	13
+ Goodwin, James L.	A	11
+ Goodwin, Robert	D	15
+ Grover, John H. L.	H	6
Ham, Charles M.	B	10
Hancock, Nath¹., U. S. C. T.		
+ Hanson, George W.	H	6
+ Hanson, John A.	K	11
Haughay, Peter	B	10
+ Hayes, Charles W. H.	H	6
+ Hewins, Otis W. (or		
Hawkins)	G	10
		1
Jackson, John	K	1
+ Jones, Charles P.	K	11
+ Jones, Samuel J.	H	6
Jones, William	B	10
	D	2
Kelley, Patrick	F	7
+ Keniston, George O.	E	13
Kennedy, Michael	K	5
+ Kent, Charles A.	E	13
+ Kingman, Col. John W.		15
Laerny, William	K	11
+ Langley, George E., Co. K,		
Cavalry	B	1
+ Langley, John F.	H	6
+ Langley, Moses B., Co. B.,		
N. H. H. A.		
+ Lees, Thomas	B	2
+ Long, George W.	E	13
+ Long, James H.	K	11
+ Long, Nicholas	E	2
+ Long, Perry	D	3
Maccaboy, James	E	5
Maloy, Dennis	B	10
	C	2
Malten, John	C	10
McDermott, F. C.	B	10
McDonnel, John, (McDon-		
ald)	H	8
McWilliams, Thomas		

NAME.	CO.	REGT.
+ Mellen, Henry B., U. S. Cav.		
Moore, Wm. J.		14
+ Moring, Andrew D.	K	11
Morton, Charles	G	5
+ Palmer, Asa D.	H	6
+ Palmer, Ezekiel U. S. A.,		
+ Palmer, George W.	F	7
+ Palmer, Henry S.	F	7
+ Palmer, Joseph 2ᵈ	K	3
+ Parker, Riley H.	A	9
+ Paul, William E.	K	11
+ Pendergast, George P.	D	2
+ Philbrick, Charles W.	B	2
+ Pinkham, Alphonso	H	6
+ Pinkham, John H.	H	6
+ Pinkham, Joshua	K	3
+ Prescott, Benjamin	F	7
+ Reynolds, Charles W.	K	
	I	5
Roberts, John A.	A	12
Rogers, John	D	10
+ Ryan, Patrick, Co. H, Navy		
& 1st Cavalry		
Saunders, George	B	10
+ Sanders, John B.	B	6
Scales, Edward	E	4
Scott, Austin	G	5
+ Shepard, John	E	2
+ Small, James R.	G	7
+ Smart, Amos M.	K	11
Smith, Daniel	F	
	S	7
Smith, James	D	15
+ Smith, Samuel E.	H	6
+ Starbird, James W.	H	6
+ Stevens, Andrew J.	I	6
+ Stevens, Samuel	H	6
Stewart, Horace M.	B	10
	A	2
+ Stimpson, Alfred	H	6
+ Stimpson, Curtis	B	2
Strunk, Isaac	A	12
+ Thompson, S. Millet	E	13
+ Tuttle, Andrew J. S.	E	13
+ Tuttle, Freeman H.	B	2

NAME.	CO.	REGT.	NAME.	CO.	REGT.
+ Tuttle, James H.	B	3	+ Willey, Henry	K	3
			+ Willey, Jonas M.	H	6
Urnback, Adam	E	5	+ Willey, James Warren	K	3
			Williams George	E	5
Valley, Franklin?	H	6			
+ Vibbert, Luke R.	H	3	Young, Charles, negro	C & G	10
				D	2
+ Walker, James F.	H	6	+ Young, George B.	K	11
+ Walker, Thomas H.,	{ D	2	+ Young, James T.	K	11
	{ K	5	+ Young, John T.	E	13
White, James			Youngblet, Friedrick	E	12

Men born in Durham, who lived elsewhere when they enlisted in the Civil War.

NAME.	CO.	REGT.	NAME.	CO.	REGT.
Adams, John	B	12		D	10
Bryant, John S.	B	3		D	2
Chesley, Joseph M.	E	2	Maj. Mellen, Henry B., U. S.		
Colomy, Jacob, not born in D.,			Cavalry		
lived here after war.	I	3	Randall, Charles D.	D	3
Dudley, Hollis O., not born in			Reynolds, Charles W.	K	
D. but lived here after war.				I	5
1st N. H. Regt. &	C	11	Ricker, Joseph	I	3
Ellison, Geo. W.	H	6	Speed, John	A	11
Fernald, William J.	G	2	Smith, Daniel[1]	F	
Farr, John	B	5		S	7
Hill, Alfred H.		3	Stimpson, William	H	7
Keyes, Phylander	D	9	Stevens, James, lived here after		
Long, Nicholas	E	2	war.		
Mendum, John, only lived here			Venner, James M.	D	2
after the war	D	3	Willey, James	K	7

Durham Soldiers who Enlisted During Civil War in Other States, as Shown by Town of Durham Records

NAME.	REGT.	CO.	STATE.	
John Conroy	28	E	Massachusetts	
Wm. Dame			Wisconsin	
Daniel Walker	1st		Massachusetts	
	Cavalry			
Edward Bickford	45	B	Massachusetts	
Michael Long			Massachusetts	
Robert H. Mathes	17		Maine	
Lysander Richardson	Navy		Massachusetts	Sept. 2, 1861
Charles Edgerly	12	E	Massachusetts	
Samuel T. Long	I	G	Massachusetts	

[1] See Genealogical notes, Smith family.

Names of men who volunteered for 9 months in other States.

NAME.	REGT.	CO.	STATE.
Edward Bickford	45	B	Massachusetts
Charles B. Jenness	48		Massachusetts
John Conroy	28	E	Massachusetts
Lysander Richardson			Wisconsin
William Dame			Wisconsin
Thomas Henney	13	H	Maine
William Henney	5	B	Maine
George Hoitt	Cavalry		Rhode Island
Daniel Mathes			Massachusetts

Durham Men in the Navy During the Civil War

NAME.	MUSTERED IN. NAVY.	TERM.	AGE.	
Chas. W. Reynolds	Apr. 25, Landsman 1861	3		reenlisted Aug. 19, 1864, 3 yrs.
Benjamin F. Jackson	May 13, Landsman 1861	3	21	
Charles W. Davis	May 13, Landsman 1861	3	21	
Charles B. Jenness	May 15, Landsman 1861	1	21	
George F. Richardson	May 16, Landsman 1861	2 or 3	27	reenlisted Oct. 12, 1862
Ebenezer S. Chapman	May 29, ordinary 1861	1	31	
Albert B. Clement	July 29, Landsman 1861	3	21	
Lysander Richardson	Sept. 2, 1861	3	25	reenlisted Dec. 2, 1864. marine
James Britton	Oct. 14, Landsman 1861			reenlisted 1863– 1 year, Aug. 19 1864–2 yr.
Sylvanus Chapman	Nov. 20, Landsman 1861	1	21	
Luke Long	Feb. 19, Landsman 1862	3	21	
Patrick Ryan	July 24, Landsman 1862	1	19	
Cephas Hepworth	Aug. 9, Landsman 1862	1	21	
John Denney (A. G. S.)	Sept. 15, Navy 1863			
John Drew	Oct. 23, Seaman 1863	1	35	reenlisted Oct. 21, 1864, 2 years.

NAME.	MUSTERED IN. NAVY.	TERM.	AGE.
William Tuttle, Jr.	Aug. 6, Navy 1864	1	
Charles S. Davis	Oct. 29, Navy 1864	2	
Charles H. Bunker	Nov. 7, Navy 1864	4	
George W. Bunker	Nov. 8, Navy 1864	2	
James L. Goodwin	Oct. 22, Navy 1864	2	
Henry Mathews (4 years)	July 6, Navy 1859	1	25
Wallace Halstead (4 years)	Aug. 23, 1859	1	23
Asa Mathes			

The accompanying group of veterans, living half a century after their services in the Union Army, are now champions of peace and fraternity. They are here presented with the gratitude and congratulations of fellow townsmen. Beginning with the upper row, at the left, they are: George P. Demeritt, Lieut. Co. K, 11th Regt. N. H. Vols.; John H. Doeg, Co. A, 9th Regt. N. H. Vols.; George P. Doeg, Co. D, 3rd Regt. N. H. Vols.; David O. Davis, Co. D, 2nd Regt. and Co. F, 5th Regt. N. H. Vols.; Silas Jenkins, Corp. Co. D, First Mass. Heavy Artillery. Those in the lower row, beginning also at the left, are: Samuel J. Jones, Co. H, 6th Regt. N. H. Vols.; True W. Lovering, Co. F, 13th Regt. N. H. Vols.; Riley H. Parker, Co. A, 9th Regt. N. H. Vols.; Joshua Pinkham, Co. K, 3rd Regt. N. H. Vols.; and David A. Stevens, Co. E, First Regt. of Heavy Artillery.

Earlier in this chapter has been presented the military record of some who were prominent in the struggle for national independence. The lapse of time has added to their laurels. Half a century has passed since the war for the preservation of the union, and perhaps this is perspective enough for history to make mention of their deeds. The following condensed statements of military services may interest some future generations even more than those who now read them.

Enoch G. Adams enlisted from Durham, 22 April 1851, at the age of 32, for three months. He reënlisted, 10 May 1861 for three years and was mustered in 1 June of the same year. He was promoted to sergeant, 1 October 1861, and was severely

SURVIVORS OF THE CIVIL WAR, LIVING IN DURHAM AND VICINITY.

wounded at Williamsburg. He was promoted to be second
lieutenant, 10 August 1862, and was commissioned captain
of Company D, First United States Volunteers, 30 April 1864.
He was mustered out of service at Fort Leavenworth, Kan., 2
November 1865, having been brevetted major for gallantry.
From May to September, 1865, he was in command at Fort
Erie, Dak., as ranking officer of the three regiments comprising
its garrison. After leaving the service he spent some years on
the Pacific Coast, being registrar of land under appointment
of President Grant, at Vancouver, and published a newspaper
there. He settled on a farm in Berwick, Me., where he died.

Capt. John B. Sanders was born in Effingham, August 1817,
and at the outbreak of the rebellion was a traveling salesman
with a good salary. He succeeded in enlisting sixty men and
received a captain's commission from Gov. Berry and was
presented with a sword by people in Durham. He was in the
Burnside expedition, had a sunstroke at Newport News in July,
1862, and was forced by ill health to resign. He belonged to
the famous Sixth New Hampshire Regiment of Volunteers,
that fought in twenty-three battles and lost two thirds of its
original number of men. Capt. Sanders after the war resided
in Dover, where he died, having suffered much from disease
contracted in the service.

The following is taken from the History of the Seventh New
Hampshire Regiment:

Major Daniel Smith was a son of Winthrop Smith, Esq., of Durham. He
was born at that place on the 27th of January, 1823. After graduation from
the public schools of his native town he attended for several terms the academies at Greenland and Pittsfield. In early life he adopted the business of
landsurveyor, which to him proved eminently successful. In 1850 he was commissioned lieutenant-colonel of the Twenty-fifth Regiment of New Hampshire
Militia, and besides filled many positions of honor and trust in his native town.
In 1854 he removed to Dover and from 1855 to 1860 he was deputy sheriff
for Strafford County, city marshal for Dover for three years, and a representative from that city to the popular branch of the New Hampshire legislature
in 1860 and 1861. For his character as a man and for the many desirable
qualities he possessed for the position he was appointed and commissioned
major of the Seventh Regiment on the 15th of October, 1861. He went with
his regiment to New York city, thence to Fort Jefferson, Fla., where he served
ably and acceptably as provost marshal, until the regiment moved to Beau-
fort, N. C., where he was seized with fever. He was permitted to go home on
a leave of absence, arriving at his house in a very enfeebled condition, and

died on the 26th of August, 1862, leaving a widow and four children. As a citizen Major Smith was highly respected and discharged all official and public duties with intelligence and fidelity. While in the army his promptness, valor and uniform cheerfulness and kindness to the officers and men won for him the confidence, respect, and affection of all with whom he became associated.

MAJOR DANIEL SMITH

It may be added that he was a selectman in Durham in 1847 and chairman of the board in 1849 and 1851-52. He and his line of ancestry made four generations who held the rank of major. [See Genealogical Notes on the Smith family.]

Lieut. Stephen Millett Thompson was born in Barnstead, 27 April 1838. In youth he fitted at Phillips Academy, Exeter, for the sophomore year of Harvard and later studied medicine for one year. He enlisted in Company E, Thirteenth New Hampshire Regiment, from Durham at the age of 24. He was mustered in 19 September 1862, as first sergeant, and was promoted to

164   HISTORY OF DURHAM

second lieutenant, 10 June 1863. He was wounded severely, 15 June 1864, in the assault on Battery 5, Petersburg, Va., and was discharged on account of wounds, 4 October 1864. He wrote the history of his regiment. After the war he resided in Providence, R. I., where he died about 1910. [See Genealogical Notes on the Thompson family.]

David O. Davis enlisted 30 April 1861 in Company D, Second New Hampshire Regiment, at age of 30. He was born at Alton. He reënlisted 10 May 1861 for three years and was mustered in as corporal 1 June 1861. He was discharged for disability, 19 September 1862, near Fairfax Seminary, Va. In August, 1853, he was drafted and assigned to the Fifth New Hampshire Regiment. He was wounded at Fort Steadman, captured at Farmville and again discharged for disability after the surrender. He lived after the war at Durham and was mail carrier and expressman. Later he removed to Newmarket. [See Genealogical Notes on the Davis family.]

Charles S. Davis, brother of Davis O. Davis, enlisted for three months, 13 May 1861, and was mustered into Company M of the New Hampshire Battalion of the First New England Cavalry, 24 December 1861. He was promoted to corporal and discharged for disability 27 June 1862. He enlisted for two years in the navy, 29 October 1864. He was buried in the Albert Young graveyard in Durham. [See Genealogical Notes.]

George P. Pendergast, born in Durham, enlisted 29 April 1861, at age of 21, in Company D of the Second New Hampshire Regiment. He reënlisted 10 May 1861 for three years and was killed at the battle of Williamsburg, Pa., 5 May 1862.

Thomas H. Walker was born in Boston, Mass., but enlisted from Durham, where he was living with his sister, Mrs. James Monroe Smart, 25 April 1861, at the age of 23. He reënlisted 10 May 1861 for three years in the Second New Hampshire Regiment, and was mustered in as sergeant 1 June 1861. He was discharged for disability at Washington, D. C., 1 August of the same year. He reënlisted 11 September 1861 in Company K of the Fifth New Hampshire Regiment as sergeant and was promoted to second lieutenant 15 December 1862, which office he resigned 11 June 1863. After the war he lived at Hyannis, Mass.

Freeman H. Tuttle, son of John Landon Tuttle and wife,

Elizabeth, was born in Durham and enlisted at age of 21 in Company B of the Second New Hampshire Regiment, 11 May 1861. He was wounded 25 June 1862 at Oak Grove, Va., and was transferred to the Invalid Corps 15 August 1863. He was discharged at Washington, D. C., 10 June 1864. He was living in Dover in 1907. His brothers, Andrew J. and James H., were also in the service.

George E. Langley enlisted as a private in Company B of the First New Hampshire Regiment, at the age of 22. He was mustered in 2 May 1861 and mustered out 9 August 1861. He reënlisted in Company K of the First New England Cavalry, afterward called the First Rhode Island Cavalry, and was mustered in 24 October 1861. He reënlisted 2 January 1864 in Company K of First New Hampshire Cavalry and was promoted to corporal 1 July 1865. He was mustered out with his regiment at Cloud's Hill, Va., 15 July 1865. His brother, Moses B. Langley, was in Company B of the New Hampshire Heavy Artillery, mustered in 19 August 1863 and discharged with his regiment 11 September 1865. [See Genealogical Notes on the Langley family.]

George P. Doeg was born in Durham and enlisted at age of 20 in Company D of the Third New Hampshire Regiment, 9 August 1861. He was wounded 18 July 1863 and was discharged by surgeon's certificate of disability 7 November 1863, at Norris Island, S. C.

Joseph Edgerly, born in Durham, enlisted 16 August, 1861, in Company D of the Third New Hampshire Regiment, at age of 26. He was discharged at Hilton's Head, S. C., 10 October 1862, by surgeon's certificate of disability. His brother, Charles E. B. Edgerly, was in Company D of the Thirteenth New Hampshire Regiment. They were sons of Jacob and Elizabeth Edgerly.

John Mendum, born in Lee, enlisted from Durham, where he was a resident for many years after the war. He enlisted, 1 August 1861, in Company D of the Third New Hampshire Regiment, at age of 34. He was discharged at Hilton's Head, 23 September 1863, for disability by reason of sickness. Described as five feet, five inches, in height, of dark complexion, blue eyes and brown hair. He reënlisted in 1863 and served through the war, having been in many severe battles. He was mustered out 19 December 1865. He received a pension for a long time and died at the Soldiers' Home at Tilton.

Joshua Pinkham was enrolled at Dover, 20 August 1861 and discharged at Bermuda Hundred, Va., 23 August 1864. He is described as five feet, nine inches, in height, of dark complexion, dark eyes and dark hair. His brother, Alphonso Pinkham, died in the service. [See Genealogical Notes on the Pinkham family.]

Samuel J. Jones was born in Lee, 29 April 1836. He enlisted, 19 October 1861 for three years in Company H, of the Sixth New Hampshire Regiment. He was promoted from corporal to sergeant 1 April 1865, after having reënlisted 2 January 1864. He was mustered out 17 July 1865, and resides in Durham. He married at Newmarket, 22 January 1856, Eliza A. Berry of Strafford, who was born 5 February 1840. They had children, Orin F. born 10 January 1857, Marianna born 21 January 1859, and Samuel born 29 January 1862.

Samuel E. Smith, born at South Andover, Mass., enlisted from Durham 2 November 1861, at age of 30, for three years in Company H of the Sixth New Hampshire Regiment. He reënlisted and was mustered in 2 January 1864. Captured 1 October 1864 at Poplar Springs Church, Va., and released. He died of disease at Durham 15 April 1865 and was buried in the village cemetery. The town records give his wife as Ann, aged 23, and children, Mary 6, George 4, and Cora 2, who became the wife of Clarence I. Smart of Durham.

James W. Starbird, son of John and Olive (Emerson) Starbird, enlisted 30 October 1851, at age of 31, in Company H of the Sixth New Hampshire Regiment, for three years, and was discharged for disability 27 November 1862 at Washington, D. C. Town records say he had wife, Angeline P., aged 27, and children, Mary 8, Martha 6, and George 1.

George W. Palmer, son of Joseph and Rebecca (Leighton) Leathers, enlisted 9 October 1861 and served over three years. He was in Company F of the Seventh New Hampshire Regiment, and was appointed wagoner. He died at Durham 18 March 1905 and was buried in Dover. He had a brother, Henry S. Palmer in the same company, aged 29, who was promoted from corporal to sergeant. Another brother, Asa D. Palmer, was in Company H of the Sixth New Hampshire Regiment. Henry S. Palmer removed to Maine. Their father was a brother to Ezekiel Leathers, who had sons, Ezekiel, George and Joseph in military service in the Civil War. All the Durham Palmers had their surname changed from Leathers to Palmer by the legislature before the war.

William E. Paul, son of James and Sarah (Jenkins) Paul, was born in Durham and enlisted 2 September 1862 in Company K of the Eleventh New Hampshire Regiment, at age of 18. He was promoted to corporal and transferred to the Veteran Reserve Corps, 1 September 1863, from which he was discharged 11 November 1863. He was killed near Shaw's House, Va., 16 January 1864.

Amos M. Smart, son of Enoch and Hannah (Glover) Smart, enlisted 18 August 1862, at age of 25, in Company K of the Eleventh New Hampshire Regiment. He died 6 April 1863, of typhoid fever, at Baltimore, Md., and was buried in the village cemetery at Durham.

Joseph W. Dame, son of Joseph and Maria, was born in Durham and enlisted, at age of 18, in Company G of the Eighth New Hampshire Regiment, 16 December 1861. He was promoted to corporal 15 March 1863. He reënlisted 4 March 1864 and was transferred to Company B, Veteran Battalion, 1 January 1865. He died at Durham, 18 May 1865.

John H. Doeg was a native of Durham. He enlisted 5 June 1862 in Company A, of the Ninth New Hampshire Regiment, aged 21. He was discharged at Washington, D. C., 13 November 1862, on surgeon's certificate of disability.

Silas Jenkins was born in Chatham, N. H., 30 March 1840. He was mustered into Company D of the First Massachusetts Volunteer Heavy Artillery, 4 April 1862, and was promoted to corporal 20 October 1863, near Fort Corcoran, Va. He was mustered out 3 April 1865. Described at enlistment as five feet, eight inches, in height, of light complexion, blue eyes, and sandy hair. After the war he lived at Natick, Mass., Greenland, N. H., and Durham since 1871. [See Genealogical Notes on the Jenkins family.]

Charles H. Bunker was born in Durham, 24 February 1839, and enlisted in the navy, 17 October 1864 for two years, on the United States ship *Vandalia* in Portsmouth Harbor. He acted as assistant ship's cook, or landsman. He was discharged 18 May 1866; was a pensioner and lived on the Mast Road, dying 25 May 1903. He was son of Ephraim and Dolly (Merrill) Bunker.

George W. Bunker, brother of Charles H. Bunker, was born in Durham, 13 October 1836. He also enlisted in the navy, 17 October 1864. He was assigned to the same ship as his brother, and was mustered out 18 May 1866. He died 29 November 1866.

James M. Stevens was a soldier, enlisting from some other town. He lived in Durham many years and carried the mails, receiving back pay and pension. The old Kincaid land was acquired by him and sold to Prof. George H. Whitcher. See page 153 and genealogy of the Stevens family.

Thus have been brought together, with painstaking research by Col. Lucien Thompson, some details of the military records of some of the best known volunteers of Durham. Others have been noticed in other chapters of this history, or incidentally mentioned in the Genealogical Notes. Earnest effort has been made to present the names of all Durham soldiers in the preceding alphabetical list. If any name has been omitted unintentionally no one will regret this more than the writer.

SKETCH OF CHURCH HISTORY

The earliest inhabitants of Oyster River Plantation worshiped at Dover Neck with all the settlers of ancient Dover, whither they went in boats. Here Richard Pinkham beat his drum to call the people to church, and here they listened successively to Revs. William Leverich, George Burdett, Hanserd Knollys, Thomas Larkham, and Daniel Maud. All this has been told at length in Dr. Quint's First Parish of Dover.

An agreement was made, 14 July 1651, that two ministers should be employed, at a salary of £50 each, Rev. Daniel Maud to remain at Dover Neck and another to be called to Oyster River. April 16, 1655, the town voted that all the rents of the saw-mills and a tax of two pence in the pound be devoted to the "comfortable maintenance of the ministry of Dover and Oyster River." A meeting house was built by Valentine Hill in 1655, near the oyster bed, on the south side of the river, about half way between the Falls and the Point. March 30, 1656, the town voted that "thear shall be a house at Oyster Reuer Billd neier the meeting house for the use of the menestrey, the demenshens as follareth, that is to say 36 feet long, 18 foett Broed, 12 foot in the wall, with too chimneyes and to be seutabley feneshed." This parsonage was burned by the Indians in 1694. The breadth of land on which it stood long remained parsonage land.

Rev. Edward Fletcher served as minister at Oyster River about one year and returned to England in 1657. He came back to Boston and died there about 1666.

In 1660 a committee chosen by the town and consisting of Valentine Hill, Richard Walderne, William Wentworth, Raphfe hall, Richard Otes, William ffurber, John Daues, Robert Burnom, William Willyames, and William Robords agreed that Oyster River should have for support of the ministry there twenty pounds from the rent of the grant at Lamprell River and two pence to the pound on taxes raised among its own inhabitants; that they should call their own minister and that he should be approved by the town or three elders; that the twenty pounds should be returned in case Oyster River were four months without a minister, they of Dover doing the like in a similar case; that fifteen pounds should be paid for preaching at Cochecho in

169

the winter season; and that Valentine Hill's now dwelling house
at Rocky Point should be within the line of division to Oyster
River.

The Rev. Joseph Hull was preaching at Oyster River in 1662,
as is incidentally learned from Quaker history. How long he
had been there does not appear, and he soon after left for the
Isles of Shoals, where he died in 1665. [See Hull family under
Genealogical Notes.]

There is no record of any preaching at Oyster River for the
next twenty years or so. Meanwhile disputes arose and some
thought that the best way to settle them would be to make
Oyster River a separate township. To this end the following
petition was sent to the General Court of Massachusetts in 1669:

To the much honored General Court assembled at Boston, May 17, 1669,
the humble petition of the inhabetants of Oyster Riuer is as followeth. The
consideration of your prudent and pious care for the carriing on the main end
of planting this colonie, in the settling religion and the promoting the welfare
of souls in evrie part of it subject to your government, doth embolden us (who
are also in some measure sensible of the great end we came into the world for
the advancement of the glory of God in our own salvation) to present this
humble address unto yourselues. It is not unknown unto some of you that
the inhabitants of Dover (of whom for the present we are part) manie years
taking into consideration the intolerable inconvenience of our traveil manie
myles, part by land, part by water, manie times by both, to the publick worship of God and the necessarie stay of manie of us from publick worship, who
can not undergo the difficulties of travel to it, it was then publickly agreed
and concluded that there should be two ministers at Douer, the one at Oyster
Riuer the other at Douer neck, as appears by a town act bearing date the
fourteenth of the fifth, fifty one, the means of calling and maintaining both
which are one, yet while we continue with them there is noe power improued
on our behalfe to that end, nor have we anie of ourselves, whereby we have a
long time and at present groan under intolerable inconveniences, our minis-
trie being greatly weakened, yea and hazarded thereby, having neither head
nor hand to move in calling when without or settling and maintaining when
obtained, and it being so difficult for us to attend civil meetings there that often
most of us cannot be there, whence we are in danger to be neglected or not
taken care of, nor our affairs so well provided for as if we were a township of
ourselves, we being in all two hundred and twentie souls, near fiftie families,
seventie and odd souldiers, a conuinient number of freemen, humbly request
this honoured Court to grant us that so beneficiall a priuilege of becoming a
township with such bounds as haue been alreadie granted us, or shall be
thought meet by this honored Court, and for this end we have sent John
Woodman, an inhabitant among us, and give him power to join anie with
him, as he shall see meet for ye managing of this our petition and prosecution
of our further reasons committed to him. Should this honoured Court whose
care we know extendeth to us among the rest of this colonie vouchsafe us
favourable answer to this request, whereas now our hands and hearts are
weakened in the work, prouision for the ministree at a stay, the old and young

in families too much neglected, others of good use who would join with us dis-
couraged until we become a township, some readie to leave us if things stand
as they doe, we trust upon your grant you will soon find our number increasing,
our hearts and hands strengthened in the work of God, our care more uigorous,
for an able orthodox minister, our families instructed according to law, ourselves growing in truth and peace to God's glorie, our content and your good,
and we shall not cease to pray God Almightie for a blessing upon you in all
your weightie concerns and subscribe ourselves

Yours in humble obseruance

John Bickford	John Meder
Richard York	Thomas Willie
John Daues	John Hill
William Beard	Thomas Edgerlie
Robert Burnam	William Perkinson
Phillip Chesley	Benjamin Matthews
Charles Adams	Davie Daniel
Steuen Jones	Thomas Drew
Walter Matthews	Joseph Field
Nicholas Doe	Zacharias Field
Vidua Elizabeth Drew	John Goddard
John Woodman	Matthew Williams
Edward Lethers	James Smith
William Randall	James Huckins
William Pitman	Robert Watson
Teag Royall	Patricke Jemison
Salathiel Denbow	James Thomas
Barnard Pope	Walter Jacson
Jos Stinson	Francis Drew
John Smith	

[N. H. Province Papers, Vol. I, pp. 308-310.]

The only effect of the above petition was that the town voted
to allow the inhabitants of Oyster River to build a meeting
house at their own expense and to appropriate their tax for the
ministry.   After 1675 two of the five selectmen were chosen from
Oyster River, and the people had their own minister, paid by the
town from the parish rates.   Who preached from 1662 till 1682
is not known.   There appears to have been no regular and
settled minister.   At the latter date John Buss began his labors
here as minister and physician, having previously served several
years at Wells, Me.   His house and library were burned at the
time of the great massacre in 1694.   If any early records of the
church existed, they were then destroyed, but there was no
organized church.   The following petition throws light on his
ministry and the character of the people:

To His Excellency Sam¹ Shute Esq' Gov' and Comander in chief in and over
his Majesties Province of Newhampshire and the Hon'ble his Majesties
Councell and Representatives convened in General assembly:

The Petition of John Buss of Oyster River most humbly Showeth—That
your Petitioner who for forty years successively has laboured in the work of
the ministry in that place even in the time of the late terrible Indian Warr
when many a score fell by the sword both upon ye right hand & the left, &
severall others forced to flight for want of bread during all which time did
watch ward and scout for the more ease and reliefe of ye Inhabitants; and
notwithstanding that, did constantly exercise in the garrison and one other
every Lords Day as god did enable him—But being now advanced to Seventy
Eight years of age and incompassed wᵗʰ a great many infirmities, and unable
to perform the usual Exercise of the Ministry the People have not only calld
another Minister but stopt their hands from my Subsistence, where upon he is
greatly reduced having neither bread to eat nor Sufficient Cloathing to in-
counter the approaching Winter—Wherefore your petitioner most humbly
supplicates that your Excellency, the councill, and Representatives would so
compassionate his miserable circumstances, as to order a competent maintenance during life—And your Petitioner shall ever pray,

                                                JOHN BUSS.

It was voted, 8 October 1718, that "the Selectmen of Dover
be advised to do their duty & take care of sd John Buss & supply
him with what he is in necessity of, according to ye law of this
Province; and that the Selectmen of Dover pay him twenty
pounds out of the town stock to be paid quarterly from year to
year." [N. H. Province Papers, Vol. XVII, p. 736.]

The following contract shows when the new meeting house
was built at the Falls, where the Sullivan monument now stands.
The original paper is in the possession of S. H. Shackford, Esq.,
of Boston. The signatures and names of witnesses have been
torn from it:

To all Christian People to whom this Covenant or instrument in writing Shall
Come and appear now Know ye that I John Tomson Sinior off the township
of Dover and Provance of new hempshir do heir by these presence grant Covenant and agree with the parties following that is to say Leuᵗ Jeramiah Burnum
Lefᵗ Abraham Bennick Jonathan Woodman Leuᵃⁿᵗ Joseph Davis Stephen
Jones Philip Chesley John Smith Junior of the foresaid towne and provane I
the forsᵈ John Tomson do by these presence bind and oblidge me to fram an
meeting house at Oyster river being in Length fortie foots and thirtie six foots
in bredth and twentie footes stude with an Belfree preportionble to the house
And to provyd and haill all the timber to the place appointed and that at or
before the thretie one day of July next ensewing the dait hereof And we the
forsaid parties do heir by these presence bind and oblidg our selves conjunctlie
and severalie to pay or cause to be payed to the forsaid John Tomson the sume
of sevintie three pounds money in Considderation of the work don by him in the
forsᵈ fram the one half to be payde in money when all the timber is haled and
laid in the place and the other half in money when the frame is fite to be

raised the fram and Belfree being in figur being lyke the new meet house off
Hemptowne And for the trew performanc heir of our hands and sealles this
nynteen day of Janwary one thousand seven hundred and twelve threeteen in
presenc of these witnesses.

Thus we know just when the first meeting house at Durham
Falls was built and something of its size and appearance. The
location was chosen not without opposition of the people living at
the Point. Indeed, another meeting house was built at the Point
soon after. July 3, 1719, Francis Mathes deeded to the inhabitants of the lower part of the parish of Oyster River one half of
an acre of land and road thereto two rods wide, on the south
side of the mouth of Oyster River, so long as the same should
be used for public worship. The deed shows that the frame
was then on the lot and was to be erected the next week. [N. H.
Province Deeds, XVI, 104.]

Dr. Quint at one time confused this meeting house at the Point
with the first one built at the oyster bed. He says it stood upon
a knoll on the land owned at the time of his writing by John
Mathes, at the extremity of Durham Point. "It is on the northern side of the road, but a few rods from the water side. It is
exactly north from the Mathes burial place; or rather this burial
place is at the edge of the knoll. The meeting house stood,
doubtless, within four or five rods, northerly of that inclosed burial
ground." This describes the location of the opposition meeting
house at the Point, built in the year 1719. There is no record
that any minister ever preached therein except the Rev. Hugh
Adams, and the frame was taken down some years after, trans-
ported to Portsmouth, and became part of the chapel of Dr.
Buckminster's church, as saith tradition recorded in the Smith
note-book.

The opposition between the Falls and the Point in the matter
of meeting house and ministry is further shown by the following
petitions. The first is signed by persons living nearer to the
Falls and was read 11 November 1715:

To the Hon.ble Geo. Vaughan, Esq., Lieut. Gov.r, Councill & representatives,
convened in General Assembly; The Humble Petition of his Maj.ties good
subjects, ye Inhabitants of that part of the town of Dover commonly
called Oyster river, Most humbly sheweth:
Whereas by mutuall agreem.t the Inhabitants of Oyster River have, for
many years past, made choice of their own Minister & paid his salary, according to ye conditions of s.d agreem.t as it appears in Dover town book of records,
refference thereto being had, & that ye selectmen of y.e town in generall, (two
whereof have been annually chosen w.thin y.e district of Oyster River) have all

along made rates for yᵉ severall ministers & taken care that the same be paid
to yᵉ sᵈ ministers according to the sallaries they have been agreed wᵗʰ for,
untill of late (viz.) yᵉ last year's rate is either by yᵉ neglect of yᵉ Constable
or yᵉ selectmen, or both, so retarded, that yⁿ minister wants subsistence;
nor can we understand that yᵉ selectmen have or are abᵗ to make any rate this
year for yᵉ minister; so that, either some few of us must maintain a minister
or we must be wᵗʰout one & return to Dover again, wᶜʰ was thought a hardship
more than forty years ago; & a liberty granted as above; & much more hard
will it be now we are increased to double the number we then were; so that
we most humbly pray yoʳ Honʳˢ will please to send for yᵉ Constable & selectmen to answer for yᵉ neglect as above, & that we may have powʳ granted us,
as yoʳ Honʳˢ were pleased at first to grant unto yᵉ Parish of Newington, (viz.)
to chuse three or five p'sons annually, wᶜʰ being chosen by a majority of voices
present at such election, may assess & tax yᵉ Inhabitants of our sᵈ Parish pro-
portionably in a rate for yᵉ discharging such a sallary as the Parish shall agree
to settle upon any minister of the Gospell that we at p'sent have, or hereafter
may be fixed amongst us; Likewise, that we may have powʳ to choose & settle
a schoolmaster upon such terms as we shall agree, wᵗʰout any other regard
to the town in generall than that yᵉ Constable annually chosen at the general
town meeting for collecting yᵉ Prov: tax in our district, may also collect our
Parish dues; And yoʳ Petitioners shall ever pray, as in Duty bound,
          Presented by Nath. Hill in behalf of ye subscribers.

Jeremiah Burnham	Elias Critchet, jun.
Stephen Jones	James Nock
Elias Critchett	John Tompson
Sampson Doe	Joseph Jones
Joseph Dudey	John Chesley
John Burnham	John x Sias,—mark.
David Davis	Job Renholds
Abraham Bennick	Samˡ Chesley, jun.
John X Gray,—mark	Samˡ X Chesley,—mark
John Rawlins	Cornelius Drisco
James Bickford	Robᵗ Burnham
Samˡ X Perkins—mark	Peter Mason
Willᵐ X Duly,—mark	Jonᵃ Simpson
John Doe	Robᵗ Tompson
John York	Samˡ Hill
Joseph Chesley	John X Renalls,—mark
John X Cromell,—mark	Joshᵃ X Davis,—mark
John Buss, jun.	Moses Davis, jun.
Philip Chesley	Willᵐ Leathers
Joseph Davis	Francis Pitman
John Tompson, sen.	Ely Demeritt
John Smith	Naphtali Kincaid
Willᵐ Jackson	James Jackson
David Kincaid	Tho: Wille
Jonathan Chesley	James Burnham
Valentine Hill	Robᵗ Huggins
Ichabod Chesley, jun.	Jonᵃ Woodman
Thomas Alin	

          [N. H. Province Papers, Vol. III, pp. 606–07.

As a result of the above petition the assembly ordered that the selectmen of Dover should "call to an account Jos. Davis, ye last years Constable for that town, in ye district of Oyster River" and see that he pay the money which he was obliged by the town warrant to collect, and that the selectmen see that a sufficient amount should be assessed for the support of the present minister, Mr. Buss, "untill another minister shall be called and settled in his room." This shows that John Buss had been regularly installed and had just claims upon the parish.

The following counter petition was presented by persons living nearer to the Point:

To the Honourable Governour Councell and Representatives Convened in Generall Assembly:

Whereas there is a petition Laid before your honours By part of the Inhabitants of oyster River Expecting thereby to Serve their own Interest though it be with much hardship to their Neighbours

We the Subscribers being Residents or free holders within those districts as in petition mentioned do humbly Referr to your Consideration these things as Reasons of objection against the said petition

1 That we ought to have had knowledge and to have Conferred with them about the said petition and whereas they keept it private from us it Showeth a Secret plotting and Contriving against our Interest

2 That Some of their Subscribers as we Suppose are neither Residents nor freeholders within the said districts

3 That Some of their Subscribers do denye part or all the petition

4 That if your honours Should See good to grant the Said Petition we being farmars Shall then be So bound up within those districts not haveing Room to advance our Estates—that we Shall not be able to subsist our familyes and to mentain a minister honourably

5 That a Settled Schoolmaster will be of no Service to us in teaching our Children because we do Live so Remote and are also divided with a River and Creeks—but rather as we have hitherto done to hire a Schoolmaster for ourselves and our adiacant neighbours

6 We are very well Satisfyed with our towns general Election of Select men Seeing we have two within our districts who are well acquainted with our affairs and we do count it hardship to be denyed our former privilidg

these Reasons we give haveing many others which we are Loath to trouble your honours withal—we humbly hope that you will not grant their petition— Except it be only to the petitioners and pleas to grant us the Libertyes that our fathers had first Settled in this place

We Remain your most Humble Servants

1	Thomas Edgerley Sen	35	John footman sener
2	John Meder Sen	36	John Smith junr
3	Edwerdus Wakeham		his
4	Thomas Drew	37	william X durgin
5	John Daniell		mark
6	Joseph Meder	38	James Thomas
7	Ichabod follet	39	Sallathan denbo
8	Joannes bunker	40	John: Smith Junr
9	John Williams	41	Samuill wille
10	Nathaneal Laimmos	42	francies Mathes Junr
11	william hill	43	william pitman
12	Henry Rines	44	John Rand
13	John Edgerley	45	Samuel Edgerley
14	Francis Mathes	46	Joseph Kent
15	Richard denbo	47	Thomas footman
16	thomas Rines	48	Joseph Stevenson
17	Samuel Williams	49	William Glines
18	Beniamen bodge	50	Batholomew Stevenson
19	Samll Smith		his mark
20	John meder Ju	51	James F Lingley
21	nicoles meder	52	william wormwood
22	Jno ambler	53	Eleazar Bickford
23	Moses davis Juner	54	Amos pinkham
24	John daves Sen	55	James Davis Juner
25	timmothy davis		his
26	Stephen Jonsones	56	John M Mondro
27	John Bickford		mark
28	beniamin mathes	57	Thomas Davis
29	Joseph Edgerly	58	Danel Mishorve
30	John willes Senior	59	Daniel Davies
31	John Rand	60	Joseph ginkens
32	John wille juner	61	James Davis the Son of Moses
33	John Pender		Davis
34	Beniamen Pender		N. H. Town Papers, XI, 567.]

This petition was probably presented to the Council by Messrs. Jno Meader and John Ambler, 20 December 1715, or 6 January 1715/6, when they appeared to prosecute the "Counter Petition." It was followed by further petitions which are here presented:

OYSTER RIVER PETITION PRESENTED APRILE 6TH 1716 MINUTED

To the Honble Geo: Vaughan Esq Lt Govr & Commandr in Cheif, to ye Honble the Councill & representatives of his Majties Prov: of N. Hampe, Convesned in Genl Assembly:—

The Petition of his Majties Good Subjects sundry ye Inhabitants of ye Parish of oyster river, wth in the township of Dover—

Most Humbly sheweth—

That, Agreeable to yo' hon' resolve (in Janr last for allowing y' Inhabitants of y' Parish of oysteriver till y' first sessions, of y' Gen': Assembly, after y' tenth of March next ensuing y' s' Janr in ord': to a friendly agreement & settlem' of y' differences among themselves.) We, the Subscrib' being Inhabitants of y' s' Parish of oyster river, or y' majr part of us, have had a meeting in s' Parish, at w' time & place, we chose a Committe, & impowered them y' s' Committe, as far as in us lay, to meet & treat w' a Committe from our adverse Pho in ord' to y' reconciling all misunderstandings & differences in s' Parish. The s' Committes had a meeting accordingly: thô altogether ineffectual & to no purpose, as we find by y' return of y' s' Committe on our behalf: Wherefore, we Psume once more to Address yo' hon' for yo' resolves on this matter as soon as yo' hon' in yo' wisdom shall see meet: (viz') y' we may be impowered to call a Parish meeting, in ord' to y' doing wh' may be necessary & proper for y' obtaining & Settling a minist' w' in our s' Parish: for y' y' means Pscribed by yo' Hon' for a reconciliation to be made among ourselves, has proved of none effect, & we plainly seeing y' a further suspension of yo' Hon' determination of this matter will much rather widen, than narrow this breach, Inasmuch, as our cheif end & design is y' speedy settlem' of a learned & authordox minist' among us, that we may no longer be sheep without a shepherd, but y' we may be in the use of means for y' Promotion of Christianity; w' is what our neighbours in y' low' part of our Parish are mainly making their Court against, w' is plainly demonstrable by their overtures made, which they so strenuously stand to, for a complyance w', (viz') y' a minister be treated w' to preach at both meeting houses, alternately w'in s' Parish, w' is so forreign from reason y' y' is no unprejudiced rationall man but w' will condemn so impracticable a project.—Our Neighboring Parish, in y' same town w' our selves are now destitute of a minist' as we are, who not long since had a settled ordained minist' among them, & who lost them upon no other consideration than for being urged & solicited to preach at two Places, w' he said was so unreasonable & hard upon him, as he could not Comply w' thereupon lost them: Now can it be reasonable to expect one man to settle und' such disadvantages & hardships w' was y' Pure cause of y' removal of another; & again y' requesting a minist' to preach at two places, is so rare y' tis scarce to be heard of, once in an age, & then you are as certain to hear a denyal as y' y' thing was asked w' Consideration (in our opinion) might have been a Sufficient disswasive to our Counter Petitioners, from insisting on so unreasonable a point: & thus y' case stands.

May it Please yo' Hon'.

We who have been at y' charge of y' new meeting house, so far as y' same is built & finished, have offered it to be a Parish house, w' this Proviso, y' all y' Inhabitants w' in s' Parish Joyn w' us in equall proportion compleatly to finish it & agree constantly to maintain y' Publick worship of God therein On y' Lords day, w' s' house stands in y' most convenient & proper place w'in s' Parish for y' accommodation of all y' Inhabitants in Gen': that now are, or hereafter may be settled w'in the same: —As to any information w' y' Hon' may have had relating to y' Scituation of s' meeting house, its being near y' head line of our Parish, they are false suggestions, for tis a positive truth, & in no wise to be doubted, y' our new meeting house stands nearer to

12

yᵉ lowᵉ part of sᵈ Parish, or next yᵉ sea, by two miles, than ic doth to our head line, so yᵗ if yᵉ sᵈ house is not well situated tis because it is not far upwᵈ enough towᵈ our head line, & tis certain yᵗ what further settlemᵇᵗˢ there will be in sᵈ Parish, or besure most of them will be above sᵈ meeting house wᶜʰ is argued from yᵉ far greater quantity of land's being above, than wᵗ is below sᵈ house,,

Nathˡ Hill	Ichabod Chesle
Jaramiah Burnham	Samuel Cheslie
Stephen Jones	Samuel Chesle Juner
Joseph Jones	John Chesle
Jonathan Woodman	William Letheres
	his mark
John Smith	James davis ‖
Philip Chesle	Elias Critchett Ju
William Jackson	Elias Critchett
Volintine Hill	Abraham bennick
John Footman	Eley demeret Junʳ.
Samson Doo	James Jakson
Cornalus Drisco	Thomus Wille
David Lyntard	Peter Mason
James Thomas	James Burnum
his	
John Ꙅ Gray	Thomas Allen
mark	
	his
Job Renels	John O Crommet
	mark
Robard Burnnum	Joseph Davis
John Burnum	his
John York	William ✕ Durgin
timothy Connor	mark
his mark	his
John s munsie	Jonathan ｜ Chesle
his mark	mark
Timothy T Moses	John Buss Juner
Joseph Daniel	Edward Letheres Siner
his	
John J Sias	James Bikford
mark	
John Doo	Joseph Chesle
William duly	James durgin
Robert Huckins	James Nock
	his
Robart tomson	Samuel ✕ Wille
John Rawlings	mark
John tomson	John Davies
	Joshua Davis
William burly	Josep Dudy
his	his
John ✛ Runals	frances ✕ footman
mark	mark

"A Petition Psened by John Ambler In behalf of sundry the Inhabitants of Oysteriver May 2ᵈ 1716." Evidently written by Elder Ambler himself in a neat quaint handwriting with small characters.

To the Honourable Lifᵗ Gouernour Councell and Representatiues conuened in generall Assembly:

May it please your honours

WHEREAS our brethren and neighbours with whome we would gladly haue had the oppertunity of agreeing according to your honours aduice haue now made their Second address to your honours by way of petition as if they are Rather willing to Inuade our priuiledg than to Comply by a brotherly or neighbourly agreement

We therefore his Maiestyes good and orderly Subjects do humbly Answer and Reply against their Second petition—as also Intimateing against their disorderly Carryings on—thus—

First—If our Late pastor at douer haue Left his Flock and people for Ends best known between god and himself and haueing Some Infermity of body did according to his thoughts declare that he supposed that his present Infermity might come by Reason of his often going between the two meeting houses we Referr this to your honours Consideration—whether his body was brought down by trauell—or whether the fatness and grossness of his body might not rather signifye to us that more Bodily Exercise might haue been helpfull against his Disease—it may be necessary therefore that we may all Consider the hand of god in it—that when the people began to trouble one another and to Inuade one anothers priuiledg then it pleased our god to Send our pastor away—for the great Shepherd & Command is that his pastor Sheep should Liue in Loue—therefore we do humbly hope that your honours will not account this any Reason why their petition Should be granted.

2 WHEREAS the Honoured Gouernour and Councell was pleased to alow us time to make offers of agreement to one another—we did offer to our neighbours ouerlooking their disorder in their building of their meeting hous—that if they would help us to build a ministers house on the personage that we would agree that the meeting should be Every other Sabbath day at the old meeting house untill Such time as we do build a new one and then to haue the meeting continued by turns att the two new meeting houses—and now whereas we haue offered so friendly and Brother Like to our neighbors who do Endeauour to Inuade our priviledg we humbly hope that your honours may Consider that our offer to them is not only fair but that we do Condescend and stoop to them in the same—and therefore that you will not see good to put us to any hardship or hazards by granting their petition—

3 WHEREAS our brethern and neighbors with whome we would gladly all along haue Joyned if they had gone to work orderly—and had placed their meeting hous something for our Conueniency and had not Set it so unreasonably beyond the Center of the Inhabitants haue now petitioned for a parish meeting we do with Submition to your honours humbly answer that as they haue without order or government built themselues a meetinghouse we do not desire to Inuade their priuiledg in the same neither are we willing to agree or Consent to a parish meeting in order to the Establishing of that meeting house that is Erected and built without either gouerment or order—but as we haue followed the order of our town and haue Closed with douer

180   HISTORY OF DURHAM

and haue thereby met with the advantage of mentaining our own priuiledg
also at oyster Riuer Lower meeting house by the Condecention and Labours
of the reuerend and faithfull Mr mathew Short—we do therefore humbly
hope that your honours will not see good to deny or deprive us of our priuiledg
and our Choyc till Such time as our neighbours minds do come down to a
Christian Complyance

1 FFRANCES MATHES	}	*in behalf*
2 JNᵒ AMBLER	}	*of*
3 JOSEPH MEDER	}	*the*
Aprill yᵉ 7ᵗʰ 1716. 4 JOHN WILLIAMS	}	*Rest*

We being conuened Together February yᵉ 20ᵗʰ 17$\frac{15}{16}$

These are to Certifye al men whom it may Concern That we the Subscribers
together with the men whome we do make Choyse of do Endeauor to stand
by our priuiledge in the ministry of the gospell in the Lower part of oyster
River and we the subscribers do meke choyce of and appoint four men or so
many of them as Shall be needfull. namely Serg Joseph Meder jur Frances
Mathes John Williams and John ambler to try to agree with our neighbours
at the head of the Riuer in order to an honourable agreement between us and
our neighbours. That we may by the blesing of god haue the gospell settled
amongst us

John Maider	John Edgerly
his X mark	William glines
Thomas Edgerley	John rand
William pirkins	Ichabod follet
his mark	Thomas Dauis
Joseph Kent	daniel danis
John Wille	Joseph hix
Thomas Footman	Beniamin bodge
Thomas Drew	William Hill
Moses Dauis Jun.	Samuel Williams
James Langle	Thomas Rines
James Dauis Junʳ	Joseph Bickfort
Stephen Jenkens	William Wormwod
John Bickford	Salathan Denmoor
John Kent	Abraham mathes
Beniamin Pinder	John pinder
Beniamin Mathes	abraham Stephenson
William Pitman	Joseph Edgerley
William Wille	Samuel Adams
Joseph Stephenson	Daniel Misharve
Samuell Wille	Napt. Kinket
John Daniall	Pl—— (illegible)
Samuel Edgerle	Philip Duly S
Francis Mathes	Philip Duly J
John Dauis sen	Joseph Meder Jun
John Wille Jun	John Williams
Edward Wakeham	John footman
timothy daues	Robard Kent
Nicolas Meder	Beniamin footman
peter denmor	Joseph footman
Eleazar Bickford	Joseph Danel iunr
William Clay	Joseph Jenkins

This petition was copied from the original document lent by Isaac W. Hammond—the original orthography preserved.

The original is now in possession of New Hampshire Historical Society.

The House voted, 4 May 1716:

That y* agreement of y* towns of Douer w*h y* part of y* toun called Oyster river ab* maintaining a minister among them at their own cost and charge be confirmed; & that y* new meeting house built there be y* place of y* public worship of God in that District, and established a Distinct parish with all rights and privileges belonging to a Parish, w*h full power & authority to call & settle a minister there & make assessm* for y* paym* of his Sallary & all other Parish charges, equally on y* several inhabitants within y* district & annually to chuse five p'sons, freeholders w*hin said Parish, to make y* tax & manage all affairs of the Parish, & y* p'sons so chosen, w*h a Justice of the Peace of this Province shall, whenever they see cause, call a Parish meeting to transact any matt* concerning y* Parish, & y* y* first meeting be on Monday y* 14th instant, at y* afores* New meeting-house, & y* John Thompson, y* present Constable of that district, notify y* inhabitants y** of; and further, that all p'sons that have of late years paid to y* minister there, shall continue to pay y* proportion to him y* shall succeed in s* office.

By order of the house of Representatives,

THEO ATKINSON, Cler.

Another petition, presented in 1717 and favorably considered was as follows:

The Petition of sundry of the Inhabitants of Oyster River in Dover, most humbly sheweth: That, Whereas sometime about a year and a half agoe, a Petition was then preferred to the General Assembly then sitting at Portsmouth, by several of our neighbors in said place to be made a District of themselves,—which being wrongly represented unto said Assembly, a vote thereupon was passed in both Houses, which being very prejudial unto the Interest of the whole:—

Your Petitioners therefore do humbly Pray that as there was only a vote, but no Act passed, that there may be a fair hearing of the whole matter before your Excellency in Council, that in your wisdom you may see good to Reverse the same; and that a reasonable proportion of land may be allotted us from the township of Dover, for a more amicable agreement between each other in carrying on the Worship of God; And seeing we have two meeting houses, we humbly pray that in wisdom you will so determine, that the Inhabitants

may go to each of them every other meeting day; And your petitioners shall
ever pray.

Thomas Edgerly	Moses Davis, jun:
Thomas Drew	John Rand
John Pinder	Edward Graham
	[Wakeham]
William Gloyns	Abraham Mathes
[Glines]	
Joseph Edgerle	John Bickford
Joseph Kent	William Wormwood
John Footman	Joseph Bickford
John Danel	Thomas Footman
John Kent	Joseph Stephenson
Samuel Edgerly	Joseph Footman
Benjamin Pinder	Thomas Davis
Benjamin Footman	Francis Mathes
Robert Kent	William Hill
John Davis	Daniel Misharve
Joseph Danel	Joseph Jenkins
Eleazer Bickford	Henery Rines
Stephen Jenkins	Daniel Davis
Benjamin Mathes	Thomas Rains
James Langle	James Davis
Francis Mathes, jun.	Abraham Stephenson
Nathaniel Randal	John Edgerle
Samuel Davis	Solomon Davis
John Williams, jun.	Salathiel Denbo
Joseph Hix	William Clary
Benjamin Body	Ichabod Follet
James Davis, junr.	William Rains
Samuel Williams	Samuel Smith
Bartholomew Stephenson	Philip Duly
Timothy Davis	John Williams
Zacharias Edgerly	John Ambler
Joseph Nudder	

In consequence of this petition we find the following voted
9 May 1718,

WHEREAS, the Parish of Oyster River, in Dover, have by a petition p'ferred
to the Gen¹ Assembly prayed that the ministry wᵗʰin sᵈ Parish may be settled,
so as may best accommodate the inhabitants of sᵈ Parish,

Voted, That the Minister for the time being do preach at both the old and
new Parish meeting-houses alternately in sᵈ Parish, excepting the three winter
months, wᶜʰ shall be left to the choice of sᵈ minister. [Provincial Papers, III,
730.]

The Rev. Hugh Adams records, under date of 8 June 1718,
"Lord's day (at my first preaching in the old meeting house,

by order of the Government) baptized Abraham Ambler, son of
Bro. John Ambler of Quochecho Ch," and again, under date of
19 October 1718, "at the old meeting house, then and there, he
being propounded in the Congregation publicly, the preceding
Sabbath for the same Office, and no person objecting in the mean
time, John Ambler, one of the Brethren of the Church, by the
Major votes, was chosen Deacon thereof." "The parsonage
lot where the old meeting house formerly stood" is mentioned in
1746.

A public parish meeting, held 1 April 1717, voted that Rev.
Hugh Adams should be their minister at a salary of £100 and use
of the parsonage, and ten acres of land granted by the town,
and £70 for his settlement to be paid within two years. The
committee met Mr. Adams soon after above date "in the eastern
chamber of Capt. Hill's house" and agreed with him for a salary
of £104, half of which was to be paid at the end of each six
months, according to depositions made by Joseph Davis, senior,
and Abraham Bennick, senior, in 1733. [See Court Files at Concord, N. H.]

The church at the Falls was organized and the Rev. Hugh
Adams was installed 26 March 1718, though Mr. Adams had been
preaching there nearly two years. Under that date Nathaniel
Hill and Stephen Jones wrote to the *Boston News Letter* as follows:

This day (through the smiles of Heaven upon us) we had a Church gathered
here, in the Decency and Order of the Gospel, and our Teacher, the Reverend
Mr. Hugh Adams was then consecrated and Established the Pastor thereof,
who then preached from that Text in Cant, 3, 11; we being then favored with
the Presence and Approbation of some Reverend Pastors of the next Neighboring Churches, with the Honoured Messengers thereof at the said Solemnity,
in our New Meeting-House, wherein they gave the Right Hand of Fellowship,
As witness our hands,

NATHANIEL HILL
STEPHEN JONES

The account of the same event, as given by the Rev. Hugh
Adams in the records of the church, is as follows:

March 26, 1718. This day through the grace of God our Saviour we had
a Church orderly gathered with the presence and approbation of the Pastors
and messengers of the churches of Newington and of Quochecho. The Rev^d
Mr. Jonathan Cushing prayed. I preached from the text Cant. 3:11, and made
a short prayer. Then I read our Confession of Faith and Church Covenant,
signed by me and Nathaniel Hill, Sampson Doe, Stephen Jones, Samuel Emer-

son, Joseph Dudley, John Allen, James Nock, James Langley and Samuel Edgerly.

Then the Rev⁴ Mr. Cushing, Pastor of Cochecho Chʰ being chosen by the Council of the Chᵇˢ present for it, made a decent speech to the said ten brethren and to the whole Assembly, whether any person had any thing to object against their establishing me the Pastor of this Church. No person then objecting, he propounded me to said Church as their Pastor. To which they all voting with uplifted hands, then I declared my acceptance.

Then the sᵈ Mr. Cushing read publicly the Testimonial of my former Ordination at Braintree, signed by the Rev⁴ Doctor Increase Mather and his son Doctor Cotton Mather of the old North Church in Boston, by Rev⁴ Mr. James Keith, the Hoary Pastor of the Church in Bridgewater, who laid their hands on my Head in that Ordination, Signed also by the Rev⁴ Nehemiah Walker, Pastor of the Church of Roxbury. Then the Rev⁴ Mr. Joseph Adams, by a pertinent speech, gave unto me as pastor and to our said Church the Right Hand of Fellowship. Then we sang Ps 132, 13-18. Then I pronounced the blessing.

The Rev. Hugh Adams, son of John and Avis of Boston, and probably of Scotch origin, was born 7 May 1676 and was graduated at Harvard College in 1697. He preached in South Carolina a few years and was ordained at Braintree, Mass., 10 September 1707. He was dismissed from there 22 August 1710 and preached at Chatham, Mass., 1711-1715. He preached for a short time in 1716 at Georgetown, Me., and in the latter part of that year came to Oyster River. He was something of a physician as well as minister and once practised the healing art on the famous Jesuit priest, Sebastian Ralle, at Georgetown. He says the cure was effected in three days and without charge.

During his pastorate of twenty-one years in Durham the church records, which cover only the first ten years, show that he added more than one hundred members to the church and baptized 694 persons. Surely this is a remarkable record and goes far to offset the discords and oppositions which troubled him during the last part of his ministry. He and Col. James Davis did not agree and both were probably too independent to be swayed by anybody else. The abusive language used by controversialists of those times is not a fair index of character but the fault of the age. Mr. Adams was strict in discipline and very plain and unsparing in his written statements, yet he had a kind and sympathetic heart. His interpretations of Scripture were sometimes fanciful, judged by modern standards, yet the habit of the century was to make an odd passage mean anything

that the preacher wanted to say, to which the allegorical method
lent aid.   He thought that he had prevailing power in prayer as
well as Elijah, the logical consequence of a literal interpretation,
and once he, too, shut up the heavens in drought for three months.
In the afflictions of his opponents he saw the hand of God, just
as the Hebrew prophets saw it in national calamities.   Indeed,
his church records and petitions to the General Assembly show
that he was saturated with the language and spirit of the Old
Testament more than of the New.   He was eccentric and opin-
ionated, spoke his mind freely and so roused opposition, yet the
great majority of the parish evidently stood by him.   He records
the observance of a day of fasting and prayer "kept by our
church at the house of Dea. John Williams on account of some
preternatural troubles about their house," when he preached from
II Cor. xii: 7 and I John iii: 8.   Evidently he considered the devil
to be the author of said troubles.   This service was a sort of
exorcism.

He had difficulty about collecting his salary, leading to considerable litigation, and no settlement was reached till after his
death.   Twice he sued the town and brought suit in court against
his successor, Mr. Gilman, for appropriation of lands granted to
the minister.   He was dismissed by Council 23 January 1739,
yet he continued to preach at the church at Durham Point.
The town voted, 28 March 1743, "that Mr. Hugh Adams shall
have twenty pounds of the new issue bills of credit yearly during
his abode in the town of Durham, Provided he set down satiesfied
and Preach no more in said town for the futer, but if he preach
any more in s^d town then this vote to be thereby voide and of
none effect."   This is believed to be the only historical instance
where a town has tried to hire a minister to stop preaching.

A petition was presented by Francis Mathes, 15 February 1739/
40, or less than a month after Mr. Adams' dismissal, signed by
fifty-seven persons, about all of the male inhabitants of the
Point and of Lubberland, asking for a separate parish.   Their
request was denied, yet the petition shows that Mr. Adams could
not have been an unworthy nor an unpopular man to have been
quite unanimously desired as their minister by a section embrac-
ing half of the town, and doubtless he had many friends in the
other half.   It shows also who the residents of the Point and of
Lubberland were in 1740:

Petition of Frances Mathes and others for a new parish in Durham. To His Excellency Jonathan Belcher Esq' Governor and Commander In Chief in & over His Majesty's Province of New Hampshire in New England, the Honble His Majesty's Council and House of Representatives for said Province in General Court Convened Jany 31st 1739. The Petition of Sundry of the Inhabitants of the Town of Durham in Said Province Humbly Shews,

That the Inhabitants of the Said Town are divided into two parties Respecting their Ecclesiastical affairs, the One such as adhere to the Reverend Mr Hugh Adams the late Minister of Said Town & who continues so to the said party, the other (who are much the greater) are such as have oppos'd his Standing in that Relation to them, & still Continue to do so. That notwithstanding it was the opinion & Result of the late Ecclesiastical Council held there that it would not be Expedient for him to be any longer the Minister of the said Town yet considering his former Services his advanced years and the unhappy Circumstances of himself & family they Earnestly Recommended and press'd it upon the said Inhabitants that they should Liberally make provision for his Support during the Stay of himself & Family among them,—which is what would be highly agreeable to your Petitioners,

That altho Several propositions have been made touching that matter yet nothing has been agreed on nor any care taken to secure the performance thereof in the manner Recommended as aforesaid,

That your Petitioners apprehend it would be a great Indecency if he who was once & so long the Minister of the said Town should have no other Provision made for his Support than what the Law provides for one of the poor of the Town and that he should be Reduced to a Necessity of Depending upon such a Subsistence,

That your Petitioners are desirous still to sit under his Ministry and are willing to support him & his family Suitable to his character & Station among them, and conceive that his being comfortably supported would have a good Tendency & be the Means of making peace in the Town (respecting Ecclesiastical matters) and would keep all parties quiet & easy. But your Petitioners however willing are not of ability to afford such Support while they are Subject to & pay toward the Maintenance of another Minister in the Town.

Wherefore they most Humbly pray that they with Such others of the said Town as will associate with them (not Exceeding the one half) may be Exempted from paying toward the Support of any other Minister & may be discharged from all charges of that nature laid upon them by Law by their Opponents from the time of the aforesaid Result and may be Incorporated as a Parish during the Life of the said Mr. Adams in order to maintain him & his Family & to Enjoy the Benefit of his Ministry.

Or that the Town in General may be Obliged to afford him a Comfortable Subsistence during his abode there Or that Such other Method may be pursued as this Honble Court in their Great Wisdom & goodness shall think proper for

the peace of the Town & the Ease of that aged Gentleman—and your petitioners as in duty bound shall ever pray &c.

Francis Mathes	Towerthey Durgin
Thomas Footman	Joshua Durgain
Thomas Drew	Hezekiah Marsh
Joseph Wheeler	Joseph Duda
William Lord	Joseph Duda Jun.
John Edgerly	Benmor Duda
Stephen Wille	John Cromet
Joseph Stevenson	Phillip Cromet
John Footman	David Davis
Joseph Footman	Jacob Tash
Benjamin Pender	Isaac Mason
John Durgen	Nathaniel Watson
Benjamin Durgen	Nathaniel Frost
Benjamin Pinder Jun.	John Smart
Francis Durgen	John Mason
Joseph Drew	Benjamin Burdet
John Kent	Pumfret Whitehouse
Moses Edgerly	Vallitin Hill
John Kent Junr	Samu Adams
John Drewe	Saml Willey
Benjamin Benet	Joseph Bickford
James Durgain Jun	Abraham Benneck
William Durgain	Benjamin Benneck
Willm Durgain Jun	William Wormwood
Joseph Durgain	Joseph Edgerly
Thomas Bickford	William Accason
Abraham Stevenson	Joseph Edgly
John Bickford	

[N. H. Province Papers, V, 23.]

It is easy to suspect that the real motive of this petition was not so much a loving regard for the Rev. Hugh Adams as it was the desire to have regular preaching at the Point, to be independent of the Falls, and to have their own sweet way in matters ecclesiastical.

Mr. Adams was not one of those "safe" men who walk in "the middle path between right and wrong." He followed his convictions and was sometimes mistaken. The Ecclesiastical Council that dismissed him censured him for "his great presumption in pretending to imprecate the divine vengeance and that the calamities that had befallen sundry persons were the effect of his prayers." They concluded that "it would not be for the honor of Christ or the interest of religion nor any way

SAMPLES OF DURHAM SCENERY

answer to the great ends of his ministry in this place for him to
continue any longer in it." He was now sixty-three years of
age, and doubtless oppositions had made him nervous and a
little more unbalanced than usual. Perhaps he needed sympathy
and coöperation; instead, after twenty-three years of faithful
service, he was censured for his eccentricities and dismissed to
poverty in his old age. This must have greatly rejoiced the heart
of Col. James Davis and other opponents.

It has been several times published that the Rev. Hugh Adams
died in 1750, but the following town record places his death two
years earlier. He was living 22 July 1748:

At a town meeting held the 12 day of December 1748 at the meeting house
at Durham Falls . . . Voted that a Committee shall be chosen to agree
with Mdam Adams & to fully settle all affairs & Demands with s⁴ Mdam
Adams widow concerning her Demands on the Town for Mr Adamses sallary.
Then voted Leut Robt Burnum, Mʳ Daniel Rogers & John Woodman be
accomtee for that service to agree & settle the affair.—Teste John Woodman
Cler. Pʳ temp.

July 9 1750. Voted that the funeral Charges of the Revᵈ Mr. Hugh
Adams shall not be paid. Leut Stephen Jones, John Woodman & Daniel
Rogers chosen accomte to agree with Susannah Adams or her son Samuel
Adams concerning the arrearages of Reverᵈ Hugh Adams Deceased. [Town
Records, Vol. I, pp. 25, 31.]

The committee reported 28 May 1751, that the town should
pay £262, old tenor, to Susannah Adams, administratrix.
Whether the town ever paid this amount does not appear.

Since the above was put in type additional information has
been obtained concerning the Rev. Hugh Adams. In 1725 he
wrote, "A Narrative of a Particular Faith and Answers to
Prayer," and offered it to the authorities of New Hampshire for
publication. In it he reviews the main events of his life, in
which he sees the gracious providence of God and claims that
God has done wonderful things for him in answer to prayer.
We learn that he had an extensive practice as a physician in
South Carolina, Massachusetts and Oyster River during twenty-
three years, and that by this profession, as much as from his
salary as a minister, he was enabled to support his family. He
speaks of "my former Travels into several Countreys of Europe
and Africa, as well as of the Continent and Islands of America,
my instruction from Sundry able Physicians & Chirurgions, my

hard studies in the best Books, and my so long Practice and
Experience" as the sources of his medical skill, declaring that he
was then toward the end of his forty-ninth year of age. Incidentally he says that he arrived in South Carolina in July or August
1698 and was sick several months in getting himself seasoned to
the country and climate. The following spring, 1699, he was
"called to settle at a large parish on both sides of Wandoe River,
where I preached two years having a Meeting House on each
side thereof builded on purpose for me. One about 13 miles
from Charles Town N. N. E. The other about 7 miles distant
about half a mile above the head of that river." The people
paid him about half his salary, which occasioned his getting in
debt sixty pounds "for the maintenance of four of my young
brethren and sisters being orphans and left to my Brotherly
care." This led to "my first Remove soon after my Marriage
in the year of our Lord 1701." He then preached for a while
in Ashley River parish, and thence he removed to South Edisto
River parish, fifty miles from Charleston. "My second son was
born there." He returned to New England in 1706, leaving
wife and boy ten months old. He preached his first sermon in
Braintree 27 October 1706.

This *quasi* autobiography relates many interesting things about
the people of Oyster River. At the time of the Indian War,
1724, he procured two horns made of the horns of cattle and
employed his "two younger sons in sounding of them when my
eldest son was gone forth a volunteer into our wilderness against
our said Indian enemies, wherein he so prospered." This was
done because of some fanciful interpretation of an odd passage
in the Old Testament. He says that in consequence "not one
of my family hath been killed, wounded, or captivated."

He tells of many remarkable cures that had been effected in
his different parishes by his medical skill and in answer to prayer,
naming the following at Oyster River, Abednego Leathers, Mary
wife of Joseph Davis, Mary wife of Benjamin Glitten at the
house of Richard Hilton seven miles away in Exeter, whither he
had been summoned at midnight, and where a son was born and
immediately baptized Benjamin, William Randall, John Buss,
Jr., Joseph Mason, wife of John Pearl of Dover, Mary wife of
Lieut. Jonathan Chesley, Moses Furber of Newington "at the

house of my near neighbor Captain Hill," 30 June 1724, Lieut.
Ichabod Chesley, widow Elizabeth Smith, James Bunker cured
of rheumatism and pestilential fever whereof his father died a
little before. "His foolish Quaker aunt had given him stone
horse dung in wine." This was in the summer of 1724. Others
cured were "my neighbor Jonathan Thompson's son, October
6, 7, 8, 1724," Hannah wife of Philip Chesley "Lieutenant of
the Troop of horse," February 1723, William Dam's wife,
Theodore Atkinson, Esq., of Newcastle, Edward Evans of Dover,
and John Dennet of Kittery, showing that he had a wide medical
practice. He does not give the names of those who died under
his treatment.

He declares that from childhood he was afflicted with many
diseases and suffered from almost all the ills that flesh is heir to,
including melancholia, and that his "particular faith" in connection with acquired medical skill had saved him out of all his
distresses. It is easy to see that his mind was unbalanced at
times in consequence of physical infirmities, and thus his impa-
tience and eccentricities are accounted for.*

The parish soon found a successor and, 14 September 1739,
voted that Nicholas Gilman be the settled minister. He was
born in Exeter, 18 January 1707/8, son of Judge Nicholas Gilman. He was graduated at Harvard in 1724 and was installed
at Durham 3 March 1742. Lieut. Jonathan Thompson, Joseph
Wheeler and Benjamin Smith were the committee that secured
him. Mr. Gilman's health was poor and for three years he was
assisted by the Rev. Joseph Prince of Barrington, who was
blind from his fourteenth year of age. He preached again at
Durham after the dismissal of the Rev. John Adams, in 1778.
He died in 1791 at advanced age and was buried in the same
church at Newburyport in which are the remains of the Rev.
George Whitefield.

Mr. Gilman was a man of piety and much beloved, yet he was
deluded by a fanatic named Woodbury, who used to arouse
him by night and lead him into the woods and swamps to pray
till morning. Jacob's wrestling with the Angel has prompted

* Manuscript in library of the Massachusetts Historical Society, Boston.

many to do likewise. Some extravagancies and disorders arose
in the church at Durham, which are best set forth in the diary
of the Rev. Samuel Chandler:

"Aug 20, 1746. I set out on a journey to Durham to a fast at y⁴ desire
of the church there, they being under difficulty. I called Mr. Wise [of Ber
wick] by the way We got to Durham about 10 o'clock, cloudy rainy weather
& the people not much expecting any minister would come had got into the
meeting house and were praying. Mr. Prince, a blind young man supplies
them during their Pastor's silence & neglect to discharge his pastoral office.
When we went into the pulpit Mr. Gilman went out & went into the pew.
I began with prayer. I was under some restraint. Mr. Wise preached from
John 15. 5, & concluded with prayer. In the exercise were a number, 4 or 5,
that were extraordinarily agitated. They made all manner of mouths, turning out their lips, drawing their mouths awry, as if convulsed, straining their
eye balls, & twisting their bodies in all manner of unseemly postures. Some
were falling down, others were jumping up, catching hold of one another, extending their arms, clapping their hands, groaning, talking. Some were approving what was spoken, & saying aye, so it is, that is true, 'tis just so, &c.
Some were exclaiming & crying out aloud, glory, glory. It drowned Mr. Wise's
voice. He spoke to them, entreated them, condemned the practice, but all
to no purpose. Just after the blessing was pronounced, Mr. Gilman stood up
to oppose some things that had been said. He read 1 John 1. 8 & 9th verse,
& began some exposition on the 9th verse what God hath cleansed let no man
call unclean & went on to prove perfection as attainable in this life. Then
Mr. Wise rose up and there was some argumentation between them. Mr.
Gilman took some particular text & turned it contrary to the general current
of scripture. Then we went into the house & were entertained. Mr. Gilman
came in & after him a number of those high flyers, raving like mad men, re-
proaching, reflecting. One Hannah Huckins in a boasting air said she had
gone through adoption, justification & sanctification & perfection & perseverance. She said she had attained perfection & yet had a bad memory: I
reasoned the point with her, but presently she broke out into exclamations
'Blessed be the Lord, who hath redeemed me, Glory, glory, glory, &c. fell to
dancing round the room, singing some dancing tunes, jiggs, minuets, & kept
the time exactly with her feet. Presently two or three more fell in with her &
the room was filled with applauders, people of the same stamp, crying out in
effect Great is Diana of the Ephesians. One of these danced up to Mr. Gilman & said, Dear man of God, do you approve of these things? Yes, said he,
I do approve of them. Then they began to increase & the house was full of
confusion, some singing bawdy songs, others dancing to them & all under a
pretence of religion. It is all to praise God in the dance & the tabret. One
woman said it was revealed to her that the minister that was to come to the
Fast was one that did not know Joseph, & that Joseph was Mr. Gilman. These
mad people prophesied that there would be great trials at the falls, that is at
the meeting house that day. . . . Mr. Gilman justified their proceedings.

They do it out of a good design, he says, and that there is no sanctity in tunes, and that the reason we cannot approve of it is because there is no light in us &c. &c. . . . A little after dark all left the house & went out into the streets when they held it till near ten o'clock. These are but some general hints. O awful melancholy scene, O tempora, O mores.

Aug. 21. I preached from Gal. 2. 20. The people appeared very devout, excepting those that were of Mr. Gilman's party. They as yesterday made wry mouths & extraordinary gestures of body, often crying out aloud, but generally approving. I desired & entreated, if they loved the souls of sinners, that they would suffer them to hear what I had to offer to them, but all to no purpose. At length the authority took hold of one & the rest all jumpt up & out they went, crying out & railing & made a hideous noise abroad, but we finished & went into the house.

Mr. Gilman says he has a witness within him that I neither preached nor prayed with the Spirit. I told him I had a witness within myself that I did both. He said how can that be when you have your thumb papers, & you could hardly read them? He seemed to speak by way of reflection & an air of disdain. Mr. Gilman says he can't receive those that don't receive Woodbury & all those persons in all their extravagancies. He allows that a regenerate man may have a strong persuasion & confidence in lesser & yet be deceived. Mr. Gilman tarried but a little while & went away & soon after him all the rest. One Mr. Woodman told me that two of these people got together by the ears last night. They struck one another with their fists, saying you are a devil & you are a devil. The persons afflicted are John & James Huckins & their wives, Ralph Hall & wife. Capt. Hardy, Scales, &c.

Such abnormal manifestations of religious enthusiasm were once very common and still are known among uneducated populations. They are best explained by erroneous teaching accompanied by hypnotic suggestion. Most people, whether awake or asleep, do and say as they are taught by a few leaders, wise or otherwise.

The Convocation of Ministers of New Hampshire, in 1747, appointed a committee to look into the troubles of the church at Durham, who reported that they found the affairs of the church in a very unhappy situation:

That their Rev⁴ Pastor Mr. Gilman had for a considerable time desisted from the work of the Ministry among them, & by all their Endeavours they could not prevail with him to reingage in s⁴ Work; but that they had had for the most part preaching on Lord's Days, & that Mr. Wooster still continued to preach to them. They also informed us that a considerable Number of their Communicants & others of their Congregation had separated from them & held a separate meeting in a private House in the Town on the Lords Days & at other Times. And the s⁴ Committee was further informed by divers of s⁴

Church that at s^d separate Meeting there were very disorderly vile & absurd things practiced (such as profane singing and dancing, damning the Devil spitting in Persons Faces whom they apprehended not to be of their Society &c) greatly to the Dishonor of God & Scandal of Religion.

(Signed)   JON⁂ CUSHING
                                                JOHN MOODY.

It may be that the spitting in the faces of some persons was not intended as an insult, but to drive out evil spirits, since the same thing is now practised in some countries at the baptism of infants. I have often seen it in the Baptistery at Florence, Italy. The "profane singing and dancing" might have been nothing more than has been practised by Shakers, like the old Israelites praising the Lord with the tabret and with the dance. Many forms of worship seem absurd and vulgar till we get used to them, and then they are too good and sacred to be disturbed.

The Rev. Joseph Roberts preached for a short time after Mr. Gilman ceased to officiate. The latter died of consumption, 13 April 1748. Sickness probably had much to do with his mental disorders. "He was buried at Exeter, whither he was carried in procession by the young men of the town. He was greatly beloved for the excellencies of his character and disposition." His seems to have been a case of religious hallucination, caused by feeble health, overstrain of nerves, and the friendly influence of an unwise adviser. No records have been preserved of the results of his ministry, and we know nothing about baptisms, marriages and deaths during his term of office. In those days such records were the minister's private property, which usually he took away with him.

Mr. Gilman married, 22 October 1730, Mary, daughter of Bartholomew Thing of Exeter, who died 22 February, 1789. They had children: Bartholomew, born 26 August 1731; Nicholas, born 13 June 1733; Tristram, born 24 November 1735, who was graduated at Harvard and became minister of the church at North Yarmouth, Me.; Joseph, born 5 May 1738, who became a judge in Ohio and died 14 May 1806, and Josiah, born 2 September 1740, who died 8 February 1801. The inventory of Mr. Gilman's estate shows that he had a good library, considerable real estate in Exeter, valuable furniture and one Negro slave, besides three gold rings and a pair of gold buttons, etc.

It was during the pastorate of Mr. Gilman that the parish of Madbury was formed of people living in Dover and Durham. The petition for the same was addressed to the Governor, Council and House of Representatives, convened the 10th day of May 1743, and was as follows:

The Petition of Sundry Persons Inhabitants of the Westerly part of the Town of Dover & the Northerly part of Durham in said Province Humbly Shews That your Petitioners live at such a distance from the meeting houses in their Respective Towns as makes it difficult for them & their Families to attend the Public Worship there especially in the Winter & spring seasons of the year which induc'd a number of your Petitioners some years since at their own cost to Build a meeting house situated more conveniently for them where they have some times had preaching in those seasons of the year at their own expense, tho they were not Exempted from paying their Proportion at the same time to the standing Minister of the Town.

That the Towns aforesaid are well able as your Petitioners apprehend to bear their annual charges without the assistance of ye Petitioners and that they might be Incorporated into a new Parish whereby they might be accommodated their children & servants (as well as themselves) have more Frequent opportunity of attending Publick Worship and all of them Keep the advantages of such an Incorporation which considering their present circumstances they think would not be a few, and the Towns not Injured.

That your Petitioners conceive a parish might be erected with out prejudice to the other parts of the Town of Dover by the Following Boundaries viz., Beginning at the Bridge over Johnsons Creek so called, where the dividing Line between Dover and Durham Cross the Country Road & from thence running as the said Road runs until it comes even with Joseph Jenkins his house & from thence to run on a North West & by North course until it comes to the head of said Township which boundaries would comprehend the estates and habitations of ye Petitioners living in Dover & the making of a parish there will greatly contribute to the settling the lands within said Boundaries & those that Lay contiguous as well as be very convenient for ye Petitioners. Wherefore they most humbly pray that a parish may be erected & Incorporated by the Boundaries aforesaid with the usual powers & Priviledges & that such of ye Petitioners as live within the Town of Durham may have liberty to Poll off into the same, or that such a part of the said Township may be annexed thereunto which would be the better way as will accommodate the Remote settlers in said Township near the said Boundaries as well as your petitioners

or that they may be Relieved in such other way & method as this Honble
Court shall see fit, & yor petitioners as in duty bound shall ever pray &c.

Thomas Wille	John Huckins
John Roberts	James Jackson
Samuel Davis	Zachariah Pitman
Samuel Chesley	Ely Demerit
Thomas Bickford	John Foay Jr.
Daniel McHame	Solomon Emerson
James Huckins	Jacob Daniel
Ralph Hall	Joseph Rines
William Bussell	Benjamin Hall
Azariah Boody	William Demeret
Timothy Moses	William Allen
	his
John Demeret	Nathiel O Davis
	mark
Zachariah Edgerly	Joseph Daniel
Francis Drew	Samuel Davis Jr.
Daniel Young	Jonathan Hanson
William Twombly	Robert Evens
Isaac Twombly	Jonathan Daniel
Joseph Evans Jr.	William Hill
John Evens	Stephen Pinkham
Henry Bickford	Benjamin Wille
Henary Bussell	John Rowe
Joseph Hicks	Hercules Mooney
John Tasker	Joseph Twombly
Derry Pitman	Abraham Clark
Paul Gerrish Jr.	Joseph Jackson
John Bussell	James Clemens
Job Demeret	William Dam Jr.
David Daniel	Morres Fowler
James Chesle	Robert Wille
Reuben Chesle	Abel Leathers
Henery Tibbetes	

[N. H. Province Papers, Vol. V.]

Nothing resulted from this petition and another petition was presented 17 January 1754, and Madbury was incorporated as a parish 31 May 1755, and impowered to raise money for the separate support of preaching, schools and paupers, but remained as before with respect to province taxes, highways, etc. This parish was vested with full town privileges 20 May 1768. The

second petition was signed by the following, here arranged alphabetically:

Azariah Boodey,
Charles Bickford,
Henry Bickford,
Thomas Bickford,
Ebenezer Buzzell,
Jacob Buzzell,
John Buzzell,
John Buzzell Jr.,
Joseph Buzzell,
Henry Buzzell,
William Buzzell,
William Brown,
Samuel Chesley,
James Clemons Jr.,
James Crown,
James Davis,
Samuel Davis,
Joseph Daniels,
Eli Demeret,
Ebenezer Demeret,
John Demeret,
John Demret Jr.,
Job Demeret,
William Demeret,
Zachariah Edgerley,
Lieut, Emerson,
John Evens,
William Fowler,
Paul Gerrish,
William Gliden,
Thomas Glovier,

Reuben Gray,
Capt. Hicks,
James Huckins,
John Huckins,
Robert Huckins,
William Huckins,
James Jackson,
James Jackson Jr.,
Joseph Jackson,
Antony Jones,
Benjamin Leathers,
Joseph Libbey,
Timothy Moses,
Timothy Perkins,
Zachariah Pitman,
John Roberts,
Joseph Ryans,
John Smith,
Ebenezer Tasker,
John Tasker Jr.
Ens. John Tasker,
William Tasker,
Nathaniel Tibbetts,
Isaac Twombly,
Joseph Twombly,
William Twombly Jr.,
Benjamin Willey,
John Winget, Jr.,
Daniel Young,
Noah Young.

The next settled minister was the Rev. John Adams, son of
Matthew Adams of Boston and nephew of the Rev. Hugh
Adams. He was born 19 June 1725 and was graduated at
Harvard College in 1745. The two factions in the church that
existed in the time of his uncle's pastorate were still quarreling,
and old Mr. Adams' party, "who had for a long time been
separated and were a distinct body by themselves," were thought
by the other party to have been too influential in the choice of
the new minister. Gradually the opposition subsided with the
lapse of time and the departure of some from the church militant.
The articles of agreement with the Rev. John Adams contain
some interesting touches of history:

Articles of Agreement made and Concluded upon the third day of October ano que Domeney 1748 and in the twenty Second year of his maiesties Reign Between John Adams now Residing in Durham in the provence of newhampshire Clerk of the one Part & Philip Chesle David Davis Stephen Jones Jun Benj* Smith Job Runals Nath Rendal Joseph Wheler Jos Glidden Sam¹ Wille Daniel Rogers Benj* Mathes & Joseph Sias all of Durham afore said as a Committee of the said town lawfully chosen & appointed to contract & agree with the said John Adams for his sallerey as the Gospel minister of the s⁴ town of the other part as follows that is to say where as the said town have lately invited & caled the said John Adams to settel among them the inhabitants of s⁴ town in the office & capasaty of a Gospel minister to them which call the said John Adams has been Pleased to accept & we being chosen for ye purpose afore said Have bargained & agreed and by the Presents Do Covenant Bargain & agree to & with the said John Adams to pay him and the s⁴ town shall hereby be obliged to pay the sd John Adams the yearly salary of five hundred pounds old tenor bills of Public Credit during the time that he shall continue in the gospel ministry in the sd town the sd yearly salary to commence the twenty fifth day of March next and for the Preventing of iniustice & dispute between the sd town & the said John Adams by the alteration & change of the Value of the said bills it is further agreed by the sd parties to these Presents that the sd bills shall be fixed according to the following Rules of Computation with Respect to the said sum that is to say comparing the same with Indian Corn at thirty shillings old tennor a bushel Pork at three shillings old tenor a pound & beaf at one shilling and six pence old tennor a pound and in case the sd specis of Provision shall be dearer & the Price thereof Rise then the said yearly salary shall be increased & such a farther sum added thereunto as shall be equilent & Proportionable t) the Rising & Increas of the Price of such Provision above the Respective Prices herein before mentioned and in case the prices of the said Kinds of Provision shall fall & be lower than the Respective sums afores⁴ than the sd yearly sallery shall be abated & such a sum deducted from the same as shall be Equelant & Proportionable to such fall & lowering of the sd Prices and in case one of said Kinds of Provision only shall alter in the price either derer of cheper then one third of the sd sum of five hundred pounds shall folow the sd price or the Rule of that Kind of Provision & be either increased or deminished in Proportion as aforesaid & the other Remaining the same then two thirds of the sd five hundred Pounds shall folow the said alteration in manner aforesaid—

AND it is hereby farther covenanted & agreed between the sd Parties to these Presents that ye said John Adams shall have hold & enioy the Parsonage house which the late Reverant Nicolas Gilman occupied & improved in said Durham and the ten acres of Parsonage land lying near to sd house which he improved also being part of the Parsonage lands belonging to sd town during the time of his ministry as afore said & the said John Adams doth hereby covenant and agree to and with the sd Commite that he will accept the afore said sum of five hundred Pounds to be paid in manner afore said with the mprovement of the said house and land as afore said in full of all demands and claims for salary from the said town for his service in the capasaty afore s l and that he will Keep the sd house in good tenentable Repair at his own

own proper cost & charge. In testemoney whereof the said Parties to these Presents have hereunto interchangably set their hands and seals the day and year first above written.

Then follow the signatures of the persons above named. The acceptance of his call is also spread upon the town records as follows:

DURHAM, NEW HAMPSHIRE, October third 1748.

WHEREAS it has pleased the Soverign Ruler & Dysposer of all things to incline and dispose the generalaty of the People of this place to attend to my Preaching amongst them with such satisfaction & approbation as that the freeholders of said town at there meeting held here on the   day last Past were very unanemus in giving me an invitation & call to settel among them in the work of the ministry & to undertake & ingage in the office & duty of the Gospell ministry of the said town and after due Deliberation upon this weighty affair & considering the great unaninity of the people in this case which is the more Remarkable because of former Divisions among them I esteem the voice of the people in this case to be the voice of God and ading to this some particuler call from God & secret intimation to my own Breast inclining me thereto I accept of the said invitation & call Promising as the Lord shall anable me faithfulley to the utmost of my ability to Discharge the Duties of that defficult and Important affair and in all things according to my Power to behave my self as becoms a minister of the Gospele of Jesus Christ & to be contented with such Satiesfaction Salery and Reward as shall be agreed between the Comtee of ye town and my self. In testemony where of I hereunto subscribe my name as in the Presents & in the favor of the Lord the day and year above writen—

JOHN ADAMS.

On account of fluctuating prices the salary of Mr. Adams was changed, in 1774, to seventy-two pounds ten shillings of lawful money, half to be paid semiannually. New difficulties arose and he was dismissed 16 January 1778, after thirty years of service. He removed to Newfield, Me., in 1781, where he preached and practised medicine till his death, 9 June 1792. He married (1) 13 October 1752, Sarah Wheeler of Durham, (2) Hannah Chesley of Durham, and had fourteen children. About a century after his departure from Durham a copy of his manuscript records of marriages and baptisms during the years 1749-63 was obtained by Miss Mary P. Thompson from one of his descendants. There are one hundred and twenty marriages and three hundred and thirty-three baptisms. The Rev. John Adams was a man of ability in mechanics and music as well as in the work of the ministry. He took an active part in the events that led to the Revolution and was chairman of the first committee in Dur-

ham of Correspondence, Inspection and Safety. It is said of
him that at times he was greatly depressed and at other times his
genius flashed out in bursts of eloquence. Toward the close
of his pastorate in Durham prejudices were excited against him
"by a false and slanderous attack on his character by a worth-
less woman." Thus the lie of a disreputable person sometimes
outweighs the truth as proclaimed and lived throughout thirty
years, and those who believe such a lie are about as guilty as the
liar. When he preached his farewell sermon in Durham, he
requested his audience to sing, after his reading, a metrical ver-
sion of the 120th Psalm, which certainly ministered to mortifi-
cation, if not to edification.

It was during the pastorate of the Rev. John Adams that the
parish of Lee was formed. A house of worship must have been
built in Lee quite early, for 28 October 1765, the town of Durham voted thirty pounds lawful money to "repair the meeting
house near Little River." The first meeting house stood
in the burial ground at Paul Giles' corner. The Rev. Samuel
Hutchins was the first minister. The Rev. John Osborne
preached there many years, though the Congregational Church
in Lee was not organized till 3 December 1867.

After the dismission of Mr. Adams the church was in a weak
condition. The members were few and scattered. A confession of faith was for the first time adopted and nine males and
ten females subscribed to it, after the installation of his successor. They were Curtis Coe, Abednego Lethers, John Edgerly,
Thomas Bickford, Benj^a Smith, Walter Bryent, Valentine
Mathes, Jeremiah Burnham, Joseph Stevens, Phebe Mathes,
Bethiah Bickford, Hannah Mathes, Margaret Frost, Sarah
Edgerly, Mary Chesle, Abigail Burnham, Hannah Small, Elizabeth Bryent, and Abigail Thomas. There may have been a few
more church members at that time, but, if so, they did not sign
the new covenant and creed.

The Rev. Curtis Coe was born in Middleton, Conn., 21 July
1750. He was graduated at Brown University in 1776. He
began preaching at Durham as early as 18 August 1779 and was
ordained and installed there 1 November 1780. It was agreed
that he have the use of the parsonage house, to be repaired, and
£75 in money annually, to be computed according to the price
of certain articles. Mr. Coe resigned his pastorate 1 May 1806

and became a home missionary in Milton, N. H., and in other
towns. He married, 22 February 1781, Ann, daughter of Judge
Ebenezer Thompson. The dismissing council declared that
"Mr. Coe's character is unspotted" and that they esteemed him
"a man eminent for piety and a faithful minister of the New
Testament." He died in South Newmarket 7 June 1829.
Descendants of his are now living in Durham.

It was during the pastorate of Mr. Coe, in 1792, that a new
meeting house was erected on the site of the former one, where
now is the Sullivan monument. The plans for this meeting
house were drawn by Judge Ebenezer Thompson, perhaps
acting as agent for Noah Jewett, to whom the town records
ascribe the plan. The meeting house was sixty feet in length,
fifty feet in width, and the posts were twenty-nine feet high.
It had a portico at the front door and another at the back door,
with "good handsome hewn stones at the doors." The house
had broad galleries around three sides and a lofty pulpit at the
east end, with a sounding board over it and deacons' pew in
front of it. At the west end was "a steeple with a spire and a
weathercock or vane thereon." In this steeple hung a bell,
which could be heard at the mouth of Oyster River. "The
plastered arch overhead" was "painted a sky color interspersed
with scattered clouds." The contract specified that the meeting house should be like that at Amherst, N. H., built also by
Edmund Thompson. The old meeting house was sold at auction to Capt. Joseph Richardson for £40. It proved to be rotten
and so the town released him from paying £20.

At vendue at the house of Joseph Richardson the building
of the new meeting house was struck off to William Smith, at
£760. April 13, 1792, the committee, which consisted of Valentine Mathes, Ebenezer Thompson, Ebenezer Smith, Joseph
Young, Bradbury Jewell, Edmund Pendergast, Zebulon Durgin,
Jonathan Woodman, Jr., Noah Jewett, Edmund Thompson and
John Blydenburgh, located the house as follows: "The sill on
the fore side or southern side shall be placed and leveled as
follows, viz., the west end to be placed exactly where the northwest corner of the old meeting house stood, and to be extended easterly exactly over the same ground where the back
side of the old meeting house was placed, and to be carried on
the same line until the sixty feet is completed, and the other sills

REV. CURTIS COE

to be squared accordingly." The house had an "electric wire," or lightning-rod, at a cost of £5, 18s.

Pews were sold at prices ranging from £19 to £34. The following persons were purchasers: John Blydenburgh, Noah Jewett, Ebenezer Thompson, Joseph Chesley, Samuel Edgerly, Stephen Cogan, Ebenezer Thompson, Jr., Jeremiah Mooney, George Frost, Jr., Zebulon Durgin, Joseph Richardson, James Leighton, William Ballard, Eliphalet Daniel, Edmund Thompson, Benjamin Thompson, George Dame, Samuel Edgerly, Jr., Jacob Crommett, Capt. Jonathan Woodman, Samuel Joy, Joseph Wormwood, Col. Samuel Adams, Stephen Evans, Samuel Edgerly, Thomas Pinkham, Lieut. Benjamin Chesley, John Stevens, Capt. Joseph Young, William Smith, Ebenezer Doe, Valentine Mathes, Esq., Valentine Wormwood, Benjamin Smith, Reuben Bickford, Jonathan Chesley, Edward Pendergast, Timothy Meserve, Bradbury Jewell, Curtis Coe, Joshua Davis, John Bennett, Stephen Durgin, John Smith, 3d, and Robert Lapish. The thirty-one remaining pews were struck off to William Smith at £4 each.

While the new church was in process of erection, meetings were held in Jonathan Edgerly's Bark House, so called, which stood near his tannery, near the Falls. Mr. Edgerly lived where Mr. David H. Fogg now lives, on the north side of the road to the Point, in the vicinity of the Pound. Town meetings were held in this Bark House in 1796, after the new meeting house was completed. Some town meetings were held in Joseph Richardson's tavern. In March 1798, the town meeting was held in the school house, erected the year before, near Widow Griffin's.

About this time towns were ceasing to pay taxes for the support of ministers and poll parishes were formed. New denominations were coming in, and the Baptist Church at Madbury, of which the Rev. William Hooper was minister, attracted some of the Rev. Curtis Coe's parishioners, who for some reason did not take kindly to his preaching. The dissenters seem to have been led by Col. Timothy Emerson, who sued the town for taxing him for ministerial support. A letter from the Rev. William Hooper is recorded in the town records, dated 31 December 1802. He stated that the following persons from Durham were regular members of his church and society and had contributed that year to his support, viz., Jonathan Steele, Andrew Simpson,

James Durgin, Jeremiah Emerson, John Ffrost, Jonathan Ches-
ley, Jonathan Chesley, Jr., John Angiers, Robert Bickford, Samuel
Langley, Samuel C. Drew, John Bickford, Nathaniel Demeritt,
Andrew Stevens, Benjamin Smith, Israel Demeritt, Robert Burn-
ham, Philip Chesley, Edward Wells, Joseph Daniels, Elijah Gove,
John Winkley, Robert Leathers, Jr., Thomas Jones, Andrew
Emerson, George Grover, John Stevens, John Emerson, Joshua
Ballard, William Emerson, Ephraim Hanson, Samuel Stevens,
Andrew Bickford, William Bickford, Anne Stevens, Elizabeth
Stevens, and Love Davis—thirty-six in all, while the total mem-
bership of the church at Durham Falls was not more than half
that number. This indicated either decided opposition to the
Rev. Curtis Coe or to the system by which they were taxed to
pay him. There was a wide call for a complete separation of
church and state. Methodists, Baptists, Quakers and others
were building denominational churches. The above persons were
temporary Baptists for financial as well as ecclesiastical reasons.
March 28, 1805, Jonathan Steele and fifty others petitioned for
a poll parish in Durham. In 1807 and 1808 nothing was voted
by the town for the support of the ministry.

After the dismissal of Mr. Coe the church was without a pastor
for more than eleven years, declining in numbers and strength.
The Rev. Samuel Greeley was paid $32, for preaching four Sab-
baths in 1807, and widow Margaret Frost was paid $16 for board-
ing him. Probably there was preaching by others from time to
time, of which there is no record. There were no additions to
the church from 30 October 1790 to 22 June 1817, nearly eighteen years. At the latter date there were only seven members
of the church. In 1814 the Rev. Federal Burt came to Durham
as agent of the Massachusetts Society for Promoting Christian
Knowledge. From that time until his ordination he preached
here at intervals, a considerable portion of that period. Thus he
became interested in the people and the people in him. With the
aid of the aforenamed society and also of the New Hampshire
Missionary Society, together with the strenuous exertions of a
few persons in Durham, provision was made for the support of a
minister, and 18 June 1817 the Rev. Federal Burt was installed
as the fifth pastor of the church. His ministry was one of un-
surpassed prosperity. Old prejudices were laid aside, and gen-
uine piety was promoted. Soon additions were made to the

church and continued from time to time. The largest addition was in 1826, following a revival, resulting in part from a meeting of the General Association. Thirty-seven new members were thus gained, not all stable converts, since five of them were afterwards excommunicated. This revival was greatly aided by the labors of the Rev. Henry Smith, son of Ebenezer Smith, Esq., of Durham, a graduate of Bowdoin Col-

REV. FEDERAL BURT

lege and of Andover Theological Seminary. During Mr. Burt's ministry the membership of the church increased from seven to about seventy.

The Rev. Federal Burt was born at Southampton, Mass., 4 March 1789 and, therefore, named Federal. He was graduated at Williams College in 1812. He married Mary Pickering of Newington in July 1819. In 1827 he suffered the amputation of a finger and then of an arm. His health being impaired, he was appointed editor of the *New Hampshire Observer*, and he edited that paper till his death, 9 February 1828. He is described as "a man of large stature, of generous, magnanimous spirit, of ardent temperament, yet of sound judgment. Possessing superior conversational powers, much ability in extemporaneous speaking, and being skilled in adapting himself to people of different classes and conditions, he was a leader among his associates." When he was called to Durham he had another invitation to Salisbury, Conn., where the prospects were more flattering, but a committee of ministerial brethren from the vicinage expressed their "desire to have the assistance of another fellow labourer in the hard & barren ground of the part of the vineyard in which our Divine Master has seen fit to station us," and so Mr. Burt accepted the call to Durham. This record may convince some that in "the good old times" the churches were not more prosperous than at present. The people were not more religious, nor did they like to go to meeting any better than now. The ministers had more trials and it was harder to collect regularly their meager salaries. The Revs. John Buss, Hugh Adams, John Adams and Curtis Coe, all had great trouble in collecting amounts due to them according to terms of contracts made.

It is recorded that Mr. Burt was accustomed to wear in the pulpit the clerical gown of black silk, and that after the preaching service the audience respectfully arose and stood while Mr. and Mrs. Burt passed down the broad aisle. Have reverence and respect decreased in these latter days?

It was during the pastorate of Mr. Burt that the first Sunday School was formed in Durham. At a meeting held at the school house, Sunday evening, 23 March, 1819, James Bartlett, Jedediah Ingalls and Abraham Perkins were chosen directors of the proposed school, whose duty it was to select instructors and have the government and management of the school. Joseph Hanson, Benjamin Mathes, Jr., and James Joy were another committee to procure clothing for the destitute and funds for the school. The following instructors and pupils are on record. Valentine Smith's class consisted of Hamilton Smith, Charles Parks, John Parks, John Odell, Daniel Holt and John Hanson. Miss Martha Leighton had under her care a class whose names are not recorded, and the same is true of Mr. Joseph Hanson.

Miss Abigail Ballard taught the following, Mary Jackson, Mary Chesley, Laura Emerson, Susan Leighton, Louisa Doe, Jane Chesley and Sarah Chesley.

The class of Miss Sarah Richardson consisted of Mary Hull 13, Eliza Meserve 11, Rebecca Pickering 11, Betsey Henderson 9, Charity Willey 8, Dorothy Garland 7, and Adaline Griffin 15.

Miss Margaret Blydenburgh had for pupils, Martha Boardman, Harriet Pickering, Sarah Garland, Harriet Libbey, Mary Thompson, Mehitable Doe, and Elizabeth Holt.

Miss Charlotte Gregg had in her class Eliza Chesley 12, Eliza Ingalls 9, Clarissa Coos 12, Caroline Tego 17, Jane Parks 5, Fanny Hull 11, Abigail Emerson and Mehitable Morse 7.

Miss Abigail Joy had as pupils Mary Davis, Caroline Follett, Lucy A. Hull, Jane Boardman, Mary Chesley, Lydia Yeaton, Elizabeth Yeaton 7, and Mehitable Bunker 7.

The successor of the Rev. Federal Burt was the Rev. Robert Page, who was born 25 April 1790, graduated at Bowdoin College in 1810, at Andover Seminary in 1815, was ordained and settled at Bradford, N. H., in 1822 and was installed at Durham 3 December 1826. He specified in accepting the call that his small salary should be paid regularly. This was not done, and so he resigned his pastorate after a little more than two years. He was dismissed by Council 31 March 1831. The Council declared him to be "an able minister of Jesus Christ, highly esteemed in our congregations and approved and beloved by his brethren in the ministry." He afterwards labored with success at Hanover, Hillsborough and Lempster and died 12 January 1876.

The Rev. Alvan Tobey, D. D., succeeded Mr. Page. He was born at Wilmington, Vt., 1 April 1808, graduated at Amherst College in 1828 and at Andover Seminary in 1831. He began preaching at Durham the first Sabbath of October of 1831 and was ordained 20 November 1833. His salary was $500, of which $100 were paid by the New Hampshire Missionary Society. In 1854 the salary was increased to $650 in consequence of Mr. Tobey's proposal to withdraw. More than once he had to stir up the brethren to make due collections for his salary, yet he remained till January 1871. In 1867 subscriptions were obtained to nearly double his salary. Before that he declared that he received only half enough to comfortably support his family. He was greatly esteemed and the church prospered under his ministry of nearly thirty-nine years. One hundred and forty-nine members were added to the church, thirty-four of them in the year 1868. Mr. Tobey removed to Somersworth, where he died 20 September 1874.

It was during his pastorate, in 1848-49, that the old meeting

REV. ALVAN TOBEY, D.D.

house was torn down and the new church was erected, which continues unto the present day. Mr. Tobey saw the need of this and advocated it several years before the work was accomplished. Elder John Adams of Adams Point bought the old meeting house and with the lumber erected some boarding houses at Salmon Falls and Great Falls. Some of the round posts under the galleries now form a part of the pagoda on the shore of the bay near the residence of Mr. Adams.

The new meeting house, or church, as some have since preferred to call it, was erected on a lot purchased of Samuel Dunstar for $250. The contractor and builder was Moses H. Wiggin, Esq. The plans cost $31, and the cost of the furnace for heating it was $150. The total cost was $3,325. In 1851 an organ was put in at a cost of $500. The church was paid for by

CONGREGATIONAL CHURCH

sale of pews, a method of church building then much in vogue, which public opinion now disapproves as hostile to the general spirit and purpose of a christian church. The rich and the poor should meet together for worship, the Lord being the maker of them all. The easiest way of getting money for religious purposes is not always the best way. The new church was dedicated 13 September 1849.

The successor of Mr. Tobey was the Rev. Henry Laurens Talbot, born 4 August 1836 at East Machias, Me. He was graduated at Andover Seminary in 1870 and was installed at

14

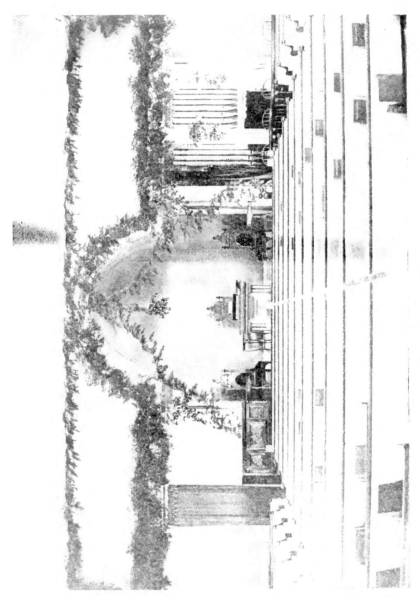

CONGREGATIONAL CHURCH

"A day in thy courts is better than a thousand."

Durham, 1 January 1873. He was dismissed at his request 13 March 1882 and made his residence in Durham until his death. During his pastorate twenty-five new members were added to the church.

The Rev. Samuel H. Barnum was the next pastor. He was graduated at Yale College in 1875 and at Yale Theological Seminary in 1879. He preached about three years at Salisbury, N. H. He began his ministry in Durham 30 July 1882 and was installed 25 April 1883. During his pastorate was organized the Young People's Society of Christian Endeavor. He was dismissed 25 March 1890, having accepted a call to Cornwall, Vt.

The church was then without a settled pastor till 30 April 1895, during which time the Rev. Charles H. Chapin acted as pastor. He was educated at Cornell University and had preached at Acworth and Lyme, N. H. During his pastorate the church was repaired and enlarged, and a new organ and a new furnace were put in.

The Rev. Oliver D. Sewall commenced preaching in Durham, 1 April 1895. He was born at Chesterville, Me., 23 January 1865 and was graduated at Bowdoin College in 1887 and at Andover Theological Seminary in 1892. He was pastor at Strong, Me., two years. He was installed at Durham 30 April 1895, and remained two years. He was assistant pastor at Brookline, Mass., from 1897 till 1909, and has since been pastor at Great Barrington, Mass.

The Rev. William S. Beard was born in Harwich, Mass., 9 June 1870, son of the Rev. William Henry and Mary Adelaide (Parker) Beard, grandson of the Rev. Spencer Field Beard. He was graduated from Phillips Academy, Andover, in 1890, from Yale Academic in 1894 and from the Yale Divinity School in 1897. After serving a short time at Westchester and at South Killingly, Conn., he accepted a call to Durham, where he began his work in July 1897. He was ordained and installed 28 September 1897, and remained till the last Sunday in June 1908. During his pastorate the parsonage was purchased and entirely remodeled; the chapel was moved from its old location to its present one and was enlarged, providing parlor, study, dining room and kitchen. The church and chapel were painted and renovated, newly cushioned and carpeted and refitted with electric lights, and water was introduced. Mr. Beard was secre-

tary of the Village Improvement Society and served six months
on the school board. He was called to the First Congregational
Church at Willimantic, Conn., where he began his work in
September 1908, and where he still is pastor.

The successor of Mr. Beard was the Rev. Telesphore Taisne,
son of Augustin and Clara (Le Vigne) Taisne, born in Caulery,
France, 29 May 1876. He was educated at the French-American
College, Springfield, Mass., graduating in 1899, and in Hartford

CONGREGATIONAL CHURCH

Theological Seminary, graduating in 1902. He was ordained to
the Congregational ministry at the French church, Marlboro,
Mass., 25 November 1902, and remained with that church two
years. From 1903 to 1909 he was pastor of the Sixth Street
Church, Auburn, Me., where he was a member of the school
board. He began preaching in Durham the first Sunday in
February 1909, and was installed as pastor 18 May of the same
year, where he remained till his death, 23 December 1911, from

typhoid fever. He married, 2 July 1902, at Westfield, Mass., Winifred N. Chisholm, daughter of Oscar H., and Julia (Cuson) Chisholm, who survives him. During his pastorate he taught very acceptably several classes in French in the college and the last year of his life he had charge of the chapel exercises. Mr. Taisne was regarded as one of the stronger preachers of his denomination, and his untimely death cast a gloom over the community.

The present pastor of the church is the Rev. Fred T. Knight, who was born in Boston, Mass., 12 August 1859. He was educated at the Boston Latin School, Harvard, 1881, Harvard Law School, 1884, Hartford Theological Seminary, 1895. He practised law ten years in Boston. His pastorates have been in Quincy, Mass., 1897–1900, Stamford, Conn., 1902–04, Northbridge, Mass., 1904–08, Harwich, Mass., 1910–12, Durham, 1 December 1912 to the present time. He married, 29 June 1898, Cara W. Hanscom.

DEACONS, AND DATES OF THEIR ELECTION

Nathaniel Hill, 1718	Valentine Mathes, 1781, declined to serve
Samuel Emerson, 1718	
John Ambler, 1718	Walter Bryant, 1781
James Nock, 1721	Abraham Perkins, 1819
John Williams, 1722	William Wiggin, 1826
James Langley, 1724	John Thompson, 1835
Joseph Wheeler, 1732	William Tuttle, Jr., 1869
Jonathan Thompson, before 1738	James M. Smart, 1869
Ebenezer Smith, before 1752	John E. Thompson, 1874
Benjamin Wheeler, before 1766	Winthrop S. Meserve, 1877
Jeremiah Burnham	Albert Young, 1894
Hubbard Stevens, before 1765	Charles H. Pettee, 1896
Lieut. John Smith	Arthur F. Nesbitt, 1907
Nathaniel Norton, before 1777	Forrest E. Cardullo, 1912
Samuel Joy, 1791	Charles E. Hewitt, 1913

PARSONAGES

The first parsonage, occupied by the Rev. John Buss, was near the first meeting house, by the oyster bed, and was burned in 1694. Just where Mr. Buss lived afterward does not appear, but there is a tradition that he lived on the parsonage lot, just south of the road from the Falls to the Point.

Another parsonage was built in 1739, on an acre of land bought of Lieut. Samuel Smith, and Lieut. Jonathan Thompson and Lieut. Francis Mathes were a committee to receive a deed for the same. The price paid was £31. This land was near the top of the hill as one goes from the Falls to the Point, on the north side of the road after passing the road to Newmarket, in

THE PARSONAGE

the rear of the small house now called the Johnson house. The town records say that this parsonage was sold in 1831 for $26.50. Here lived the Rev. John Adams and the Rev. Curtis Coe.

The house built about 1720 by the Rev. Hugh Adams, a few rods south of the so-called Sullivan house, was occupied by him and later by the Rev. Mr. Tobey, and has been called a parsonage, though it was never owned by the parish. It was removed to the north side of Denbow's brook, on the road to Newmarket, was repaired and is still in good condition.

The present parsonage of the Congregational Church was built by Capt. Andrew Lapish Simpson before his marriage to Lydia Kelley, 23 September 1840. The barn was the old house owned and occupied by William Odiorne, ship-builder and commissioner for the preservation of forests. He married Avis, daughter of the Rev. Hugh Adams. He sold his "mansion house" to Timothy Meader in 1770. Afterward it was owned by Robert Lapish, and then by his son-in-law, Andrew Simpson, and by Capt. Simpson until about the time of his marriage. His widow, Mrs. Lydia (Kelley) Simpson, died 31 May 1895, aged 81 years and four months. She joined the church in Durham, 10 February 1833, and was always liberal in its support. She is remembered as kind and benevolent, a friend to the church and to all in need, one whose social qualities drew around her many friends. She bequeathed this house to the Congregational Society in Durham and to the Durham Library Association. The latter sold their half to the former, and the house has been used as a parsonage since 1895. Capt. Simpson was a noted sea-captain and doubled Cape Horn twenty-six times. He was representative several years in the State legislature. He died 18 December 1870.

THE FIRST CHRISTIAN CHURCH IN DURHAM

The organization of this church was due to the efforts of the Rev. William Demeritt, who was ordained at Lee, 11 July 1816, together with the Rev. Israel Chesley. The audience was so large that the meeting house could not hold them. A hay-rack was turned upside down, and the bottom of it was used as a platform for the ordination ceremonies.

Elder Demeritt was a minister of commanding presence and popular gifts. He served in the ministry gratuitously on principle. He also acted as selectman in 1812, 1833 and 1834. He is said to have baptized and married more persons than any other minister in his region of country. The baptisms were by immersion just below the bridge, and sometimes the ice was cut from the river in preparation for the solemn rite.

The First Christian Church was organized 4 December 1819 and held its first meetings in private houses and in the old school house west of the residence of Mrs. Albert L. Comings. The brick meeting house was built on the site of the old George

Chesley dwelling house, which was burned 24 September 1823, when widow Sarah Chesley and Patrick Cogan, who had been a quartermaster in the Revolution, perished in the flames. The brick church was dedicated 20 January 1825.

The following brief but sufficient agreement was made by the first members of this church:

> We the subscribers, professed followers of Jesus Christ, agree to strive to walk together in the spirit of a Church of Christ, to take the scriptures for our guide and Christ our head, to watch over each other for our benefit, the strong to bear the infirmities of the weak, and so fulfill the law of God, to be known by the name of the First Christian Church in Durham.

The organizing members were Daniel Mathes, Robert Mathes, James Chesley, Benjamin Mathes, Ebenezer Doe, Richard Kent, John Meader, Ebenezer Parsons, Benjamin Dame, Isaac Waterhouse, William Demeritt, Aenon Barhew, Deborah Chesley, Mrs. Lapish, Elizabeth Durgin, Sally Chesley, Susan Mathes, Betsy Mathes, Sally Doe, Olive Emerson, Mary Demeritt, Comfort Laskey, Sally Parsons, Susan Chesley, Mary Dame, Drusilla Wiggin, Hannah Pendergast, Nancy Fowler, Abigail Demeritt, Betsy Randall, Lovey Whitehouse, Margaret Appleton, Lois Smart, Mrs. Henderson, Loisa Doe, Abigail Leighton, Lovey Edgerly, Olive Smart, Avis Bodge, and Sally Mathes.

Elder Elijah Shaw became the minister of this church in 1842, when there were thirty-four male members and fifty female members; notwithstanding twenty-three members had died since its organization and forty had joined other churches. Rev. Elijah Shaw was born at Kensington, N. H., 19 December 1793 and died at Fall River, Mass., 5 May 1851. He served as pastor at Salisbury, Mass., Portland, Me., Lowell, Mass., Durham, Franklin, N. H., and Fall River, Mass., and also as editor of the *Christian Journal*. Elder Mosher was chosen pastor in 1850 and Elder J. S. Smith in 1862.

The Christian Society was incorporated in 1850 and the following persons signed its Constitution: James Langley, Daniel Mathes, Stephen Reynolds, Gideon C. Pitman, James Smart, Jacob Sheppard, Thomas B. Mathes, Clement M. Davis, Thomas Bartlett, Samuel Runlett, Richard Follet, Daniel Lee, John Ellison, William J. Chesley, William Walker, Samuel E. Mosher, William W. Jackson, Timothy Demeritt, Nathan Keniston, Caleb G. Cloutman, Albert L. Gleason, J. S. Smith,

H. W. B. Grover, Charles H. Whitehorn, Willard C. Tufts, William D. Langley, Marcus M. Estabrooks, Albert Young, and Job. R. Giles.

The church gradually declined and the brick meeting house was sold at auction, with the land adjoining, 11 June 1889, to the Town School District, for $255. The proceeds were divided among the pew owners, the final dividend being made in 1894.

ROADS

For some years after the first settlements in Dover the rivers were the only highways, and the only vehicles were boats. When horses came into use, bridle paths were made through the forests, following probably in some instances old Indian trails. These were gradually widened to permit the hauling of masts and timber. The winding paths of least resistance were followed, little care being taken to avoid steep hills or to cut them down. The brooks and shallow streams were forded. Bridges and carriage roads came much later. For the Mast Roads in Durham see Miss Mary P. Thompson's Landmarks in Ancient Dover for a full description.

The first road of which there is any historical mention is that from Oyster River Point, now Durham Point, to "Hills Mill," at the Falls, in 1659, when this highway was presented at Court because of its bad condition. The path at the head of Johnsons' Creek was presented at the same time. This was the path leading from the Falls to Cochecho.

In 1663 Philip Chesley and Patrick Jameson were chosen "to lay out the heigways from Oyster River to Cochechae and make the heigways fitt for horse and foot and bring thear a Compt of thear charges to the Townsmen."

In 1664 Capt. Ralph Hall and Dea. John Hall were ordered to lay out a highway from Lamprill River fall to the water side in Great Bay, through what was afterward called Doe's Neck, in Newmarket, then a part of Dover. See page 32.

In 1686 John Woodman, Thomas Edgerly, Nicholas Harrison, John Wingate, and John Tuttle, selectmen, reported that they had laid out highways as follows: "from Willies Creeke near Bickfords Ferry unto Oyster River fall," and also a road to "Bellimans banke falls, neare along as the path goes fouer Rods in breadth as it was formerly laid out by John Bickford and John Woodman by a Towne order." They also reported that they had "bin Uppon the high wayes betwixt Oyster River and Lamperele River & have laid out the high wayes as the path goes to be fouer Rod wide from Oyster River falls to Lampriele River falls, or about fortie Rods above it as may be most conuenient,

LAMPREY RIVER SECOND FALLS, OR SULLIVAN'S FALLS

In this vicinity Gen. John Sullivan had six mills. The water power has not been used for a long time.

and we have Laid out a highway from oyster River falls unto
the freshett or over the River into the Commons by Edward
Smalls of fower Rod wide near as the Path now goes."

In 1701 it was voted in Dover town meeting "that a highway
be laid out from the mast path to the Cheslies mill on Oyster
River over the freshet, to run by Edward Smalls and so clear
threw to the old way formerly Laid into the commons by
Edward Smalls and so to Lampercle Second Falls maintaining
the same breadth." This is the southerly branch of the Mill
Road, after crossing Oyster River at Chesley's Mill, where the
ruins of the old dam are plainly seen. On this road or near it
lived Jabez Davis and Dea. John E. Thompson in more recent
times, whose lonely abandoned house is perched upon the bank
close to the railroad cutting. Here was once a fine farm, with
beautiful shade trees and orchard and five miles of well laid stone
wall. Further out on this road, now abandoned, lived Edward
Small two hundred or more years ago. In Mr. Caverno's lower
field and near the river is an old cellar, where some say Mr. Ballard built a house, but the land seems to be described in a deed
from Jonathan Woodman and his wife, Elizabeth, of Dover, for
"yᵉ Natural Love & affection wᶜʰ I have & bear to my Sister
Mary Small of Moniemay." The conveyance was of twenty
acres on the "south Side of Oyster River Betwixt yᵉ Mill Pond
& yᵉ River" and the date was 10 June 1707.

In the year 1719 there was a petition for the reopening of the
old road from the Falls along the northwesterly side of the
freshet, or mill-pond. The original petition is of great interest,
since it has the autograph signatures of over forty of the men of
Oyster River at that time. The petition is here given with the
names underwritten, except two or three that can not be de-
ciphered easily.

To the Worshipfull Justices now siting at porthmouth the Compleint of us the
Subscribers hombly shueth that where as the town of Douer have granted
and Laid out highways at the hed of oyster River and also Land Laid out for
a Landing place for Laying of Timber & other goods which now fenced up by
Cap Nathanil Hill and sons is great damage to the Inhabiten⁻ there for their

RESIDENCE OF THE LATE DEA. JOHN E. THOMPSON

halling of timber wood and fencing which we hope your Worships will consider
the matter and do his Majesties subjects Justice in that affair.

Solomon Davis	Thomas Davis
David Kincaid	Moses Davis
Joshua Davis	———— ————
John Tasker	Abraham Clark
Edward Pomry	Thomas Drew
James Clark	William Drew
Tomas Drew	Eli Clark
Clement Drew	Samuel Davis
Joseph Jenkens	Peter Mason
Joseph Smalle	William Pitman
Benjamin Smalle	Daniel Davis
Joseph Davis	———— ————
Stephen Jones	Timothy Davis
James Davis	Joseph Jenkins
Joseph Hicks	Nathaniel Randel
Daniel Meserve	Thomas Leighton
Nichlos Meader	Jeams Basford
Gorg Chesle	James Davis
Elias Critchett	Benja Thomas
Job Renells	John Smith.

The matter was considered in court and the following depositions are filed in connection with the case.

The Deposition of Moses Davis Testifieth & saith that Nathaniel Hill or
p'sons by his order hath fenced up the high way that Leads from Oyster
River falls unto ye freshet by Edward Smalls and also the Landing Place at
Oyster River falls by Georg Chesles fence and have also in croch upon the
thorow fair Rhod that Leads to Cochecho & hath maintained the fence from
the first of march last past unto the 2 day of June 1719, and Daniel Davis
Testifieth to all that is above writen. Sworne in Courte June 2d 1719.

THEODORE ATKINSON, *Clerk.*

The Deposition of John Williams Testifieth and sayeth that for thirty years
and upwards that he was a Long with Bartholomew Stevenson that Capt
Peter Coffen came a Long by and told ye afores^d Stevenson y^t h^e must not
fence in that way for it was a Loud for a high way: which way was upon y^e
north side of oyster River falls from ye falls near ye freshett and so by Edward
Smalls. [Sworn in Court in the same action. No date. See Court Files,
No. 17372.]

This indicates that the old cellar above mentioned, where
Mr. Ballard is said to have built a house, marks the former abode
of Edward Small, and that the road along the north side of the
mill-pond antedated by several years the road now known as the
Mill Road.

OYSTER RIVER FRESHET
(View above the dam at the Falls)

The continuation of the Mill Road toward the west is mentioned in the records of a town meeting held 28 May 1718:

"Beginning at the End of Highway formerly laid out to Chesleys mill on the south side of s⁴ River, the way to be fouer Rods wide along the old way Leaving Moses Davis Junᵉ his forty acre Lott on the south & Bartholomew Staveson his ten acre Lott on the North & so along the Comons Leving Daniel Missarve his Thirty acre Lott on the Northwest and so on the Comons Leving Moses Davis senᵣ his four score acre Lott and Thomas Stephsons Three score acre Lot on the west and so on the comons to William folletts hundred acre Lott at Maharamuts Marsh, to two Trees marked H fower Rods Distance. This way Laid out by us the thurteenth Day of June 1719." Signed by James Davis and Thomas Tibbetts.

This road is still traveled. At its end lived, a century ago, on the north side, Lieut. David Wiggin, and his old house is still standing. The family burial place, surrounded with an iron railing, is a little west of the house. The Stevenson family, on the south side of the road, long ago disappeared, and their only remembrancer is a lonely graveyard in the eastern part of a large field. Hilliard F. Fogg owns and lives on this old Stevenson farm.

Turning to the south at the end of the road above described one soon passes the Griffiths burial ground and comes to the beautiful residence of the Griffiths brothers, with shaded and well-kept lawn and broad, fertile acres of Moharimet's Marsh, which stretches away into Croxford's swamp.

March 18, 1689.
Then laid out at the head of William Beards Creek a Certaine percell of Land there on the west side of the Creeke for the Conuenience of a landing place and high wayes; the bounds of the said land and high wayes as followeth:
At the Creeke 8 rods wide & from thence following North & by West unto the North side of John Woodmans land North Nor west unto the King his high waye & from the head of the said Woodman his land ffourty rods North east unto a Certaine p'cell of Rocks there, where wee have appointed & Laid out two high wayes of 4 rods wide, and Runs ouer the Brooke neare North west & then north north east & by east unto the high waye unto Newtowne: and from the afore said Rocks Another high waye runs North west & by North on the North side of the aforesaid John Woodman his land into the Commons,
These landing places and high wayes were laid out by virtue of an order from the townsmen bearing date Sept. 24, 1688,
By us—JOHN WOODMAN
JAMES HUCKINS.

The above named landing place was sold, by vote of the town, to Jonathan Woodman in 1779.

15

The landing place at the Falls, though in use from the time of
the erection of the first mill there, about 1650, was formally laid
out by vote of the town taken 27 October 1701. A portion of
the report of the committee has been given on page 71. Beginning where that leaves off the report reads, "and alsoe the mast
path is laid out fower Rods in bredth as ye sd path now lyeth or
Leadeth from ye sd Landing place to the outmost of our Towne
bounds for a publick Heywaie. Wee have alsoe Laid out a high-

THE ROAD TO BAGDAD
(Not far from Beard's Landing.)

way from ye Chesley mill at Oyster Riuer to the mast path to
be fower Rods in bredth a Long as ye path now Ledeth from sd
mill to ye mast path as may appear by fower trees markt H and
standing at ye fower Corners of ye said way." Laid out 14 June
1703.

Another road was laid out the same year, which is described
as follows:

We the subscribers hereof have laid out the highway from oyster bed to
oyster Riuer, through the Country road to durty gutt by Abraham Clark his
house, beginning at ye Usuall wadeing place att oyster bed at a Pine tree on
the East and white oak on the West at 4 Rods distance markt H each of them,
from thence North Easterly to the west side of ffollet his Rocky hill, aboue
ffollet his barn, and then it Runes on the East side of the next Rocky hill by

James Bunker his barn and from thence to the Cartway at the head of Bunker Creek and so a Long threw as the old way formerly Lay till it comes to a Rock at the southwest Corner of Nath Lamos his Land, from thence as it is markt till it comes to the bridge at Durty gutt, to lye 4 Rods wide Clear threw, and allso a highway from that leads from Ltt Dauis his house, beginning att a white oak marked H I B and 4 Rods in bredth a Long by the head of Joseph Bunker his land from thence to the King's thorrofair Road.

Laid out this 9th of Aprill 1703 by us

JNO TUTTLE
JERE BURNUM
JAMES DAUIS
    of the Comittee.

Abraham Clark lived near the boundary line between Oyster River parish and Dover proper, now Madbury. The highway above described was a continuance of the road from Cochecho. After fording Oyster River to some point near the old church the path continued along the highway between the parsonage lot and that of William Williams, later of Stephen Jenkins, and so in a direct course through Long Marsh to Lamprey River, now Newmarket. This part of the road or path was discontinued long ago. The part of it north of the river is spoken of in a deed dated 3 October, 1720, from Joshua Davis to Amos Pinkham, as the road "leading from James Bunker's into ye main road that goes to Cochecho."

WHEREAS we the subscr hereof being chosen with others to be a Comitte to survaie and Lay out highwaies in the seueral parts of the Towne of douer for the Conueniency of the Inhabitants, and being desired by Lt. James Daues and Joseph Meader to lay out a highway from the heads of their Lottes to the King his road, thoro fair Road according to a vote in generall Towne meeting, ye 27th October 1701, and being Apon the place or ground with John Gerrish Esqr., one of his Majts Justes of Peace, haue laid out as followeth Viz— from two stumps at or near the aforesaid Dauis and Meader their land at about fower Rods distance and to Rune about 12 Rods north westerly, Then turning moer westerly keeping the hey land till it comes to a hemlock tree in the nor west Corner of Mathew Williams his forty acre grant, in the tenure of Joseph Smith, and so to the old path that leads to Abraham Clarks and so Clear Thoro to the king his thorofair Road as the way now goes, to be fower Rods wide.

Given under our hands this 29th of October 1701.

JNO TUTTLE
WILL FFURBER
TRISTRAM HEARD
    of the Comitte
JONE GERRISH, Just. Pe.

In response to a petition of James Langley, dated 25 July 1715, in which he states that Bartholomew Stevenson had penned him up to a way only eight feet wide or thereabout, a road was laid out from his house to the main road.

Wee whose names are under Written being chosen by the Towne of douer with others to suruaie and Lay out high waie in the seuerall pts of the Towne and being desired of James Langley to Lay out a way of too Rod wide beginning at will Drews old possession joyning to the bond high way so running sow west and by west to a pine tree on the south East side of this highway and so keeping the two Rods in breadth to a little hill Leaueing the Spring Seuen Rods on the nor west side of the highway, keeping the same breadth south southwest to the highway that goeth from Willeyes Creek to Oyster Riuer falls to a white oke markt H. I. S. and william drews wood lott on the south east of this highway.

> JAMES DAVIS
> JEREMIAH BURNUM
Recorded may ye 28, 1716   THOMAS TEBBETS

This old road over the "little hill" can now be easily traced, though its course has been changed toward the west, to avoid the hill. William Drew's house and wood lot are mentioned, though he had been dead forty-six years. There was an old landing on Giles' Creek, that was connected with this road, as shown by a deposition made about 1710 by "Bat Stimson," [Bartholomew Stevenson], aged about 50, that "there is a landing place laid out against Thomas Drew's dore on ye south side of Mathew Goyles [Giles'] Creek and buts against the waye that goes to Oyster River falls, and Thomas Pitman have got a marked tree in his possession as the waye was laid out." [Court Files, 17372.]

Here is the Long Marsh Road:

It is the request of thirty eight of the Inhabetance of the Parrish of oyster Riuer to haue a high way of three Rods to bee Laid out from a highway that Leads to willeys Creek to ye Kings Thorowfare Road that Leads to Lampercel Riuer and it is laid out as followeth, beginning att the hed of the Lane att a Place Called Team hill and so along between fransis Matheus Twelue Acre Lot and the Lott hee bought of John Wille and ouer the South Corner of Matheus his Seauenteen acor Lott and ouer the north Corner of the Poynt wood Lott and soe along whear the Path now goes and on the north East side of a grate Rock and soe on the north side of John Willeys indwelling hous and so Down to the Long marsh and over the Marsh to the highway that Leads from oyster Riuer falls to Lamperell Riuer Bridg. This highway Laid out and bounded the 22 Day of February 1720/21 by us,

> THOMAS TEBBETS
> JOHN SMITH
> FRANSIS MATHUES.

At a General Session of the Peace, 6 March, 1710/11, complaint having been made about the want of roads from town to town, a committee was appointed in each town to run such roads as they thought necessary, laying them out four rods wide. The Dover committee consisted of Capt. Tuttle, Capt. James Davis and Joseph Jones. The laying out of the road through Durham was as follows:

From Lampereal River as Strait as it may be to the old Bridge by ye Moat so as ye way goes to Graves [William Graves] his Land thence to the falls, to make the whole four rods wide, and there ye way is to open on ye Left at Stimsons [Bartholomew Stevenson's ?] and at Robert Huggins [Huckins] his house. So at Wm Jacksons pasture to ye head of Jacksons Creek Strait as ye old Road went then Joseph Jenkins to open on ye Left & all others to make ye way four Rods wide to Fields Garrison.

At the last point it entered the Back River Road to Cochecho. [N. H. Town Papers, XI, 539.]

June 9, 1738, a road was laid out from the highway at Newtown saw mill, on the south side of Oyster River, in a southwest direction by the land of John Sias, following the old way to Solomon Sias' land, and so on to the mast road that leads from Little River. [See Town Records, Vol. I, p. 21.] This mill was afterward known as Layn's Mill. It is in Lee.

Aug. 10, 1745:

Then laid out a high way from a picked Rock by Thomas Willeys new house where he now dwelleth and from thence on a straight Course to James bunkers northwest Corner bound of his twenty five acrees, it being a great oak Stump, then East & by north forty Rods to said bunkers north bound then near north East to the Maple brook so called, this high way to be on the north side of the above sd Courses three Rods wide tell it Comes against the Rock first mentioned, laid out by us,

DAN¹ SMITH *Select*
JOHN WILLIAMS *men.*

Here is a road in the western part of the town:

A highway laid out on the Common Land from a place called Camsey [Campsie], from the head of Mr. Robert Tomsons fence to Mr. William Drews and So to the River be Low Deans mash and from thence to the head of the Town, by a partition [petition] under their hands directed to us, the present Selectmen for said town, and by their request we have laid out the way and bounded it as followeth, beginning on the north side of the Mast Road on the south or west corner of Mr. Robert Tomsons fence called Camsey and from that fence is bounded by the Spoted Trees as they now standeth Runing westerly four Rods from Joseph Jones barn then by the spoted trees so between Mr. Wil-

liam Drews and Ely Clarks house. Then by the spoted trees to Newtown
River below Deans mash and then by the Spoted trees Runing near Richard
Glovers House and then by the spoted Trees to a way called Willes way so
as that way leads to the head of the Town being fouer Rods wide; Laid out
and bounded by us the present Selectmen this 29 day of January in the year:
1733/4. [Signed by Joseph Jones, John Williams and John Woodman as
Selectmen.]

Dean's Marsh, doubtless, took its name from the John Dean
who was the first one killed in the massacre of 1694, and "the
place called Camsey" is explained in connection with the Kincaid family.

The road known as the Wine Cellar Road was laid out as follows:

By and at the Request of sundry of the inhabitants of the town of Durham
we have laid out a high way from Luberland to the Kings Rode between Richard Denbos field and John Buss Junᵣ. We began at a great Rock between
John Smiths house and John Does marsh & from thence by said Does marsh
and so between Jos Whelers land & John Smith Junᵣ land to Thoˢ Langles
land & from thence to the wine selers & so along on the sow west of Joseph
Edgerleys land and so along on the N Est side of John Willes Junᵣ house to
the Rode between John Burnum fence and the sᵈ Willes land to a great rock
marked H and from thence by John Buses fence to the Countrey Rode this
Rode is three Rods wide from the last Rock marked H the other part from ――
town to luberland is laid out four Rods in wedth all along sᵈ Rode. Laid out
and bounded by us this 16 day of March 1735/6. [Signed by Jonathan Thomson, John Woodman and Samuel Smith, Selectmen.]

In company with Dea. W. S. Meserve I rode over this road in
April 1913, and probably no wheeled vehicle will ever go over it
again. The carriage as well as the lives of the horse and riders
should be well insured before making the attempt. Such de-
clivities and superabundance of ledge and boulders make us won-
der how any selectmen ever dared to lay out a road there; but
the people living at Lubberland wanted a shorter route to the
meeting house at the Falls. The road started near the house of
the late Valentine Smith and from there to the Back Road,
through Horn's Woods, it is known by the name of Simon's Lane,
most likely from Joseph Simons, who, 8 February 1727/8, married Elizabeth, daughter of Elder James Nock, who lived in this
vicinity. Perhaps it is the lane through which Joseph walked
to woo Elizabeth, for we may well believe that this road was
used as a bridle path some years before it was "laid out." After
reaching the Back Road it followed that easterly for perhaps
twenty rods; then it struck through the woods and rocks again

to the Long Marsh Road and followed that, as it formerly ran, to the Newmarket Road near Denbo's Brook, or Horsehide Brook, as it is now sometimes called. John Buss seems to have been living here, perhaps on the ten acres of ministerial marsh land granted long before by the town and concerning which there was a law suit between the Rev. Hugh Adams and the Rev. Mr. Gilman. Most of this old road was long ago abandoned. Only Mr. Patrick Connor lives on it now, without whose kindly assistance we would hardly have gotten through alive. He disowns all relationship to the Timothy and James Conner who were from Ireland and residents of Durham about the time of its incorporation.

There is a huge overhanging boulder along this abandoned road, that according to tradition was the sheltering place of wine in the old days, and hence the name of the Wine Cellar Road, but notice that in the return of the road, given above, the phrase is "wine selers." Were there those who sold wine living there? The names in the return of the road indicate owners of land along the way rather than residents, for there is hardly room between the rocks for more than one family to live.

The northerly end of this road seems to be further described in a highway granted 20 May 1727 and laid out 15 June 1734. It was granted to John Willey, Jr., "from His House to ye Contre Rode between John Buss and Richard Denmor [s] Field," a road three rods wide, "by s^d Willeys House and From thence to a grat Rock marked H on ye west Side of said way which is called John Buss Corner Bound next to s^d Willeys House so from s^d Rock Bounded between John Buss and Richard Denmor to ye^e Contre Rode."

At the request of several of the inhabitants of the town of Durham that we the subscribers should lay out a highway for the Priviledg of the town above said from the Kings highway to the Salt water and for a Priviledg to Pass to the meeting house at the falls in sd town and according to their Request we have laid it out Beginning at the East Side of the Kings high way on the South Side of the Bridge at Oyster River falls in sd town sow Running by the Kings high way to the Land of Daniel Rogers where he now lives and then Running Partly by sd Daniel Rogers Land and Partly by the Land of Mr. Hugh Adams down to the salt River and bounded by the River up to said bridge a high way laid out and bounded by us for the Benefit of the Town.

The 14 Day of March 1742 3.

JOSEPH ATKINSON
EPHRAIM DAVIS   } Selectmen.
EBENEZER SMITH

This highway ran around the old meeting house. Some claimed
about this time that the house of Dr. Samuel Adams, now called
the Sullivan house, stood partly on land belonging to the town
landing, and a committee was appointed to investigate the matter. No report has been found. June 29, 1744, an article in
the town warrant was to see if the town will build a bridge over
the falls "where the old bridge now standeth also what manner of bridge whether a cart Bridge or a horse bridge and what
breadth the bridge shall be built." It was voted to build a cart
bridge fifteen feet wide. It is probable that the old one,—how
old can not now be said,—was a horse bridge for the accommodation of those riding horseback and very narrow.

October 12, 1737, John Woodman and Samuel Smith, selectmen, "Capt. Francis Mathes being present and assisted in Laying out this High way But deceased before Sinning" [signing],
laid out a road as follows:

> We began at Wensday Brook the said Road is three Rods wide Running
> by Nathaniel Meaders Land so along by a great Hill and then it Runeth over
> the South Side of Said Hill to a gutter between Thomas Stevensons Land and
> Thomas Footmans Land so Running between said lots till it Comes to the
> Turn and then Runing between Meaders and Smiths Land till it comes to
> Joshua Woodmans Land." [See Town Book, Vol. I, p. 40.]

April 4, 1752, Samuel Smith, Joseph Wheeler, and Joseph
Thomas, Selectmen, laid out a road two rods wide, beginning
"at Moses Davises fence seventy nine Rods from Leut Joneses
fence so caled near folets Swamp at the head of John Woodmans
land next to or near Jonathan Monses [Munsey's] land and from
thence it Runs west north west seventeen Rods to or near a stone,
then it Runs near north to sd Moses Davises Land, this high way
laid out at his Request and for his use for ever." [Town Book,
Vol. I, p. 33.]

April 9, 1753, Joseph Wheeler and Joseph Thomas, selectmen,
laid out "a small peice of Land for a high way," "beginning at
the sd Rode or high way that leads from ye Point to sd Oyster
River falls at where Joseph Wheler joins to sd Rode or high way
and Running bounding on sd last mentioned high way untell it
comes to the above sd high way that leads from sd Oyster River
falls to Lampercel River falls then Running by sd last mentioned
highway to land in possession of Ichabod Chesle then Running
by sd Chesles possession to land in possession of Joseph Wheler

then by sd Whelers possession to where we bagan, to be an open highway for the use of the town forever." This seems to be the piece of land in front of the old pound, at the intersection of the roads coming from the Point and from Newmarket. [Town Book, Vol. I, p. 36.]

On petition of Miles Randall and others the Court of General Sessions of the peace ordered a highway to be laid out in Durham, which was done 20 July 1763, beginning at the "northwest corner of Joshua Woodman's land by Col. Smith's land and running by land of John Langley to Lampereel River where the bridge formerly stood, over said river to land of Stephen Pendergast, then past Samuel Joy's land to David Davis's land, thence to Major Thomas Tash's land, thence to land lately John Smart's, to pisscassick mill priviledge, then over the bridge to the dividing line between Newmarket and Durham." [Town Book, Vol. I, pp. 57, 58.]

March 4, 1765, a road two rods wide was laid out from Joseph Stevens' land on the east side of Johnson's Creek unto Dover line, bounded on the southeast by land of Nathaniel Lammos.

March 13, 1758, a road was laid out from Wadley's mill pond in Lampereel River to Little River, in what is now Lee. Mention is made of lands of John Durgin, Joseph Durgin, Edward Woodman and Ebenezer Smith.

At the General Court convened 11 February 1768, there was a petition for a highway two rods wide from Lamprey River bridge to the road leading from Durham Point to Durham Falls. Lands of the following parties are mentioned along the route proposed, Joseph Ham, Walter Bryant, Esq., Abraham Bennet, Samuel Smith, Joseph Chesley, heirs of Ebenezer Smith, Esq., deceased, John Smith, Thomas Stevenson, Joseph Footman, Dependance Bickford, John Durgin, Heirs of Ebenezer Smith, to Mathes Creek, so called, near the mill, and over the creek between lands of the Hon. Peter Livius, Esq., and John Kent, John and Joseph Drew, to road leading from Durham Point to the Falls. This petition was signed by David Davis, Moses Edgerly, Jr., Trueworthy Durgin, Jr., Stephen Wille, Jr., Nathaniel Norton, George Bickford, Valentine Mathes, John Mead, Ede Hall Burgin, Zebulon Doe, Jr., Jonathan Doe, Edward Smith, Bradstreet Doe, James Cram, Thomas Stevenson, Joseph Drew, John Drew, Joseph Wormwood, Jr., Dependance

Bickford, Francis Mathes, John Edgerly, John Smith, George Tuttel, Timothy Murray, and John Mundro. March 7, 1768, Capt. Thomas Chesley was appointed agent for the town to answer this petition. This road, or path, must have been in use for more than a century. It is a hard, rough road now, much of the way, and it would impoverish the town to fit it for automobiles.

March 24, 1752, a road was laid out from a small pitch pine bush on the north side of the way or path by the Spruce hole,

SPRUCE HOLE
Near boundary of Lee, 100 feet deep, five acres.

running south southwest to the pitch of the hill by James Hall's house, thence to Jethro Furber's land, thence as the way now goes to John Davis' grist mill, then crossing the Little River about two rods above said mill it runs southwest and by south to Samuel Chesley's line and then on Chesley's and Smith's lines. Laid out by Joseph Thomas, Samuel Smith and Joseph Wheeler, Selectmen.

March 15, 1771, Ebenezer Thompson and John Smith, Selectmen, laid out a road at the request of Joseph Stevens,

leading from said Joseph Stevens Pasture to the highway near Chesleys Grist Mill in Durham as follows, Viz., Beginning at said Stevens Pasture at a saplin pine markt I on three sides standing on land of Francis Mathes thence through said Mathes land North nine degrees East Eleven Rods to land in Possession

PASCATAQUA BRIDGE

From "A Tour of the Eastern States in the Year 1797," by Robert Gilmor, of Baltimore. This is a pen-sketch by the author. Published by the Boston Public Library.

of George Chesley, Thence North Forty one degrees East Eleven Rods thence
North forty four degrees East Twenty Rods thence North Eleven degrees
East Eight Rods to a heap of stones, the highway laying on the Eastern side
of the aforesaid lines and from thence to the aforesaid highway to Chesleys
mill as the fence now stands between the aforesaid George Chesleys land and
land in Possession of the heirs of Edward Small Deceased, said fence to be
accounted the middle of the highway and the highway to be Two Rods wide
the whole length. Said highway being laid out as near as can be ascertained
where a highway was formerly laid out and a return thereof entered on Dover
Town Book of Records Leading from Chesleys mill to Second Falls on Lam-
pray River." [Town Book, Vol. I, p. 532.]

A petition, dated 23 November 1791, and signed by certain
inhabitants of New Hampshire, was addressed to the General
Court, asking for a road from Concord to Durham. The petition represents that the roads from the sea coast inland are

RELICS OF PASCATAQUA BRIDGE

crooked and indirect and that the trade would be greatly facili-
tated by straightening the same; that a road can be built from
Durham Falls to Concord in thirty miles, and will save to the
consumer the expense of forty-five miles of carriage, all of which
has been demonstrated by survey and plans already drawn. The
General Court appointed a committee, 10 December 1791, with
full powers to survey and establish a road from Concord to Durham Falls and to Newmarket Bridge. This first New Hampshire Turnpike was followed by fifty-two more in the state before
the year 1812. After a time most of them failed to yield revenues
and their charters were surrendered. Others were dissolved
under a legislative act of 1838, which gave the towns the right
to convert a turnpike into a highway upon appraisal and payment of damages.

In the laying out of this Turnpike mention is make that it
"joins the now road at the end of a causeway near John Thomp-
sons" and goes on to "the road leading to the Lee meeting house,
thence leaving Lee road." Damages were allowed to Jonathan
Warner, Col. Stephen Evans and John Thompson. The report

was signed 16 June 1792, and accepted by General Court 21 June of the same year.

This Turnpike was continued on the north side of the river, to Meader's Neck, after the construction of Pascataqua bridge in 1794. This bridge was 2,362 feet long and 38 feet wide, built from Fox Point in Newington to Rock Island, thence to Goat Island by an arch of 240 feet, thence to Meader's Neck or Tickle Point, where there was a toll gate. The architect was Timothy

BOSTON & MAINE RAILROAD STATION, DURHAM
Erected 1911

Palmer of Newburyport, Mass. There was a draw for the passage of vessels. A sketch of it was made by Robert Gilmor of Baltimore in 1797. The original cost of this bridge was $65,-947.34 and it was sold half a century later for $2,000. It gave way in 1830 and again in 1854, and 600 feet of it, on the Newington side, was carried away by ice, 18 February 1855. It was not rebuilt. The construction of the railroad turned the course of travel. The vicinity of the Durham terminus is still known as Pascataqua Bridge, and the school district here is known by the same name. For more minute description of this bridge see Miss Thompson's Landmarks in Ancient Dover.

As early as 1792 a stage was run through Durham to Boston from Dover but was discontinued through lack of patronage. Twenty years later two lines of stage were started from Dover to Boston, one running by the way of Haverhill and the other through Newburyport. They continued to run till 1841, when the Boston and Maine Railroad Company opened its line from Exeter to Dover.

The road from the Falls to Madbury formerly led around through Bagdad, where Dea. W. S. Meserve now lives. It was straightened early in the nineteenth century, so as to pass directly by the Judge Thompson house. March 12, 1811, it was voted in town meeting that the selectmen let the building of this road to the lowest bidder, although for two years the building of it had been opposed.

The ferries from Fox Point in Newington to Meader's Neck and to Oyster River Point, the latter called Bickford's Ferry, Furber's Ferry from Furber's Point in Newington to Mathes Neck and to Durgin's farm on the west side of the mouth of Crommett's Creek, the ferry across Lamprey River, etc., have been repeatedly and sufficiently mentioned in this book and in the Landmarks in Ancient Dover.

BURIAL PLACES

The oldest graveyard of which we have any knowledge was near the meeting house, built in 1656, on the south side of Oyster River, in the vicinity of the oyster bed. The site was sold with the parsonage lands to Daniel and Robert Mathes, 13 April 1837, and no reservation of the burial ground was made. All traces of the old meeting house, the parsonage and the graveyard have disappeared, except that near the river may be seen some flat, oblong pieces of rough granite, scattered about, that may have marked the resting places of some of the first settlers in this vicinity. It is believed that careful investigation, with the use of the spade, would reveal this earliest cemetery.

Only a few families, however, availed themselves of this resting place for their dead. On nearly every original farm may be found a sacred spot, marked with granite, unlettered stones and low mounds. The new owners of the old farms have sometimes respected such spots, and sometimes they have not. The dead were buried near the garrisons or private houses, where the graves of loved ones could be seen and cared for every day. Nobody knew how to polish and chisel granite, and slate headstones were expensive and hard to be obtained at any price. A mound and two roughly split stones were the usual memorials, and doubtless, while relatives survived, flowers grew and faded on those little mounds. Even to this day new residents sometimes place a handful of flowers upon graves of the unknown. Ought not the many prosperous descendants of the first settlers to fence and properly mark the resting places of their ancestors? This has been well done in several instances.

On the north side of Oyster River, and near its mouth, several generations of the Meader family lived, died and were buried, on land now owned by Edward L. Emerson. Other portions of the Meader farm are owned by Elisha R. Brown, Stephen P. Chesley and others. Tradition says that six or seven persons from Durham Point, on their way to the boat from a religious meeting held at the garrison house of Col. James Davis, were waylaid and slain by Indians on the Meader land, just below

Davis' Creek. Their bodies were discovered a few days later and buried where they lay. Their graves can still be pointed out.

On the other side of the Turnpike road, on the Odiorne farm, now owned by David W. Watson, are the graves of the Odiorne family.

On the Emerson farm, a little further up the river, are the graves of the early Knight family.

Above Davis' Creek, in the field overlooked by the site of the garrison, were buried the families of Ensign John Davis and of his distinguished son, Col. James Davis.

Still further up the river are the graves of Joseph Smith and many descendants. His headstone states that he was the first European to till the soil where he is buried. This burial lot has a split stone wall around it, and the present owner of the farm, Forrest S. Smith, keeps the place in admirable condition. Near by are the graves of Col. Gilmore's family.

Crossing Bunker's Creek we see the remains of the old Bunker garrison, on the hill north of the highway. Near by is the house sold by Fred M. Bunker to Clarence Fowler a few years ago, near which are some of the Bunker graves, but the oldest Bunker graves are in the field across the highway and near the river. The field is now owned by Mrs. Joseph Smith. Here were buried James Bunker, the emigrant, Benjamin Bunker who took part in the siege of Louisburg, and others.

On the farm owned by Clarence Fowler, across the road from his house, are the graves of some of the Twombly family, once resident on this farm.

There are Ransom graves on the farm of Friend Pinkham.

Passing up the highway, or Turnpike as it is called, and crossing Jones' Creek we come to the land first owned by Stephen Jones about 1663. Down to the present generation the Jones family have been buried on a high knoll, in sight from the Turnpike. A massive stone wall has been built around a spacious burial lot. It ought to stand for centuries. It is the best built burial enclosure to be found in this section of the country.

On the south side of the Turnpike is the farm of the late John T. Emerson, at one time owned by the Leathers family. Near the river is the Emerson tomb. On another farm near by, owned by the heirs of the late George P. Emerson, are more Emerson graves.

On the north side of the Turnpike, west of the Jones farm, on land now owned by the heirs of the late William P. Ffrost, formerly the town farm, and before that owned by the Chesley family, is the old Chesley burial place, where Philip Chesley, the emigrant, Col. Samuel Chesley and many others of the Chesley family were buried. A later Chesley burial ground is fenced about in the open field. Near by, on land owned by Samuel Kidder, are Foss graves.

On the George B. Palmer farm, formerly the Jackson farm, are Jackson graves, which were near the barn, but not visible at the present time, as the plow has removed all traces of the graves within a few years.

Near the point of intersection of the Dover road with the Turnpike road is the Coe burial lot, where Joseph Coe, ship-builder, son of the Rev. Curtis Coe, is buried.

Passing over the creek near the Coe farm we come to the farm of the late Dea. Albert Young, and here are buried his father's family and also his Chesley ancestors, descendants of George Chesley. Here also lies Charles S. Davis, a soldier of the Civil War, the father of Walter S. Davis, who lives in this neighborhood. There are graves on the land owned by the heirs of the late Samuel Runlett.

Durham has no public cemetery. The nearest approach to it is the graveyard near the village school house. March 24, 1796, Jonathan Woodman, Jr., of Durham sold one acre of land near Durham Falls "for the sole and exclusive use and purpose of a burying place of them and their several posterities forever to Ebenezer Smith, Jonathan Steele and Ebenezer Thompson Junr, esquires, Joseph Richardson, James Durgin and Jacob Woodman, gentlemen, John Blydenburgh, Benjamin Thompson, Robert Lapish and William Ballard, traders, John Angier, physician, Noah Jewett, joiner, James Leighton, tailor, Joshua Ballard, hatter, John Stevenson, cordwainer, Curtis Coe, clerk, Thomas Pinkham, hatter, Samuel Yeaton, Cooper, and John Langley, blacksmith, all of Durham." There is little space left in this graveyard for burials. The Rev. Federal Burt and wife are buried here, also Dea. Abraham Perkins and wife, and families of men above mentioned.

The New Hampshire College has a residence for its president, built upon the site of a former house erected by Lieut. Benjamin

16

Chesley, born 24 January 1743. He is buried across the Turnpike in the field that the College bought of the heirs of the late
John McDaniel. On the college farm, on land formerly owned
by John W. Emerson, are more graves.

Near the village on the Mill Road, lie the bodies of Moses
Davis and his son, killed by Indians, 10 June 1724. His negro
slave avenged his death by killing one of the leaders, a son of
Baron de St. Castine. Love Davis, daughter of Moses, in view
of the slave's fidelity gave orders that he should be buried at
her feet. This was done and their graves may still be pointed out.
Further from the village, on same farm, were buried the parents
of Love Davis and there is a stone marked "Aaron."

Near the residence of Lucien Thompson is the Thompson
burial ground, where are buried many generation, including
John Thompson, Sr., Robert aad Judge Ebenezer.

On the next farm are buried Capt. John Woodman, builder
of the old Woodman garrison, as well as his descendant, John
Smith Woodman, a noted professor at Dartmouth College.
This burial place, often called the Indian burying ground, perhaps because it was once used by the Indians as a place of burying their dead, is cared for by a trust fund held by the town of
Durham. The Woodman monument is a conspicuous object.

Near the Woodman garrison was the Huckins garrison, and
in sight, August, 1689, eighteen persons were massacred by the
Indians.

On the college farm, near the railroad station, on land bought
of J. W. E. Thompson, are graves of the early Hill family. They
are unmarked, on the brow of the hill, among the oak trees
close to the road. Close by, on land formerly owned by a
daughter of Timothy Hussey, are some graves of the Joseph
White family. North of the road and westerly of the college
farm, on land owned by Miss Martha A. Stevens, are Stevens
graves. Among those buried here are two of her brothers, who
served as soldiers in the Civil War, Samuel Stevens and James
M. Stevens.

In the rear of the George Mathes place is a burial ground,
where Lemuel Woodman and family are buried.

Not far from the Oyster River boundary line, in the woods,
lies buried Eli Demeritt, the emigrant from the Isle of Jersey.
Capt. Samuel Demeritt, his grandson, settled on land granted

to his grandfather before 1700 and left parts of his homestead to his sons, Nathaniel and Israel. On each of these farms are Demeritt burial places.

Close to the Madbury line, on the farm owned by Edward Pendexter, are the graves of the Pendexter and Joy families. On another part of the same farm are Marden graves. There are Woodman graves on the Moses G. Woodman farm. On land owned by Ira B. Hill are Indian graves mentioned 4th of 9th month, 1652, and also Chesley graves. Nearer Munsey's bridge, on land owned by the first Munsey of Durham, are graves of that family.

On the farm owned by George G. Hoitt, formerly the farm of the late Demeritt McDaniel, is the McDaniel tomb, where are the remains of at least two generations of the McDaniel family.

There is an old burial ground nearly opposite the residence of Leonard B. Bunker, on the Mast Road leading toward Lee, where are numerous graves, unmarked, belonging to the Thompson family.

In this vicinity, over the line in Lee, is a large cemetery where many of the Durham people are buried. Passing by the residence of George E. Chesley in Lee towards Packer's Falls, we go by the Corson place, where the Corsons are buried. Then we reach the David Wiggin place, and back from the road in the woods are Wiggin graves.

Across the road, on the Hilliard F. Fogg farm, are two burial places, one of which contains the remains of the Stevenson family.

Next is the Griffiths farm, on which are the Meader and the Griffiths burial places. On the George Dame farm is the Dame place of sepulture.

In this section are the burial place and tomb of the descendants of the late Dea. Samuel Hayes. In this tomb are also relatives by the names of Bennett and Young. The Hayes place is now owned by the Morse family, and the granddaughter of Dea. Hayes, Miss Alice Hayes of Cambridge, Mass., has filed with the town clerk a list of those whose bodies are in this tomb. A trust fund has been left to the town, the interest of which is to be used in caring for this burial place.

On the farm owned by Albert Brown, formerly known as the Young place, are graves of the Young family.

On the Pendergast garrison farm, now owned by John H. Scott, the Pendergast family lie buried.

On the farm owned by H. H. Dame, formerly the Joseph R. Chesley place, are Chesley graves, and in this place George Chesley was killed by lightning, 12 June 1878.

On the Joy farm, now owned by Mr. John Gooch, is the Joy cemetery, well cared for, in which are buried the Joy family, one of whom was Dea. Samuel Joy. Here also is the $3,000 monument in memory of David F. Griffiths and his wife, Sarah E. Griffiths. Mrs. Griffiths gave a trust fund to the town to insure the care of this monument.

On the Eben M. Davis farm, near the Newmarket line, once stood the David Davis garrison, and on this farm four or five generations of the Davis family have lived and died and been buried.

On the Daniel T. Woodman farm are three burial places, the oldest of which is the Pitman, then the Moses Wiggin, then the Woodman. There are graves on a farm in this vicinity owned by Joseph Bascom.

On the farm now owned by Herbert Tuttle and formerly onwed by the Bennett family are the Bennett graves. Here lies Capt. Eleazer Bennett, who was one of the party that captured the gunpowder at Fort William and Mary in December 1774. On the George Dame place are graves of the Dame family.

On the Ezra Parsons farm, formerly the Clough farm, are Clough graves. There are Bickford graves on the farm owned by Roscoe Otis. On the Newmarket road leading toward Durham village, near the residence formerly of Lester Ladderbush, is the Mooney burial place, enclosed by a stone wall. Here are buried descendants of Col. Hercules Mooney. Cogans are buried on the Levi Davis farm, now owned by Frank E. Doe.

In Lubberland, on the farm of Peter Smith, are Chesley graves, and the garrison built by Joseph Chesley about 1707 was located in this vicinity.

On the farm owned by Frank Emerson, at Lubberland, are graves of the Drew family, among which is that of Nicholas Drew. On the old Smith farm are buried Judge Valentine Smith and his ancestors.

On the farm owned by John B. G. Dame are the graves of the Dame family and also of the Bickford family, the remains of some of the Bickford family having been taken up near the residence of Hon. Jeremiah Langley and reinterred here.

On the farm of Joseph M. R. Adams, formerly known as Mathes Neck, is the Adams tomb, where lie the remains of Rev. John Adams, known as "Reformation John Adams."

On the Eben Kent farm are buried eight generations of the descendants of Oliver Kent. On the next farm north, formerly that of Thomas Drew, lie buried Thomas and his wife, Tamsen, and many of their descendants, in the middle of the field, west of a little gully.

On the Rollins farm, commonly called the Clark Mathes farm, are buried many of the Fernald family who once lived here.

On the farm owned by James D. Meader are some old graves unmarked by headstones, whence some bodies of the Edgerly family were removed.

At Durham Point, on the farm owned by Hon. Jeremiah Langley, down in the pasture back of an old Bickford cellar, are the graves of the Bickford family.

The Mathes cemetery, at the Point, is the burial place of many generations of that family. It is well fenced and cared for. Near by is the mound where the family of Charles Adams, all massacred by the Indians in 1694, are buried.

The graves of "Deacon Langley and Mary his godly wife," as the record of the Rev. Hugh Adams has it, are said to be on the old Langley farm, earlier that of William Drew. On the Stevenson place, next west, and in the middle of a field are indications of early graves.

On the Clarence Smart farm, once owned by Abijah Pinkham, at least a part of it, is a burial place overgrown with bushes. The marble headstones have all fallen, but the inscriptions can be read. Here lie the remains of Abijah Pinkham and some of his family. This is about half way between the Falls and the Point, and not far from the road.

The Burnham cemetery is situated in the field of the old Burnham farm, between the river and the hill on which the garrison of Ambrose Gibbons was built. It is well fenced. There are a dozen graves with granite headstones. Here also are buried Samuel Pickering, who died 15 July 1856, aged 55, and Simeon Pickering, who died 1854, aged 80 years, 3 months.

On the hill back of the Sullivan house is an old burial place, which has recently been cleared up and well walled. The oldest inscription here is that of Phebe Adams, wife of Dr. Samuel Adams, showing simply that she died in 1743. A row of low mounds indicates that probably her husband and his father and mother, the Rev. Hugh Adams and wife, Susannah, are buried here. They ought to have suitable memorial stones, for in spite of his eccentricities the Rev. Hugh Adams and his son, Dr. Samuel, did many good deeds for Durham. This place is also honored as the resting place of Maj. Gen. John Sullivan and family, and Judge Jonathan Steele.

A few rods distant is the Simpson graveyard, where the old sea captain and his wife lie buried, who left their property of $18,000 to the church in Durham and the Durham Library Association, and a small legacy to the town, the interest of which is to be used in caring for these graves.

The Lapish family and the Drew family are buried on the farm now owned by the Ffrost family. Here in an unmarked grave lies the body of James Britton, a soldier in the Civil War in both army and navy. Close by are many rough granite headstones that indicate the graves of early members of the Smith family, for James Smith and his descendants owned this farm many years.

Above the tidal part of the river, on a sightly knoll, lies buried the late Hamilton Smith, Durham's only millionaire. His widow erected a costly stone chapel, in which services are sometimes conducted in memory of him and his wife, for whom the citizens of Durham had the greatest respect.

On the Olinthus Doe farm, near the moat, now owned by the town of Durham are at least four generations of the Doe family.

On the Leonard Bunker farm, on the Mast Road, are the graves of Ichabod Chesley's family. On the Coe place, between the turnpike and Bucks hill, in the pasture, are probably the graves of Jonathan Chesley's family, as he owned this place, and there are graves of the family of Ezekiel Leathers.

On the Walker farm, close to Beech hill, owned by the late Albert DeMeritt, are the graves of the family of Joshua Chesley.

Near the Huckins graves, on the farm of Dea. W. S. Meserve, are buried four generations of Capt, Samuel Emerson's family. In another spot on same farm are the graves of four slaves.

Money has been bequeathed to the town, only the interest of

which can be used, to insure perpetual care of the Woodman, Simpson, Griffiths, Wilson, Furness, and Hayes cemeteries and graves. All families having ancestors buried in the town would show love and respect, if they would give or bequeath money to the town for a like purpose.

SLAVERY

The first African slaves in America were brought by Dutch ships in 1619 and sold to Virginian planters. At that time slavery was quite common in old England, and the American colonies followed the old custom. No law was necessary to legalize the traffic in slaves nor the custom of holding them. Slavery had been a concomitant of war from time immemorial. Hence Indians taken in war were held as slaves and sold into slavery. A large number of those captured in the sham fight at Dover, managed by Maj. William Waldron and Maj. Charles Frost, were sold as slaves in the West Indies.

Slavery was not profitable in the northern states, and most of the slaves were house servants. In 1767 there were in Portsmouth one hundred and twenty-four male and sixty-three female slaves, probably more than in any other part of New Hampshire. As early as 1649 William Hilton sold to George Carr an Indian slave named James, and the bill of sale is on record. In 1767 there were 633 slaves in New Hampshire and in 1775 there were 657. The Revolution virtually put an end to slavery in the North. In 1790 the census shows only 158 in New Hampshire, and these were old servants held and maintained out of kindness, for in 1800 the census shows only eight in New Hampshire. In 1840 one is reported. Durham reported only three slaves in 1790, belonging to Samuel Burnham, Timothy Emerson and Stephen Jones. Lee and Madbury did not report any slaves, though there were free colored persons living there. No emancipation law was ever passed by New Hampshire, though an act in 1789 seems to show the intention of legislators to regard slavery as a dead letter.

Among the earliest slave owners at Oyster River was William Drew, in the administration of whose estate, 1669, mention is made of a man servant and a maid servant. The will of Nicholas Follett, 1700, mentions "my Negroe Man Caezer."

The Rev. Hugh Adams records among his baptisms the following, 17 December 1719: "At a lecture at Loverland, on account of her faith and engagement for its education, our sister Sarah Bennick, having an infant maid servant born in

her house of a Negro father and Indian mother, had her baptized
Mary Robinson." And again, 5 January 1723/4, he records,
"Then at our house, Simon Teko, Indian man servant, owning
his Baptismal Covenant, I baptized our Indian woman servant
Maria, and their Infant born in our house, Scipio," and June 23
1728, "Phillis, our servant child, born in my house of Maria,
our Indian Woman Servant." He baptized, 30 August 1724,
"Peter, the Negro servant of Peter and Sarah Mason" and 5
March 1726/7, "Caesar Sanders, Free Negro."

The inventory of the estate of the Rev. Nicholas Gilman,
1748, names Peter, a negro man, valued at £150.

The Rev. John Adams recorded the marriage of Belmont
and Venus, 1 January 1760. Their surname was Barhew and
they are said to have been brought from Africa and belonged
to Jeremiah Burnham. The Rev. Curtis Coe recorded the
burial of Venus, November 1783. The Barhew family lived
on a part of the Burnham farm called Nigger Point. They had
seven children, Aenon, Caesar, Jubal, Titus, Peter, Candace, and
another daughter. Aenon, when only four years old, was
bought for $100 by Col. Timothy Emerson, brother of Mrs.
Jeremiah Burnham, and became free after the Revolution. He
died 16 December 1827 and was buried, with other slaves owned
by the Emerson family, near the residence of Dea. Winthrop
S. Meserve. Caesar was noted for his singing at prayer meetings. He was acquired by Vowel Leathers, and died in Newmarket after having obtained his freedom. [See Landmarks of
Ancient Dover, p. 162.]

The following bill of sale may be of interest and further follows
the fortunes of the Barhew family:

Know all men by these presents that I Jeremish Burnum Junr of Durham
in the County of Strafford and State of New Hampshire, yeoman, for and in
Consideration of the sum of thirty pounds rightful money to me in hand
before the delivery hereof well and truly paid by my daughter Elizabeth
Burnam of said Town, single woman and Spinster, the receipt whereof I
do hereby acknowledge, have given, granted, bargained and sold and by these
presents do give, grant, bargain and sell unto my said Daughter Elizabeth,
my Negro boy named Jabal now about Seven Years old.

To have and to hold the said Negro to her the sd Elizabeth, her heirs or
assigns, to her or their only proper use and benefit during the term of his

natural life. In witness whereof I have hereunto set my hand and seal this 29th day of June A.D. 1778.

JEREMIAH BURNUM JUNr.

Signed, Sealed & dela
in presence of
JOHN SMITH
JAMES SMITH.

Jabal or Jubal was afterward acquired by Capt. Smith Emerson. Candace, his sister, was given to Elizabeth Burnham at the time of her marriage, and Peter, the youngest, remained with the Burnham family. His sleeping place, called Pete's hole, could be seen in the ruins of the old Burnham mansion.

Robert Thompson was the owner of several slaves, three of whom are mentioned in the settlement of his estate, 1752, viz., John Battles valued at £350, Page £120, and Nan £350. The wife of Robert Thompson in her will gave to her brother, Solomon Emerson, her negro woman, Dinah.

A negro servant of Solomon Emerson, named George, about to go to war, made his will, 5 June 1777, giving property to wife, Phillis. A negro slave named Sidon is mentioned in the inventory of Samuel Thompson, 1755.

The inventory of the estate of Capt. Samuel Emerson, 1743, shows the appraisal of one man negro at £55, one woman negro at £80 and one young man negro at £130.

The inventory of Capt. Samuel Demeritt, 1770, shows that he owned a negro named Prince.

A negro man, Peter, belonging to Hon. George Frost was buried 16 July 1785, according to record of the Rev. Curtis Coe.

Judge Valentine Smith used to mention a female slave named Phillis, who took excellent care of his mother, Lydia Millett Smith, in her sickness. The slave was buried in the family burial grounds at Lubberland.

Col. Thomas Tash had a slave named Oxford Tash, who died 14 October 1810, aged sixty. He fought in the Revolutionary War and was wounded in action. He refused a pension so long as he could support himself.

A slave of Capt. Nathaniel Randall served in Capt. Thomas Tash's company in 1758. His name is enrolled as "Cesar Durham, negro, by the consent of his master Nathaniel Randal, enlisted April 29, 1758, age 45." Another negro served in the same company and is enrolled as "Sippo Negro Servant to Doctor Joseph Atkinson, enlisted April 8, 1758, age 26."

Peter Adams, negro, served in the Revolution, 1777, from Durham, perhaps slave or servant of the Rev. John Adams, perhaps belonging to Lieut.-Col. Winborn Adams.

Robert Lapish of Durham, in 1777, bought of Jacob Sheafe of Portsmouth a negro slave named Joseph, aged about 37 years.

Gen. John Sullivan had his slaves and special quarters for them erected in the rear of his house. They often rowed him down the river thirteen miles to Portsmouth. One was named Noble.

The following exact copy of a liberation paper will be of interest:

Know all men by these presents that I, John Woodman, of Durham in the county of Strafford and State of New Hampshire, yeoman, for and in consideration of the sum of sixty pounds lawful money to me in hand paid before the delivery hereof by my negro man Dan, a servant for life, about twenty-eight years of age, the receipt whereof I do hereby acknowledge, have given, granted, bargained & sold & by these presents do give, grant, bargain and sell unto the aforesaid Dan his time for life, liberating & making him a free man to all intents as tho' he had been born free, hereby engaging for myself, my heirs, exec⁫ & admin⁫ that no person or persons claiming from, by or under me or them shall have any right to demand any service of him in future as a slave.

In witness whereof I have hereunto set my hand & seal this 23d day of June Anno Domini 1777.

Signed Sealed & delivered   JOHN WOODMAN.
    in presence of
    JOHN SMITH
    JONᵃ. CHESLEY.

This slave took the name Dan Martin and served as a soldier in the Revolution. According to the records of Durham Dan Martin, "late a soldier for Durham," received £17. He and his family used to live on the landing, near the wharves, near the Gleason house. He used to work upon the boats that carried freight to Portsmouth. He died at Greenland June 1839. His wife died 2 March 1830. He was sometimes called Dan Woodman, and he named a son Archelaus, for the brother of his former master. They were buried in the Chesley-Young burial lot.

"Duke Smith" and "Black Pegg" were among the paupers bid off to those who would board them for the least money, 1783-86. The price varied from three to four shillings per week. In 1786 the town was charged "for a Sheet and Shift to bury

Black Pegg in." She had been kept by Robert Wille, and Duke Smith lived with Moses Edgerly at the expense of the town.

The records of Durham show that Portsmouth or Porch was the negro dog-whipper in the meeting house, in 1751, 1754 and 1755. The dog-whipper was once a well-known official in England. In many cases he was the sexton. Perhaps they remembered the saying of the revelator, "Without are dogs."

During the Revolution, 1779, twenty slaves of New Hampshire petitioned the Honorable Council and House of Representatives for their freedom. Among them was Peter Frost, slave of the Hon. George Frost of Durham. They express the desire "that the name of Slave may not more be heard in a Land gloriously contending for the Sweets of Freedom." No action was taken on this petition, "postponed to a more convenient opportunity." Nero Brewster headed the petition, called King Brewster, slave of Col. William Brewster of Portsmouth.

The census returns for 1767 show that Durham then had twenty-one male slaves and eleven female slaves; in 1773 there were fifteen male slaves and nine female; in 1775 Durham had twenty-five slaves for life; in 1786 there were only three in Durham and nine in all Strafford County.

Agitation for the abolition of slavery began in New Hampshire soon after 1830, amid much opposition. A Strafford County Anti-Slavery Convention was held at Gilmanton Center, 27 April 1836. Among those who signed the call were the following from Durham, John A. Richardson, Joseph Coe, G. W. Thompson, Richard Steele and John I. Kelly. An anti-slavery address was given at Durham 17 November 1836 by the Rev. David Root of Dover, on Thanksgiving evening, and at the close of the address an Anti-Slavery Society was formed, consisting of sixty-three members. The officers of the society were Dea. Abraham Perkins, president; Dea. Daniel Mathes, vice-president, and Richard Steele, Esq., secretary.

The great change in public opinion that had gradually come about in Durham, on the subject of slavery, is well illustrated in the following letter addressed to Miss Mary P. Thompson by the Rev. Alvan Tobey, on the occasion of her request for a church letter to join a Presbyterian church at Maysville, Ky. The letter is dated 4 May 1847:

Your request for a dismission from the Congregational church in this place and a recommendation to the Presbyterian church in Maysville, Ky., was laid before the church last Sabbath, and the matter was referred to a committee consisting of the pastor and deacons, on the ground that the circumstances are somewhat peculiar. The peculiarity of the circumstances does not relate to you personally, but to the fact that Maysville is in a slave state, & the Presbyterian church there probably has members who are slave-holders. It is the first instance in which a direct act of fellowship with a church in a slave-holding state has come before us. It is important that we should decide upon the right action in this case, as it may be a precedent in time to come, and our whole course should be regulated by correct principles. Probably a majority of this church would not consider the fact of another church having some members who are slaveholders a reason for withholding from it all fellowship. But if a church and its pastor should defend slavery as right, as a good institution, and its members should hold slaves & manage them for purposes of gain, like any other property, it is hardly probable that we should think it right to have fellowship with them. In this case it seems to us desirable to have more information before we act.

We should be glad to know whether there are slaveholders in the Presbyterian church in Maysville? if there are, on what ground they are considered justifiable in continuing the relation of master and slave? And whether slavery is approved and cherished by the church as a good thing? Or is it lamented and its removal sincerely desired?

Perhaps,—probably, I think, it would have been granted, if all the church had the same views on the subject that I have. But such is not the case. A few years ago the subject of slavery & abolition was discussed in the church & created such a difference of opinion & feeling as threatened to produce serious difficulty. The alienation caused by it then has apparently been healed, & none of us, I believe, wish to have it come back again. We wish & we mean, I think, to act together if we can, but we all are strongly opposed to slavery and ready to express our disapprobation of it and our desire for its removal, if we can in any way that is proper & promises to do good. In my own opinion slavery should not be a bar to christian fellowship.

I believe there are Christian slaveholders & that for us to separate from them is neither wise nor right. It is not the way most likely to promote the abolition of slavery & it rejects those whom, not withstanding their imperfections, I believe God accepts.

The church at Durham decided not to grant the desired letter, after learning that there were slaveholders in the church at Maysville. Had all northern advisers been as wise and considerate as the Rev. Mr. Tobey, perhaps much trouble might have been avoided. Who can say? Both North and South now rejoice that slavery is no more forever in this "land of the free."

The will of Margaret Blydenburgh of Durham was signed 30 May 1849 and approved the first Tuesday in January 1862. In it a bequest is made to "William Lloyd Garrison, the editor

of the newspaper called the *Liberator*, . . . through my
regard to his devotedness and valuable services to the cause of
truth, religion and liberty." The sum was $1,000. Also she
gave the residue of her estate to him, to Wendell Phillips, to
Parker Pillsbury and to Frederick Douglass, the well-known
advocates of anti-slavery principles, as a trust fund for the
benefit of the fugitive slaves who may be in the free states.

EDUCATION

The first record of any public school in Dover is dated 5 April 1658, when it was voted that twenty pounds be appropriated for the maintenance of a schoolmaster for all the children. He was to teach reading, writing, casting accounts and Latin. Charles Buckner was then employed. Probably private schools had existed before this date. Massachusetts, about 1647, required that towns of fifty householders should have a school.

The early ministers, like Daniel Maud, were teachers of schools as well as preachers of the Gospel. Sometimes they were physicians also and they did much law business. Ministers and schoolmasters were exempted from Province rates as early as 1692, and also from military duty.

A petition, dated 1715, shows that the people at the Point were accustomed "to hire a Schoolmaster for themselves and adjacent neighbors." They objected to having one schoolmaster for the whole town, as the school, in that case, would be too far distant for their benefit. When Oyster River became a parish, in 1716, the people were permitted and required to have a schoolmaster. Dover petitioned, in 1722, to be released from the obligation to have a grammar school during the Indian War.

The first reference to schools after the incorporation of Durham as a town is found under date of 8 October 1736, in a preamble to a call for a town meeting, signed by the selectmen, "And itt is the Desire of our Reverant pasture Mr. Hugh Adams that ye town should vote that he should have the one half of his salary paid him on or before the first week in October annually from time to time and whereas his son Winbon Adams was the schoolmaster of this Town for the present year and Deceast in that ofice in the Town service to see if the Town will vote that sum certain Part of his funeral charge be Paid out of the town stock." Winborn Adams was born in Boston and at the time of his decease was 21 years of age.

The earliest schoolmasters in Durham were Hercules Mooney, 1751-66, and John Smith, who is first mentioned in this office in 1757. Both of these were noted in their profession. Dr. Joseph Atkinson taught in 1758, and Dr. Samuel Shepard in 1759, 1762

MODERN SCHOOL HOUSE
PACKERS FALLS DISTRICT
ERECTED 1888

NO 10 SCHOOL HOUSE
PACKERS FALLS

NO 5 SCHOOL HOUSE
PACKERS FALLS

and 1764. Dea. Nathaniel Norton was a teacher in 1767, and William Parsons taught in that and the following year. John Marshall is mentioned as a teacher in 1772. Up to 1754 there seems to have been but one public school. In 1764 it was voted that the school money be divided. In 1768 the town voted to keep a grammar school. In 1769 six districts and committees were voted, and forty pounds were raised for the support of schools. After the close of the Revolutionary War seventy-five pounds were voted to maintain schools.

In the town warrant, dated 8 April 1794, was an article as follows, "to see if the town will vote to build a house for the purpose of holding town meetings in the future or vote a certain sum to be laid out in conjunction with subscribers who propose to build a house for an academy and to have both under one roof." The proposal was defeated. The next year the town voted "that money should be raised sufficient to build a school house in each district in the town." At a subsequent meeting the same year this vote was reconsidered. In 1797 a committee of eight was appointed to locate and build schoolhouses in the several districts. The town warrant, dated 26 March 1798, called the meeting "at the schoolhouse lately erected near the Widow Griffin's in said Durham." Miss Mary P. Thompson attended school there when she was but three years and a half old. She writes, "The old wooden school-house, where I first went to school in my childhood stood between the Griffin house (now Buzzell's) and the present house of Samuel Runlett, opposite the Richardson house."

The Durham school districts are mentioned in the records of 1794 as 1, Falls, First North District, i. e., in Durham village; 2, Falls, Second North District, i. e., the district around Buck's Hill; 3, Falls, South District, now the Broth Hill District; 4, Lubberland; 5, Point District; 6, Packer's Falls; 7, District below Jones' Creek; afterward called the Bridge District; 8, District above William Spinney's. The last was called the Mast Road District in 1797.

In accordance with a law passed in 1805, providing for the separation of towns into districts for school purposes, Durham was divided into ten school districts and until 1885 the duty of providing teachers was taken from the selectman and imposed upon a prudential committee of the several districts. In Durham,

during this period, a superintending school committee, consisting
of from one to three persons, was annually chosen to supervise
the schools, often the pastor of one of the churches filling this
office for a very small remuneration.

Benjamin Thompson, who founded the college, taught school
three months in 1825 for $12 per month in District Number
Two and $14 per month in District Number Four, as receipts
show. During this time he was informed by a note as follows:

MR. THOMPSON:

SIR—I would inform you that Ivory has Come home with a peace pinched
out of his Check he says by James Langley Between Schools. you will En-
quire into it. From yours &c.   WEAR COLCORD.

Mr. Thompson preserved a list of fifty-seven boys and forty-
three girls who were his pupils in the two districts. The list,
alphabetically arranged, is as follows: Boys—John Burnham,
Joseph Burnham. Langdon Burnham, Moses Burnham, William
Chesley, Ivory Colcord, William Colcord, Caleb Davis, Enoch
Davis, George Davis, Charles Follett, Richard Follett, John
Farnham, Daniel Holt, Henry Holt, Stephen Holt, Joseph Hoit,
Robinson Jones, John Keniston, Nathan Keniston, Andrew
Langley, Gilman Langley, James Langley, John Langley,
Thomas Langley, Alfred Langley, Moses Langley, John Langley
and James Langley again, David Laken, Ezekiel Leathers,
Stephen Nudd, Alfred Paul, Howard Paul, James Paul, Stephen
Paul, Frederic Parks, Timothy Parks, Charles Parks, Alfred
Pinkham, Daniel Pinkham, Stephen Pinkham, William Pink-
ham, James Presson, William Shackford, Mark W. Walker, James
Wiggin, George Wiggin, John Wiggin, William Wiggin, Jacob
Willey, Henry Willey, Ira Willey, James Willey, Ira Tego and
John Tego.

The girls were Caroline Burnham, Eliza Burnham, Hannah
Burnham, Hannah Burnham again, Jane Cox, Jane Davis, Mary
Davis, Sarah Ann Colcord, Temperance Ann Edgerly, Susan
Farnham, Abigail Farnham, Caroline Follett, Elizabeth Holt,
Elizabeth Hussey, Caroline Jenkens, Mary Keniston, Lucia Ann
Keniston, Abigail Langley, Abigail Langley again, Abigail Lang-
ley, 3d, Martha Langley, Mary Ann Langley, Sophronia Langley,
Sarah Langley, Deborah Langley, Caroline Mathes, Jane Nudd,
Caroline Paul, Mary Paul, Susan Paul, Temperance Ann Paul,
Jane Parks, Sarah Ann Parks, Eliza Pinkham, Caroline Pinkham,

Sally Pinkham, Fanny Pinkham, Maria Tego, Harriet Willey, Mehitable Willey, Susannah Willey, Mary Willey, Lydia Wiggin.

George Frost was a teacher near the close of the eighteenth century, and one of his pupils was Judge Valentine Smith. The school was in one of the chambers of the Smith homestead at Lubberland. Judge Smith himself taught at Lubberland.

Among the teachers in the village, in the thirties, were Samuel Burnham, Sarah Odell, Hannah Ela, Edmund J. Lane, Susan R. Wilson, George P. Edney, Timothy Hilliard.

Stephen Mitchell taught in 1802; Edward Wells in 1802, 1804, 1805 and 1808; Charles Hardy in 1807.

There was a petition for "a woman school," for the benefit of small children, in 1804. Mrs. Mary Hardy, widow of Theophilus Hardy, and sister of Gen. John Sullivan, was teaching in 1812. She rented the front room in the old schoolhouse between the Runlett and the Griffin houses, and this was called the "girls' room." Here she lived, cooked in the open fireplace, and taught.

Sarah S. Blunt taught in 1835; Abigail H. Folsom in 1838; Preston Rand, Jr., and John S. Woodman in 1839; and Hiram Kelsey in 1840. Other natives of Durham who have become noted as teachers are Edward Lancaster, Edwin DeMeritt, Prof. B. F. Dame, John S. Hayes of Somerville, Mass., George W. Ransom, and Calvert King Mellen.

In the year 1846 the amount raised for schools was $546, divided among the ten districts of the town. About fifteen years later and until the time the district system was abolished the amount so expended annually varied from $1,200 to $1,500. In 1902–03 the amount expended in three schools, with five teachers, was $2,835.

In 1859–60 the number of pupils enrolled was 292; in 1884–85 the number was 148. The length of the school year in 1857 and in 1884 varied in the different districts from fifteen to thirty-two weeks. Now there are four schoolhouses and thirty-six weeks of school. The equipment is excellent, and there is state aid in supervision of the schools.

We have seen that Durham academy was talked of in Durham as early as 1794. It was not till 1839 that the New Hampshire Christian Baptist Conference decided to establish "an Academy where the youth both male and female may be taught the various branches of education free from the leaven of sectarianism."

They further stated that "their wish and intention is to establish
an Academy of a strictly literary character, without any reference
to the profession the students may be disposed to choose afterward." The conference invited requests from any villages or
neighborhoods that wished to have such an institution. In
response to this appeal Elder William Demeritt of Durham, pastor
of the Christian Baptist Church, and other citizens of Durham
became interested in securing the location of this academy. They
were successful in their efforts, and the act of incorporation was
passed in 1840, locating the institution at Durham, to be known
as the Durham Academy. Elder Demeritt was the chief financial and business manager. The original design was to have an
institution that would accommodate 250 pupils, and donations
were solicited throughout the conference. A large share of the
expense, however, was paid by Elder Demeritt, who left his farm
and moved into the house now occupied by C. E. Hoitt, where
he boarded pupils. The academy was located on an acre of
land between the village cemetery and the brick church, bought
of Widow Hannah Young. It was a two-story edifice built of
brick and stone and consisted of a large room and two class rooms
on each floor, besides a basement. The lower story was devoted
to the boys, and the upper story to the girls, while the basement
was used by the Christian Society as a vestry. The building had
a tower and bell. The site can be seen easterly of the present
schoolhouse fence.

The first term of the academy commenced 27 August 1841,
with Joshua D. Berry as principal, assisted by his sister. Among
those who taught in the academy might be mentioned Trueman K.
Wright, Miss Martha Bridgman of Hanover, who married Mr.
Wright, Maurice Lamprey of Hampton, Mary F. Kent, O. D.
Adams, Mr. Hills, Mr. Pease, Mr. Courser, Miss Richardson,
Miss Allen, Orrin Payson, Edward Lancaster, Ira G. Hoitt,
James Bates, Dr. John G. Pike, Joshua M. Pitman, Mary E.
Kelley, George K. Hilton, Abraham Burnham and George F.
Kelton.

Among the pupils who attended were Hon. Joshua B. Smith,
Miss Mary P. Thompson, Maj. Enoch G. Adams, Dr. John G.
Pike, Dr. T. J. W. Pray, Hamilton Smith, John S. Hayes, J. W.
Coe, John E. Thompson, Dr. R. L. Hodsdon and Dea. Winthrop
S. Meserve.

Elder William Demeritt died in 1842 and the academy severely felt his absence. An effort was made to cancel the debt and to raise an endowment. The tuition and other resources were not sufficient to meet expenses, and thus the institution gradually declined. Higher institutions of learning must give much for little in order to attract students. Education has to be about as free as the Gospel before many will be induced to receive it.

VILLAGE SCHOOL HOUSE
Erected on site of the Brick Meeting House

But while Durham Academy flourished, it ranked high in efficiency and was a credit to the town.

In one term sixty-eight males and forty-four females were enrolled as pupils, about thirty per cent. being non-residents and some coming from other states. The academic year consisted of four terms of eleven weeks each. Students were fitted for college, and there were other courses of four years. The tuition was $4 per term, with additional expense for extras. Board was from $1.25 to $1.50 per week, including everything except wood.

In 1864 John S. Smith, pastor of the First Christian Church, proposed that the academy building be sold at auction and the seats used for the brick church that had been built near by. The walls were cracked and the building was unsafe. The brick and stone were taken to Portsmouth. The bell was stored in Mark Willey's shop, and in 1879 it could not be found, and an effort was made to collect $42 for it.

For about sixty years the people of Durham have missed the advantages of the academy and have been obliged to pay tuition and car-fares to have their children attend the high school, academy, or seminary in Dover, Newmarket, Exeter or other towns. Some families have removed from town in order to educate their children, and other families have not moved into town because of this lack of educational facilities. This has been a serious loss to the town. The growing college and increasing population demand a preparatory school of first grade. Such an institution would help Durham in many ways. The consequent increase of value to real estate would indirectly pay for the building. It would attract students and families to the town. It is hoped that some generous person may imitate the noble example of Benjamin Thompson and give or bequeath funds sufficient to establish an institution that shall even surpass in honor and usefulness old Durham Academy.

The following is Durham's Collegiate Roll of Honor: John Sullivan, James Sullivan and George Sullivan, Harvard, 1790; Jacob Sheafe Smith, Harvard, 1805; Henry Smith, Bowdoin, 1810; John A. Richardson, Dartmouth, 1819; Richard Steele, Dartmouth, 1815; John Thompson, Harvard, 1822; Hamilton Smith, Dartmouth, 1829; Charles Ingalls, Dartmouth, 1829; George P. Mathes, Dartmouth, 1834; William B. Smith, Dartmouth, 1840; John S. Woodman, Dartmouth, 1842; Enoch George Adams, Yale, 1849; Hilliard Flanders, Union Seminary, 1849; John Isaac Ira Adams, Yale, 1852; George T. Wiggin, Dartmouth, 1859; William A. Odell, Harvard, 1864; George S. Frost, Dartmouth, 1865; Gen. Charles W. Bartlett, Dartmouth, 1869; Edwin DeMeritt, Dartmouth, 1869; Frank DeMeritt, Dartmouth, 1870; George E. Thompson, Dartmouth, Chandler Scientific, 1879, and Harvard Medical, 1884; George W. Ransom, Dartmouth, 1886; Miss Ada M. Thompson, Wellesley, 1886; Rev. William J. Drew, Berea, 1891; Miss Margaret A. Coe, Smith College, 1896; Miss Anne H. Coe, Smith College, 1902; Roy W. Mathes, Dartmouth Medical, 1906; John R.

Mathes, Dartmouth, 1900; James M. Mathes, Dartmouth, 1911; Miss Ruth E. Thompson, Denver University, 1912; Calvert King Mellen, Norwich University, 1884.

The following residents of Durham have graduated at the New Hampshire College of Agriculture and Mechanic Arts:

Miss Carrie L. Comings, 1897; Miss M. E. Comings, 1897; Leslie D. Hayes, 1897; Miss Mabel L. Hayes, 1898; Miss Etta L. Simpson, 1899; Miss Fannie Burnham, 1900; Charles E. P. Mathes, 1900; Miss Alvena Pettee, 1900; Miss Blanche M. Foye, 1900; Harold M. Runlett, 1901; Eugene P. Runlett, 1902; Ernest F. Bickford, 1903; David A. Watson, 1903; Frank R. Brown, 1903; Everett G. Davis, 1903; Albert N. Otis, 1903; Horace J. Pettee, 1905; Warren C. Hayes, 1905; Miss Lucia S. Watson, 1907; Miss Sarah E. Pettee, 1908; Miss Katharine DeMeritt, 1908; Miss Margaret DeMeritt, 1908, M. A., 1912; Mary A. Chesley, 1908; Stephen DeMeritt, 1912; Miss Bernice M. Hayes, 1912; Myles S. Watson, 1912; Charles F. Scott, 1913; Miss Marie L. Robertson, 1900.

THE NEW HAMPSHIRE COLLEGE OF AGRICULTURE AND MECHANIC ARTS

It was a great day for Durham when this institution, which began its existence in 1866 at Hanover, was removed here. The inducement was the bequest of Benjamin Thompson, of which mention is made in the biographical sketch of that benefactor. The bequest, by accumulation of interest, now amounts to an endowment of nearly $800,000, and its annual income of about $32,000 became available first in 1910. The State appropriated $100,000 for building in 1891 and an additional appropriation of $35,000 in 1893, when the college entered upon its new career. New buildings have been added from time to time, made necessary by the rapidly increasing number of students and by new courses of study. Its halls and campus are taking on the appearance of the old New England colleges, except that the campus is larger and has greater variety of landscape, with much natural beauty. The college owns 380 acres, of which seventy acres are forest and one hundred and twenty acres are in tillage. There are hill and dale, orchard and woodland, meadow and stream, gardens and greenhouses, race-track and ball-ground. A special

NEW HAMPSHIRE COLLEGE

MORRILL HALL

NESMITH HALL

CONANT HALL

SMITH HALL

THOMPSON HALL

GYMNASIUM

GREENHOUSES

LIBRARY

FARM BUILDING

dormitory has been built for young ladies, and the young men in clubs hire spacious houses with all needed accommodations. The removal of the railroad track toward the west and the disappearance of several unsightly buildings have made possible the further beautifying of the campus.

The growth of the college has been phenomenal. In 1893 the enrollment of students numbered only thirty and there were only seven professors in the Faculty. Now there are 354 students enrolled and the Faculty has forty-two instructors. Nearly 2,000 students have already availed themselves of the privileges of this institution, perhaps induced in many cases by the reasonableness of expense, which need not exceed $300 annually. There are also a goodly number of scholarships, besides opportunities for partial self-support. Here may be found an earnest set of young people, who go to college for hard intellectual work more than for athletics and a general good time. However, they get athletic exercises and good times incidentally, the way happiness must always come. There is an excellent gymnasium and the play-ground adjoining welcomes often enough teams and ball clubs from other New England colleges.

The buildings of the college can not be described in a few words better than by quoting from the last bulletin:

Thompson Hall is the main administrative building and contains the offices of the President, the Dean, the Registrar and the Purchasing Agent. Here also are located the departments of Drawing and Machine Design, Modern Languages, Mathematics and Zoölogy.

Conant Hall is given over wholly to the departments of Chemistry, Physics and Electrical Engineering.

Morrill Hall contains the Experiment Station Library of over twenty-five hundred volumes, the office of the Director of the Experiment Station, and the laboratories, lecture rooms and offices of the departments of Agronomy, Animal Husbandry, Horticulture and Forestry.

Nesmith Hall is occupied by the departments of Chemistry and Botany of the Experiment Station and contains the laboratory and lecture room of the department of Botany of the college.

The Mechanical Engineering Building contains a wood shop, a machine shop, a forge shop, a foundry and the laboratories of the Mechanical Engineering department.

In the Armory are the lecture rooms and offices of the Military department, the rooms of the College Club and a large drill hall or gymnasium.

The Dairy Building is arranged and equipped in the most up-to-date and sanitary manner. It contains a commercial creamery, with separator room, churning room and cold storage room; laboratories for giving instruction in

THOMPSON HALL

milk testing, milk inspection, farm butter and cheese making and bacteriology; a reading and exhibition room; a class room and offices.

The college has also an insectary, a large modern dairy barn, several smaller barns for sheep, horses, etc., and a range of greenhouses especially planned for carrying on up-to-date work in greenhouse management.

Smith Hall, the woman's dormitory, was made possible by the generosity of Mrs. Shirley Onderdonk, of Durham, who gave sixteen thousand dollars as a memorial to her mother, Mrs. Alice Hamilton Smith. The remainder of the cost, ten thousand dollars, was provided by the State. The building furnishes accommodations for thirty-two students.

In accordance with an act of consolidation between the libraries of Durham and the college, the books of the Durham Public Library and the college are all shelved in one building and form the Hamilton Smith Public Library. This consolidation makes an especially good collection, the scientific books of the college supplementing well the more popular books of the town library. The consolidated libraries number about 30,000 bound volumes and 10,000 pamphlets.

On the thirteenth day of April 1913, the Governor of New Hampshire signed the bill appropriating $80,000 for a new engineering building, which will be erected at once.

Thus have been brought together in twenty years buildings and property to the value of about half a million of dollars, besides the endowment fund. Surely a firm basis has been laid, and the future growth of the college is assured. The application of science to agriculture has made farming in New England a new and attractive business, demanding brains as well as brawn. The trolley, the telephone and the rural delivery of mail no longer leave the farmhouse in lonely isolation. Good roads are bringing the markets nearer. Will women become farmers, and is this the reason why they are admitted to New Hampshire College? Why not? Indeed, this is actually the fact and one of growing importance. It has been proved that women have business enterprise and scientific knowledge sufficient to manage large farms successfully. There is reason to think that they will soon compete with men in this vocation, as they are now doing in many trades and professions that were once closed to them. Good agriculture is the basis of human welfare in material things, and should be considered an honorable occupation and made sufficiently lucrative.

Look at the list of subjects taught and wish yourself young again, such as the study of soils, seeds, farming machinery, domestic animals and their proper care, dairying, orcharding, horti-

KAPPA SIGMA   BETA PHI   THETA CHI
        GAMMA THETA   ZETA EPSILON ZETA
Houses now or once used by College Fraternities

culture, forestry, botany and chemistry. Thus equipped the young farmer begins his work, knowing what to do on his particular farm and how to do it. He can raise a profitable crop of something almost anywhere, if he only knows how. He can draw nutriment out of the air, by proper rotation of crops. If one does not like farming, one can here become fitted to be a chemist, an electrical or mechanical engineer, a surveyor, a machinist, a teacher, and to handle a great variety of tools. The student learns to do things as well as to philosophize about them. Here is pragmatism in contrast with speculative philosophy.

The military drill, optional in the senior year, is a useful training for many, but will be abandoned with the growth of the college into a State University, for the time is hastening on when international arbitration will keep the peace of the world and the nations shall learn war no more.

Education by the State is taking the place of education by Christian denominations, and the former is no less Christian than the latter. New Hampshire ought to have at least one institution of learning, where women have equal privileges with men and both may pursue any lines of study they may choose. A course in Domestic Science and Household Arts is the latest attraction. Why not have also courses in architecture, sculpture, painting, music, and literature? All these departments will be added in due time. An endowment by some noble patron or alumnus will hasten the desired end.

It is gratifying to know that the college recognizes that it should be an educator of the people at large as well as of the students that flock to Durham. Bulletins of very valuable information go forth from the Experiment Station. "A College on Wheels" is the name given to its Extension Service, that sends lecturers throughout the State to teach farmers how to raise fruit, hay, stock, etc., that makes exhibits at fairs, and enrolls whosoever will in agricultural reading courses.

The first president of the college, after its separation from Dartmouth and removal to Durham, was Dr. Charles S. Murkland, who took charge in the fall of 1893 and served for ten years. Perhaps the richest legacy left by this able and erudite president is the spirit of true scholarship which characterized his administration and which still remains. President William D. Gibbs

Edward Thomson Fairchild, LL.D.
President of New Hampshire College

served as chief officer during the past nine years. He was singularly strong in his administration of financial affairs, and during his term the college prospered greatly. Several buildings were added and the number of students more than doubled.

Edward Thomson Fairchild, Ph. D., LL. D., was elected president of the college in August, 1912. He is a native of Ohio, educated at Wesleyan and Wooster Universities. His whole life has been devoted to educational work. He taught in Ohio Normal School and served as state superintendent of schools. Later he was city superintendent of schools in Kansas and for eight years was

RESIDENCE OF THE COLLEGE PRESIDENT

a member of the board of regents of the Agricultural College. Three years he was state superintendent of public instruction in Kansas, when he formulated workable and up-to-date courses of study in rural, graded and high schools throughout the state. At the time of his election as president of New Hampshire College he was president of the National Educational Association and also superintendent of public instruction for Kansas. The latter position he resigned upon coming to New Hampshire. He has already impressed himself upon the college and town as a man of unusual graciousness and tact in handling administrative prob-

18

DEAN CHARLES H. PETTEE, LL.D.

lems and as a scholar particularly well informed in educational matters.

Mention ought to be made of the work of Prof. Charles H. Pettee, LL. D., who has served as dean of the college fourteen years. After graduating from Dartmouth in 1874 and from the Thayer School of Civil Engineering in 1876 he accepted the chair of Mathematics and Civil Engineering in the New Hampshire College, then at Hanover. He assisted in planning and providing for the erection of the buildings at Durham and has been a positive force in the development of the town. He is a deacon and constant helper in the church and in the prosperity and future growth of the town he shows his faith by his works.

At the commencement exercises held 11 June 1913 the president of the college conferred the degree of LL. D. on Dean Pettee in the following words:

Charles Holmes Pettee, Dean of the College, for thirty-eight years you have served this institution faithfully and well. Your loyalty has been such that no task has been too humble or too difficult to enlist your quick sympathy and earnest action You have worked for its interests in season and out of season. Ever ready with kind advice or sympathetic assistance, you have been a consistent friend of the thousands of students who have been enrolled in this college. Hundreds of former students and the alumni of this institution will join in approval of the action of the trustees in bestowing upon you the honorary degree of Doctor of Laws, and I now declare you entitled to all the rights and privileges belonging thereto.

LIBRARIES

The educational history of Durham demands that something should be said about the public libraries that have done so much to stimulate desire for sound learning and to enrich the minds of readers. The Durham Social Library was incorporated in 1815, and the Durham Agricultural Library was incorporated in 1862. For a long time the books of both were on the upper floor of lawyer Richardson's office and were in constant circulation. After Squire Richardson's death no use was made of them until Mr. Albert DeMeritt initiated a movement to secure them as a nucleus for a new library. Money was raised, Benjamin Thompson being a liberal contributor, and, 9 March 1881, the Durham Social Library was organized. The books of all the libraries were kept in the Congregational Church and Maj. H. B. Mellen was librarian. The Durham Library Association was incorporated 8 March 1883, and the Richardson law office and land were purchased, the building remodeled, and the upper floor leased to Scammell Grange. Maj. H. B. Mellen continued as librarian on the lower floor, and he was succeeded by Hon. Joshua B. Smith, Miss Mary E. Smith and Miss Charlotte A. Thompson.

Mrs. Lydia Simpson died in 1895 and left about $8,000 to the Durham Library Association, in trust, the income to be used. March 8, 1892, the town voted to accept the provisions of an act to establish free libraries.

March 18, 1893, the town and Durham Library Association signed a contract, securing the union of the library of the town with that of the association.

January 13, 1906, a contract was signed by the New Hampshire College, the town of Durham and the Durham Library Association, whereby the three libraries were consolidated, all three contributing toward its support. The running expenses are paid by the college, and the library is open to all the citizens of Durham. The funds for the Hamilton Smith Public Library building were contributed by Hamilton Smith and Andrew Carnegie, and the building was furnished by the State of New Hampshire. There are 30,000 volumes in the library, five daily papers, twenty New Hampshire weekly papers and a large number of magazines. Thus it is seen that Durham has exceptional library advantages.

In connection with the libraries of Durham honorable mention should be made of Maj. Henry B. Mellen, who was born in Durham 2 March 1828. He served during the Civil War in the Second California Cavalry, continuing in military service till 4 October 1872, when he was retired "for loss of right foot at ankle and left leg below the knee, from injuries rceived in line of duty." His service was in California, Louisiana and Texas, and he had charge of the erection of several frontier forts. Beginning as first lieutenant, he gradually rose to the rank of major. Soon after his retirement he settled in Durham and became interested in the Library Association, serving gratuitously as librarian and on the book committee. He died in Durham 20 June 1907, aged 78.

LAWYERS AND LAW STUDENTS OF DURHAM

Ichabod Bartlett was born in Salisbury, 24 July 1786. He graduated at Dartmouth in 1808 and was admitted to the bar in 1812, beginning at once to practise law in Durham. He removed to Portsmouth about 1818, where he resided till his death, 19 October 1853. He was one of the ablest lawyers in the State. He was clerk of the senate in 1817 and 1818, representative from Portsmouth seven times and speaker of the house in 1821. In 1822 he was elected to Congress and served as representative three terms.

James Bartlett was born in Salisbury, 14 August 1792. He graduated at Dartmouth in 1812 and studied law with his brother, Ichabod Bartlett, in Durham, and practised in partnership with him a few years. He was appointed registrar of probate for Strafford County in 1819 and removed to Dover. He married, 28 June 1820, Jane, daughter of Joshua Ballard of Durham. He served four terms as representative from Dover in the legislature, 1823–26 and as State senator, 1827–28. He married (2) June 1831, Jane M., daughter of George Andrews of Dover.

William Boardman was born in Newmarket, 31 July 1779. He was educated at Phillips Academy, Exeter, and studied law with Ebenezer Smith in Durham. He began practice in Farmington about 1806 and within two years returned to Newmarket, where he died soon after.

Joseph Clark was born in Columbia, Conn., 9 March 1759, and graduated at Dartmouth in 1785. He studied law with Gen. John Sullivan and began practice at Rochester about 1788. About 1810 he removed to his native town, where he died, 21 December 1828.

Nathaniel Cogswell was born in Haverhill, Mass., 9 January 1773. He graduated at Dartmouth in 1794 and studied law with Ebenezer Smith in Durham. He commenced practice in Gilmanton, in 1805, and removed to Newburyport, Mass., about 1808, where he died in 1813 or 1814.

Richard Ela was the son of Joseph and Sarah (Emerson) Ela, born in Lebanon, 21 February 1796. He studied law with Ichabod Bartlett in Durham and was admitted to the bar in

1819. He practised law in Durham from 1819 to 1830. He removed to Portsmouth, and in 1835 he was appointed to a position in the Treasury Department in Washington. He died in Washington, D. C., 8 January 1863.

Peter French was born in Sandown in 1759. He graduated at Harvard in 1781. He studied law with Gen. John Sullivan and practised for a short time in Durham. He died in Maine.

John Ham was born in Dover, 30 December 1774. He graduated at Dartmouth in 1797 and studied law with Ebenezer Smith at Durham. He was admitted to the bar in 1800 and began practice at Gilmanton, where he died 7 March 1837. He served as selectman, member of the legislature, and trustee of Gilmanton Academy.

Winthrop Atkinson Marston was born in Nottingham, 14 June 1804. He studied law in Durham, in the office of Stephen Mitchell. He was admitted about 1829 and practised law at Somersworth and Dover. He died 30 March 1850 at Somersworth.

Stephen Mitchell, son of Benjamin and Martha (Steele) Mitchell, was born in Peterborough, 29 March 1780. He graduated at Williams College in 1801 and studied law with his uncle, Jonathan Steele, in Durham, where he began practice in 1805. In behalf of his townsmen he made the address of welcome to Gen. Lafayette, in the summer of 1825, in a "very handsome and appropriate manner." He taught school in Durham in 1802. He married, 9 November 1809, Sarah, daughter of Joseph Mills of Deerfield, born 22 June 1788. He died in Durham 18 February 1833. He was one of the incorporators of Durham Academy and a member of the Congregational Church, whence he and his wife took letters in 1830, recommending them to the Episcopal Church in Portsmouth.

Moses Parsons was born in Newbury, Mass., 13 May 1744. He graduated at Harvard in 1765 and studied law with Gen. John Sullivan, practising in Newmarket and Durham. He removed to Amherst, N. H., in 1773, and was a delegate from that town to the third and fourth Provincial Congresses. He is said to have been in Kingston in 1775, in Newmarket in 1778 and in Massachusetts in 1779. Governor Bell relates the following story about him. "When he was once about to return to Durham from a visit to his father, the latter gave him some seasonable religious advice. 'That reminds me,' replied the son, rather irreverently "of my mortality. I have one request to make. If I die at Durham, don't bury me there.' His father answered that it was of little consequence where the body was deposited, if the soul was properly fitted for the other world. 'True,' responded his son, 'but the people of Durham are so uncivilized and quarrelsome that I should be ashamed to be seen rising in their company at the last day.'"

John Adams Richardson was born in Durham, 18 November 1797. He was son of Capt. Joseph Richardson, who was born in Boston, 25 December 1756, and married Sarah Hanson of Dover. He graduated at Dartmouth in 1819. He was a teacher in Haverhill, Mass., in 1818 and 1820 and read law there with John Varnum. He was admitted to the bar in 1823 and at once began practice in his native town, continuing therein till his death, 25 August 1877. In 1846 he was clerk of the state senate. In the latter years of his life he was president of the bar association of Strafford County. He is described as a very social and gentlemanly man, having a fondness for the peaceful side of the law, and a reader of general literature. He married (1) Marcia A., daughter of Maj. Alexander and Sally (Adams) Rice of Kittery and had two daughters, Marcia and Frances. His first wife died 8 October 1832, and he married (2) in 1835, Mrs. Frances J., daughter of Hon. Daniel Farrand of Burlington, Vt., and widow of Rev. Thomas J. Murdock.

Arthur Rogers was the son of Maj. Robert Rogers, who became celebrated in the last French and Indian War of 1754 as a leader of a company of rangers. He was born in 1770 and studied law with Gen. John Sullivan in Durham and with Edward St. Loe Livermore of Concord, where he began practice in 1793. He removed to Barrington in 1794, to Pembroke in 1797, to Plymouth in 1800, to Pembroke again in 1803, to Concord in 1812 and to Portsmouth in 1832, where he died in 1841.

Hon. Ebenezer Smith was born at the garrison house in Lubberland, Durham, 13 March 1758, son of Dea. Ebenezer Smith. He was educated at Dummer Academy, Byfield, Mass., and studied law with Gen. John Sullivan, beginning practice in 1783. He was the secretary of Gen. Sullivan while the latter was a member of Congress, 1780–81. He served his native town as moderator, selectman seven years, representative six years.

He was councilor two years, justice of the Court of Common Pleas, 1784-87, aide on the staff of Governor Gilman in 1798, and president of the bar association of Strafford County nearly twenty years. According to Governor Bell he was "very sucessful in his profession and became one of the most prominent lawyers in his section of the State." In 1783 he purchased the Thomas Pinkham residence in Durham village and built an office west of the house, which was used in recent times as a grocery store with tenement overhead. This real estate is now owned by George W. Jennings of New York. Mr. Smith died in Durham, 24 September 1831. [See Genealogical Notes.]

Hamilton Smith, born in Durham 19 September 1804, graduated at Dartmouth College in 1829 and studied law in Washington, D. C., with Levi Woodbury, senator from New Hampshire, and with William Wirt of Virginia. In 1832 he went to Louisville, Ky., where he practised law and engaged in business enterprises, being president of corporations that owned cotton mills and coal mines. He removed to Cannelton, Ind., in 1851. He served as a member of the Indiana legislature in 1858 and was a delegate to the National Democratic Convention at Chicago in 1864 and to the similar convention at New York in 1868. He died in Washington, D. C., 7 February 1875, after an honorable and successful career in law and business. For family see Genealogical Notes.

Judge Jonathan Steele, son of Capt. David and Janet (Little) Steele, was born in Londonderry, N. H., 3 September 1760. He studied law with Gen. John Sullivan and was admitted to the bar in 1787, practising in Nottingham and Durham. He married, Lydia, only daughter of Gen. Sullivan. He first rented a small house near the Durham ship yard. As his fortunes improved he bought one half of the house lot of Ephraim Folsom deceased, where he was living before 12 March 1790. This house was burnt in 1867 after passing into the possession successively of James Durgin, Jr., Dr. Jedediah Ingalls, Samuel Dunster, Ira Cheney and Mrs. Alfred Chesley. This lot was opposite the residence of Mrs. Hamilton Smith. Judge Steele served some time as clerk of court, but declined the position of United States attorney for the District of New Hampshire. He was a justice of the Superior Court from 1810 to 1812, but the position was uncongenial and the salary was insufficient. So he resigned the office and spent his last days in the practice of law in Durham and in the care of his farm and residence, which he built, now occupied by Mrs. Joseph W. Coe. He is said to have been diffident and sensitive to criticism. As a lawyer he had more than ordinary learning and skill. He died in Durham, 3 September 1824.

David Steele, nephew to Judge Steele, was born in Peterborough 27 November 1793 and studied law with Stephen Mitchell in Durham. He was admitted to the bar in 1824 and settled in New Durham in 1825. He removed to Dover in 1850, and died there 6 July 1882.

Jonathan Steele, another nephew of Judge Steele, was born in Peterborough 8 February 1792 and graduated at Williams College in 1811. He studied with Stephen Mitchell of Durham and Charles H. Atherton of Nashua. He was admitted in 1815 and practised in Epsom and Sandwich. He was solicitor of Rockingham County, 1818-23 and died at Epsom September 1858.

Gen. John Sullivan, who was the most prominent lawyer Durham ever had, needs no further mention here. See chapter on Military History.

George Sullivan, son of Gen. John Sullivan, was born in Durham 29 August 1771. He graduated at Harvard in 1790 and studied law with his father. He commenced practice at Exeter in 1793 or 1794, was county solicitor in 1802, representative in 1805 ,and attorney general two years. In 1811 he was elected a member of Congress. In 1814-15 he was State senator, and served again as attorney general from 1815 till his resignation twenty years later. He died at Exeter, 14 April 1838. Governor Bell says, "By universal consent he ranked among the half a dozen foremost lawyers in the State."

John Thompson was born in Durham 2 December 1801. He was educated at Phillips Academy and Harvard, where he was graduated in 1822. He studied law with Stephen Mitchell of Durham and with Levi Woodbury of Portsmouth. In 1825 he established himself as a lawyer in Center Harbor, where he died, unmarried 22 January 1854. His house took fire and, in trying to save a chair which he valued as a gift from his mother, he perished in the flames.

James Underwood is supposed to have been son of James

Underwood of Litchfield. He read law in the office of Wiseman Clagett of Litchfield and in that of Gen. John Sullivan. He was with the party that captured the stores at Fort William and Mary, December 1774, and afterward enlisted in the army and served at Cambridge. In 1776 he became adjutant of Col. Joshua Wingate's regiment raised for the Canada campaign. He practised law in Bedford about six years and is said to have become insane.

John Sullivan Wells, son of Edward and Margery (Hardy) Wells, grandson of Theophilus and Margery (Sullivan) Hardy, was born in Durham, 18 October 1803. He practised law in Lancaster and in Exeter, where he died 1 August 1860. He was admitted to the bar in 1828 and first practised at Guildhall, Vt., for seven years. Thence he removed to Bangor, Me., and in 1836 to Lancaster. He soon became county attorney and served two terms. He was representative in the legislature, 1839–41, being speaker of the house the last year. He was appointed attorney general in 1847 and resigned within a few months. In 1851 and 1852 he was president of the State senate. In January 1855 he was appointed United States senator to fill a vacancy and served till the following March. He was a candidate for Governor in 1856 and 1857, but was defeated. Dartmouth College conferred on him the honorary degree of A. M. in 1857. As a lawyer he was successful, and he was distinguished for his work as jury lawyer.

John Smith Woodman was educated for the law, but turned from this vocation to that of teaching and so is mentioned elsewhere in this book.

Col. John W. Kingman, who once lived in Durham, in the Coe house, practised law with Daniel M. Christie in Dover. He served in the Civil War with distinction as a colonel. He married a daughter of Mr. Christie and removed to the West, serving as United States judge in Wyoming for a time. He then removed to Iowa and died at Cedar Falls at the age of 82 years.

James F. Joy was a native of Durham, who became a very able lawyer in Detroit, Mich. He was born 2 December 1810, son of James and Sarah (Pickering) Joy. He was graduated at Dartmouth in 1833 and studied for a year at the law school of Harvard. He then taught in Pittsfield Academy and as tutor of Latin at Dartmouth College. He completed his

HON. JAMES F. JOY

studies at Harvard and in 1836 entered the law office of Augustus
B. Porter in Detroit and was admitted to the bar the following
year. He became interested in railroad construction and secured
the building of the Michigan Central, and also organized the
Chicago, Burlington and Quincy Railroad. Several other lines
are due to his activity. He nominated James G. Blaine for the
presidency. He was a large owner of real estate and railroad
stock and was numbered among the millionaires. He was also
a classical scholar and a profound student of railroad law. All
this did not hinder his serving one term in the State legislature
nor from taking an active part in the Congregational Church.
Mr. Joy drew the will of Benjamin Thompson, his cousin, and
was one of the executors of the same. He came on and gave a
public address in the State House at Concord in behalf of the
acceptance of the terms of the will, thus helping to secure the
College of Agriculture and Mechanic Arts. Mr. Joy received
the honorary degree of LL. D. from Harvard, Iowa University
and University of Michigan, all in 1869.

PHYSICIANS

The records are not abundant concerning those who have practised medicine in Durham. The knowledge we have is derived from incidental mention in town records and elsewhere.

The first physician, of whom we have any knowledge, was the Rev. John Buss. Most of the ministers of his time had some training in medicine as well as theology, like many of the missionaries now sent out to foreign lands. Hence John Buss cared for both body and soul in Wells and Oyster River. In a deposition, dated 1705, he is called Dr. Buss. He lived beyond the age of ninety-eight, and the town assisted in his support in his old age and in the support of his widow for many years, not because he had been a physician, but in consideration of the fact that he had been the settled minister.

Dr. Jonathan Crosby is mentioned 22 October 1718, when he bought land of James and Mary Burnham. He sold this land to the Rev. Hugh Adams, living on lot adjoining. The Dover records say that he had wife, Hannah, and children born as follows: Jonathan, born 16 August 1719; John, born 3 October 1721, and Sarah, born 18 January 1723-4. His marriage intentions with Mary Dill were recorded in York, Me., 16 August 1729, and he had children, Daniel and Elizabeth, baptized in Dover, 4 July 1731. Since his daughter, Sarah, was baptized in Dover 2 February 1724, it is probable that he removed to Dover before that date. He sold his eighteen acres at Oyster River to Joseph and Samuel Smith, 18 September 1722, and bought of Joshua Cromwell twelve acres on Dover Neck, 21 August 1723. He and wife, Mary, sold this, 16 July 1731, to Nicholas Hartford and probably left Dover about this time. June 1, 1723, the House and Council "allowed Doct^r Crosby for administering to the men under Capt. Gilmans Command as per his acc^t on file £1,12,11."

The Rev. Hugh Adams was something of a physician. He makes mention of practising the healing art at Georgetown, Me., on the famous Sebastian Rasles before he settled in Durham. He probably taught his son, Samuel, the greater part of his theoretical knowledge of medicine, and Dr. Crosby, living at the next house, may have done the rest. Cf. pages 189-91.

Dr. Samuel Adams built the so-called Sullivan house and practised medicine till his death in 1762. The following bill in his own hand-writing, has been preserved. "March the 25th 1759—Sam[ll] Demerit D[r] to Sam[ll] Adams for a visit Blooding & medicians Aply[d] to him £5 = 0 = 0 old Tenor." The Province papers mention Dr. Adams repeatedly as ministering to soldiers. For further particulars see Genealogical Notes.

Dr. Samuel Merrow, son of Henry and Jane (Wallis, or Wallace) Merrow, was born in Reading, Mass., 9 October 1670. His father was probably one of the Scotchmen sent to Boston in 1651. Dr. Samuel Merrow began practice in Dover about 1720 and lived within the Oyster River parish till about 1733. He removed to Rochester, N. H., and died there about 1740.

Dr. Joseph Atkinson came to Durham about the year 1734 and bought the Huckins farm, on the road to Madbury, and probably built the house still standing. He married the widow of Timothy Emerson and had no children. He married (2), 9 December 1777, Elizabeth Waldron and died in 1780. His widow married, 15 June 1788, John Heard Bartlett of Kittery, now Eliot, Me. Dr. Atkinson was one of the selectmen in 1742 and 1743, and was moderator of town meetings in 1762-64, 1771, 1773-74. Judge Ebenezer Thompson, who studied medicine with him and settled his estate, acquired his real estate by purchase from the heirs, and perhaps some property was given by Dr. Atkinson to his young friend.

The Rev. John Adams practised medicine to some extent, especially after he removed from Durham to Newfield, Me.

Dr. Stephen Swett was born in that part of Exeter which is now Newmarket, 3 January 1733 4, son of Moses and Hannah (Swett) Swett. He married, 8 August 1756, Sarah, daughter of Dr. Samuel Adams, and probably learned the arts of a physician from his father-in-law. He is named in 1757 as a soldier or militiaman under command of Samuel Demeritt, ordered to be fitted and ready to march at a quarter of an hour's notice. It is probable that he practised medicine in Durham to some extent, since his first two children were born there. He lived in Pembroke and Epsom, N. H., and removed to Gorham, Me., about 1770. Here he was the first and only physician for many years. He served as surgeon in Col. Edmund Phinney's Thirty-first regiment of foot for three months in 1775, going to Cambridge, and on the sixth of October of that year was recommended by Gen. Washington for a surgeon's commission, which one of his descendants still possesses. In his old age he lived for a short time in Windham, Me., and died in Otisfield, Me., 6 January 1807, at the house of his son, William, who was then keeping a store on Otisfield Hill. He has a host of descendants, among them the writer of this book.*

Dr. Samuel Wigglesworth, son of the Rev. Samuel Wigglesworth of Ipswich, Mass., was born 25 August 1734 and was graduated from Harvard in 1752. After practising medicine in Ipswich a short time he removed to Dover about 1768. He was evidently living in Durham in 1774, for then "Dr. Samuel Wigglesworth" appears as one of the Association Test Committee. He was taxed in Durham in 1777. He was a surgeon in the Revolutionary Army, in two different regiments. He married, 9 September 1779, Mary, daughter of George Waldron of Dover, where he taught school and practised as a physician till about 1792. Then he settled in Lee, where he died about 1800.

Dr. Samuel Shepard is mentioned in 1762. He married Elizabeth Hill, 21 October 1761. Perhaps he was son of Samuel Shepard who married, 23 March 1726, Margaret Creighton and had son, Samuel, baptized by the Rev. Hugh Adams, 24 December 1727. Dr. Shepard was doubtless the same who taught a school in Durham in 1759, for whom Dr. Samuel Adams received pay. June 24, 1765 Dr. Samuel Shepard conveyed to John Edgerly half an acre of land, with house and barn, for £1,500, "on ye southerly side of ye Falls Hill," on the Mast Road. He seems to have practised medicine in Nottingham at the time of the Revolution and afterward to have been a Baptist minister at Brentwood. Rev. Samuel Shepard of Brentwood married Ursula Pinkham of Madbury, 11 July 1781.

Dr. John Angier was born 11 July 1761; married in Durham, 31 August 1794, Rebecca Drew, born 10 March 1766. The following children are recorded in the town book: Sophia, born 5 June 1795; John, born 10 April 1797; Luther, born 23 March 1799; Calvin, born 30 May 1801; Charles, born 14 March 1803, and Joseph, born 24 April 1808. He lived in a house that was moved and is now a club house, near the college.

Dr. Jedediah Ingalls was born in Andover, Mass., 26 July 1768 and graduated at Harvard in 1793. He commenced medical practice in Durham in 1796 and died there 1 August 1847. He married, 3 February 1802, Eliza Currier of Gilmanton. She died 26 October 1851. He lived just across the street from the Hamilton Smith house, in a house that was burned more than thirty years ago. He had a large practice and was regarded with popular favor. A daughter, Eliza, married Mr. Doyle, an engineer on the B. & M. R. R. Another daughter, Harriet, married William Fowler. A son, Charles, was a physician in Andover, Mass.

Judge Ebenezer Thompson was also a physician. [See chapter on Leaders in the Past.]

Dr. Richard Steele, son of Judge Jonathan Steele, was born in Durham, 6 January 1797. He was graduated from Dartmouth College in 1815 and from the Medical College in 1825. He practised medicine successively at Portsmouth, Durham, Peterborough, Dover, Lowell, Mass., Great Falls, N. H., Boston and Newburyport. He returned to Dover in 1867 and died there 13 June 1869.

John Gilman Pike, son of Nathaniel, grandson of John and great-grandson of the Rev. James Pike of Somersworth, was born in Somersworth, now Rollinsford, 17 August 1817. He was graduated at Bowdoin Medical College in 1847, having previously studied three years in the classical department, in the class of 1845. He practised at Durham, 1847–48; Salmon Falls, 1848–68; Boston, Mass., 1858–71, and resided at Dover, N. H., till his death, 31 July 1905.

Dr. Alphonso Bickford, son of Thomas Bickford of Dover, was born 12 December 1817. He was graduated at Bowdoin Medical College in 1837. He practised in Durham, 1837–48, whence he removed to Exeter, thence to Boston and thence after one or two years to Dover. He was Mayor of Dover in 1861 and 1862 and Alderman in 1866 and 1867. He was a skillful physician and had an extensive practice. He died in Dover 31 December 1869. His daughter married Elisha R. Brown of Dover, President of Strafford National Bank.

Dr. William Parker Sylvester was born in Charlestown, Mass.,

2 July 1821. He was graduated from Bowdoin Medical College in 1847 and practised successively at Poland, Me., North Pownal Me., Durham, before 1875, Dover, 1875–78, and South Sherborn, Mass. He died 18 September 1894.

ALPHONSO BICKFORD, M.D.

Dr. Silver is said to have practised in Durham about the time of the Revolution. There was later a Dr. Flanders, and Dr. O. G. Cilley, now of Boston, Mass., practised here. Dr. Woodhouse of Barnstead was here a little while in the 60's.

Dr. Samuel H. Greene son of Simon P. and Mary Augusta (Smith) Greene, was born 12 February 1837 in Newmarket; graduated at Harvard Medical College in 1860, and the same year settled in Durham, continuing in practice here six years.

He removed to Newmarket but still held a large practice in Durham. He was a selectman of Newmarket six years and postmaster eight years and also represented the town in the State legislature. He married, 12 July 1860, Mattie Ross Baker, daughter of Andrew and Mary Jane (Sawyer) Baker and had one son, Walter Bryant Greene. Dr. Greene died at Newmarket 17 December 1911.

Dr. A. E. Grant was born in North Berwick, Me., 30 July 1873. He was educated in the public schools of that town and in Oak Grove Seminary, Vassalboro, Me., He was graduated from Dartmouth Medical College in 1896 and settled in Durham 1 March 1897, where he still resides. Before him Dr. James Roberts and other physicians lived in Durham a short time.

LEADERS IN THE PAST.

Some who properly belong in this class have been sufficiently mentioned in previous chapters. Here can be named only a few of those who were prominent in the civil history of the town and in business activities. Valentine Hill, merchant, was admitted to church in Boston, the 12th of 4th month, 1636, and was made freeman, 13 May 1640. He had a brother, John Hill, who lived in London and named Valentine and other relatives in his will. He was proprietor, town officer and deacon in Boston, member of the Ancient and Honorable Artillery, and chief owner in a wharf. He had numerous grants of land by the town of Dover, between 1643 and 1652, chief of which were a large tract on the north side of the mouth of Oyster River, the mill privilege and five hundred acres where Durham village now is, and the mill privilege at Lamprey River with accommodations of timber on land a mile wide on both sides of the river, for which he was to pay to the town twenty pounds annually. In 1660 "the house of Mr. Valentine Hill, which is his now dwelling house at Rocky Point" is mentioned in fixing the division line of Oyster River parish. This must have been on his tract at the mouth of the river. He had a house also at the Falls.

Valentine Hill was the leading man of Oyster River for more than a dozen years. He built the first church. He was a selectman in 1651 and 1657. He was deputy to the General Court at Boston from 1652 to 1657, inclusive. By petition of the inhabitants of Dover he was made one of the associate judges in 1652 and probably continued in that office till his death in 1661. For further particulars concerning him see incidental mentions in this history and especially the Genealogical Notes.

Capt. John Woodman came from Newbury, Mass., as early as 1656. When the inhabitants of Oyster River petitioned to be made a separate parish they sent John Woodman to represent them at the General Court. He was selectman of Dover seven years, moderator of the town meeting in 1675, justice of the peace, and deputy to the Provincial Assembly in 1684, when resistance was made to the oppression of Cranfield. Upon the overthrow of Andros, a convention was called to form a govern-

ment, and Capt. John Woodman's name appears at the head of
the Dover delegation of six. This convention drew up a form of
government, one branch of which was to be a Council, and in
January 1690, Mr. Woodman was chosen a member of this Council. He was again provincial deputy from 1692 to 1696, 1699,
1703, to the time of his death in 1706. He was also justice of
the peace and a justice of the Court of Common Pleas, 1702–1706.
He held a commission as captain prior to 1690, which was renewed
several times. His garrison was one of the most noted, resisting
all attacks and continuing till it was accidentally burned in 1896.
He was a wise and trusted leader in councils of war and of peace.
[See Genealogical Notes.]

Col. James Davis was born at the garrison house near the
mouth of Oyster River, 23 May 1662, and died at the same place
8 September 1749. His career was one of marked activity and
leadership and shows him to have been a man of superior abilities,
which were readily recognized by his fellows. His name gleams
brightly from the pages of colonial military history and appears
upon the records of New Hampshire as one of the most important
in the formative period of the state. He participated actively
in the affairs of town and colony. Before reaching the age of
twenty he had organized and led scouting parties against the
Indians for the defence of the colony and had received the rank
of lieutenant. This rank was recognized by the Massachusetts
government, 19 March 1689, and renewed by Governor Usher, 20
September 1692, extending through the period of King William's
War. He held the rank of captain during the period of
Queen Anne's War. In the spring of 1703 he was on a scouting
tour in the lake regions of New Hampshire, at the head of sixty
men, and in 1704 he took part in an expedition against the French
and Indians in Maine, for which he received a special award of
five pounds for honorable service. On the 18th of October 1707
he was appointed by the New Hampshire government a member
of the Council of War. In June 1709 he reported that one of
his scouting party (Stevenson) was killed. In 1710 he had command of another scouting party of 110 men, when he was allowed
nine pounds for snowshoes and moccasins. In 1712 he led a party
of 370 men for five months. He was in one or more of the ex-
peditions against Port Royal. Before 1719 he was advanced to
the rank of lieutenant-colonel, and in 1720 was made colonel.

He was moderator of the Dover town meetings in 1702, 1713, 1715-17, 1720-21, 1728-31, and moderator of the first town meeting held in Durham, 1732, in which capacity he served at nine of the following meetings. He served repeatedly as commissioner of highways and assessor. He was one of the selectmen of Dover in 1698 and 1700-01. He also was deputy to the General Court, 1697-1701, and 1715-27. He was justice of the peace and, 9 December 1717, was appointed judge of the Court of Common Pleas, which office he held at the time of his death. On account of disagreement with the Rev. Hugh Adams he and his wife withdrew from the church at Oyster River and joined the church at Dover, in 1723.

Col. Davis received large grants of land in Dover, Durham, Madbury, Rochester, Barnstead, Canterbury and Bow. In 1694 he had a one-eighth share in the entire Lamprey River for the purpose of erecting saw-mills. His lands and riches he distributed among his sons and daughter. [See his will and Genealogical Notes.] Altogether he was the most prominent man of his time in Durham, and few were his equals in the Province of New Hampshire. Strength, courage, conscientiousness, intelligence, enterprise and an iron will mark his career.

Capt. Francis Mathes was the leading man at the "Point" for many years. He served as selectman in Dover thirteen years and four years in Durham. He was deputy, or representative, 1728-30 and 1731-32, and moderator in 1728. He was the town clerk of Durham from its first meeting, 26 June 1732, until 29 March 1736. He is called "Sargent" in 1707, "Ensign" in 1714, "Captain" in 1728. Frequent and honorable mention is made of his services in the State and Provincial Papers. He was active in religious affairs, promoting the building of a meeting house at Durham Point, on his own land, and he sought to make the Point District a separate parish in 1739. He was one of the proprietors of Rochester and was chosen chairmen of its first board of selectmen, in 1727. Some of the meetings of the proprietors were held in Durham. [See Genealogical Notes for further particulars.]

Capt. Jonathan Thompson's name appears on the muster roll of Capt. James Davis in 1712. He was selectman in Dover, 1729-30, and in Durham, 1732-41 and 1746. He acted as moderator in 1733, 1737 and 1745. He was representative in the General Court, 1741-44 and 1748-51, when he served on a large number of committees. He was a deacon in the church during the pastorate of the Rev. Hugh Adams but withdrew and joined the church at Dover when the Rev. John Adams became pastor. He died in 1757, aged about 64.

Col. Samuel Smith, son of Joseph, was born 16 June 1687, and lived on the ancestral farm on the north side of Oyster River, where he died 2 May 1760. He was selectman of Dover in 1727–28 and 1731–32, and was chairman of the first board of selectmen in Durham, 1732, being reëlected in 1734, 1735, 1737 and from 1744 to 1752 inclusive. Five times he served as moderator of town meetings. He was town clerk from 29 May 1736 until his death. He was councilor from 13 January 1742 till 2 May 1760. He also served as colonel in the militia.

Hon. John Smith, 3d, was born 24 December 1737, called "Master" John Smith from the fact that he taught school. He inherited the Smith homestead nearly opposite the Sullivan monument, where later lived Maj. Seth H. Walker and, more recently, John Drew. He died 24 May 1791. He was town clerk 1774–91, dying in office. He was selectman thirteen years, beginning with 1766, and representative from 1776 till 1782. He was a member of the town's Committee of Correspondence, Inspection and Safety, 1774–79, delegate to the third congress at Exeter, 1775, clerk of the House of Representatives, 1781–83, member of the New Hampshire Committee of Safety, 1776–77 and 1781–84. He was justice of the peace after 1780 and registrar of deeds for Strafford County, 1781–91. A petition that he be appointed justice of the peace was signed by eighty-one of his townsmen, stating that he was a "Gentleman who has not only distinguished himself as a patriot but from his early youth by an upright and irreproachable conduct gained the Esteem and Confidence of all his fellow citizens who have had the pleasure of his acquaintance." It adds, "The proficiency he has made in Literature is not equalled by many." [See N. H. Town Papers, XI, 592–94.]

Hon. George Frost, born at Newcastle 26 July 1720, was son of Hon. John and Mary (Pepperrell) Frost. Upon the organization of Strafford County, in 1773, he was appointed one of the associate justices of the Court of Common Pleas and held that office till 1791, for the last few years being chief justice. He was delegate to the Continental Congress in 1777, 1778 and 1779, councilor in New Hampshire, 1780-84, moderator of town meetings seven times, selectman four times. He was delegate to the fourth Provincial Congress convened at Exeter 17 May 1775. He was also a member of the town's Committee of Correspondence Inspection and Safety. He lived in the Smith garrison at Lubberland, having married Margaret, widow of Dea. Ebenezer Smith. [See Genealogical Notes.]

Judge Ebenezer Thompson was born in Durham 5 March 1737. He studied medicine but soon abandoned medical practice for public duties. He was elected one of the selectmen at the age of twenty-eight and held that office ten years, by annual reëlection. He also represented for ten years the town of Durham in the General Assembly at Portsmouth, beginning this service in 1766. He took an active part in the events that led up to the American Revolution. He was among those who seized the military stores at Fort William and Mary, 14 December 1774, for which he was deprived of his commission as justice of the peace. He was a member of all the Provincial Congresses that met at Exeter and acted as clerk, and after the formation of a state government he was the first secretary of State, reappointed for eleven years in succession. He was also clerk of the senate from 1776 to 1786. He was secretary of the State Committee of Safety all through the Revolutionary War and was also a member of the Durham Committee of Correspondence, Inspection, and Safety. He was one of the committee to draw up a plan of government for New Hampshire and to frame a constitution. He held the office of councilor for five years. He was a commissioner to meet delegates from other states at New Haven in 1778. He was employed to settle the boundaries of several towns, being an expert land surveyor and draughtsman. He drew the plans for the church built at Durham in 1792. Twice he was appointed to represent the State of New Hampshire in the Continental Congress, but he declined these honors because of feeble health. He was State senator, justice of the Inferior Court of Common Pleas and in 1795 justice of the Superior Court of Judicature. In 1796 he accepted the office of judge of the Court of Common Pleas for Strafford County and held it till his death in 1802. In the midst of all these cares of State he found time to serve his town as clerk for eighteen years, selectman, assessor of taxes, commissioner and auditor, besides being on most of the committees of

the parish and acting as one of the school committee.   He was
often consulted for legal advice, though he never was admitted
to the bar.   He was one of the presidential electors at the choice
of Washington and also of Adams.   No native of Durham has
held so many public offices nor won more esteem from his fellow

JUDGE VALENTINE SMITH

citizens.   His record is one of honesty, patriotism, unusual ability
and usefulness.*

Judge Valentine Smith was born in Durham (Lubberland)
26 May 1774, son of Dea. John Smith, and died 2 March 1869.
He was town clerk twenty-eight years, from 1802 to 1819, and
from 1827 to 1838.   Besides being teacher and surveyor he served

*See Memoir published by Miss Mary P. Thompson.

as selectman eleven years and as representative six years.   He was
justice of the Court of Common Pleas, 1819–21, chief justice of
Sessions, 1822–25, and was for fifty-six years a justice of the
peace.   He was interested and helpful in the church, in education
and in the Durham Social Library, a highly useful citizen

Hon. Stephen DeMeritt was born 19 December 1806, and died
27 January 1867.   He took an active part in town affairs and

HON. STEPHEN DEMERITT

was often employed in the settlement of estates, being named
in 1856 as one of the executors of Benjamin Thompson's will.
He died, however, before Mr. Thompson.   He served as
moderator in town meetings seven times, and selectman in
1836, 1837, 1841, 1843, 1844, and 1850.   He represented the
town in the legislature in 1837, 1838, and 1844, once being
unanimously elected, and was State senator in 1845.   He is

remembered as honest, able and popular, a strong friend of the temperance cause and a man whose influence was for the good of the town. [See Genealogical Notes.]

Prof. John Smith Woodman was born 6 September 1819, and died 9 May 1871. He fitted for college at South Berwick Academy and was graduated at Dartmouth in 1842, after which he studied law with John A. Richardson, Esq., and with Hon. Daniel M. Christie. Meanwhile, he taught four years in Charleston, S. C., and went abroad, traveling for more than a year in France, Belgium, Holland, Switzerland, and Italy, publishing his Observations in the *New Hampshire Patriot* and the *Charleston News*. He made a special study of art and agriculture. He was admitted to the bar in 1848 and opened an office at Salmon Falls. In 1850 he was appointed commissioner of schools for Strafford County. In January 1851 he was chosen professor of mathematics in Dartmouth College and in 1857 was made professor of civil engineering, to have general charge of the Chandler Scientific Department of Dartmouth College.

Meanwhile he had served as commissioner of schools for Grafton County with remarkable success. After twenty years of service in the Scientific Department of Dartmouth he retired because of ill health and went to Florida for a short time. He returned to Durham and to the old Woodman homestead to end his days and was buried in the Woodman cemetery. He was probably the most prominent and successful educator that Durham has produced. His property, amounting to some $20,000, was bequeathed to the institution he had served so long and well.

Benjamin Thompson was born at Durham 22 April 1806, and died there 30 January 1890. He was never married. His father was Benjamin, and his grandfather was Judge Ebenezer Thompson, mentioned heretofore. He inherited, among other property, his father's residence in Durham village, with neighboring lands, and the so-called "Warner farm," originally a part of the 500 acres granted to Valentine Hill. By strict economy and good management in the course of half a century he increased his property to over $400,000. He taught school two terms in his youth. No public office was held by him save that of auditor one year. He was never strong physically. Nearly all his property was willed to the State of New Hampshire in trust, "The object of this devise being to promote the cause of agri-

culture by establishing . . . an agricultural school to be
located on my Warner farm, so called, and situated in said Durham, wherein shall be thoroughly taught, both in the school-room
and in the field, the theory and practice of that most useful and
honorable calling." The real estate so bequeathed was valued

Benjamin Thompson

at $17,100, and the Benjamin Thompson Trust Fund amounted
to $363,823. Thus he very wisely chose to perpetuate his
memory by honoring his native town and conferring blessings
upon untold generations.

Hamilton Augustus Mathes was born 16 July 1843, son of
John and Pamela (Mathes) Mathes, and died 2 December 1891.

He was educated at Colby Academy, New London. He filled various offices in the town of Durham, being moderator of town meetings seven times, selectman in 1871–72, supervisor 1878–82, and treasurer, 1872, 1885 to 1890. He was one of the prime movers in establishing the Durham Social Library and was its president till his death, in ten years having missed only one meeting of the board. He began to manufacture brick at the

HAMILTON A. MATHES

age of twenty-one and the last year of his life he sold 8,000,000 of bricks. He was president of the Pascataqua Navigation Company, which he helped to organize. He lived at Durham Point till about 1883, when he removed to the village. He employed about 200 men in his five brickyards. He was actively interested in the work of the Grange and was an influential member of the Congregational Society.

Miss Mary Pickering Thompson was born in Durham 19 November 1825, and died there 6 June 1894, daughter of Ebenezer and Jane (Demeritt) Thompson, great-grand-daughter of Judge Ebenezer Thompson. After studying at Derry and Durham Academies, where she took first rank, she attended Mount Holyoke Female Seminary, where she graduated with honor in 1845. A little later she took post-graduate studies at the same institution, then under charge of that famous educator, Mary Lyon. She taught at Oakland Female Seminary, Hillsborough, Ohio, and at Aberdeen, Ohio. Here, in 1847, she asked

MISS MARY PICKERING THOMPSON

for a letter from the Congregational Church in Durham to the Presbyterian Church in Maysville, Ky., just across the river from Aberdeen. Her request was refused on the ground that "Maysville is in a slave state, and the Presbyterian church there *probably* has members who are slave holders." This refusal led her to study into ecclesiastical questions, and the result was that she united with the Roman Catholic Church and, 31 August 1847, she entered the Notre Dame Convent at Cincinnati, Ohio. She taught for a while in the Ursuline Convent at Galveston, Tex., and she was one year, as vice-president, at St. Mary's Female Seminary, Md. During the years 1854-56 and again in 1873-77 she traveled in France, Italy, Switzerland, Germany, Austria, Spain, Belgium, and Holland. The rest of the time during this period and thereafter she spent in literary work at the house which she purchased in Durham village, and in such work, which was her delight, she excelled in quantity and quality. She contributed one hundred and thirty-five articles to the *Catholic World*, historical, biographical, descriptive and religious, besides many newspaper contributions. She was specially interested in everything that pertained to her native town and to ancient Dover, and she devoted years to research work among the New Hampshire Province Deeds, Probate Records, and Court Records, original and copious sources of historical information. The records of Durham and Dover were minutely examined by her. Wherever she looked scarcely anything seems to have escaped her notice. The new things of this history of Durham have been derived from sources printed or indexed since her death or from examination of places which she could not visit. She gathered up a great amount of interesting and valuable folk-lore and interwove it with the facts of history, so as to make everything she wrote interesting as a novel. The beauty of her style arises from the fact that she knew so much to say and the study of several languages enabled her to choose the appropriate word, while her knowledge of general literature is attested by constant allusions to standard prose and poetical works. Her Landmarks in Ancient Dover is a compendium of refined knowledge, indispensable to the historian and full of interest to the general reader. It was completed in the midst of physical pain, yet the whole work is joyous. Her Memoir of Judge Ebenezer Thompson shows a proper family pride and is a loving tribute to the memory of a distinguished ancestor. Durham has produced many honorable and able men and women, but no one of them has done more for the town and merits more gratitude and praise than Mary Pickering Thompson. I know her only in the spirit, and I wish, with many others, that she could have lived to write this history of Durham, as was her desire and intention. Certainly she has contributed more than any other to make it as full and accurate as it is. Durham owes to her some permanent memorial.

Dea. John Emerson Thompson, born 25 September 1815, was

the son of Dea. John Thompson and the great-great-grandson
of Dea. Jonathan Thompson. Thus this family has rendered
distinguished service to the church. He served as deacon from
the year 1870 till his death, 10 January 1892. His father held
that office forty years. The latter was a master carpenter and
built three meeting houses, one of them being the church erected
in Durham in 1792. His ancestor, the first John Thompson of

DEACON JOHN THOMPSON

Durham, built the historic meeting house on the same spot,
about 1712.

Dea. John E. Thompson had a ready and tenacious memory
and was fond of relating stories of old times and people. He
lived about a mile from the village, near to the Jabez Davis
garrison. He is remembered as a staunch supporter of the church
and a useful and honored citizen. He held the office of selectman in 1862. The most of the old shade trees in Durham

Village, especially along the street next the New Hampshire College land, were grown and set out by him and are a good memorial. For family see Genealogical Notes.

Dea. Albert Young was born in Durham 3 February 1837, and died 21 September 1910. He was son of Daniel and Hannah (Chesley) Young. His father was a soldier in the War of 1812

DEACON JOHN EMERSON THOMPSON

and afterward kept the toll-gate on the New Hampshire Turnpike, where Edward A. Marston now resides, and had a tan yard on the Fowler land easterly. Dea. Young was educated in Durham and Strafford Academies. He was an incorporator of the Christian Society in Durham and for many years was an active leader in that denomination. After services ceased in

the brick church he united with the Congregational church and
was made a deacon therein in 1894, which office he held until ill
health compelled him to resign. He managed a shoe shop and
a good farm, the old estate of maternal ancestry. He served as
selectman. He was also an Odd Fellow and a charter member of
Scammell Grange. For years he was president of the George

DEACON ALBERT YOUNG

Frost Temperance Society. His memory was remarkable and
he could tell much about the old residents and houses of Durham.
He was a man of deep and staunch moral convictions, unselfish
and devoted especially to home life. Patient and uncomplain-
ing through years of ill health, he left behind the memory of an
upright citizen and loyal friend. He left one daughter, Mary E.,
20

OLD SAWMILL AT WIGGINS FALLS

OLD GRIST & SAWMILL WIGGINS FALLS

born 4 August 1869, who married 24 April 1893, Charles A. Smart, and has a son, Albert Monroe Smart, born 5 December 1907.

Thomas H. Wiswall was born in Exeter 28 January 1817, son of Thomas and Sarah (Trowbridge) Wiswall. He was educated in Exeter schools and Wakefield Academy and began apprenticeship at the age of sixteen in his father's paper-mill at Exeter. He left Exeter in 1846 and for five years had charge of a paper-mill

THOMAS H. WISWALL

at Dover, after which he was employed two years in the Russell paper-mill at Exeter. In 1853 Mr. Wiswall removed to Durham and in partnership with Isaac Flagg, Jr., the son of his father's partner, purchased a saw-mill on the Lamprey River, in that part of Durham known as Packer's Falls.

Here may be the proper place to say a few words respecting the industries of this region. In 1835 the original dam and a

saw-mill were built by Moses Wiggin, and another building was
added for a grist and flour mill, both two-story buildings.   In
the second story of the saw-mill gingham cloth and blankets were
manufactured by a Mr. Talbot.   Other articles manufactured in
these mills were shoe knives, hoes, pitch forks, wooden measures,
nuts, bolts, bobbins, ax handles, hubs, carriages, sleighs, chairs,
matches, and spokes, by various persons.   In 1854 Moses Wiggin
built a canal and purchased the old Brooks machine shop which
formerly stood where Elmer Kent's stable is now, opposite Lang's
blacksmith shop in Newmarket.   This building was removed to
Wiggin's Falls, then so called, and was the original paper-mill,

WISWALL'S PAPER MILL

a building 34 by 80 feet.   It was leased the same year, with water
power, to Messrs. Wiswall and Flagg.   After three months Mr.
Flagg sold his interest to Howard Moses, and he soon sold out
to his father, C. C. P. Moses, and the business continued under
the name of T. H. Wiswall & Co., until the death of Mr. Moses
in August 1883.   Previous to this Mr. Wiswall had acquired full
ownership of all the mills, and gradually all other manufactures
ceased, and paper became the sole product.   Additions to the
mill were made, including an L, 15 by 20 feet, and a stock house
was built, 30 by 50 feet.   In 1868 a completely new dam was built.
Houses were erected for the workmen, and a store was kept by

Austin Doeg. This continued to be the busiest spot in town till 1 November 1883, when the paper-mill and all adjoining buildings were totally destroyed by fire. Only the dam and saw-mill were kept in use till the spring of 1896, when a freshet swept a portion of the dam away. November 25, 1899, the privilege was sold to James W. Burnham, president of the Newmarket Electric Light, Heat and Power Company, and an electric power station was built at once, Durham seeing its first electric light, 20 February 1900, in the houses of James W. Burnham, Mrs. Sarah J. Woodman (the Highland House), and the Griffiths brothers. The plant has been owned, since 7 April 1912, by the Newmarket Electric Light Company, and a concrete dam and head gates have been built.

Mr. Wiswall married, 22 June 1841, Miss Hannah Thing of Brentwood. He was a deacon in the Congregational church at Newmarket, director of the Newmarket Bank and representative from Durham in 1872 and 1873. He retired from active business in 1883, and died 7 March 1906.[1]

Hamilton Smith, although born in Louisville, Ky., 5 July 1840, regarded Durham as his own home as well as the home of a long line of ancestors. Here he built his summer residence and here he died, 4 July 1900, while on a sail down Oyster River. He became an expert mining engineer. His office was for years in London and later in New York. He was interested in mines in South America, Alaska and South Africa, as well as in the United States. He published a book on hydraulics, a treatise on "The Cost of Mining and Milling Free Gold Ores," and papers written at different times on "The Flow of Water through Pipes," "Water Power at High Pressure," and "The Temperature of Water at Various Depths." An obituary notice spoke of him as "one of the world's great mining experts." He gave $10,000 for the Valentine Smith Scholarships in New Hampshire College, and his widow gave as much more for the dormitory for young ladies, called Smith Hall. Both were very fond of Durham, and their beautiful private grounds were open to all. Mrs. Alice Smith survived her husband and died in Washington, D. C., 15 March 1906. Both were buried in a chapel built on their Durham estate. They were highly esteemed by the people of

[1] The material for the above sketch was kindly furnished by Col. Arioch W. Griffiths.

Durham and will long be remembered for their kindness and generosity.

Ebenezer Thompson was born in Durham 15 August 1821, and died 15 May 1869. He was a man of keen, active mind and intelligent tastes. He was educated in the academies of New London, South Berwick and Andover. He was specially

HAMILTON SMITH

familiar with the early history of the New England colonies and began to collect materials for the history of Durham. For a time he was with his grandfather, Benjamin Thompson, merchant, and Gov. Ichabod Goodwin, Portsmouth. In the early days of the Boston & Maine Railroad he was station agent at South Berwick Junction, and later he was wood agent of the

New York and Erie Railroad, living some years at Dunkirk, N. Y. He returned home in 1854 and the following spring was elected chairman of the board of selectmen and the same year was appointed justice of the peace. He took a strong interest in politics, held several town offices and was a county commissioner.

He was greatly interested in the public schools of the town and was so efficient a superintendent that he received a vote of thanks

EBENEZER THOMPSON

at the annual town meeting in 1861 "for his assiduity and interest taken and zeal manifested in the cause of common schools in this town,"—one of the few votes of similar nature in the records of the town. In his section of country he was the pioneer in growing the Baldwin apple, in which he was very successful. He was also engaged in lumber business, insurance agent for several companies, and director of Newmarket National Bank and

Strafford National Bank. [See Genealogical Notes, and **accompanying portrait.**]

Mark Henry Mathes was born in Durham 2 October 1840, and died there 8 June 1911. He lived on the old Mathes homestead at Durham Point, as a successful farmer, serving the town as selectman and representative to the legislature. In

MARK H. MATHES

the last years of his life he was compelled by rheumatism to walk with crutches. He is characterized as honest, outspoken and kind. [For family see Genealogical Notes.]

Gen. Alfred Hoitt was born in Northwood, 11 January 1806. He removed from Lee to Durham soon after the building of the Boston and Maine railroad and erected a fine residence close

to the station. His buildings were destroyed by fire, caused
by sparks from an engine of the railroad. This led to litigation
with the railroad for four years, and Gen. Hoitt at last won the
suit. For years he conducted a lucrative business in shipping
produce to Boston. He was a major general of the New Hampshire militia and a sturdy representative of the Jeffersonian type

GEN. ALFRED HOITT

of democracy. He served as representative and State senator
for Lee and was once unanimously elected selectman of that
town. He also represented Durham in the legislature. Within
less than a year after his removal to Dover, about 1880, he ran
for mayor and lacked only one hundred and seven votes of de-
feating the opposing candidate in a city of one thousand Republican majority. He died in Dover 9 November 1883.

SOME MEN OF THE PRESENT

In the previous chapter it has been a pleasure to extol the virtues of the departed, and nobody can complain because of this, since death glorifies our beloved. It is now necessary to say something about some who are living, and here words must be carefully chosen and a severe simplicity is demanded. Somehow most of us poor mortals cannot well bear to hear our own living acquaintances praised beyond ourselves. It is impossible to mention all the good people of Durham in this chapter. Modesty should be a prominent trait of the living, and the writer wishes to avoid any accusation of flattery and of having kissed the Blarney Stone. Therefore, the following statements deal with facts only, which must speak for themselves. The names are arranged to suit the illustrations, without any reference to preëminence.

Hon. Joshua B. Smith, son of Hon. Valentine Smith, was born in Durham 28 July 1823. He has served as moderator ten times, as town clerk, 1851–56, selectman nineteen years, treasurer eleven years, representative in 1865, 1866 and 1878, state senator 1875–77, councilor 1877–78, and delegate to the Constitutional Convention in 1876. He was one of the leaders in the organization of the Durham Social Library and was for a long time librarian and then president of the Durham Library Association. He is a member of the Congregational church and, like his father, has done much to support and advance it, both having been active in the building of the present church edifice. He has been a member of the State Board of Agriculture and a justice of the peace.

His sister, Miss Mary E. Smith, has been associated with him in all good works. For years she played the church organ gratuitously. Her private library has been at the service of many, and for a long time she was president of the board of trustees of Durham Library Association, a director, librarian, and on the committee for the selection of books, without any compensation except the thanks and good will of the people. And is not that enough for generous souls? The poor have had in her a benefactress, and many others owe to her more than money can pay. They who give themselves to society give most.

Dea. Winthrop S. Meserve, son of Smith and Abigail (Emerson) Meserve, was born in Durham 7 February 1838. He studied at Durham, Berwick and Hampton Academics. At the age of eighteen he assumed management of the old Emerson farm, which he acquired later. He has been a leader in the Congre-

HON. JOSHUA B. SMITH

gational church, serving as clerk of the church since 1871 and of the society since 1875 and as deacon since 1877. To the business of a farmer he added that of lumbering. He has served two years as county commissioner. In politics he is an independent Democrat, and both parts of that name have hindered advancement in political office in Durham. This has never weighed heavily upon his spirit, nor has it lessened the public esteem in which he is held. In town affairs he has often acted as moderator,

overseer of the poor, selectman and on various committees. He
is also a justice of the peace. As a member of the committee to
collect material and publish a history of Durham he has been
zealous and efficient, the acknowledged superior of all in knowledge of genealogical details of the town's old families. He has
gathered and imparted such information by patient search of

FORREST S. SMITH

public records and by an extensive correspondence of many years.
He has done this *con amore*, for the mere love of it—the trait of
the expert genealogist. [See frontispiece of Vol. II.]

Forrest S. Smith, seventh in descent from Joseph Smith, was
born 30 June 1857, and owns the same acres on which his first
American ancestor settled. He was educated at Exeter Academy

and passed examination for admission to the Yale Scientific School, but the death of his father threw upon him the care of the farm. He taught school in Durham and served some years on the school committee. He made a specialty of raising hay and cattle. In 1887 he went to Boston and secured a position in a wholesale commission house, that deals largely in hay and grain. In 1892

HON. JEREMIAH LANGLEY

he became a member of the firm known as Hosmer, Robinson & Co., and they do the largest wholesale hay and grain business in the world, as is claimed. Although he keeps his legal residence in Durham and maintains a summer home on the ancestral estate, he lives most of the year in Brookline, Mass. His office is at the Chamber of Commerce building.

Mr. Smith married, 1 September 1887, Sarah Adla Thompson, daughter of Dea. John E. Thompson, and they have traveled extensively in America and Europe. He is a member of the Algonquin Club, of the Boston Athletic Association, of the Boston Art Club, of the Grae Burn Country Club of Newton, and of the Masonic order.

Hon. Jeremiah Langley was born in Durham 25 March 1841. He was educated in the public school and at the age of fifteen had learned the trade of a shoemaker. He also learned to manage a farm and raise hay, and, knowing the value of this product, he has bought and sold a good deal of it. In 1890 he and sons bought a line of barges for transporting coal from Portsmouth to Dover, Exeter, Newmarket and Durham. He has taken great interest in political affairs and has served his town in varied offices, as moderator, selectman three times, representative and senator. While in the legislature he did much toward securing the removal of the agricultural college from Hanover to Durham. As senator he served on the committees on railroads, agriculture, incorporations, elections and soldiers' home. He has been president of the Republican Club of Durham and a recognized leader in that party for twenty years. The Grange and Public Library acknowledge his services, and the Newmarket Bank has had him as director. He is a Mason and an Odd Fellow, speaking after the manner of lodges, and to speak plainly he is an energetic farmer, business man and political leader.

Hon. Lucien Thompson was born at the old Thompson homestead in Durham 3 June 1859. When he was ten years old his father died and the family removed to Manchester, where Lucien graduated from the high school at the age of eighteen, being the salutatorian of his class. Preferring farming to a course of classical study in college he returned to the homestead in Durham and became a successful farmer; yet he has found time to serve his town and state in various offices, such as supervisor, treasurer and moderator of ten town meetings. He has been a justice of the peace since 1886 and for a long time notary public. From 1887 to 1892 he was a member of the State Board of Agriculture, and since 1892 he has been a trustee of the New Hampshire College of Agriculture and Mechanic Arts and is secretary of the board. At the age of twenty-seven, he was elected representative to the legislature. He was a member of the senate in 1893-94, and served as chairman of the committee on agriculture and as member of committees on education, state prison and industrial school, labor, and public improvements. He was on Governor Bachelder's staff with rank of colonel.

Col. Thompson, for so he is popularly called, inherited the valuable library of his aunt, Miss Mary P. Thompson, and has written historical articles for the newspapers and the *Granite Monthly*. He assisted his aunt in gathering material for her Landmarks in Ancient Dover and for more than a score of years has been collecting material for the history of his native town. The facts pertaining to military history, cemeteries, old houses, slavery, post offices, and many details of educational and ecclesiastical history, that are recorded in this book, are the result of his long and painstaking research. Indeed, without his coöperation the history of Durham must have been incomplete.

Col. Thompson drafted the by-laws of the Durham Social Library and has been secretary of that and of the Durham Library Association since 1881. He is a charter member of Scammell Grange, its secretary many years, lecturer and overseer of the Pomona Grange, and a member of the State Grange executive committee. He is a charter member of the New Hampshire Genealogical Society and has been a trustee and the treasurer of the same, and belongs to the Sons of the American Revolution. When in the legislature he was a member of the special committee that erected the present Strafford County court house.

As a working member of the Congregational church he gave much assistance in editing its historical manual. He has also edited and published several historical pamphlets and papers read before patriotic societies. It is to be regretted that the health of himself and his family does not permit him to live continuously in Durham. For several years his winter home has been in University Park, Denver, Col. [See Genealogical Notes and frontispiece of Vol. I.]

Hon. Daniel Chesley, son of Daniel and Margery Steele (Woodman) Chesley, was born in Madbury 11 October 1859. He lives on the old farm that has been in the possession of the Chesley family from the earliest beginnings of Durham and is a practical and successful farmer as well as a general contractor, doing a lot of building in stone, brick and wood. He has

served on the board of selectmen. as representative to the
legislature and as a member of the State Constitutional Convention of 1902.   He is now filling the office of State senator for
the term of 1913 14 and is chairman of the committee on towns
and parishes and a member of committees on military affairs,
agriculture, state hospital, and fish and game.   He belongs to

HON. DANIEL CHESLEY

the orders of Odd Fellows, Knights of Pythias and Patrons of
Husbandry.   His portrait tells the rest of the story.

Charles Wentworth, son of Charles H. and Ann Elizabeth
(Stacy) Wentworth, was born in North Berwick, Me., 10 July
1872, eighth in descent from Elder William Wentworth, one of the
earliest settlers of Dover and bearing a surname that was been

21

honored in history. He was educated in the North Berwick
High School and in New Hampshire College. He has served as
town clerk of Durham since 1904 and represented the town in the
legislature, 1905-06, serving as secretary on the standing committee on agricultural college, and partly by his influence money
was appropriated for the college gymnasium. He has also been

CHARLES WENTWORTH

on the school board five years and has been station agent of the
Boston and Maine Railroad since 1900. He is a member of the
Sons of Veterans, his father having served three years during the
Civil War in Company F. 4th New Hampshire Volunteers. He
married, in 1898, Evelyn Jenkins of Lee, a student of New
Hampshire College, and they have one daughter, Valerie. A
social companion, an artist in telling a story and in illustrating

it with pen or brush, a faithful and accommodating official, a
modest and unassuming man of worth,—such is the impression
that he makes upon one who knows him a little below the surface.

Col. Arioch Wentworth Griffiths was born in Packer's Falls
district 31 August 1851. He was educated in the common
school, Newmarket High School and the Franklin Academy of

COL. ARIOCH W. GRIFFITHS

Dover. Together with his father and brother he has developed
one of the best farms in Strafford County. The set of buildings,
twelve in number, includes a handsome two-story residence,
equipped with electric lights, steam heat and telephone, and a
spacious barn, 41 by 110 feet, which has a capacity for 150 tons
of hay. An electric mill has been built, capable of producing

600 barrels of cider per day. The output averaged 1,000 barrels per year for thirty-five years. Owing to change of laws
and failure of the apple crop the mill is now idle. Mr. Griffiths
is a Republican in politics, has served two years as selectman
and as moderator of town meetings twelve years in succession, holding that office now. He also holds at the present time
his seventh commission as deputy sheriff. Since 31 May 1888
he has been an active member of the Knights of Pythias, being a
member of Pioneer Lodge, No. 1, of Newmarket. He was
actively instrumental in the organization of Sullivan Lodge, No.
26, of Durham. He filled the various chairs and became a
member of the Grand Lodge in 1891. He was a charter member
of W. A. Frye Company, No. 5, U. R. He was second lieutenant
at its organization, afterward elected five times first lieutenant,
and was promoted to the rank of major on regimental staff. After
holding this position two years he was elected lieutenant-
colonel and held the position two years. He was then appointed
assistant inspector general on the brigade staff with the rank of
colonel, in which position he served two terms of four years each.
He was then appointed assistant quartermaster general with
same rank, in which office he is now serving his second term. He
belongs to the Sons of the American Revolution and was for many
years a director of the Newmarket National Bank.

Albert DeMeritt was born in Durham 26 August 1851. Besides
caring for a farm of three hundred acres and doing much in lumber business he has held many public offices, such as moderator
of town meetings eleven times, and two terms representative
in the legislature, where he served on the standing committee
on agricultural college and on the committee on appropriations.
In appreciation of his work in the legislative session of 1911 the
faculty and trustees of New Hampshire College each unanimously
passed resolutions of commendation.

Mr. DeMeritt was a member of the Constitutional Convention in 1889 and again in 1912. He served on the State Board of
Agriculture nine years and has been one of the trustees of the
college. He has taken great interest in education, serving on the
school board nine years. He drafted the free text-book bill,
which became a law in 1887 and remains in force unchanged,
so complete that almost all the other states have adopted it.
Through his efforts the Durham Lyceum was organized, which

ran for a decade with remarkable success, attracting people from the neighboring towns.

Mr. DeMeritt is a member of Scammell Grange and past chancellor commander of Sullivan Lodge of Knights of Pythias. He is also a justice of the peace. New Hampshire College has conferred upon him the degree of Master of Science.*

ALBERT DeMERITT

Charles E. Hoitt, son of Gen. Alfred Hoitt, was born 8 March 1849. After spending a few years in Concord he settled in Durham, buying and remodeling the old Ballard house. Like his father he belongs to the Democratic party. His popularity is shown by the fact, that, although Durham always casts its presidential vote for Republican electors, and has chosen only four Democratic representatives since the Civil War, he and his father are two of that four. He has been elected selectman

* Mr. DeMeritt, shot accidentally, died 22 August 1913, much esteemed and lamented by a host of friends.

sixteen times and still holds that office.   He has filled every chair
in Sullivan Lodge of Knights of Pythias, including grand chancellor.   He is also a prominent officer in Scammell Grange.   He
is now serving his second term as county commissioner.   His
popularity is due to his cordial way of meeting all people and
to honesty and economy in handling the people's money, the

CHARLES E. HOITT

necessary expenses in a new college town demanding wise and
strict calculation.

Valentine Mathes was born in Durham 13 February 1846.   At
the age of eighteen he began river freighting to Portsmouth,
Exeter and Newmarket.   After three years he turned his attention to railroading in New York and Boston for a year.   Then

he bought out Joseph W. Coe at Durham village, where he kept a general country store and served as postmaster from 1872 to 1880. He then removed to Dover, where for sixteen years he did a large business in groceries, coal, wood, hay and grain. This business was sold in order that he might devote all his time to the lumber business, in which he had been interested actively

VALENTINE MATHES

from boyhood and which had grown extensively. In this business his son, John E. Mathes, is associated with him.

Mr. Mathes owns and rents to tenants one hundred and sixteen tenements, offices and stores and is the largest individual taxpayer in Dover. He and his brother, Hamilton A. Mathes, organized the Pascataqua Navigation Company, with a capital of $100,000, and have two boats and twelve barges engaged in river freighting from Eastport, Me., to Boston, Mass.

He has been representative to the legislature and has served in the common council of Dover. He is a Mason, Granger, Red Man, Elk, Odd Fellow, and, last but not least, a member of the Congregational church.

CHARLES S. LANGLEY

Charles S. Langley, son of Hon. Jeremiah Langley, was born in Durham 11 October 1867. He has been a member of the school board eighteen years and represented the town in the legislature, 1903–04. serving on the committee on Agricultural College. Since boyhood he has been associated with his father in the hay and lumber business and in river freighting. In addition he deals in automobiles and has planned and built several houses in Durham Village. He has been a director of Newmarket National Bank about fifteen years. He is affiliated with the Grangers, the Knights of Pythias, and the Elks. The Langley home is one of hospitality, prosperity and ambitious contentment. [For family see Genealogical Notes.]

GEORGE W. RANSOM

George W. Ransom was born in Durham, 1 January 1858, son of Alonzo and Isabella (Hook) Ransom. He brushed aside all obstacles to his way through preparatory schools and college by working on a farm after he was fourteen years of age at eighteen dollars per. month and by chopping white oak cord wood in the winter at fifty cents a cord, and he has made himself richer

than those who allowed him to do it. He fitted for college at
Franklin Academy, Dover and New Hampton Literary Institution and graduated at Dartmouth in 1886 with the degree of
A. B. Meanwhile he taught school in Middleton, Wolfeboro
and the village school at Durham three years. This kept him
away from his work in college twelve weeks of each year. The
writer hereof knows just what that means by happy and profitable experience. One learns to study as well as to teach by
teaching.

After graduation Mr. Ransom taught in Walpole, N. H.,
Pepperell, Mass., Warner, N. H., and since 1893 in Boston, Mass.,
where he has served as submaster and master of schools in Dor-
chester, Roxbury and the city proper. He is now master of
the Abraham Lincoln School, which has 2,400 pupils, perhaps
the largest school in New England. He has also been principal
of the South Boston Evening High School. He has taken several
courses of study in the Boston School of Technology and in Harvard University and has traveled extensively in Europe and in this
country. He certainly has an aptitude for hard work and for
work that counts for something. He has honored the history of
Durham more than the History of Durham can honor him.

Mr. Ransom married in June, 1893, Eliza B. Taylor at Alex-
andria Bay, New York, a graduate of Oswego Normal School
and a teacher of large experience. She graduated from the
Boston University Medical School in 1900 with degree of M. D.,
and afterward took postgraduate courses in New York and in
Johns Hopkins University. She has been instructor in the
Boston University Medical School in the chair of Histology and
is now practicing as a specialist in nervous diseases, in Boston.
They have children, Ruth, born 24 December 1903, and Eleanor
born 22 December 1905.

POST OFFICE AND POSTMASTERS

The earliest post office in New Hampshire was established at Portsmouth previous to 1695, and it did business for the entire province. Durham was first included in a mail route in 1786, and Samuel Dearborn was the post rider, at a salary of twenty-four pounds per annum. The cost of sending a letter forty miles was six pence. After 1691 the rate was reduced to eight cents for distances under forty miles and increasing gradually to twenty cents for over three hundred miles, and twenty-five cents for over five hundred miles. Every letter composed of two pieces of paper paid double these rates, and so the rates went up in proportion to size and weight. Then letters were necessities or luxuries, and the art of compact writing was cultivated.

The building of Pascataqua bridge and the New Hampshire Turnpike put Durham on the main line of travel, and then caravans a mile long, composed of loaded teams from Portsmouth and from Durham wharves might be seen on their way to Concord. Thus a post office at Durham became almost a necessity, and Benjamin Thompson was appointed the first postmaster, 1 October 1796. He was son of Judge Ebenezer Thompson and served for twenty years as clerk of the Court of Common Pleas in Strafford County. He was also a justice of the peace and a trustee of Durham Academy. The post office was then in a building near the location of the present office, in a store that was burned several years ago.

Mr. Thompson was succeeded, 1 October 1802, by Edward Wells, who served during the administration of President Thomas Jefferson. Mr. Wells was taxed in the Lubberland district in 1794. A deed from Benjamin Chesley to Joseph Coe, dated 21 July 1804, conveying land adjoining on which now stands the Town Hall, contains the following clause, "adjoining land in possession of Edward Wells as his store now stands," and here was the post office. Mr. Wells married Margery, daughter of Theophilus and Mary (Sullivan) Hardy, and taught school in Durham several terms between 1802 and 1812. His sons became noted men, Samuel being governor of Maine, Joseph

331

lieutenant-governor of Illinois, John A., United States senator from New Hampshire and candidate for Governor.

Benjamin Underwood Lapish was the next postmaster, taking office 1 January 1808 and holding it only six months. The post office at this time was in the Alonzo Ransom house.

George Ffrost was the fourth postmaster in Durham. He was appointed 1 July 1808, and he or his son, George, held office till 5 January 1848. The office during this time was in a store on the north side of the road at Durham Falls bridge. Mr. Ffrost was a magistrate, merchant and extensive farmer, representing the town in the General Court in 1807.

William J. Chesley was the successor of George Ffrost and served till 25 July 1849, a little more than one year. He inherited his grandfather's, Benjamin Chesley's, homestead, living on the spot where now is the residence of the president of the college. He kept the post office in the southeast corner of his residence. He served as selectman, moderator, and delegate to the Constitutional Convention in 1850.

Mrs. Mary A. Page succeeded Mr. Chesley and held the office till 23 May 1853. She was Mary Ann Gilman and married Joseph W. Page, 30 November 1823. She kept the post office in the west front room of the house east of the house in which was the post office in 1902, and Mr. Page kept a store over the well between his dwelling house and the residence of Mrs. Hamilton Smith. He died 9 March 1834, aged 42. Mrs. Page lived in the house here mentioned till her death, in 1882.

Alfred D. Hoitt was appointed postmaster 23 May 1853, and held the office about four years, during the administration of President Franklin Pierce. Mr. Hoitt kept a general store in a building formerly standing opposite the old railroad station and now removed to Thompson Avenue. Here was the post office.

Mr. Hoitt removed to Charlestown, Mass., and became prominent in politics, serving as alderman and in the common council. He was a hay and grain merchant on Canal Street, Boston, for thirty years, removing to Arlington in 1873, where he served on the water board and board of assessors as chairman. He was a director of the Metropolitan Bank and vice-president of the Arlington National Bank. He served several times as delegate to Democratic national conventions and was superintendent of the Arlington branch of the Boston post office.

Joseph W. Coe became postmaster 9 July 1857. He kept the office in the old brick store in the Town Hall building and in the Perkins store across the street. He was educated at Durham Academy and was engaged in mercantile pursuits for twenty years. He purchased the beautiful Steele residence, where he long resided. Being a Union man he identified himself with

JOSEPH WILLIAM COE

the Republican party in 1861. The income of the post office in his time was only about $200 annually. [See Genealogical Notes.]

Valentine Mathes, Jr., was appointed postmaster 12 August 1872, to succeed Mr. Coe. He served under the administration of President U. S. Grant, and kept the office in a store opposite the Town Hall building. He was also town clerk. He sold out his business to Jasper R. McDaniel, and removed to Dover.

Jasper R. McDaniel became postmaster 15 November 1880. He was the son of the late John R. McDaniel, Esq., and lived in the house afterward owned and occupied by Prof. Charles L. Parsons. The post office was continued in its previous quarters. Mr. McDaniel sold his business to Chauncey E. Hayes, and removed to Malden, Mass.

Alvin Jackson began his duties as postmaster 24 August 1885. He was born in Madbury in 1848, and for many years was engaged in business in the store belonging to Miss Louise S. Smith, residing in the tenement over the store. He served under both President Cleveland and President Harrison.

Chauncey E. Hayes was appointed postmaster 5 April 1889, and the office was again removed to the Town Hall building, in the room now used as the town safe. Mr. Hayes carried on a general store and was town treasurer, 1892–96. He is still living in Durham village and all four of his children have graduated at New Hampshire College.

Alvin Jackson again came into office 17 June 1893 and served till 1 July 1897, when George D. Stevens was appointed postmaster. The removal of the post office from the Town Hall under the hill to a point nearer the college occasioned some contest. The store east of the Benjamin Thompson residence was fitted up and again the post office was located here, in the same building where it was kept under the first postmaster, 1796–1802. Mr. Stevens occupied the tenement over the store for a dwelling. The post office remained here but a few months. On a Sunday afternoon, 12 December 1897, the Alvin Jackson store was discovered to be on fire. As this building was about two feet from the post office building, the contents of the latter were hurriedly removed to the grocery store of Walter S. Edgerly in Whitcher's block, where it remained a few days. The post office building and the Benjamin Thompson residence, at that time used as a girls' dormitory, were completely destroyed.

Within a few days the post office was removed to the annex of the store of Gorham H. Sawyer, opposite the Alvin Jackson store. March 20, 1899, it was removed to the Mary P. Thompson house, so called, owned by Hon. Lucien Thompson, who fitted up the west side of the house for the accommodation of the public.

Mr. Stevens occupied the rest of the house for a residence. The post office was first lighted by electricity in the spring of 1900. Mr. Stevens served sixteen years as town clerk and is justice of the peace. He was prominent as an officer in the Scammell Grange and in Sullivan Lodge of the Knights of Pythias having filled the chairs and been chancellor commander. He was born

GEORGE D. STEVENS

16 November 1860, son of David and Hannah (Lee) Stevens, and married, 14 September 1892, Gertrude Isabelle Davis. They have two daughters, Marjorie Pearley Stevens, born 6 November 1896, and Louise Esther Stevens, born 21 June 1907.

The income of the post office greatly increased after the removal of the college to Durham, and by order of the Post Office

Department at Washington it became a third-class post office on and after 1 January 1904. The rural free delivery route was inaugurated 1 December 1902. Previous to this time Dover rural route, No. 6, served Pascataqua Bridge section and continues to do so.

Owing to need of more suitable quarters for the rapidly increasing amount of mail the post office department agreed with Mr. Lucien Thompson that if he would build and equip a new post office building, not connected with any other building and not used in part for dwelling or store, and suitably furnish the same, they would lease it for a long term of years. The building was erected in 1907 and occupied on the first day of November of that year. It is an up-to-date building with first class furnishings for postal business, electric lights, steam heat, and flagpole.

SOME OLD HOUSES

In deeds cited on page 59 it is shown that Dr. Samuel Adams built the Sullivan house previous to the year 1741, on land deed d to him by his father, the Rev. Hugh Adams, in 1743. Here Dr. Samuel Adams lived till his death, in 1762, and his widow, Rebecca (Hall) Adams, sold the house and three acres of land to John Sullivan, 19 December 1764. Here lived Gen. Sullivan till his death, in 1795, and his widow lived here till her death, in 1820. Mr. Amory described it as "a large square house of two stories, with handsome carved balusters to the staircase, and other richly moulded wood work. It was the center of a cluster of attached or surrounding buildings, his library and office, dairy, granary, stables and bee-hives, some of which have been removed. . . . Here he had his council chamber, as President Governor, and here public affairs were transacted. Various distinguished persons from all parts of the country and Europe were his guests."

The road leading to the wharf ran between this house and the old meeting house. Maples and poplars surround the house now, and probably did in the early days. The land sloping down to the wharf was terraced long ago. The house contains fourteen rooms, and a sun-parlor has recently been added to the rear. The large rooms have fireplaces about the central chimney, and in some rooms the wall-paper of Revolutionary times has been preserved. Ornamental panelings and carvings attest the taste and luxury of original owners.

There was a dilapidated building in the rear of this house, which some say was the abode of Gen. Sullivan's slaves. Others think it was his law office.

About 1834 Capt. Ebenezer Thompson bought the house and here he and his wife died the same night, 26–27 January 1853. His son, Charles A. C. Thompson, inherited the place and died here 4 December 1868. It then passed into the possession of Miss Lucetta M. Davis. After her death it belonged to Charles H. Mitchell of Dover. In 1912 it was purchased and thoroughly repaired by Mr. Lynde Sullivan, a lawyer of Boston and great-grandson of Gov. James Sullivan of Massachusetts, who was

RESIDENCE OF GEN. JOHN SULLIVAN

brother to Gen. John Sullivan. Since Gov. James Sullivan
married Hetty Odiorne, grand-daughter of the Rev. Hugh
Adams, it follows that Mr. Lynde Sullivan has acquired his
own ancestral estate, which the Rev. Hugh Adams bought in
1717. Long may the Sullivan family own, preserve and enjoy
the house and land made famous by occupants of two centuries.

About three rods south of the Sullivan house is the site of
the house built between 1717 and 1720 by the Rev. Hugh Adams,
for at the latter date John Drew, carpenter, of Portsmouth sued
said Adams for twelve pounds, wages of himself and son, John.

INN OF MASTER JOHN SMITH
Built soon after 1700

Here lived the Rev. Hugh Adams and later it was the home
of the Rev. Alvan Tobey, D. D., when he first came to Durham.
It was called a parsonage, though it seems never to have been
owned by the town or the church. Valentine Smith lived in
this house when he removed from Lubberland. Many years
ago it was hauled to its present location, on the road from the
Falls to Newmarket, on the north side of Denbow's brook,
on land that once belonged to Benjamin Thompson, Sr. In
his will, 1838, he called it his "Long Marsh Farm." The house
has been repaired and slightly remodeled and is in good condition. Israel P. Church once lived in it.

A little south of where the Rev. Hugh Adams lived there is a

RESIDENCE OF MISS MARGARET B. FFROST

A part of it was built by Valentine Hill, about 1649

house, the rear part of which, or L, has the appearance of being very old. There was a house here in 1682, when John Mighell sold it to Samuel Burnham. See page 58. James, son of Samuel Burnham, sold it to Dr. Jonathan Crosby in 1718. Capt. Daniel Rogers, blacksmith, bought this place, or a place near by, of Peter Mason, in 1735. He died in 1785.

On the west side of the road is a very old house. James Smith was licensed to keep a public house here in 1686. His grandson, John, is called "innkeeper," and he died in 1739. Master John Smith lived here in Revolutionary times, and his daughter, Sarah, married Seth S. Walker in 1810. This location was reckoned within the region called "Broth Hill" and the rhyme has been handed down:

> "Broth Hill, the city of Seth;
> Were it not for Joe Coe,
> They would all starve to death."

Joseph Coe was a ship-builder, and many of his workmen lived in cottages on Broth Hill. After Walker's time the old Smith mansion was dwelt in by John Drew. It now belongs to the Ffrost family.

Next north of the old Smith inn is a stone house, built in recent times by Howard and James Paul. James was killed in taking down the staging. Here lived Rev. Mr. Barnum and Rev. C. H. Chapin. Next to this is the house built by Lieut.-Col. Winborn Adams, who acquired land here of Derry Pitman. Here he and his wife, Sarah, kept an inn, and town meetings were sometimes held here. The place is now owned by Fred E. Jenkins. The frame and the foundation for the chimney are about all that remains of the old house. The latter is of massive stone and fills about half of the cellar. The first meetings of the proprietors of Holderness were held in this inn, from 1762 to about 1768. Later they were held in the inn of John Layn at Newtown, in Lee.

Evidence abundant has been cited in the chapter on Early Settlers and Estates, page 70, to prove that Valentine Hill built a house on the north side of the river and not far from his mill as early as 1649. In the Dover rate-list for 1661 is found "Mr. Hills mill and house and lands." Capt. Nathaniel Hill, son of Valentine, lived here. Bartholomew Stevenson built a house on the hill, not far from Hill's house, about 1687. Tradition says that the house built by Valentine Hill is now the so-called Ffrost house. Additions and repairs have been made, but the appearance of the oldest part of the house warrants the belief that here is the original house built by the leading man of Oyster River, about 1649. Its location, both for defence and for commanding view, was the only suitable place for the wealthy mill-owner to live. There is no record that the Indians even attempted to capture it in 1694. The house and land about it passed into the possession of Jonathan Woodman, who sold it to George Ffrost after 1796, and it has been occupied by the Ffrost family

INTERIOR OF RESIDENCE OF MISS MARGARET B. FFROST

The portraits on the wall are of her great-great-grandfather, John Frost and his wife, Mary (Pepperrell) who was sister of Sir William Pepperrell

until now. The rare, antique furniture well befits the abode. Here for over two centuries and a half has been the home of comparative wealth, comfort and beautiful surroundings.

The house once owned by Capt. Joseph Richardson was a licensed hotel. Here town and jury meetings have been held. Capt. Richardson was born in Boston, 25 December 1756. He served six years in the Revolutionary War and was twice wounded. His son, John A. Richardson, lived and died in this house. His daughter, Mrs. Frances P. Treadwell, sold the place and after extensive repairs it became the residence of Mr. and Mrs. George H. Mendell. Mrs. Mendell was formerly Miss Mary B.

Smith, daughter of Hon. Hamilton Smith, grand-daughter of
Judge Valentine Smith.

The Hamilton Smith house was built by the Rev. John Blydenburgh and afterward was owned by his daughter, Margaret. It
has been owned by Prof. John S. Woodman, George Ffrost,
Joshua B. Smith, Irene Cheney, Mary H. Chesley, Mary E.
Smith and Hamilton Smith, who bought it 2 December 1895.
He made extensive improvements in the place, adding quite a
portion of the Buzzell field in the rear as well as the Mary H.

RESIDENCE OF MR. AND MRS. GEORGE H. MENDELL

Chesley lot in front, making it the most valuable homestead
in Durham. The house is known as "Red Tower" and is
owned by Mrs. Shirley Onderdonk, daughter of Mrs. Hamilton
Smith by her first marriage. The spacious garden in front, on
the opposite side of the road, is free to all lovers of the beautiful. The accompanying picture describes the exterior of the
house far better than words can do. The interior is the abode
of comfort, artistic elegance, peace and happy memories. The
village school was located on the vestry lot east of this house

RED TOWER, RESIDENCE OF THE LATE HAMILTON SMITH

until 1854, when the schoolhouse was built where now the grange hall is located. When the Mary H. Chesley lot was sold, in 1895, the house thereon was removed to a lot near the college, owned by Dea. W. S. Meserve, and was extensively repaired. This old house was located very near the Joshua B. Smith house and was owned by Ephraim Folsom, who died in 1785. Robert Lapish, Jr., Dr. John Angier and Jacob Odell, lived here. There was a house on the east side of the Mary H. Chesley house until 1867, when it was destroyed by fire. It was then owned by Mrs. Alfred Chesley. Judge Jonathan Steele owned this place and lived here till he built the present Coe house. Steele sold the place, 17 February 1813, to James Durgin, Jr. Dr. Jedediah Ingalls once owned and occupied this house.

The house now owned by Joshua B. Smith and his sister, Miss Mary E. Smith, was bought by their father, Hon. Valentine Smith, at auction sale, 7 December 1814. It had been previously owned by William Ballard, who was born 6 February 1787, and died 26 October 1811. Prior to him it was owned by Stephen Cogan, and before him James Drisco, a mariner from Portsmouth, owned the place. He died 31 January 1778. Before Drisco the place was owned by John Layn, blacksmith, who bought it of Nathaniel Hill, 23 May 1763. Tradition in the Layn family says the house was built in 1735. When the Rev. George Whitefield passed through Durham, he dined in the east front room.

The land where the Ebenezer Smith house stands was originally owned by Valentine Hill and was sold by Nathaniel Hill to Jonathan Clough, 16 January 1761. After being owned by various members of the Clough family it was sold by Zaccheus and Love Clough to Thomas Pinkham, 7 June 1777, when mention is made of a dwelling house thereon. Thomas Pinkham sold to Ebenezer Smith, 10 November 1783. Smith built the present house, which long has remained in the Smith family. Here have visited many of the notable men of a century ago.

The Mary P. Thompson house was owned by Abraham Perkins, born 20 January 1771, who died 16 January 1863, and before him by Mrs. Mehitable (Sheafe) Smith. Oliver C. Demerit acquired it in 1837, and he and wife, Sarah, sold it to Miss Mary P. Thompson, 2 November 1860, for $1,035. Through

RESIDENCE OF THE LATE JUDGE VALENTINE SMITH

her will it was inherited by Hon. Lucien Thompson. Here Miss
Thompson lived and wrote her Landmarks in Ancient Dover
and pursued her genealogical and historical researches. William
Ballard traded in a little shop on this lot.

The Benjamin Thompson house was purchased by Benjamin

RESIDENCE OF EBENEZER SMITH

Thompson, Sr., 2 April 1790, of his brother-in-law, James Leighton. Benjamin Thompson, Jr., inherited it by will of his father,
in 1838. Here he was born and died. He bequeathed this
place, in 1890, to the State of New Hampshire for the use of the
college. Miss Lucetta M. Davis remained in the house a short
time. It was afterward repaired and was occupied by President

House Built by James Joy, Father of the Hon. James F. Joy
Afterwards residence of Deacon Abraham Perkins

C. S. Murkland till 1895. It was then used as a girls' dormitory until it was destroyed by fire, Sunday, 12 December 1897.[1]

The house now owned by Charles E. Hoitt was built by Joshua Ballard, who bought the land 1 October 1782. The land had been previously owned in succession by Valentine Hill, Nathaniel Hill, Dea. Hubbard Stevens, Moses Emerson, Capt. Abednego Leathers, Daniel Hardy. The house passed from Joshua Ballard to his daughter, Elizabeth Smith, and has since been owned by Joshua B. Smith, Eugene Thurston and Gen. Alfred Hoitt. The Rev. Alvan Tobey, D. D., lived in this house during the last of his long pastorate in Durham.

The house now owned by Mrs. Ann M. Jenkins was built by Stephen Mitchell, Esq., who began practice as a lawyer in Durham in 1805. It was afterward owned by a Mr. Flanders, who died in 1833. It has since been owned and occupied Dr. Thomas Flanders, Dr. Alphonso Bickford, Zilla B. Burbank, and Mrs. Silas Jenkins.

The Mathes-Talbot-Parsons house is said to have been built by Daniel Mathes, because his wife would not live at Durham Point. Daniel Mathes married, 26 January 1806, Abigail, daughter of the Rev. Curtis Coe. She died 11 January 1807, aged 23, and he married Betty Folsom, and moved back to the Point. The house was afterward owned and occupied by Maj. Benjamin Mathes, John McDaniel, Rev. Henry L. Talbot, and Prof. Charles L. Parsons. The last two made extensive improvements in the house and grounds, making it one of the best residences in town. It is now occupied by a club of students.

The first house below J. W. Coe's, going toward Pascataqua bridge, was brought up the river from "Franklin City by John T. Emerson," he having bought the same from Ballard Pinkham in 1821. The land once belonged to the Jackson and Leathers families, and was bought by Mr. Emerson of Philip and Joseph Chesley. It has recently been acquired by Prof. C. Floyd Jackson and extensively repaired.

Not far from the Falls, in the low ground called Follett's swamp or Moharimet's swamp, Eli Demeritt built his log cabin on land granted before 1700. It had one room and no cellar. Later he built a log house of two rooms. His grandson, Capt. Samuel Demeritt, built upon the same spot a framed house of two stories

[1] A picture of this house appeared in *Granite Monthly*, vol. xxxiii, page 420.

RESIDENCE OF ALBERT DeMERITT

in front with a lean-to. The brick for the chimney were from old
England, and the bottom of the oven was of tiles, eight inches
square, which had a crown stamped on one side with lettering.
In the present house, in possession of Albert DeMeritt, the
doors of the cupboards in the kitchen and dining room were from
the old house, and the upper part of the beaufet is in the attic.
In the sitting room and dining room hearths the tiles may still
be seen. Some of the windows were of diamond-shape, leaded
panes. The house was unpainted, ceiled and paneled. From
Capt. Samuel Demeritt the place was inherited by his son,
Israel, who built the present house in 1808. The brick were
made on the farm. Israel Demeritt was succeeded in ownership
by his son, Stephen, and from him it passed to the present owner,
who has added many acres to the farm. He is the great-great-
great-grandson of the Eli Demeritt to whom the land was granted
and laid out 31 May 1699. The farm is one of the largest and
most productive in Durham, and the house and well-shaded lawn,
with outlook upon broad meadows, are a delight to one who
appreciates home comforts and rural scenery.

Across the fields another Demeritt house was built by Capt.
Nathaniel Demeritt, brother of Israel above named. It was
rebuilt by Capt. Nathaniel and his son, the Rev. William Demeritt, about 1819. The first was a one story and a half
house. The present house, beneath the old elms, is owned by
George P. Demeritt, son of the Rev. William.

The Bunker garrison house was probably built by James
Bunker soon after 1652, when he bought the land on which
its ruins now lie. The walls, except the gable ends, were of hewn
hemlock logs, nine inches in thickness. There were loopholes
for defence, afterward enlarged into windows. This was the
last remaining garrison of Oyster River that was attacked by the
Indians in 1694. It seems to be decayed and fallen beyond
the power of restoration. The plan of this garrison is presented through the courtesy of the Society for the Preservation
of New England Antiquities. See page 63.

Woodman's garrison was built by Capt. John Woodman
soon after 1656, when he came to Oyster River. In 1660 he
had a grant of twenty acres between lands of William Beard
and Valentine Hill. Miss Mary P. Thompson thus describes it:
"It is beautifully situated on the eastern slope of a hill at the

head of Beard's creek, with brooks and deep ravines on every
side of the acclivity, except at the west. It has a fine outlook
for an approaching enemy, as well as a charming view in every
direction, except in the rear, where the rise of land intercepts

WOODMAN GARRISON

the prospect. Durham village, which did not exist when this
garrison was built, lies at the south in full view, embosomed
among trees; and at the east may be traced the windings of
Oyster River on its way to the Pascataqua. At the north, through

an opening between the hills, can be seen the spot where the
Huckins garrison stood; and nearer at hand, but separated from

WOODMAN GARRISON
Destroyed by fire November 1896

it by a profound ravine, is the field where occurred the massacre
of 1689."[1]

This garrison was destroyed by fire, 8 November 1896, a

[1] Landmarks in Ancient Dover, p. 179.

23

RESIDENCE OF COL. LUCIEN THOMPSON

LIBRARY OF COL. LUCIEN THOMPSON

loss that caused sadness to every lover of the town's historic memorials. Fortunately good photographs exist of the garrison as it was in its best days, and some thoughtful and prompt artist secured snap shots of it while it was burning.

The garrison built by David Davis at Lubberland in 1695 is probably the same as the Smith garrison, having been acquired by Lieut. John Smith some time after David Davis was killed by Indians, 27 August 1696. Later it was known as Frost's garrison and Blydenburgh's garrison. It was taken down only a few years ago and the road now runs over its site. A good picture of it has been preserved. See page 34.

Another garrison was built by David Davis, son of the above named, at Packer's Falls, early in the eighteenth century, where five generations of David Davises have lived. The original garrison was located on a knoll in the center of the field back of its present location, to which it was moved prior to 1790 in order to be on the highway. Additions have been made by later generations, so that the garrison of pre-Revolutionary times forms but a part of the present building, occupied by Eben Meserve Davis.

The Pendergast garrison is still standing and occupied. It was probably built by Stephen Pendergast, who acquired land here near Packer's Falls, in 1735.

Half a mile from Durham village, toward Madbury, on an elevated space to which the road gently ascends, is the house built by Judge Ebenezer Thompson soon after the Revolution on land that has been in possession of the Thompson family from the first grant, in 1694. The house was erected on the site of an older one, in which Judge Thompson was born. It is a typical rural dwelling of the well-to-do persons of that time, squarely built around a huge chimney, with large rooms of low ceiling, a fireplace in every room, heavy mouldings and cornices and a lot of wainscoting. It is still painted white, with green blinds, the best combination of house colors New England has ever had. It was a year's work for a carpenter to prepare the exterior and interior finishing material. In the hall-chamber, specially reserved for guests, the same paper is on the walls that was there a century ago. On this spot Judge Thompson entertained many of the leading men of the Revolutionary period, and in this house he was often consulted on politics, medicine and law. It was in the "hall-room," or parlor that he fell from his chair and instantly expired, in 1802.

An east two-story wing was added to the house by its present owner, Col. Lucien Thompson, in 1895, and in it he has the rare library, photographs and souvenirs that his aunt, Mary P. Thompson, gathered during her years spent in Europe. Here is a very valuable collection of historical and genealogical material that several generations have been acquiring. One would have to search long in New Hampshire to find its equal in any private house.

The spacious lawn and shade trees, the commodious barn, stable and carriage house, the fertile acres and the orchard of five hundred trees, make the visitor envy or congratulate the owner. If the visitor has the true riches of the soul, then it is congratulation and not envy.

The residence of Forrest S. Smith was built in 1803 by Major Daniel Smith and his son, Major Winthrop Smith. The former house stood farther back from the turnpike, on ascending ground down the lane which led to the Dover road. It was a two-story house in front, sloping off to one story in the rear. Tradition says that Major Daniel Smith insisted on having the big chimney in the center of this house after the style of those days, so that at the gatherings of the militia they could march around the chimney at the evening festivities, after the training was over. This was the grand promenade that preceded the dancing.

The present house is beautifully situated among shade trees and affords a fine view of Oyster River and Little Bay. It has been extensively repaired. Heat, running water and bathroom bring the modern conveniences of the city to the roominess, quiet, restfulness and hospitality of the country. At many a week's end a party from Boston alights from a large touring car at the front gate, for the old-fashioned front yard, filled with flowers and shrubs and protected by ornamental fence, still preserves one of the best rural traditions. Several hundred acres of fertile land certainly add to the attractiveness of the place. It is said that the difference between the farmer and the agriculturalist is this, that the farmer makes his money in the country to spend it in the city, while the agriculturalist makes his money in the city to spend it in the country; but Forrest S. Smith was a successful farmer before he began to be an agriculturalist. Here the re-

RESIDENCE OF FORREST S. SMITH

markably youthful mother of four score years finds rest and offers
it to friends, contented to linger longer amid beautiful earthly
surroundings before moving into the mansion in the skies.

The last illustration of this chapter is presented, not because
it is one of the old houses, but it is a new house on an old site
and serves to contrast former days with the present.   It is the

SUMMER CAMP OF ELISHA R. BROWN
Near site of Meader Garrison

summer camp of Elisha R. Brown of Dover, president of the
Strafford National Bank.   It is built near the site of the Meader
garrison, at what was first known as "Hills Neck."   The land
was long in the possession of the Meader family.   On this neck
of land, between Royall's Cove and the mouth of Oyster River,
the three towns, Dover, Madbury and Durham, meet at Tickle
Point.   The view from Mr. Brown's camp takes in Little Bay
and its islands and the Newington and Durham shores.   Dover

Neck is in the distance toward the east.   Mr. Brown married
Frances, daughter of Dr. Alphonso and Mary Joanna (Smith)
Bickford, and thus is connected with two of the oldest families
of Durham, as may be seen in the genealogical part of this
history.   It may be added that on this neck of land was once

INTERIOR OF MR. BROWN'S CAMP

laid out Franklin City, a booming town on paper, which the
building of Pascataqua bridge was expected to develop.   The
dream soon vanished.   The lots are there still, but the only
house built there was long ago moved up toward the Falls.[1]

[1] For further description of this place and its surroundings, as well as biography of Mr.
Brown, see *Granite Monthly* for September 1912, article written by John Scales, A. M.

LISTS OF TOWN OFFICERS

MODERATORS

Before the separation of Durham from Dover, 1732, the following men from Oyster River Parish served as moderators of Dover town meetings, Capt. John Woodman in 1675, Col. James Davis in 1702, 1713, 1715, 1720-21, 1728-31, Capt. Francis Mathes in 1728, and Capt. Stephen Jones in 1730 and 1731. The moderators since the formation of the town of Durham have been the following.

1732, Col. James Davis.
1733, Lieut. Jonathan Thompson.
1734, Lieut. Samuel Smith.
    Col. James Davis.
1735, Lieut. Samuel Smith.
    Col. James Davis.
1736, Col. James Davis.
1737, Lieut. Jonathan Thompson.
1738, Col. James Davis.
1739, Col. James Davis.
    Lieut. Stephen Jones.
1740, James Davis, Esq.
1741, Col. James Davis.
1742, Capt. Stephen Jones.
    James Davis, Esq.
1743, John Woodman.
1744, Samuel Smith, Esq.
    Stephen Jones.
1745, Capt. Jonathan Thompson.
1746, Samuel Smith.
1747, Samuel Smith.
1748, Lieut. Philip Chesley.
1749, Lieut. Philip Chesley.
1750, Joseph Thomas.
1751, Joseph Thomas.
1752, Joseph Sias.
1753, Joseph Thomas.
1754, William Drew.
1755, Lieut. Philip Chesley.
1757, Benjamin Smith.
1758, Hubbard Stevens.
1759, William Drew.
1761, Joseph Thomas.

1762, Joseph Atkinson, Esq.
1763, Joseph Atkinson, Esq.
1764, Joseph Atkinson, Esq.
1765, Capt. Benjamin Smith.
1766, Dea. Hubbard Stevens.
1767, Ephraim Davis.
1768, Maj. Stephen Jones.
1769, Joseph Atkinson, Esq.
1770, Dea. Hubbard Stevens.
1771, Joseph Atkinson.
1772, Valentine Mathes, Esq.
1773, Joseph Atkinson, Esq.
1774, Valentine Mathes, Esq.
    Joseph Atkinson.
1775, Valentine Mathes.
    Moses Emerson.
    George Frost, Esq.
    Maj. Stephen Jones.
    Mr. Ephraim Davis.
1776, George Frost, Esq.
    Mr. Ephraim Davis.
1777, George Frost, Esq.
    Maj. Stephen Jones.
    Valentine Mathes, Esq.
1778, Maj. Stephen Jones.
    Valentine Mathes, Esq.
1779, Col. Samuel Chesley.
    Hon. George Frost, Esq.
1780, Valentine Mathes, Esq.
1781, George Frost, Esq.
    Maj. Gen. John Sullivan.
1782, Valentine Mathes, Esq.
    Hon. John Sullivan, Esq.

1783, Hon. John Sullivan. Esq.
Ebenezer Thompson, Esq.
1784, Hon. John Sullivan.
1785, Col. Samuel Chesley.
1786, Hon. M. G. John Sullivan.
Capt. Joseph Young.
1787, His Excellency, John Sullivan,
Esq.
1788, His Excellency, John Sullivan,
Esq.
1789, Hon. George Frost, Esq.
1790, Hon. Ebenezer Thompson, Esq.
1791, Hon. Ebenezer Thompson, Esq.
1792, Col. Samuel Adams.
Ebenezer Thompson, Esq.
1793, John Blydenburgh.
Valentine Mathes, Esq.
1794, John Blydenburgh.
Valentine Mathes.
1795, John Blydenburgh.
1796, John Blydenburgh.
Samuel Adams.
Capt. Joseph Young.
1797, Ebenezer Smith, Esq.
Col. Samuel Adams.
1798, John Blydenburgh.
William Ballard.
Col. Samuel Adams.
1799, Ebenezer Thompson, Jr.
1800, Ebenezer Thompson, Jr.
Ebenezer Smith, Esq.
Andrew Simpson.
1801, John Blydenburgh.
1802, Col. Timothy Emerson.
Jonathan Steele, Esq.
1803, Col. Timothy Emerson.
1804, Andrew Simpson.
Jonathan Steele, Esq.
Col. Timothy Emerson.
1805, Mr. Andrew Simpson.
1806, Ebenezer Smith, Esq.
Ebenezer Doe.
1807, Ebenezer Smith, Esq.
1808, Ebenezer Smith, Esq.
Mr. John Frost.
1809, Andrew Simpson.
1810, John Frost.
1811, Jonathan Steele.

1812, George Frost.
Jonathan Steele.
1813, George Frost.
1814, George Frost.
George Hull.
1815, Ichabod Bartlett.
1816, Ichabod Bartlett.
Benjamin Mathes, Jr.
1817, Daniel Mathes.
1818, Joseph Coe.
1819, Joseph Coe.
1820, Joseph Chesley, 3d.
Jacob Odell.
1821, Joseph Chesley, 3d.
1822, Joseph Chesley, 3d.
Winthrop Smith.
1823, Joseph Chesley, 3d.
1824, Joseph W. Page.
1825, James Langley.
1826, John A. Richardson.
1827, George Hull.
1828, George Frost.
Richard Ela.
1829, Moses Noble.
1830, Joseph Chesley, 3d.
1831, Joseph W. Page.
1832, Joseph W. Page.
1833, John A. Richardson.
1834, George Hull.
1835, John A. Richardson.
1836, Benjamin Doe.
1837, George Hull.
1838, Dr. Richard Steele.
1839, Benjamin Kelly.
1840, Stephen Demeritt.
1841, Stephen Demeritt.
1842, James Langley.
1843, Stephen Demeritt.
1844, Stephen Demeritt.
1845, Stephen Demeritt.
John A. Richardson.
Seth S. Walker.
1846, William J. Chesley.
1847, John S. Shaw.
1848, William J. Chesley.
1849, Joseph S. Burnham.
1850, Joseph S. Burnham.
1851, Daniel Smith.

1852, Daniel Smith.
Greenleaf Nute.
1853, Stephen Demeritt.
1854, Stephen Demeritt.
1855, Cyrus G. Hull.
1856, John S. Woodman.
1857, Joseph S. Burnham.
1858, Henry A. Drew.
1860, Henry A. Drew.
Cyrus G. Hull.
William Wiggin.
1861, William Wiggin.
1862, Cyrus G. Hull.
1863, Cyrus G. Hull.
1864, James M. Bunker.
1865, James M. Bunker.
1866, Joseph Smith.
1867, Joseph S. Burnham.
1868, Joseph S. Burnham.
Joseph C. Bartlett.
1869, Joseph S. Burnham.
1870, Hamilton A. Mathes.
1871, Hamilton A. Mathes.
1872, Hamilton A. Mathes.
Jeremiah Langley.
1873, Joshua B. Smith.
1874, Joshua B. Smith.
1875, Joshua B. Smith.
1876, Joshua B. Smith.

1877, Joshua B. Smith.
1878, Joshua B. Smith.
1879, Albert DeMeritt.
1880, Albert DeMeritt.
Joshua B. Smith.
1881, Joshua B. Smith.
1882, Cyrus G. Hull.
Albert DeMeritt.
1883, Cyrus G. Hull.
1884, Hamilton A. Mathes.
1885, Albert DeMeritt.
1886, Albert DeMeritt.
1887, Albert DeMeritt.
1888, Albert DeMeritt.
1889, Albert DeMeritt.
1890, Albert DeMeritt.
Hamilton A. Mathes.
1891, Hamilton A. Mathes.
1892, Lucien Thompson, for two years.
1894, Lucien Thompson, for two years.
1896, Lucien Thompson, for two years.
1898, Winthrop S. Meserve, for two years.
1900-13, Arioch W. Griffiths.
1913, Albert DeMeritt, pro tem.

Town Clerks

1732-36, Francis Mathes.
1736-61, Samuel Smith.
1761-66, Joseph Smith.
1766-74, Ebenezer Thompson.
1774-92, John Smith, 3d.
1792-93, William Smith.
1793, 1802, Ebenezer Thompson.
1802-19, Valentine Smith.
1819-23, Alfred Smith.
1823-27, Moses Noble.
1827-38, Valentine Smith.
1838-40, Samuel Burnham.
1840-44, Benjamin Kelly.
1844, Samuel P. Chesley.
1845, John A. Richardson.

1846-51, Joseph Coe.
1851-56, Joshua B. Smith.
1856-64, Samuel Runlett.
1864-68, John W. E. Thompson.
1868-72, Samuel Runlett.
1872-74, Valentine Mathes, Jr.
1874, Samuel Runlett.
1875, Calvin Sanders.
1876-80, Valentine Mathes, Jr.
1880-87, Samuel Runlett, Jr.
1887, Jasper McDaniel, resigned.
1887, Samuel Runlett, Jr.
1888-1904, George D. Stevens.
1904-13, Charles Wentworth.

364 HISTORY OF DURHAM

REPRESENTATIVES FOR DOVER FROM OYSTER RIVER PARISH

1652-57, Valentine Hill.
1684, John Woodman.
1690, Capt. John Woodman.
1692-95, John Woodman.
1696, Thomas Chesley.
1697-98, James Davis.
1699, Capt. John Woodman.
1701, James Davis.
1703, Nathaniel Hill.

1704-06, Capt. John Woodman.
1706-09, Lieut. Nathaniel Hill.
1715, Stephen Jones.
1715-17, James Davis.
1722, James Davis
1727, John Smith.
1728, Capt. Francis Mathes.
1731, Capt. Francis Mathes.

REPRESENTATIVES OF DURHAM

1732, Francis Mathes.
1733-34, Lieut. Samuel Smith.
1735, Jonathan Chesley.
1736-40, Samuel Smith.
1741-44, Jonathan Thompson.
1745-47, Jonathan Chesley.
1748-51, Jonathan Thompson.
1752-55, Joseph Thomas.
1756-58, Stephen Jones, Jr.
1759-65, Joseph Smith.
1766-75, Ebenezer Thompson.
1776-83, John Smith, 3d.
1784, Ebenezer Smith, Esq.
1785-86, Maj. Gen. John Sullivan.
1786-87, Ebenezer Thompson, Esq.
1788, John Sullivan, Speaker of the House.
1789-90, Ebenezer Smith, Esq.
1791, No election.
1792-93, Ebenezer Smith, Esq.
1793-95, Ebenezer Thompson, Jr.
1796, Voted not to send.
1797-99, Ebenezer Thompson, Jr.
1800-03, William Ballard.
1804, Capt. Jonathan Chesley.
1805, Jonathan Steele, Esq.
1806, Valentine Smith.
1807, George Frost.
1808-10, Valentine Smith.
1811-13, Joseph Coe.
1814-15, Valentine Smith.
1816-17, Joseph Coe.
1818-19, Daniel Mathes.
1820, Robert Mathes.

1821-22, Benjamin Mathes, Jr.
1823, Robert Mathes.
1824-25, John Mooney.
1826-27, Andrew G. Smith.
1828, No election.
1829-30, Benjamin Kelly.
1831-32, George Hull.
1833-34, Samuel Burnham.
1835-36, Abraham Mathes.
1837-38, Stephen Demeritt.
1839, John Mooney.
1840-41, Samuel Burnham.
1842, Winthrop Smith.
1843, Mark Willey.
1844, Winthrop Smith.
1844, Stephen Demeritt.
1845-46, Ebenezer Thompson.
1847, James Langley.
1848-49, George J. Wiggins.
1850, Mark Willey.
1851-52, Moses H. Wiggins.
1853-54, Joseph S. Burnham.
1855, Leonard B. Smith.
1856-57, Benjamin Doe.
1858-59, Andrew L. Simpson.
1860-61, Andrew D. McDaniel.
1862, William F. Jones.
1863, Henry A. Drew.
1864, William F. Jones.
1865-66, Joshua B. Smith.
1867, James M. Bunker.
1868-69, Lafayette Hall.
1870, Jacob Mathes.
1871, James M. Smart.

1872-73, Thomas H. Wiswall.	1892,	Ira B. Hill.
1874, Alfred Hoitt.	1894,	Jabez H. Stevens.
1875-76, Hamilton A. Mathes.	1896,	Daniel Chesley.
1877-78, Eben M. Davis.	1898,	Charles E. Hoitt.
1878, Joshua B. Smith.	1900,	James W. Burnham.
1880, John W. E. Thompson.	1902,	Charles S. Langley.
1882, Cyrus G. Hull.	1904,	Charles Wentworth.
1884, Mark H. Mathes.	1906,	Charles A. Smart.
1886, Lucien Thompson.	1908,	David H. Fogg.
1888, James W. Burnham.	1910,	Albert DeMeritt.
1890, Jeremiah Langley.	1912,	Albert DeMeritt.

SELECTMEN

The selectmen of Dover, before Durham became a separate township, have been published in the Historical Memoranda of Ancient Dover. A few Oyster River men figure in those lists, such as Valentine Hill, Robert Burnham, John Davis, John Bickford, John Woodman, James Davis, Nathaniel Hill, Stephen Jones, Thomas Chesley, Francis Mathes, John Smith, Capt. Samuel Chesley, etc. The following is the list after Oyster River Parish became the town of Durham:

1732, Lieut. Samuel Smith, Francis Mathes, Lieut. Jonathan Tomson, Thomas Drew, Capt. Jonathan Chesley.

1733, Lieut. Jonathan Tomson, Frances Mathes, John Williams, Jr., John Woodman, Joseph Jones, Jr.

1734, Mr. Thomas Drew, Lieut. Jonathan Tomson, Lieut. Samuel Smith, Mr. John Woodman, Francis Mathes.

1735, Lieut. Jonathan Tomson, Francis Mathes, Mr. Thomas Drew, Mr. John Woodman, Lieut. Samuel Smith.

1736, Lieut. Stephen Jones, Jr., Mr. Joseph Drew, Mr. Nathan' Randal, Mr. Joseph Thomas, Walter Bryant.

1737, John Woodman, Samuel Smith, Francis Mathes, Jonathan Tomson, Wm. Drew.

1738, Jonathan Tomson, John Williams, Jr., Joseph Whelor.

1739, Jonathan Tomson, Benjamin Smith, John Williams.

1740, Jonathan Tomson, Benjamin Smith, John Williams.

1741, Jonathan Tomson, John Williams, Jr., Benjamin Smith.

1742, Ephraim Davis, Ebenezer Smith, Joseph Atkinson.

1743, Ebenezer Smith, Joseph Atkinson, Ephraim Davis.

1744, Samuel Smith, Esq., Joseph Whelor, William Drew.

1745, Samuel Smith, John Williams, Joseph Chesley.

1746, Samuel Smith, John Williams, Jonathan Tomson.

1747, Samuel Smith, Joseph Whelor, Joseph Thomas.

1748, Samuel Smith, Joseph Whelor, Joseph Thomas.

1749, Samuel Smith, Joseph Whelor, Joseph Thomas.

1750, Samuel Smith, Joseph Whelor, Joseph Thomas.

1751, Samuel Smith, Joseph Thomas, Joseph Whelor.

1752, Samuel Smith, Joseph Thomas, Joseph Whelor.

1753, William Drew, Benjamin Mathes, James Smith.

1754, William Drew, Benjamin Mathes, James Smith.

1755, Ebenezer Smith, Joseph Smith, Joseph Sias.

1756, Ebenezer Smith, Joseph Smith, Joseph Sias.

1757, Benjamin Smith, Joseph Smith, Joseph Sias.

1758, Miles Randal, Jeremiah Burnum, Jr., Joseph Smith.

1759, Joseph Smith, Jeremiah Burnum, Jr., Miles Randal.

1760, Miles Randall, Jeremiah Burnum, Joseph Smith.

1761, Joseph Smith, Miles Randal, Jeremiah Burnum.

1762, Joseph Thomas, Robert Thompson, Jr., Jonathan Woodman.

1763, Lieut. Joseph Thomas, Joseph Smith, Esq., Lieut. Joseph Sias.

1764, Joseph Smith, Joseph Thomas, Joseph Sias.

1765, Joshua Cromet, Hercules Moony, Ebenezer Thompson.

1766, Joshua Crommet, Ebenezer Thompson, John Smith, 3d, Nicholas Duda, and Robert Thompson for Lee.

1767, Joshua Cromet, Ebenezer Thompson, John Smith, 3d.

1768, Joshua Cromet, Ebenezer Thompson, John Smith, 3d.

1769, Joshua Cromett, Ebenezer Thompson, John Smith, 3d.

1770, Joshua Cromet, Ebenezer Thompson, John Smith, 3d.

1771, Joshua Cromet, Ebenezer Thompson, John Smith, 3d.

1772, Lieut. John Smith, Alpheus Chesley, Jonathan Woodman, 3d.

1773, John Smith, Esq., John Smith, 3d, Lieut. Samuel Chesley.

1774, John Smith, 3d, Lieut. Samuel Chesley, John Smith, Esq.

1775, Samuel Chesley, John Smith, 3d, Trueworthy Durgin, Jr.

1776, Col. Samuel Chesley, John Smith, 3d, Trueworthy Durgin, Jr., George Frost, Esq., appointed as Durgin had died.

1777, Dea. Nathaniel Norton, Mr. Jonathan Chesley, Mr. Nathaniel Hill.

1778, Mr. Jonathan Chesley, Capt. Timothy Emerson, Mr. Elijah Drew.

1779, Mr. Jonathan Chesley, John Smith, 3d, Col. Samuel Chesley.

1780, Col. Samuel Chesley, John Smith, 3d, Mr. Jonathan Chesley.

1781, Col. Samuel Chesley, John Smith, 3d, Jonathan Chesley, Honble., George Frost, Esq., Mr. Andrew Drew.

1782, Lt. John Smith, 4th. Capt. John Griffin, Mr. Stephen Cogan.

1783, Capt. John Griffin, Mr. Stephen Cogan, Ebenezer Smith.

1784, Capt. John Griffin, Mr. Stephen Cogan, Mr. Ebenezer Smith.

1785, Mr. Ebenezer Smith, Mr. John Clough, Capt. John Griffin.

1786, Capt. John Griffin, Mr. Ebenezer Smith, Mr. John Clough.

1787, Capt. John Griffin, Mr. Ebenezer Smith, Mr. John Clough.

1788, Col. Samuel Chesley, John Smith, 3d., Mr. John Blydenburgh.

1789, Ebenezer Smith, Esq., Mr. John Clough, Col. Timothy Emerson.

1790, Ebenezer Smith, Esq., Mr. John Clough, Mr. James Leighton.

1791, Ebenezer Smith, Esq., Mr. John Clough, Capt. Joseph Young.

1792, John Clough, Robert Lapish, Jr., William Ballard.

1793, John Clough, William Ballard, Joseph Richardson.

1794, John Clough, William Ballard, Jonathan Woodman, Jr.

1795, John Clough, William Ballard, Capt. Jonathan Woodman, Jr.
1796, John Clough, Jonathan Woodman, Zebulon Durgin.
1797, John Clough, Jonathan Woodman, Zebulon Durgin.
1798, John Clough, Capt. Jonathan Woodman, Joseph Richardson.
1799, John Clough, Jonathan Woodman, Daniel Smith.
1800, Jonathan Steele, Jonathan Chesley, Zebulon Durgin.
1801, Capt. Jeremiah B. Mooney, John Clough, Capt. Daniel Smith.
1802, Valentine Smith, William Jones, Lt. Robert Mathes.
1803, Valentine Smith, William Jones, Robert Mathes.
1804, Valentine Smith, Ebenezer Doe, Robert Mathes.
1805, Valentine Smith, Ebenezer Doe, Daniel Mathes.
1806, Ebenezer Doe, William Cogan, Jacob Odel.
1807, Joseph Jones Torr, Jonathan Woodman, Andrew Emerson.
1808, Valentine Smith, James Joy, Abraham Perkins.
1809, Valentine Smith, James Joy, Joseph Jones Torr.
1810, Ebenezer Doe, Zebulon Durgin, Thomas Jones.
1811, Daniel Smith, Joseph Coe, Samuel Langley.
1812, William Demeritt, Daniel Smith, Joseph Coe.
1813, Valentine Smith, Joseph Coe, Jacob Odell.
1814, Valentine Smith, Jacob Odell, William Wiggin.
1815, Winthrop Smith, William Wiggin, Andrew G. Smith.
1816, Winthrop Smith, William Wiggin, Samuel Yeaton.
1817, Daniel Mathes, Winthrop Smith, Ebenezer Doe.
1818, Valentine Smith, Joseph Coe, George Hull.
1819, Joseph Coe, George Hull, James Chesley.
1820, Seth S. Walker, Andrew G. Smith, Joseph Chesley, 3d.
1821, Andrew G. Smith, Joseph Chesley, 3d, Daniel Mathes.
1822, Andrew G. Smith, William Wiggin, Joseph W. Page.
1823, Joseph Coe, William Wiggin, Joseph W. Page.
1824, Ebenezer Thompson, Andrew G. Smith, James Langley.
1825, Ebenezer Thompson, Andrew G. Smith, James Langley.
1826, Ebenezer Thompson, Andrew G. Smith, James Langley.
1827, Andrew G. Smith, William Wiggin, John Farnham.
1828, Andrew G. Smith, John Mooney, George Dame.
1829, Andrew G. Smith, John Mooney, George Dame.
1830, Andrew G. Smith, William Wiggin, William J. Chesley.
1831, Valentine Smith, William J. Chesley, Edward Griffiths.
1832, Valentine Smith, Edward Griffiths, Benjamin Kelly.
1833, Valentine Smith, William Demeritt, William Jenkins.
1834, Valentine Smith, William Demeritt, William Jenkins.
1835, Samuel Burnham, James Furnald, Jonathan Dockum.
1836, Samuel Burnham, Stephen Demeritt, Benjamin Kelly.
1837, Stephen Demeritt, William Jenkins, Moses H. Wiggin.
1838, Samuel Burnham, Abraham Mathes, John Yeaton.
1839, Samuel Burnham, William Chesley, Winthrop Smith.
1840, Benjamin Kelly, Winthrop Smith, Washington G. Mathes.
1841, Winthrop Smith, Moses H. Wiggin, Clark D. Thompson.
1842, Winthrop Smith, George J. Wiggin, Joseph Young, 2d.

1843, Stephen Demeritt, George J. Wiggin, Winthrop Smith.
1844, Stephen Demeritt, Joseph Young, 2d, John Mathes.
1845, Edward Griffiths, John Mathes, Joseph Burnham, Jr.
1846, Oliver C. Demeritt, John S. Shaw, William J. Chesley.
1847, George J. Wiggin, Daniel Smith, Alfred Smith.
1848, Joseph Young, 2d, Greenleaf Nute, William J. Chesley.
1849, Daniel Smith, Greenleaf Nute, Jacob B. Thompson.
1850, Stephen Demeritt, Benjamin Doe, Jacob B. Thompson.
1851, Daniel Smith, Benjamin Doe, Jacob B. Thompson.
1852, Daniel Smith, Jeremiah Drew, Stephen Meader.
1853, Joseph Young, 2d, Jeremiah Drew, Nathaniel E. Thompson.
1854, Joseph Young, 2d, Nathaniel E. Thompson, Greenleaf Nute.
1855, Ebenezer Thompson, James Butler, Smith Emerson.
1856, Greenleaf Nute, Thomas J. Haines, Rufus W. Willey.
1857, Greenleaf Nute, Thomas J. Haines, Jacob B. Thompson.
1858, Charles F. Woodman, James M. Bunker, John Drew.
1859, Charles F. Woodman, Joseph S. Burnham, John Drew.
1860, Joseph S. Burnham, William Wiggin, John Emerson.
1861, William Wiggin, John Emerson, James M. Smart.
1862, Joshua B. Smith, John E. Thompson, George W. Butler.
1863, Joshua B. Smith, Solomon H. Brock, Cyrus G. Smith.
1864, Joshua B. Smith, Jacob Mathes, George W. Butler.
1865, Joshua B. Smith, Jacob Mathes, Warren Smith.
1866, Joshua B. Smith, Warren Smith, Eben Kent.
1867, Joseph S. Burnham, Eben Kent, Joseph C. Bartlett.
1868, Joseph S. Burnham, Joseph C. Bartlett, John H. Mathes.
1869, Joseph S. Burnham, Joseph C. Bartlett, Nathaniel Stevens.
1870, Joseph S. Burnham, Ephraim Jenkins, Winthrop S. Meserve.
1871, Ephraim Jenkins, Winthrop S. Meserve, Hamilton A. Mathes.
1872, Hamilton A. Mathes, Joshua B. Smith, Calvin Sanders.
1873, Joshua B. Smith, Calvin Sanders, Daniel T. Woodman.
1874, Joshua B. Smith, John S. Chesley, Moses G. Woodman.
1875, Joshua B. Smith, Daniel T. Woodman, Jeremiah Langley.
1876, Joshua B. Smith, Jeremiah Langley, Hilliard F. Fogg.
1877, Joshua B. Smith, Hilliard F. Fogg, Albert Young.
1878, Joshua B. Smith, Albert Young, William B. Langmaid.
1879, John McDaniel, William B. Langmaid, David A. Stevens.
1880, John McDaniel, Joseph C. Bartlett, Mark H. Mathes.
1881, Joseph C. Bartlett, Mark H. Mathes, Joshua B. Smith.
1882, Mark H. Mathes, Joshua B. Smith, Frank E. Giles.
1883, Joshua B. Smith, John S. Chesley, Stephen Rand.
1884, Joshua B. Smith, Stephen Rand, Charles E. Hoitt.
1885, John Dennison, Charles E. Hoitt, Frank E. Doe.
1886, Charles E. Hoitt, Frank E. Doe, Samuel Runlett, Jr.
1887, Frank E. Doe, Samuel Runlett, Jr., Joseph M. R. Adams.
1888, Samuel Runlett, Jr., Eben M. Davis, Daniel Chesley.
1889, Eben M. Davis, Daniel Chesley, Samuel H. Craig.
1890, Daniel Chesley, Andrew E. Meserve, Jabez H. Stevens.

1891, Jeremiah Langley, Edward A. Marston, Charles A. Smart.
1892, Jeremiah Langley, Jabez H. Stevens, Joshua B. Smith.
1893, Jabez H. Stevens, Joshua B. Smith, Arioch W. Griffiths.
1894, Jabez H. Stevens, Joshua B. Smith, Arioch W. Griffiths.
1895, Daniel T. Woodman, Daniel Chesley, Frank E. Doe.
1896, Daniel Chesley, Frank E. Doe, George S. Caverno.
1897, James W. Burnham, George H. Whitcher, Charles E. Hoitt.
1898, James W. Burnham, Charles E. Hoitt, Stephen P. Chesley.
1899, James W. Burnham, Charles E. Hoitt, Stephen P. Chesley.
1900, James B. Burnham, Charles E. Hoitt, Stephen P. Chesley.
1901, Charles E. Hoitt, George G. Hoitt, James W. Burnham.
1902, Charles E. Hoitt, Frank E. Doe, Patrick J. Connor.
1903, Frank E. Doe, Charles E. Hoitt, Ira B. Hill.
1904, Ira B. Hill, Frank E. Doe, Charles E. Hoitt.
1905, Frank E. Doe, Charles A. Smart, Patrick J. Connor.
1906, Charles A. Smart, Patrick J. Connor, David H. Fogg.
1907, Charles A. Smart, Patrick J. Connor, David H. Fogg.
1908, David H. Fogg, Charles A. Smart, Wilbert S. Chesley.
1909, David H. Fogg, Wilbert S. Chesley, Charles E. Hoitt.
1910, Wilbert S. Chesley, Harry R. Hill, Charles E. Hoitt.
1911, Charles E. Hoitt, Harry R. Hill, James G. Smart.
1912, Harry R. Hill, James G. Smart, Charles E. Hoitt.
1913, James G. Smart, Charles E. Hoitt, Fred Philbrick.

HEADS OF FAMILIES IN DURHAM, N. H.

FIRST CENSUS OF THE UNITED STATES, 1790

Name of Head of Family	Free white males of 16 years and upwards, including heads of families	Free white males under 16 years	Free white females including heads of families	All other free persons	Slaves
Adams, Samuel	1	1	4		
Appleby, Joseph	1		2		
Appleby, Thos	1	1	1		
Angier, John	1		1		
Appleby, Wm	1	2	1		
Boynton, Joseph	1	4	2		
Burnham, Edward	1	1	1		
Blydenburgh, John	1		4		
Bunker, Benjamin	2	3	6		
Ballard, Joshua	3	2	5		
Ballard, Wm	1				
Burnham, Pike	1	1	3		
Bennett, Abrahm					
Bennett, John	4		4		
Burnham, Jeremh	3	1	2		
Bickford, Esther	1		3		
Burnham, Robert	1		1		
Bunker, Ephm	1	4	6		
Bickford, Reuben	2	1	4		
Burnham, John	2	3	3		
Burnham, Saml	1		2		1
Bickford, Benja	1				
Bickford, Winthrp	3		3		
Bennett, Eleazr	1	1	6	1	
Brock, Wm	2		4		
Butler, James	1				
Burleigh, Isaac	2	1	4		
Chesley, Joseph	3	1	3		
Coe, Curtis	2	3	4		
Critchet, James	1				

371

Name of Head of Family	Free white males of 16 years and upwards, including heads of families	Free white males under 16 years	Free white females including heads of families	All other free persons	Slaves
Chesley, Benja	2	1	2		
Chesley, Benja., Jr	2	5	6		
Crocksford, Daniel	1		6		
Chesley, Isaac	1	1	4		
Coldbath, John	1	1	2		
Chesley, Mary	1		4		
Cogan, Stephen	1	4	3		
Chesley, Col. Saml	2	4	1		
Chesley, Sarah			1		
Clough, Ephm., Jr	1				
Clough, John	4		3		
Crummett, Jacob	2	1	6		
Crockett, Jona	2	1	3		
Daniels, Elipht	3	1	2		
Doe, Wiggin	1	3	2		
Drew, Saml	1				
Durgin, Mary					
Drew, Andrew	2	1	4		
Durell, Benmore	3	2	5		
Davis, Ephm	2		3		
Dame, George	1	1	7		
Denbo, Ichabod	2		2		
Demeritt, Israel	1	1	6		
Dame, Joseph	1	2	3		
Davis, James	1				
Davis, Daniel	1	1	2		
Demeritt, Nathl	2	1	4		
Durgin, James	1	3	4		
Davis, Love			1		
Doe, Benja	4		3		
Davis, David	4		4		
Davis, Thos	1				
Doe, Ebenzr	1	1	1		
Dame, John	1	3	7		
Durgin, Joseph	1	1	3		

Name of Head of Family	Free white males of 16 years and upwards, including heads of families	Free white males under 16 years	Free white females including heads of families	All other free persons	Slaves
Durgin, Trueworthy					
Durgin, Zebulon	3	1	4		
Davis, Levi	1		4		
Dearbon, James	2	3	3		
Durgin, Wm	2	2	2		
Durgin, Eliza		1	1		
Durgin, Stephn					
Emerson, Timothy	2	1	4	1	
Edgerly, Ebenzr	1	4	3		
Edgerly, Samuel	4	1	3		
Edgerly, John	1		2		
Edgerly, Moses	1	1	2		
Edgerly, Moses, Jr	3	2	2		
Edgerly, Saml. Jr	1	2	2		
Emerson, Edward W	1	2	2		
Emerson, Joseph	1				
Frost, George	2	2	5		
Furnass, Patrick	1	3	2		
Folsom, James	1		1		
Griffin, Hannah	1	2	3		
Gillmore, James	2	1	1		
Grover, John	2	1	3		
Grant, Thos	1		2		
Hardy, Theops	1	1	5		
Ham, Thos	3	3	6		
Jackson, Laskey	1	2	3		
Jones, Stephn	3	1	5	1	
Jenkins, Nathl	1	1	1		
Joy, Saml	2	3	4		
Jewett, Noah	3	2	5		
Jewell, Bradbury	1	1	3		
Jackson, Enoch	2	3	7		
Jones, Robert	1	1	4		
Knight, John	1		3		
Kent, Richd	1	3	1		

Name of Head of Family	Free white males of 16 years and upwards, including heads of families	Free white males under 16 years	Free white females including heads of families	All other free persons	Slaves
Kent, Lydia	2		1		
Leathers, Abednego	2		2		
Leathers, Benja	1	1	1		
Leighton, James	4	1	6		
Langley, Joseph	2	2	2		
Libby, John	1	2	3		
Lapish, Robert	2	4	6		
Leathers, Saml	1	1	1		
Leighton, Tobias	1	1	8		
Lapish, Robert, Jr	3	1	1		
Leathers, Robert	2	1	2		
Langley, Valentine	3	1	2		
Meserve, Timo	1	1	2		
Meader, Isaac	1	3	6		
Mathes, Valentine	4	6	3		
Mathes, Benja	1		2		
Meserve, Ebenzr	1	2	3		
Munroe, John	1		3		
Neal, Joshua	2		4		
Nutter, Christopher	1	2	2		
Nutter, Lemuel	1				
Pinkham, Thos	2	1	7		
Pindexter, Thos	1	5	3		
Pendergast, Dennis	2		1		
Pendergast, Edmund	2	2	3		
Pendergast, John	2	1	5		
Pitman, George	1		3		
Pindar, Thos	1	4	2		
Perkins, Wm	1		1		
Pindar, Wm	1				
Pindar, Jeremh	1	1	4		
Pinkham, Abijah	1		3		
Ryan, Michael	2	3	3		
Richards, Bartho	1	3	2		
Richardson, Joseph	1	1	5		

Name of Head of Family	Free white males of 16 years and upwards, including heads of families	Free white males under 16 years	Free white females including heads of families	All other free persons	Slaves
Spinney, Wm.	2	2	2		
Sullivan, Jno.	6		6		
Smith, Benja.	4	1	1		
Smith, John 3d	1		3		
Smith, Robert	1		2		
Smith, Jno.	2	1	4	1	
Smith, John, Jr.	4	1	4		
Smith, Ebenzr.	1	4	2		
Stephen, Cornelius	1		5		
Stephens, Benja.	2	2	4		
Stevens, John	3	1	2		
Stevenson, John	3		7		
Steel, Jona.	1		3		
Starboard, John	1	3	4		
Spencer, Abednego	1		3		
Spencer, John	2		2		
Spencer, Levi	1	1	1		
Smith, Joseph	1	1	7		
Thomas, James	1				
Thomas, Joseph					
Thomas, Joseph, Jr.	2	4	6		
Thompson, Ebenz.	3	1	4		
Thompson, Ebenz., Jr.	1	1	3		
Thompson, Jona.	1	3	4		
Thompson, John	1	1	3		
Thompson, Edmund	1	2	3		
Thompson, Thos.	1		4		
Tucker, Henry	2	3	8		
Taylor, Thomas	1	3	2		
Thompson, Benja.	1				
Tripp, Benja.	1		2		
Thompson, Samuel	2	1	1		
Woodman, Jona., Jr.	2	5	3		
Woodman, Jona.	4	4	5		
Williams, Jona.	2		2		

Name of Head of Family	Free white males of 16 years and upwards, including heads of families	Free white males under 16 years	Free white females including heads of families	All other free persons	Slaves
Welch, John	I	4	3		
Wiggin, Issachar	I	5	3		
Wormwood, Joseph	4		3		
Willey, Benja	3		4		
Willey, Jeremh	I	3	3		
Willey, James	2	I	5		
Willey, Robert	I	I	2		
Willey, Theodore	3	2	4		
Willey, Jeremh., Jr	I		3		
Woodman, Jacob	I		4		
Woodman, Lemuel	I		5		
Willey, Valentine	I		I		
Young, Joseph	3	I	3		
Yeaton, Saml	I	4	5		
Watson, Henry	I		I		
Jackson, James	I	I	2		
Dealing, Abigail		I	3		
Davis, Micah	2		5		
Leathers, Ezekl	I		I		
Willey, Thos	I	2	3		
Bunker, Zachr	I	4	2		
Cromwell, Saml	I		I		
Cromwell, Saml. Jr	2	2	2		
Bickford, Jona	I	2	I		
Bickford, Eliakim	I	I	3		
Smart, John	I		3		
Smart, Bartho	I		3		
Beck, Abigail	I	I	2		
Rollings, Sarah			I		
Coldbath, Sarah			2		
Durgin, Henry	I	I	2		
Durgin, Philip	I		2		
Sharp, Abigail		I	2		
Gerrish, Peggy			I		
Dearbon, Mary		I	2		

Name of Head of Family	Free white males of 16 years and upwards, including heads of families	Free white males under 16 years	Free white females including heads of families	All other free persons	Slaves
Willey, Mary			3		
Smith, John, 4:	1	1	1		
Noble, Stephn	2	2	3		
Drisco, Sarah			1		
Bean, Ebenez	1	1	2		
Flint, Polly		1	3		
Marston, Levi	3	3	3		
Simson, Wm	1	2	4		
Banter, John	1	3	3		
Folsom, Joseph	1	1	2		
Langley, Jno	1		1		
Eastman, Wm	1	1	1		
Webster, Reuben	1				
Chace, Oliver	1				
Drew, Joseph	1		1		
Smith, Jonatha	1		2		
Dutch, Jno	1				
Nutter, Matthias	1	1	2		
Crocket, Jno	1		1		
Hunskum, Lucy			2		
Swain, Razar	1		2		
Durant, John	1	2	1		
Parsons, Jona	1		1		
Cromwell, Mary		1	3		
Evans, Stephen	1		5		

Copied by Lucien Thompson, Durham N. H., May 14, 1908.

MARRIAGES NOT ELSEWHERE MENTIONED IN THIS HISTORY*

By the Rev. Hugh Adams

March 25, 1719, William Miles and Hannah Heth.

May 18, 1727, Nathan Taylor and Mary Barber.

Nov. 23, 1727, Joseph Whitten and Elizabeth Gray.

Jan. 16, 1727, James Lindsey and Ann Gypson.

May 2, 1728, Joseph Hill of Kittery and Abigail Libbey.

Dec. 19, 1728, Pomfret Whitehouse and Jerusha Shepherd.

Jan. 12 1728/9, Samuel Drown and Martha Tibbets.

April 10, 1729, John Borman of Falmouth and widow Elizabeth Fisk of Newmarket.

May 29, 1729, Ichabod Tibbets, widower, and Patience Nock.

By The Rev. John Adams

Feb. 1, 1749/50 James Morrison and Mary Kelsey, both of Barrington.

Feb. 26, 1750/51, Thomas Young of Newmarket and Mary Huntress of Newington.

May 22, 1751, Amos Howard and Sarah Damm, both of Somersworth.

Nov. 14, 1751, John Moe and Elizabeth McCutchin, both of Barrington.

Oct. 11, 1752, Lazarus Rowe and Mary Webber, both of Greenland.

Nov. 16, 1752, John Johnson and Mary Kenniston, of Newmarket.

July 24, 1754, Thomas Evans and Hannah Buzzell, both of Dover.

Nov. 1, 1754, James Nelson and Hannah Kenniston, both of Newmarket.

Aug. 1, 1754, Samuel Chapman and Mary Barber, both of Newmarket.

Dec. 3, 1754, Hugh Little and Hulda Rines, both of Durham.

Dec. 26, 1754, John Sanborn of Newmarket and Mary Glidden of Durham.

* In the following records the original spelling has been retained.

Feb. 7, 1755, Samuel Wallis and Sedeny Tilley, both of Barrington.

March 9, 1755, Joseph Applebee and Eleanor Kenniston, both of Durham.

July 4, 1755, Jonathan Fiske and Sarah Welch, both of Durham.

Dec. 11, 1755, John Hartford and Bethiah Rollins, both of Newmarket.

May 18, 1756, Benjamin Hall and Patience Tibbetts, both of Durham.

Dec. 31, 1756, Christopher Gould and Elizabeth Waters, both of Durham.

July 19, 1757, Joseph Simpson of Greenland and Anne Simpson of Durham.

Sept. 19, 1757, Benjamin Evans and Hannah Chiles, both of Durham.

Nov. 17, 1757, Zebulon Glidden of Durham and Temperance Whidden of Newmarket.

Dec. 15, 1757, Joseph Palmer of Hampton and Lydia Glidden of Durham.

Sept. 21, 1758, Ebenezer Townsend and Mary Glidden, both of Durham.

May 8, 1760, Nathaniel White and Grace Roberts, both of Durham.

Jan. 18, 1761, Benjamin Glazier and Mary Brown, both of Durham.

Feb. 28, 1761, Elisha Tool [Towle] and Anne Sanborn, both of Durham.

Sept. 6, 1761, Richard Bowers and Mary Barnet, both of Durham.

Dec. 30, 1762, William Foss, 3rd, and Elizabeth Clay, both of Durham.

By The Rev. Curtis Coe

Jan 2, 1781, Levi Robinson of Nottingham and Rachel Rines.

Aug. 2, 1781, Samuel Field and Miss Anna Nock.

March 13, 1783, Samuel Bickford and Miss Deborah Elwell.

June 7, 1783, Benjamin Tripp and Mrs. Hannah Gage.

Nov. 14, 1784. George Bunker of Barnstead and Miss Alice Smith.

Dec. 28, 1784, John Smart and Miss Molly Adams.

March 26, 1785, Levi Davis and Olive Noble.

May 16, 1785, Donald McDonald and Miss Rhoda Grover.

July 24, 1785, Moses Drew and Miss Hannah Willey.

Sept. 18, 1785, Jeremiah Willey, Jr., and Miss Sally Johnson.

March 20, 1786, Solomon Davis and Miss Temperance Colbath.

Dec. 18, 1786, John Knowlton of Boscawen and Elizabeth Langley.

Feb. 21, 1787, Ebenezer Bean and Anne Whitham.

April 8, 1787, William Applebee and Mrs. Sally Langley.

June 24, 1787, Jonathan Drew of Windham and Miss Eleanor Hicks.

June 21, 1788, Matthias Nutter, Jr., of Newington and Miss Betsey Colbath.

Dec. 31, 1789, Valentine Willey and Miss Hannah Hearne.

Jan. 7, 1782, Joseph Kent of Gilmanton and Miss Margaret Jordan.

Oct. 1, 1789, William Nute of Dover and Miss Polly Davis of Madbury.

July 12, 1791, Reuben Cook and Miss Elizabeth Bickford.

Oct. 2, 1791, Oliver Chase and Miss Polly Chase.

Nov. 24, 1791, Samuel Willey and Miss Jennie Follet.

Dec. 9, 1791, Stephen Brock of Durham and Miss Abigail Bunker of Madbury.

Jan. 18, 1792, Nicholas Robinson of Epping and Miss Mary Willey of Hampton.

Sept. 18, 1792, John Clark of Rochester and Miss Betsey Langley.

Nov. 7, 1793, William Campbell and Miss Elizabeth Bunker.

March 16, 1794, John Bickford and Miss Sally Bracey.

April 6, 1794, Thomas Bennett of Newmarket and Miss Patience Ham.

Nov. 2, 1794, Rufus Wiggin of Stratham and Miss Sally Edgerley.

May 10, 1795, Benjamin French Brown and Miss Sally Bickford.

Aug. 16, 1795, Samuel York and Miss Miriam Frye, both of Lee.

Dec. 31, 1795, Anthony Vincent of Newington and Miss Betsey Rogers.

Feb. 21, 1796, William Shepard of New Holderness and Miss Hannah Hill of Madbury.

Jan. 8, 1797, James Carter of Tamworth and Miss Nancy Edgerley.

Feb. 11, 1798, Joseph French of Epping and Miss Hannah Ham.

March 1, 1798, Daniel Hanson and Miss Sally Smith.

May 8, 1798, Jonathan Elliott of Epping and Mrs. Elizabeth Glidden of Lee.

Dec. 30 1799, Joseph Pitman of Ossipee and Mrs. Ruth Colbath.

Jan. 1, 1801, Hugh Cox of Lee and Miss Sally Davis.

March 29, 1801, William Simpson of Boston and Miss Betty Hanson.

April 26, 1801, James Fogg and Miss Deborah Woodlock.

April 26, 1801, Joseph Ballard of Rochester and Miss Sally Perley.

July 2, 1801, Joseph Hodgdon of Rochester and Miss Abigail Pitman.

Jan. 13, 1803, Josiah Folsom of Portsmouth and Miss Sally Hull.

Sept. 1, 1803, John Smith of Barrington and Miss Sarah Clark of Madbury.

Dec. 8, 1803, Thomas Willey of Madbury and Miss Mary Meader.

Oct. 14, 1804, John Smith and Miss Abigail Crocket.

Sept. 19, 1805, Samuel Marsh and Miss Hannah Johnson.

By The Rev. Federal Burt.

Nov. 19, 1817, Ebenezer Hanson of Dover and Abigail Paul of Somersworth.

Jan. 18, 1818, Stephen Starbird and Miss Tamson Nute.

Jan. 15, 1818, John P. Neal and Miss Sally Clements, both of Dover.

March 15, 1818, Thomas Kief of Stratham and Miss Abigail Cole of Madbury.

June 15, 1818, Daniel Fowler, Jr., and Miss Nancy Buzzell.

June 21, 1818, Charles Woodman, Esq., and Miss Mary W. Gage, both of Dover.

Dec. 17, 1818, Samuel Hayes and Miss Lydia Young.

Jan. 11, 1819, Asa Seaver of Rochester and Miss Abigail Turner of Dover.

April 5, 1819, William J. Tomson of South Berwick and Miss Abigail M. Wentworth of Somersworth.

April 14, 1819, Robert Martin of Newcastle and Miss Sarah Ann Tuttle of Dover.

Jan. 13 1820, John Leathers and Miss Nancy Morse.

April 5, 1820, John H. Prescott of Gilmanton and Miss Sally C. Meserve of Northwood.

Aug. 19, 1821, Stephen Davis and Miss Clarissa Trickey.

Sept. 13, 1821, John Smart and Miss Prudence I. Tuttle.

Sept. 16, 1821, Samuel Cate of Alton and Miss Catherine Jenkins of Madbury.

June 30, 1822, Enoch Chase of Boston and Miss Maria Lord of Somersworth.

July 9, 1822, Jeremiah Buzzell and Miss Ann Winkley, both of Barrington.

June 10, 1823, Ebenezer Ford of Nottingham and Miss Eliza Sherburn of Northwood.

Nov. 30 1823, Joseph W. Page and Miss Mary Ann Gilman of Dover.

Dec. 10, 1823, Stephen Quint and Miss Nancy Clay.

Aug. 15, 1824, Richard Downing of Newington and Miss Ann Twombly.

Sept. 9, 1824, Benjamin Ford and Miss Sarah York, both of Dover.

Sept. 12, 1824, George W. Prince and Miss Martha Ham, both of Dover.

Nov. 28, 1824, John Wentworth, 2d, of Somersworth and Miss Statira Godwin of Berwick.

Nov. 28, 1824, John L. Thorndike and Miss Maria Joy, both of Pittsfield.

Jan. 5, 1825, Daniel Cram and Miss Edna Ela, both of Newmarket.

May 8, 1825, Joseph Hanson, Jr., and Miss Hannah March, both of Rochester.

May 19, 1825, Alonzo Roberts and Miss Mary Torr, both of Dover.

May 19, 1825, Andrew Varney and Miss Susan Footman, both of Dover.

Oct. 23, 1825, Benjamin Gerrish of Milton and Miss Margaret H. Howard of Dover.

Nov. 20, 1825, Jeremiah O. Legg and Miss Jane Clarke, both of Dover.

Feb. 9, 1826, David Manson and Miss Jane F. Grover, both of Dover.

July 6, 1826, Josiah Sanborn and Miss Harriet Bean.

Dec. 25, 1826, Micajah Leathers and Miss Hannah Whipple, both of Dover.

Oct. 14, 1827, Nathaniel Clarke of Somersworth and Miss Charlotte Ham of Dover.

By The Rev. William Demeritt.

Oct. 16, 1816, George Hooper and Hannah York.

June 16, 1818, Thomas Limber and Phebe Chesley.

June 22, 1817, Joseph Patten and Olive Edes.

Dec. 2, 1817, Jonathan Glover and Betsy Langmade.

Dec. 14, 1817, John Tibbetts and Mary Hanson.

April 26, 1818, Andrew B. Shute and Patience Grover.

April 30, 1818, Job Clay and Eleanor Daniels.

Jan. 14, 1819, Daniel Young and Eleanor Smith.

Aug. 8, 1818, John Ham and Joan McNeal.

Sept. 9, 1819, Paul Henderson and Ann Drew.

Dec. 1, 1819, Samuel Lamos and Susan Langmade.

Jan. 8, 1820, Richard James Harvey and Abigail Hall.

May 25, 1820, Benjamin Waterhouse and Rebecca Manson.

June 10, 1820, Samuel Quint and Abigail Glover.

July 23, 1820, John Ham and Lydia Ham.

Aug. 20, 1820, David Bickford and Elizabeth Jenness.

Aug. 20, 1820, Ephraim L. Bickford and Sally Davis.

Jan. 7, 1821, James McDuffee and Hannah Ham.

April 22, 1821, Samuel Drew and Sally Tuttle.

June 24, 1821, John Twombly and Mary Ham.

July 4, 1821, Miles Davis and Betsey Rendell.

July 29, 1821, Joseph Young and Mary Tibbetts.

Oct. 22, 1821, Stephen Jenness and Anna Seavy.

Nov. 28, 1821, Samuel Hall and Mary Grover.

Nov. 29, 1821, Warren Langley and Mary Peirce.

Jan. 24, 1822, Jacob Hayes and Margaret Hayes.

March 17, 1822, Ebenezer Buzzell and Hannah Caldwell.

April 4, 1822, Curtis Clay and Lattice Colbath.

Aug. 8, 1822, John Sherborn and Sally Gear.

Nov. 1822, James Thompson and Elizabeth Clarenbrook.

Feb. 2, 1823, Samuel Hanson and Sarah H. Snell.

March 27, 1823, Joseph Knight and Tamsen Carswell.

——, 1823, Jonathan Ham, Jr., and Sally Wiggins.

March 30, 1823, Moses Nute and Clarissa Pinkham.

May 11, 1823, James Bickford and Ann Arlin.
May 18, 1823, John Sant and Comfort Willey.
May 25, 1823, George P. Savory and Lydia Ham.
Nov. 13, 1823, Elezer Young and Keziah Rowe.
Jan. 11, 1824, Solomon Jenness and Phebe Taylor.
Feb. 5, 1824, Moses Hodgdon and Eliza Daniels.
May 3, 1824, Jacob Hall and Abigail Daniels.
Sept. ——, 1824, Timothy Brewster and Eliza Young.
Nov. ——, 1824, Thomas Jackson and Ann Turner.
March ——, 1825, Bartholom Berrey and Nancy P. Whitehouse.
May ——, 1825, Nathaniel Brock and Nancy Drew.
       ——, 1825, Thomas Verner and Sophia Canald.
Nov. ——, 1825, Rufus Wilkinson and Catherine Bunker.
Nov. ——, 1825, John S. Whitehouse and Abigail Bickford.
Dec. ——, 1825, William Palmer and Penniel Hall.
——, 1825, John Flanders and Mary McNeal.
——, 1826, Timothy Hanson and Abigail Chesley.
Jan. ——, 1826, Levi Cram and Lovey Bunker.
Feb. ——, 1826, Ransom Haines and Mary Chesley.
March 5, 1826, Francis P. Channell and Olive H. Chapman.
Aug. 24, 1826, William Hooper and Sarah Demeritt.
Oct. 8, 1826, Hiram Cockran and Mary Emerson.
Nov. 23, 1826, James Hanson and Mary Gear.
Dec. 23, 1826, Joel Mirison and Emely Underwood.
Jan. 23, 1827, Nathaniel Church and Patience Hanson.
Jan. 29, 1827, Joseph Putney and Sarah Whitmore.
Dec. 9, 1827, Robert Stacey and Lydia Ann Wiggins.
Dec. 23, 1827, Joseph Gear and Margaret Gear.
April 4, 1827, John Tibbitts and Ann Buzzell.
April 9, 1827, Samuel Langmade and Elizabeth Woodman.
June 14, 1827, Oliver Chadbourne and Mary Torr.
Sept. 4, 1827, Ebenezer Boynton and Mary Ann Pinkham.
Oct. 14, 1827, John Hayes and Mary Bunker.
Nov. 4, 1827, David Robinson and Martha Ham.
March 30, 1828, Ezekiel Cutler and Eliza N. Nudd.
May 4, 1828, Nathaniel Garland and Harriet Pickering.
June 5, 1828, John Cram and Phebe C. Ricker.
June 22, 1828, John Frost and Mary Ann Savory.
July 8, 1828, Benjamin Prescott and Charlotta Jackson.
Aug. 8, 1828, Oliver Tuttle and Sarah Ham.

25

Aug. 31, 1828, Samuel Libbey and Malenda Hussey.

Sept. 4, 1828, Richard Stevenson and Sally Wintworth.

Nov. 13, 1828, Oliver Varney and Abigail Ham.

April 12, 1829, Joseph Downing and Elizabeth Holland.

April 23, 1829, Daniel Ham, Jr., and Sarah Bickford.

June 4, 1829, William Weeks, Jr., and Sarah Richardson.

Oct. 8, 1829, James L. Clark and Martha Jackson.

Jan. 27, 1830, Stephen H. Nute and Nancy Allen.

April 18, 1830, Miles Tuttle and Lucinda H. Davis.

Oct. 7, 1830, George York and Mary Haddock.

Nov. 18, 1830, Michael B. Tuttle and Mary Hull.

Nov. 24, 1830, Asa Clay and Polly Lamos.

Dec. 16, 1830, Dan Woodman and Lucy Campbel.

Feb. 24, 1831, Johnson Loveren and Caroline Glover.

April 7, 1831, George Smith and Mary P. McDaniels.

May 12, 1831, John Knight and Hannah Drew.

June 29, 1831, George W. Caverno and Hannah Ricker.

July 12, 1831, Samuel Sherborn and Elizabeth Swain.

July 26, 1831, Abraham B. Snell and Olive Gear.

Aug. 18, 1831, Alexander Tuttle and Lucinda A. Bennett.

Oct. 18, 1831, Paul Snell and Lydia Tibbetts.

Nov. 27. 1831, Edward V. Perkins and Sophia Watson.

Dec. 25, 1831, Charles H. Parkes and Lucy Ann Scriggins.

Feb. 6, 1832, Nathaniel Snell and Avis Williams.

Feb. 19, 1832, George W. Thompson and Harriet P. Shepperd.

March 5, 1831, Solomon Jenness and Elizabeth Alen.

March 25, 1832, Archalus Martin and Hannah G. Campbell.

April 15, 1832, Minot Langmade and Loisa Willame.

Sept. 30, 1832, Calvin Pickering and Mary Bunker.

Oct. 3, 1832, Hail P. Daney and Permela C. Furnold.

Nov. 15, 1832, Stephen P. Smith and Mary P. Clark.

June 3, 1833, Thompson Jackson and Mary Ann Page.

June 16, 1833, Amos H. Gerry and Lucy Ann Keniston.

March 30, 1833, William H. Trip and Mary Boin.

April —, 1833, Wingate Twombly and Loisa Curtis.

May 2, 1833, Daniel Tuxbury and Sarah Ann Sherburne.

June 23, 1833, Samuel B. Gerrish and Milenda C. Eliot.

Aug. 29, 1833, Horatio Fogg and Mary L. Durgin.

April 26, 1834, Mathew Hodgdon and Susan Snell.

April 4, 1835, Richard Pinkham and Martha Clay.

June 2, 1835, Shurburne Smith and Abigail P. Runlett.

Aug. 5, 1835, Thomas Glover and Alice Barker.

Sept. 20, 1835, Jonathan Young and Sophia M. Ricker.

Oct. 25, 1835, Joseph H. Joy and Jane Straw.

Nov. 25, 1835, Nathaniel Adams and Presella Foss.

Nov. 25, 1835, Tobias Bunker and Sally B. Buzzell.

May 18, 1836, John Shurborn and Nancy Shackford.

June 18, 1836, Nathaniel Tuttle and Martha Ann Ham.

Nov. 29, 1836, William H. Clark and Mary E. Hoite.

Jan. 22, 1837, Oliver Tuttle and Francis Gray.

Aug. 10, 1837, John B. Furber and Louisa T. Bachelder.

Oct. 19, 1837, Charles Young and Permela P. Snow.

Nov. 12, 1837, Edward Doer and Sophia Hanson.

Dec. 17, 1837, Nathaniel Stevenson and Olive Wintworth.

June 24, 1838, Pike H. Harvey and Mary Ann Chapman.

Nov. 4, 1838, Nicholas Pinkham and Olive Murphey.

Nov. 14, 1838, Joseph Jenkins and Mehitable Bunker.

Nov. 7, 1838, John Williams and Sally G. Doe.

Dec. 2, 1838, Phinehas Wintworth and Abigail Willey.

April 23, 1840, Henry Davis and Ann M. Housmer.

MISCELLANEOUS MARRIAGES

Aug. —, 1807, George Smith and Miss Betsey Garland.

July 12, 1808, Benjamin Trickey and Miss Betsey Appleby.

July 3, 1810, Dr. Jonathan Greeley of Dover and Miss Susanna Richardson.

May 30, 1811, James Huntress of Bartlett and Miss Salle Wille.

Sept. 19, 1814, William French and Rebecca Ricker.

Oct. 15, 1828, Joseph Hartwell of Canton, Mass., and Miss Betsey Riley of Dover.

June 9, 1829, Daniel Martin, Esq., of Wolfeborough and Sophia W. Fernald.

Jan. 3, 1830, George Knight and Elizabeth Twombly.

Jan. 11, 1833, Oliver Colman and Mehitable Clark.

April 6, 1834, James Woodes and Miss Meribah Jones.

April 17, 1834, Plato Waldron and Elizabeth Kelly, both of Dover.

July 10, 1834, John Clay and Miss Lydia Daniels.

Sept. 14, 1834, Jacob Barney of Lowell, Mass., and Miss Elizabeth Pickering.

Sept. 6, 1836, Joseph Garland, Jr., of Rye and Miss Elizabeth Garland of Nottingham.

Dec. 21, 1836, John D. Goodwin and Miss Susan B. Chase' both of Newmarket.

Aug. 21, 1836, William H. Gage of Lowell, Mass., and Miss Harriet C. Libbey.

Oct. 11, 1836, William French, Jr., and Miss Sarah A. Cate.

Nov. 30, 1836, Isaac M. Nute of Dover and Miss Mary Ann Jenkins of Madbury.

Dec. 14, 1836, Joshua Blunt and Miss Jane Chesley, both of Haverhill, Mass.

June 6, 1837, David Frost and Sarah Ann Nutter, both of Newmarket.

Oct. 10, 1837, William Perkins of New Durham and Mrs. Deborah Spinney.

Nov. 20, 1837, Micajah Sinclair and Miss Abigail Willard, both of Stratham.

Nov. 27, 1837, George W. Furber and Miss Sarah Hill, both of Newmarket.

April 5, 1838, William H. Hayden and Miss Mary Jane Bowles, both of Newmarket.

Nov. 29, 1838, William Taylor of Northwood and Miss Eliza Jackson.

Jan. 23, 1839, Reuben Higgins of Portland, Me., and Miss Calista L. Smith.

July 9, 1839, Richard Furber of Meredith and Miss Ednah Cram of Newmarket.

Oct. 29, 1839, Jacob Tilton of Epping and Miss Elizabeth B. Lock of Lee.

Feb. 16, 1840, Benjamin F. Neally and Miss Susan E. Bartlett of Lee.

Oct. 20, 1839, Enoch S. Davis and Palnia Staples, both of Portsmouth.

Jan. 29, 1839, Wear Davis of Lee and Miss Sarah Dockum.

Nov. 19, 1840, William Marshall and Miss Abigail Sawyer of Newmarket.

April 5, 1840, Ebenezer C. Garland and Miss Maria Edgerly both of Somersworth.

Sept. 30, 1840, William H. Robinson of Exeter and Miss Mary G. Colman.

March 7, 1840, William Tego and Miss Nancy Smith.

Nov. 7, 1841, Leonard Smith and Sally Doe of Newmarket.

Jan. 4, 1842, Ira Wright and Harriet Small.

Jan. 19, 1842, Albert G. Doyle of Dover and Miss Eliza Ingalls.

May 5, 1842, Joseph Kelley of Woburn, Mass., and Miss Mary Shaw of Exeter.

Aug. 28, 1842, Cyrus G. Hull and Miss Harriet Willey.

Dec. 20, 1843, Chesley D. Hazelton and Miss Lydia B. Channel.

May 8, 1843, Edward Sherman of Lowell and Miss Mary S. Parsons.

May 28, 1843, Levi Wilson of Rochester and Miss Mary S. Pickering.

July 10, 1845, Joseph Ham and Miss Elizabeth Berry of Barrington.

Jan. 8, 1846, Charles R. Meserve and Miss Sophronia R. Tucker, both of Dover.

May 18, 1845, Edmund E. Leighton and Miss Hannah D. Chesley, both of Newmarket.

Sept. 20, 1846, John H. Odiorne and Miss Nancy Meserve of Madbury.

March 15, 1846, James Follett and Miss Sally Giles of Barrington.

Dec. 17, 1846, Jeremiah B. Hoitt of Manchester and Miss Angeline Magoon.

Oct. 11, 1846, Alfred A. Cox and Miss Susan C. Stearns, both of Newmarket.

Oct. 28, 1846, James M. York and Miss Lucy A. Willey, both of Dover.

Dec. 29, 1847, James Tucker of Boston and Miss Mary E. Savage.

March 14, 1848, Frederick B. Balch of Lancaster and Miss Thankful H. Vincent.

June 11, 1848, Alsom H. Evans and Miss Mary J. Quint.

March 12, 1848, Augustus Richardson of Dover and Miss Lydia P. Davis of Madbury.

Feb. 6, 1849, Noah Davis, 2d, of Nottingham and Miss Mary Ann Sulivan of Lee.

May 10, 1848, Edgar E. Philbrick and Miss Hannah F. Gilman, both of Exeter.

June 11, 1848, Charles C. Shaw of Boston and Miss Hannah A. H. Pickering.

Nov. 8, 1849, Thomas J. French of Nottingham and Miss Susan C. Bassett.

Aug. 25, 1849, Charles E. Clark and Miss Ariana S. Batchelder, both of Exeter.

Sept. 4, 1849, Mathew Englin and Miss Ann Bassett, both of Dover.

Nov. 8, 1849, Joseph Page and Miss Hannah Leighton, both of Lee.

Jan. 24, 1850, Leonard Balch of Bradford, Mass., and Miss Hannah J. Parsons.

Sept. 12, 1849, Nahum Heard of North Berwick, Me., and Miss Jane Spencer of Limerick, Me.

Oct. 22, 1849, Rufus Ham of Somersworth and Miss Elizabeth B. Pierce of Barrington.

Feb. 11, 1850, Joseph A. James of Lee and Miss Mary E. Fernald of Madbury.

March 31, 1850, Moses Lamos of Lee and Sarah Grey of Newmarket.

Nov. 7, 1850, Rufus Philbrick of Rye and Miss Hannah F. Mosher.

April 26, 1850, Mark F. Nason of Dover and Miss Marietta Nute.

May 1, 1850, George F. Peckham of Newmarket and Miss Caroline E. Odell.

BAPTISMS

The baptisms of the Rev. Hugh Adams have been published in the New England Historic Genealogical Register, Vol. XXXIII, and by far the greater part of them are interwoven with the genealogical portion of this history. The baptisms of the Rev. John Adams have never been published. Those that have not been used in tracing the families of this history are here given. See page 199.

July 16, 1749, Charity, dau. of Joseph Evans.

July 23, 1749, John, son of Thomas Ford of Nottingham.

July 30, 1749, Martha, dau. of Nathaniel Frost.

July 30, 1749, Dorothy, dau. of same.

Aug. 6, 1749, Joseph and William, sons of William and Hannah Glynes.

Aug. 20, 1749, Sarah, dau. of James Brown.

Aug. 20, 1749, Moses, son of James Hall.

Aug. 23, 1749, Samuel, Daniel and Joseph, sons of John Shaw. At a place called Two Miles, in Barrington.

Aug. 23, 1749, Cunningham and Abigail, ch. of Federis McCutchin. At Two Miles.

Aug. 23, 1749, Margaret, dau. of Nehemiah McDaniel. At Two Miles.

Sept. 3, 1749, Shadrach and Molly, ch. of Shadrach and Mary Walton.

Nov. 19, 1749, Priscilla, dau. of Joseph Glidden, Jr.

Feb. 2, 1749/50, John, son of Eulice (sic) and Hannah Felker of Barrington.

April 11, 1750, James, son of Nathan Fulsom of Newmarket.

April 29, 1750, Sarah, dau. of Shadrach Watson (sic)

June 10, 1750, Nicholas, son of Nat Frost of Durham, in ye Hook.

June 24, 1750, Rhoda, dau. of Walter Briant.

July 29, 1750, Moses, son of Pomfret Whitehouse.

Sept. 9, 1750, Mary dau. of James Hall.

Sept. 16 , 1750, Gideon and Dorothy, ch. of Josiah Johnson.

March 13, 1750/1, Jonathan, son of Nathan Fulsom of Newmarket.

March 31, 1750, Mary, dau. of Nathan Fulsom of Newmarket.

April 28, 1751, Samuel and Abigail, ch. of Joshua Trickey.

April 28, 1751, Mary, dau. of Thomas Ford.

June 2, 1751, Margaret, dau. of Eulice Felker.

May 10, 1752, Jean, dau. of Shadrach Walton.

June 7, 1752, Daniel, son of Charles Runlet of Newmarket.

July 12, 1752, Nathaniel, son of Nathaniel Frost.

Aug. 15, 1752, Peter, Simeon and Josiah, ch. of Jeremy Folsom, Jr., at his house.

Sept. 13, 1752, James, son of James Morrison

Sept. 11, 1752, Pierson, son of Christopher Hunt.

May 13, 1753, Thomas, son of Thomas Ford of Nottingham.

May 20, 1753, Pomfret, son of Pomfret Whitehouse.

July 5, 1753, Dorcas and Moses Bennet, ch. of Benjamin Burdett.

July 19, 1753, Susanna, dau. of John Shaw of Nottingham.

Oct. 19, 1753, Rachel, dau. of Thomas York.

Nov. 18, 1753, Phebe, dau. of John Johnson, Jr.

Jan. 24, 1754, Jean, dau. of William Kelsey.

Jan. 31, 1754, Hugh, Margaret and George, ch. of William Kelsey.

April 29, 1754, Obediah, son of Ephraim Clough.

May 5, 1754, Martha, dau. of Joshua Trickey.

July 7, 1754, Levi, son of Nathan Fulsom of Newmarket.

Aug. 15, 1754, Mary, Dorothy and Mehitabel, daus. of Samuel Watson.

Oct. 13, 1754, Anna, wife of David Davis, 3d, and Molly, their dau.

Nov. 22, 1754, Agnes, dau. of John McDaniels. Of Two Mile.

Nov. 22, 1754, Nehemiah, son of Nehemiah McDaniels. Of Two Mile.

Nov. 22, 1754, Jean, dau. of Federis McCuthins. Of Two Mile.

Feb. 7, 1755, Abigail, Hannah and Dodavah, ch. of Dodavah Garland.

March 11, 1755, Anna, dau. of Walter Bryant.

April 11, 1755, George, John, Esther and Bethia, ch. of Josiah Dam.

Sept. 21, 1755, Johnson of John Johnson.

Nov. 2, 1755, Anna, dau. of William Glidden.

Dec. 3, 1755, Levi, son of Jeremiah Fulsom, Junr.

Dec. 3, 1755, Sarah, dau. of Samuel Call.

March 28, 1756, Phebe, dau. of John Chapman.

Aug. 22, 1756, Deborah, dau. of Moses Weymouth.

June 30, 1757, Eleanor, dau. of Nehemiah McDaniels. At ye
    Two Mile.

June 30, 1757, James ,son of William McDaniels. At ye Two
    Mile.

Oct. 23, 1757, Mary, dau. of Josiah Johnson.

July 23, 1758, Joseph, son of Josiah Johnson.

Sept. 3, 1758, Stephen, son of Stephen Call.

Sept. 15, 1758, Anna, dau. of Ephraim Clough.

Sept. 29, 1758, Mary, dau. of Ephraim Clough.

April 8, 1759, Mary, dau. of John Fulsom.

April 8, 1759, Joseph, son of Thomas George.

July 7, 1759, Aaron, Elizabeth and Stephen, ch. of Solomon
    Drown.

July 7, 1759, Robert, son of John McDaniels.

July 7, 1759, Mary, dau. of William McDaniels.

March 23, 1760, Elizabeth, dau. of Joshua Trickey.

Aug. 31, 1760, Betty, dau. of Mark Spinney.

Aug. 31, 1760, Andrew, son of Joseph Bussell.

Sept. 20, 1761, Nathan, son of John Johnson.

DEATHS RECORDED BY THE REV. FEDERAL BURT

Aug. 2, 1817, Mr. Samuel Knight.
Oct. 26, 1817, Miss Susan Downing.
Dec. 18, 1818, Mr. Theodore Willey, aged 81.
April 14, 1818, Mr. Humphrey Richardson, aged 33.
June 21, 1818, Mr. Robert Willey, aged 58.
Aug. 12, 1818, Sarah Henderson, aged 5.
Aug. 30, 1818, Nathaniel Kidder Pendergast, aged 14.
———, 1818, Mr. Thomas Bickford.
Dec. — 1818, Mrs. Tuttle, the wife of Levi Tuttle.
Feb. 27, 1819, Mr. James Folsom, aged 72.
April 1819, Mr. James Critchett, town pauper.
May 22, 1819, Miss Sarah Denbo, aged 70.
June 29, 1819, Clarrisa Hall, aged 92.
Aug. 10, 1819, Mr. Samuel Jackson, aged 75.
Oct. 10, 1819, Mr. George F. Smith, aged 39.
Oct. 11, 1819, Mr. John S. Pinkham.
Oct. 22, 1819, Hamilton Young, son of Daniel Y.
May 4, 1820, Mr. Ichabod Bodge, Jr., aged 24.
Sept. 26, 1820, Widow Elizabeth Dutch, aged 87.
Sept. 29, 1820, Mary Elizabeth, child of John Parks.
Sept. 30, 1820, Miss Abigail Buzzell, aged 18.
Nov. 30, 1820, Miss Lydia Garland, aged 46.
Jan. 3, 1821, the widow Mary Folsome, aged 66.
Aug. 27, 1821, the wife of Mr. Robert Jackson, aged 56.
Sept. 29, 1821, Mr. Samuel Smart, aged 73.
Oct. 1, 1821, Miss Hannah Clough, aged 78.
Oct. 23, 1821, Mr. Daniel Taylor, bled to death by a wound,
  aged 47.
Jan. 5, 1822, Mr. Bartholomew Stimson, a pauper, aged 52.
Jan. 14, 1822, Mrs. Lydia Hanson, wife of Jos. Hanson, Esq.,
  aged 33.
Feb. 20, 1822, Abigail Channel, dau. of Mr. Abraham Chan-
  nel.
March 3, 1822, Sally Garland, dau. of Mr. John Garland.
April 15, 1822, Flora, a Black woman, and a pauper.
April 23, 1822, Caroline, dau. of Joseph Hanson, Esq.

April 23, 1822, Mr. Samuel Fowler, aged 36.　Drowned from a gondola.

April 23, 1822, Mr. John Jenkins, Jr., aged 23.　Drowned from a gondola.

May 1, 1822, Widow Mary Young, aged 82.

May 5, 1822, John the youngest son of William Curtis.

Aug. 29, 1822, Mrs. Rosamond Daniels, a pauper, aged 94.

Sept. 7, 1822, Mr. Aaron Twombly, drowned in the river, aged 33.

Sept. 30, 1822, Mr. Tobias Tuttle, aged 54.

Oct. 23 1822, Widow Sarah Hull, aged 77.

Oct. 27, 1822, Mr. Samuel Nutter, a pauper, aged 82.

Nov. 22, 1822, Mr. John Bean, aged 31.

Nov. 24, 1822, Mr. Nathan Kenniston, aged 40.

Dec. 27, 1822, Mr. James Fowler, aged 23.

Jan. 5, 1822, Mr. Edward Furness, aged 35.

Jan. 7, 1822, Mrs. Elizabeth Jenkins, a pauper, aged 75.

Jan. 13, 1822, Mrs. Abigail Davis, a pauper, aged 75.

Feb. 11, 1822, Mr. Jonathan Leathers, a pensioner, aged 65.

April 21, 1823, Mrs. Abigail Roberts, aged 104.

June 2, 1823, Mrs. Molly Willey, widow of Mr. Theodore W., aged 84.

June 20, 1823, Miss Maria Mills, aged 21

Aug. 23, 1823, Miss Mary Nutter, aged 45.

Nov. 9, 1823, Miss Betsey Keating, aged 66.

March 15, 1824, Mr. John Libbey, aged 35.

Aug.—1824, an infant daughter of Mr. Jonathan Clay, aged 3 weeks.

Oct. 1, 1824, an infant son of Mr. Simon Pickering, aged 2 years.

Oct. 27, 1824, an infant son of Mr. Joseph Page, aged 5 months.

Jan. 8, 1825, Mr. Daniel Willey, aged 31.

Feb. 1, 1825, Mr. Micajah Davis, a pauper, aged 86.

Feb. 9, 1825, Mrs. Rebekah Starbird, wife of John Starbird, aged 66.

Feb. 3, 1825, Mrs. Sarah Savage, aged 78.

Feb. 22, 1825, Mr. Phinehas Willey, aged 27.

March 28, 1825, Mr. Reuben Clark, a ship carpenter, aged 28,

April 16, 1825, Mr. Timothy Davis, aged 29.

May 16, 1825, an infant daughter of Mr. William Curtis, aged 11 days.

June 1, 1825, Mr. Brackett Furnald, aged 22.

July 18, 1825, Mr. Benaiah Phillips, aged 24.

July 26, 1825, Miss Alice Tuttle, aged 18.

Aug. 3, 1825, Stephen Henry, the infant of Mr. Samuel Hall, aged 6 months.

Aug. 9, 1825, George Libby, the infant of Mr. John Parks, aged 6 months.

Aug. 18, 1825, Mr. James Cogan, aged 47.

Sept. 1, 1825, an infant daughter of Mr. Daniel Cram, aged 3 weeks.

Sept. 10, 1825, an infant daughter of Mr. Samuel Willey, Jr., aged 1 year.

Sept. 21, 1825, an infant son of Mr. Daniel Fowler, aged 11 months.

Nov. 1, 1825, an infant son of Mr. William Furnald, aged 9 months.

Nov. 15, 1825, Capt. Samuel Starbird, aged 44.

Nov. 16, 1825, Mr. Hiram Glover, drowned from a gondola, aged 20.

Nov. 28, 1825, Abigail Tuttle, the infant of the Widow Tuttle, aged 3.

Jan. 23, 1826, William, the son of William Tego, aged 7.

Feb. 19, 1826, Mr. Winthrop Scriggins, aged 67.

March 7, 1826, Miss Sally Cheswell, aged 23.

March 17, 1826, Master John Woodhouse, aged 17.

May 5, 1826, Widow Betsey Patrick, aged 80.

Aug. 2, 1826, Mr. Daniel Cram, aged 34.

Sept. 1, 1826, Hannah, a child of Mr. Daniel Fowler, aged 3.

Sept. 11, 1826, an infant daughter of Mr. Jacob Watson, aged 1.

Oct. 4, 1826, Miss Betsey Stevens, aged 60.

Oct. 12, 1826, Mr. Nathan Foss, aged 43.

Oct. 15, 1826, Mr. Hugh Cox, aged 70.

Dec. 12, 1826, Mrs. Mehitable, wife of Samuel Furber, aged 25.

Dec. 12, 1826, the Widow Grover, aged 84.

Jan. 5, 1827, Mrs. Elizabeth Wiggin, aged 70.

INDEX OF PLACES AND SUBJECTS

26

INDEX OF NAMES

418 INDEX OF NAMES

Haddock, Mary, 386.
Haines, Ransom, 385.
  Samuel, 3, 6.
  Thomas J., 368.
Hale, Colonel, 149.
  Samuel, 112.
Haley, Michael, 154.
Hall, Abigail, 384.
  Benjamin, 114, 132, 196, 380.
  Clarissa, 395.
  Hester, 98.
  Jacob, 385.
  James, 20, 24, 132, 234, 391.
  John, 3, 6, 20, 32, 132, 219.
  Lafayette, 154, 364.
  Mary, 391.
  Moses, 391.
  Penniel, 385.
  Ralph, 3, 16, 31, 81, 169, 193, 196, 219.
  Samuel, 384, 397.
  Stephen H., 397.
Halloway, Henry, 11.
Halstead, Wallace, 160.
Ham, Abigail, 386.
  Charles M., 157.
  Charlotte, 384.
  Daniel, Jr., 386.
  Hannah, 381, 384.
  John, 28, 278, 384.
  John F., 154.
  John, Jr., 28.
  Jonathan, 384.
  Joseph, 233, 389.
  Lydia, 384, 385.
  Martha, 383, 385.
  Martha A., 387.
  Mary, 384.
  Nathaniel, 151.
  Patience, 381.
  Rufus, 390.
  Sarah, 385.
  Thomas, 373.
Hammond, Isaac W., 181.
Hance, John, 11, 12.
Hancock, Nathaniel, 157.
Hanscom, Moses, 152.
Hanscomb, Aaron, 26.
  Cara, 213.
  Lucy, 377.
Hanson, Aaron, 127.
  Betty, 382.
  Caroline, 395.
  Daniel, 381.
  Ebenezer, 382.
  George W., 157.
  James, 28, 385.
  John, 206.
  John A., 154, 157.
  Jonathan, 28, 196.
  Joseph, 111, 206, 395.

Hanson, Joseph, Jr., 383.
  Lydia, 395.
  Mary, 384.
  Nathaniel, 28.
  Patience, 385.
  Samuel, 28, 384.
  Sarah, 279.
  Sophia, 387.
  Stephen, 28.
  Timothy, 28, 385.
  William, 204.
Hardy, Captain, 193.
  Charles, 261.
  Daniel, 349.
  Margery, 282, 331.
  Mary, 261, 331.
  Theophilus, 128, 261, 331, 373.
  Thomas, 118.
Harris, Nicholas, 11.
Harrison, Benjamin, 334.
  Nicholas, 219.
Hartford, John, 380.
  Nicholas, 283.
Hartwell, Joseph, 387.
Harvey, Pike P., 387.
  Richard J., 384.
Haughey, Peter, 157.
Hawkins, Otis W., 157.
Hayden, William, 388.
Hayes, Alice, 243.
  Bernice M., 265.
  Charles W. H., 157.
  Chauncey E., 334.
  Daniel, 28, 113.
  Ezra, 154.
  Ichabod, 28.
  Jacob, 384.
  John, 385.
  John S., 154, 261, 262.
  Leslie D., 265.
  Mabel L., 265.
  Margaret, 384.
  Samuel, 243, 247, 382.
  Warren C., 265.
Hazelton, Chesley D., 389.
Hazen, ———, 148.
  Lois, 148.
Heald, James, 20.
Heard, John, 3, 6.
  Reuben, 113.
  Tristram, 70, 227.
Hearne, Hannah, 381.
Henderson, Betsey, 207.
  Mrs., 216.
  Paul, 384.
  Sarah, 395.
Henney, Thomas, 159.
  William, 159.
Hepworth, Cephas, 159.
Hewins, Otis W., 157

420   INDEX OF NAMES

Hutchins, Samuel, 126, 200.
   Thomas, Jr., 126.

Ingalls, Charles, 264.
   Eliza, 207, 289, 389.
   Harriet, 288.
   Jedediah, 206, 280, 288, 345.
Irwin (see Erwin).

Jackman, Charles, 154.
Jackson, ———, 241, 349.
   Alvin, 334.
   Andrew, 151.
   Ann, 99, 102.
   Benjamin, 26, 126, 159.
   Bennan, 126.
   C. Loyd, 349.
   Charlotte, 385.
   Eliza, 388.
   Elizabeth, 80.
   Enoch, 128, 130, 373.
   Hannah, 28, 97.
   James, 10, 16, 28, 80, 174, 178, 196, 197, 376.
   James, Jr., 28, 187.
   Jane, 80.
   John, 156.
   Joseph, 24, 28, 115, 196, 197.
   Laskey, 373.
   Lemuel, 128, 130.
   Martha, 386.
   Mary, 207.
   Mrs., 102.
   Patience, 26.
   Robert, 395.
   Samuel, 20, 24, 126, 395.
   Thomas, 385.
   Thompson, 386.
   Walter, 10, 65, 66, 80, 82, 97, 99, 171.
   William, 14, 20, 28, 102, 103, 107, 130, 174, 178, 229.
   William W., 216.
Jacobs, Daniel, 28.
   Daniel, Jr., 28.
James, Joseph A., 390.
   Thomas, 152.
Jameson, Patrick, 10, 68, 69, 80, 171, 219.
Jefferson, Thomas, 331.
Jeffrey, George, 83.
Jenkins, Ann, 91, 92.
   Anna M., 349.
   Benjamin, 111.
   Caroline, 260.
   Catherine, 383.
   Elizabeth, 396.
   Ephraim, 368.
   Evelyn, 332.
   Fred E., 341.
   Jabez, 91.
   John, 20, 56, 110.
   John, Jr., 392.

Jenkins, Joseph, 14, 64, 176, 180, 182, 195, 223, 229, 387.
   Joseph, Jr., 223.
   Keziah, 148.
   Nathaniel, 124, 132, 373.
   Rebecca, 56.
   Reynolds, 81.
   Robert, 10, 66.
   Sarah, 167.
   Sarah A., 388.
   Silas, 160, 167, 349.
   Stephen, 20, 52, 55, 56, 91, 92, 102, 150, 180, 182, 227.
   Stephen, Jr., 125.
   William, 20, 28, 111, 125, 367.
   William, Jr., 125.
Jenness, Charles B., 159.
   Elizabeth, 384.
   Solomon, 385, 386.
   Stephen, 384.
Jewell, Bradbury, 201, 203, 373.
   Mark, 26.
Jewett, Noah, 201, 203, 241, 373.
Johnson, Abraham, 28.
   Andrew, 132.
   Benjamin, 124.
   David, 26.
   Dorothy, 391.
   Gideon, 391.
   Hannah, 392.
   John, 124, 125, 132, 379, 392, 393.
   John, Jr., 392.
   Johnson, 392.
   Joseph, 393.
   Josiah, 24, 391, 393.
   Mary, 393.
   Nathan, 393.
   Phebe, 392.
   Sarah, 381.
   Stephen, 176.
   Supply, 151.
   Thomas, 10, 26, 46, 47, 64, 66, 113.
   William, 11, 26, 58.
Jones, Abigail, 26.
   Anthony, 28, 197.
   Benjamin, 16, 26, 28, 126.
   Benjamin, Jr., 126.
   Charles O., 154.
   Charles P., 157.
   Ebenezer, 20, 22, 26, 126.
   Ebenezer, Jr., 24, 26, 126.
   Eliza A., 166.
   George, 126.
   Harriet D., 65.
   John, 16, 20, 126.
   John P., 152.
   John Paul, 147.
   Joseph, 14, 15, 16, 20, 126, 174, 178, 229, 230, 232, 365.
Jones, Joseph, Jr., 16, 18.

Pinder, Jeremiah, 110, 133, 374
  John, 11, 14, 20, 35, 36, 97, 176, 180, 182.
  Thomas, 374.
  William, 374.
Pinkham, Abijah, 24, 54, 133, 245, 374.
  Alfred, 260.
  Alphonso, 153, 157, 166.
  Amos, 28, 176, 227.
  Ballard, 349.
  Caroline, 260.
  Clarissa, 384.
  Daniel, 124, 151, 260.
  Eliza, 260.
  Fannie, 260.
  Friend, 240.
  Isaac, 133.
  James, 28.
  John, 152.
  John H., 157.
  Joshua, 157, 160, 166.
  Mary A., 385.
  Moses, 28.
  Nicholas, 387.
  Paul, 28, 133.
  Rachel, 54.
  Richard, 3, 6, 169, 386.
  Richard, Jr., 28.
  Samuel, 28.
  Sarah, 260.
  Solomon, 20, 28.
  Stephen, 28, 196, 260.
  Thomas, 128, 133, 203, 241, 280, 345, 374.
  Ursula, 287.
  William, 260.
Piper, Colonel, 149, 150.
Pitman, ——, 14, 244.
  Abigail, 382.
  Connor, 28.
  Deliverance, 100.
  Derry, 16, 196, 341.
  Ezekiel, 11, 56, 57, 90, 102.
  Francis, 11, 13, 14, 51, 52, 174.
  George, 374.
  Gideon C., 216.
  John, 13, 20, 110.
  Joseph, 103, 126, 382.
  Joshua M., 262.
  Nathaniel, 100.
  Samuel, 24, 99.
  Sarah, 99.
  Thomas, 228.
  William, 10, 13, 51, 56, 57, 58, 59, 108, 171, 176, 180, 223.
  Zachariah, 28, 196, 197.
Polluck, John, 133.
  Thomas, 124.
Pomfret, William, 3, 6, 9, 64.
Pomrey, Edward, 223.
Poor, Enoch, 123.
  Thomas, 149.

Pope, Barnard, 171.
Porter, Augustus B., 284.
Pray, Thomas T. W., 262.
Prescott, Benjamin, 157, 385.
  John H., 383.
Presson, Harvey, 151.
  James, 260.
Priest, Quick, 26.
Prince, George, 383.
  Joseph, 191, 192.
Putnam, John, 126.
Putney, Joseph, 385.

Quimby, John, 37.
Quint, Alonzo, 125, 169, 173.
  Mary J., 389.
  Samuel, 384.
  Stephen, 383.

Raines, Thomas, 182.
  William, 20, 108, 182.
Rand, David, 123, 133, 151.
  Francis, 44.
  John, 11, 16, 43, 44, 45, 95, 96, 102, 103, 108, 133, 176, 180, 182.
  John, Jr., 44, 176.
  Miles, 366.
  Nathaniel, 44, 365.
  Preston, Jr., 261.
  Remembrance, 44, 95, 96, 102.
  Samuel, 96.
  Stephen, 155, 368.
Randall, Betsey, 384.
  Charles D., 158.
  Ebenezer, 24, 26, 126.
  Elizabeth, 216.
  Hezekiah, 115.
  Israel, 24.
  John, 20, 26, 119.
  Jonathan, 26, 114.
  Joseph, 114, 124, 130, 133.
  Mary, 26.
  Mason, 24, 26, 115.
  Miles, 20, 24, 26, 126, 233.
  Miss, 105.
  Nathaniel, 24, 182, 198, 223, 251.
  Samuel, 113.
  Simon, 28, 126.
  William, 20, 24, 26, 110, 113, 171, 190.
  William, Jr., 115.
Ransom, Alonzo, 155, 332.
  Eleanor, 320.
  Eliza B., 320.
  George W., 261, 264, 329, 330.
  Reuben M., 155, 240.
  Ruth, 320.
Rasle, Sebastian, 108, 264, 329, 330.
Redford, William, 102.
Reid, Colonel, 148.
Remich, John, 16.

Trickey, Abigail, 392.
  Benjamin, 387.
  Clarissa A., 383.
  Elizabeth, 393.
  John F., 155.
  Joshua, 392, 393.
  Martha, 392.
  Samuel, 392.
Tripp, Benjamin, 375, 380.
  William H., 386.
Trowbridge, Sarah, 307.
Tucker, Henry, 375.
  James, 389.
  Sophronia R., 389.
  Stephen B., 133.
Tufts, Henry, 24, 127, 133.
  Henry, Jr., 127.
  Samuel B., 155.
  Thomas, 127.
  Willard C., 155, 217.
Turner, Abigail, 382.
  Ann, 385.
Tuttle, Abigail, 397.
  Alexander, 386.
  Alice, 397.
  Andrew, J. S., 157, 165.
  Ann, 148, 149.
  Benjamin, 152.
  Charles H., 155.
  Elizabeth, 165.
  Freeman H., 157, 164.
  George, 24, 115, 127, 133, 150, 234.
  Herbert, 244.
  Isaac, 124, 133.
  James H., 158, 165.
  John, 3, 70, 219, 227, 228.
  John, Jr., 213.
  John L., 164.
  Levi, 395.
  Michael B., 386.
  Miles, 386.
  Mrs., 395.
  Nathaniel, 387.
  Nicholas, 24, 124, 127, 133.
  Oliver, 385, 387.
  Prudence I., 383.
  Sarah, 384.
  Sarah A., 382.
  Stoughton, 24.
  Thomas, 127.
  Tobias, 396.
  William, Jr., 155, 160.
Tuxbury, Daniel, 386.
Twombly, ———, 240.
  Aaron, 396.
  Ann, 383.
  Elizabeth, 387.
  Isaac, 28, 196, 197.
  John, 384.
  John R., 155.

Twombly, Joseph, 28, 196, 197.
  Reuben H., 155.
  Stephen, 152.
  William, 196.
  William, Jr., 197.
  William 3d., 28.
  Wingate, 386.

Ugroufe, John, 6.
Underhill, John, 3, 6.
Underwood, Emily, 385.
  James, 122, 125, 133, 281, 282.
  John, 133.
Urnback, Adam, 158.

Valley, Franklin, 158.
Varney, Andrew, 383.
  Esther, 150.
  Mercy, 150.
  Moses, 113.
  Oliver, 386.
Vaughan, George, 173, 176.
  Major, 89.
Veasey, George, 79, 83.
Venner, James M., 158.
Verner, Thomas, 385.
Vibbert, Luke R., 158.
Vincent, Anthony, 381.
  Thankful H., 389.
Vines, Henry, 14.

Wakeham, Caleb, 52, 110.
  Edward, 14, 51, 52, 176, 180, 182.
  Sarah, 51.
  William, 21.
Waldron, Elizabeth, 286.
  George, 287.
  James, 81.
  Plato, 387.
  Richard, 6, 17, 86, 89, 109, 150, 169, 249.
  William, 6.
Walker, ———, 246.
  Charles W., 156.
  Daniel, 158.
  James F., 158.
  Mark W., 260.
  Nehemiah, 184.
  Seth S., 294, 362, 367.
  Thomas H., 158.
  William, 216.
Walles, Jane, 84.
  Samuel, 380.
Wallingford, Samuel, 150.
Wallis, Jane, 286.
Walton, George, 3.
  Jacob, 397.
  Jean, 392.
  Mary, 391.
  Molly, 391.
  Sarah, 391.

CPSIA information can be obtained
at www.ICGtesting.com
Printed in the USA
LVHW111507030221
678262LV00017B/604